reflections of a filmmaker

robert gardner

foreword by charles simic

edited by ted perry

designed by jeannet leendertse

Production Editor: Robert D. Hack

10 9 8 7 6 5 4 3 2 1

Library of Congress Cataloging-in-Publication Data

Gardner, Robert, 1925-
    The impulse to preserve : reflections of a filmmaker / by Robert Gardner ; foreword by Charles Simic.
        p. cm.
    Includes bibliographical references.
    ISBN 1-59051-236-7 (hardcover : alk. paper) 1. Motion pictures in ethnology.
2. Indigenous peoples in motion pictures. I. Title.
    GN347.G37 2006
    305.8–dc22
                            2005022672

preface   viii

foreword   ix

a human document   1

dead birds   7

a kind of sacrifice   73

creatures of pain   75

the nuer   81

rivers of sand   101

the hanging   161

ladakh   163

deep hearts   181

ika hands   217

rushes: forest of bliss   277

city of light   307

stone, birds, air, and water   309

going back   313

fixing time   331

meadows and carved choirs   337

holy men   339

isle of dogs   343

just representing   353

passenger   357

camera visions   365

illustrations   366

notes   371

relevant books   371

acknowledgments   372

preface

This book has been long in coming. In fact, it has been more than forty years since the oldest piece in it first appeared. The years passed as I sought some purpose for it, its title forever changing, from Beyond the Pale to Human Documents to Captured Light to what it is now, *The Impulse to Preserve,* borrowed words meant to convey my belief that the individual frames in the miles of film and thousands of photographs I have exposed contained light that was reflected into my eyes through a camera and then preserved in particles of silver.

But capturing light or preserving the objects of our senses with words or any other medium, though lying at the bottom of art as Philip Larkin has so aptly put it, does not guarantee it will become art. It is only the way light or any other medium is shaped that finally matters.

I have also learned that neither filmmaking nor bookmaking can be done alone and so I am grateful to many but give especially abundant thanks to Ted Perry, a friend of long and constant duration who consented to be my editor. There are few, perhaps no others, with a deeper knowledge and wider love of film and filmmaking.

On visual matters, I have had another gifted collaborator, Jeannet Leendertse, whose talents for design are a delight for all eyes. For her, putting images on a page is a matter of deep concern both for meaning and beauty.

Finally, I am indebted to another friend, Charles Simic, whose talents with words (and images) are entirely breathtaking. I would follow to whatever shore he proposes and know that I am in the hands of a magical guide.

This was never to have been a book relying on words alone or on images exclusively of my making. So, although most of the illustrations come from films or photographs I have made, a few are the work of friends and collaborators who have joined me in my journeying. In fact, everything in this book has been shared with essential companions in the unfolding and subsequent transformation into pictures and prose of what we saw and heard.

There would have been no *Dead Birds* or its sequel in progress, *Roads End,* without Peter Matthiessen, Karl Heider, Wali, Weyak, Pua, Dick Rogers and Susan Meiselas, no *Rivers of Sand* without Clark Worswick, Omali Inda and Stewart Gardner, no *Forest of Bliss* without Ákos Östör, Mithai Lal, Ragul Pandit and the Dom Raja, no *Deep Hearts* or *Ika Hands* without Robert Fulton and no *Passenger* without Sean Scully and, again, Robert Fulton.

Had there never been Fulton and Rogers, both of whom have left for the "farther shore," my filmmaking would have been much poorer and my life would have been, is now, far lonelier. Without my wife Adele Pressman, much of it would have been unimaginable.

foreword

This is an unusual book by a very unusual man. Robert Gardner is a filmmaker whose films on the stone-age Dani society living in New Guinea, the Hamar people of southwest Ethiopia, the ceremonies and cremation rituals associated with death and regeneration in the old city of Benares, India, as well as dozens of other projects, have made him into a renowned figure whose works are regarded as classics of documentary cinema. *The Impulse to Preserve* collects some forty years of journals and notes he kept intermittently while working on his films. It also includes a few short pieces and essays that arose out of these projects. The amount of good writing in all of them is astounding.

At their best, journals can provide a rich narrative of what any life was like and convey an individual's sensibility. They are a place to record brief insights, recount minor incidents, and note memorable details that gave meaning to a particular day without worrying how it adds up in the long run. Journals are kept in the belief that a key to the mystery of our existence lies in the ordinary course of our lives.

Gardner's journals, however, because of their exotic subject matter, read at times like a narrative of an early explorer discovering some strange land and at other times like a collection of imaginary travels to imaginary places composed by a contemporary Jonathan Swift. Again and again, Gardner sets out on a journey into the unknown in the hope of escaping the rigors of settled life, in pursuit of a dream. His hope is to locate some little known community of people who lead a life hitherto scarcely imaginable, shamans in India, nomadic herdsmen in Africa or the naked fisherwomen in Korea who use bare teeth to catch their prey, and who are most likely being dispossessed of their customs along with their land.

As in any good adventure story, the narrator of these journals is beset with endless obstacles to goal, including his own doubts in the mission. Everything that can possibly go wrong does. Vehicles break down. The locals are uncooperative or their behavior is mystifying. We keep turning the pages of his journals to see how it will all end and in the process find ourselves not only wonderfully entertained but inevitably confronted with a range of questions about ourselves and our values in relationship to other cultures.

"There was something about the old lady, as she came by default of the imagination to be called, which defied description," Gardner writes in one of the most moving pieces in the book. As he travels around, or as he lingers to study the locals, he seeks some transfiguring metaphor, some striking image to describe and even unmask their way of life. Finding words for what one sees is ordinarily hard enough, but how does one do it with a camera? Gardner is well aware that to see anything clearly is also to see oneself in the act of looking. He is a self-conscious artist who worries about the authenticity of what he is doing. The photographer is a man from Mars, Dorothea Lange once said, who must learn how to become a familiar member of a family. His behavior, she continues to observe, must be that of an intimate rather than that of a stranger. This is excellent advice that is far easier to attempt closer to home than in some desert or jungle in a remote corner of the world.

Reading Gardner's book, one keeps asking oneself, who are these strange people who are so unlike us and yet so like us? The Dani of New Guinea, for instance, with whom he spent six months in 1961, have almost weekly wars with their neighbors. The killing of an enemy and the celebrations that follow, we are shocked to learn, are the most important events in their lives, the one from which all other sacred and mundane meanings derive. In Niger, the men of the Borroro tribe, we discover, paint their lips and eyes when the time comes to compete in their seasonal beauty contests for the best looking male. In other societies, too, men seem mostly to have themselves on their minds as they fret about their standing among other men. Women farm, cook and raise the children. Everyone's trapped in systems of belief that both provide them with an identity and sap their spirits. Endless strictures and taboos regulate the private lives and leave them few choices to assert their individual will. Among the Hamar in Ethiopia women speak of themselves as resembling dogs, living on scraps for which they have to beg. It's not much better elsewhere. Paradoxically, despite their inferiority, women in many of these societies appear to be happier than men. Work, as Gardner notes, is an apparent tonic for them. One tends to trust his conclusions. He neither judges harshly nor romanticizes the people he encounters. Some he likes more, some less, and he gives persuasive reasons for his preferences. He doesn't hide behind cultural relativism.

"The idea of linking the techniques of cinema to the purposes of anthropology in the hope of getting new and different takes or angles on what it means to be human goes back to the invention of the medium itself, almost exactly 100 years ago," Gardner writes. Some of the earliest films were records of everyday activities like workers leaving a factory or a baby being fed. The impulse to capture and preserve some bit of life is what all arts are about. The camera will engage the eye, and the mind and the imagination will follow, is the premise.

When it comes to a science like ethnography, the assumption is that representation of reality ought to have an impersonal quality, that the factual can be presented objectively. Over his long career in documentary film and in the course of this book, Gardner discovers that maintaining a boundary between nonfiction and fiction is not only a mistaken principle, but also a limiting strategy. As all artists and writers know, distorting the image can often be a way of getting closer to some kind of truth about reality. The unacknowledged conflict between fact and truth, document and insight, observation and vision is the growing concern of this marvelous book. Gardner comes to realize that when he makes an image he is not only responding to the powerful impulse to preserve, but that his own aesthetic sense inevitably comes into play. "As a filmmaker," he says, "I find enormous excitement in realizing that the experience has not been replicated but that it has been recast or transfigured using the medium of light."

The false discord between reality and imagination is what Gardner keeps trying to resolve. What he found out making films and writing these journals and essays is that one can't exist without the other. The art of documentary filmmaking turns out to be a literary art. Gardner is a fine writer, a man made wise by a lifetime of seeking a way to employ the medium of film to capture the splendor of the real. *The Impulse to Preserve* is a record of that noble quest.

—Charles Simic

P1

a human document

There was something about the old lady, as she came by default of the imagination to be called, which defied description. This may have been one reason she seemed from the very beginning an ideal subject for film. Age had all but erased the customary signs of sex. Her only clothing was a clump of frayed rags that she clutched between her legs with ancient modesty; sometimes she could pull it apart enough to wrap a piece around her waist and maybe over her shoulders, but usually she was concerned only about her loins.

Like the rest of her people, she was small, perhaps sixty-five or seventy pounds. In filming, there is always a problem of conveying a true indication of scale; on the screen the head of a fly can look like a monster, and a toy boat on a tiny pool like a ship at sea. This may be why there are so many pictures of anthropologists with their hands on pygmies' heads. So size was the first thing to be considered, the first problem to be solved especially by someone three times larger. Sometimes when the old lady was picked up she would protest and ask if she was going to be thrown away.

Her skin was like the bark of one of the common but infrequent desert trees, gray and wrinkled. It hung in folds and seemed to subsist in a detached way, drawing food and moisture from somewhere other than the body it still encased. Once she lost her way crawling back to her bed in the rain and blazed her leg on an assegai that someone had not properly put away. Under the hard skin her flesh was orange and wet but did not bleed. She had long feet and hands, these being the only organs that functioned at her command. She had to see with her hands and had to be propelled by her feet. She was blind and nearly alone. Her vast and incalculable age seemed a mockery of those who lived about her, and her being there was a constant source of irritation as well. She had lived too long and could not now find food, or even, when it was given to her, eat it very well. Often, instead of asking for food, she would sweep away the little twigs and bits of straw that lay on the sand near her and scoop a few handfuls of it into her mouth. But she managed to get enough to be satisfied.

To sit all day watching her was like waiting for someone to come to life. She rarely spoke except to ask, "Where is my pipe?" or, "When are we going to Nyae Nyae?" Nyae Nyae was where she was born and where she had had her children. She wanted to go there because she felt that if she did she would be happy once again. But she could not get there by herself and there was no one among her own people who wanted to take her. She spent most of her time asleep, occasionally shifting and adjusting her handful of clothing so as to protect herself from the cold night wind and the drying sun of the day. At first she was allowed the use of one of the little straw and branch shelters these people put up in the winter. The one she lived in belonged to her nephew by marriage. It was used to store the immense assortment of broken goods and worthless junk he had collected at a farm where he had once worked for a short time. She enjoyed this privilege even though it could not have been very comfortable lying on the boxes and bottles that contained her nephew's property. Then one day her bowels opened without warning and her nephew, swearing, dragged her off his possessions, and then his possessions out of the little house. Later the same day she crawled back to it, finding her way with the help of insulting directions and, perhaps, the smell of her own indiscretion. She lived alone in the house from then on and she could keep it the way she wanted.

Near her were the same little houses of other people who were all in some way her kin. Usually these houses are not more than ten yards from one another, and altogether they might number from ten to twenty-five. Except for the animals, both large and small, that live around these tiny villages, the only sounds are those of people, the thin murmur of their whispering conversations, food being eaten or gotten ready to eat, a pipe or a mother's breast being sucked, children screaming with delight or hunger. The old lady lay as if she heard nothing. The complicated pattern of life that flowed and eddied around her seemed to have no relation to her own. Only when one of the younger women teased or rebuked her for her foolish and useless old age did she show any sign of even wanting to be included. She would piteously haggle for consideration, her voice cracked and monotone. She rarely succeeded in stimulating sympathy and would subside amid the burst of renewed acrimony her pleas invariably provoked.

As time passed, she grew accustomed to the alien sounds of intruders, though the noise of the camera motor troubled her for quite a while. Her long periods of rest were interrupted by times when the one or two inescapable physiological activities that had not ceased had to be performed. These were the events of her day, and it upset her to be joined in them by such a clamorous witness. At first she lay back, hoping the noise would stop and she could have privacy. But the camera was more constant than her taunting young relatives, and perhaps, because the camera never raised its voice, she detected in it no malice or contempt. Later she talked to the camera, asking it for water, or tobacco, or some fire. It nearly always responded with what she wanted. One day she was given a cigarette that she put into her mouth burning end first. She smiled lightly at her own folly and bore no resentment whatever.

Her diet continued to be mainly sand, which she ate with as much relish as any-

where she is or even, I suspect, why she is with them. She cries quietly in total confusion and asks to be taken to the place where she was once comfortable. I tried with 100' to describe this forlorn sack of brittle bones and dried flesh on a lonely speck upon this desert' floor. I wanted to see her also against the ten ce backs of younger women and then, small children. I must find out more about her, who she is and what she remembers.

thing else she might be given, such as some soup made from the husks of a meaty nut all the other people were eating at this time of year. But it embarrassed her to eat sand in front of the camera. Everyone laughed at her insane

P2

fondness, and she tried to hide her craving. But finally she gave up attempts at deception and surrendered openly to this final lust of hers. When she had finished eating, and had sucked violently and mostly unsuccessfully on a crude pipe she stuffed with some borrowed tobacco, her long fingers would reach out to find shade and she would crawl to it, pushing with her feet and leaving a trail like a dry and broken tree stump dragged from its roots. As the sun moved across the sky it would find her and usually wake her and prod her into a new retreat. Sometimes, though, the sun was too low to disturb her and she would lie in it and absorb its warmth. Often she would be visited by butterflies that always love the sun, especially if there is the simultaneous excitement of some nearby moisture. Wherever two of her limbs had been crossed or where the flap of one of her empty breasts had lain on some other part of her, little patches of moist skin would tantalize the dancing butterflies. They would hover ecstatically in the invisible vapor, drinking in the feeble steam of her being. Then they would flutter off to a drier place such as her ear or knee. She moved so little and so stuporously that these creatures never panicked and would drift away when neither light nor liquid remained.

Weeks passed, during which no change could be detected in her circumstances or condition, though around her people and events moved with the ordinary intensity of everyday life. In the house next to hers a new bride had recently given birth to her first child. Then, late at night, in spite of the beads that had been put around its fat neck and in spite of the rich milk that dripped from its mother's breasts, its eyes dulled and its cries weakened and it quietly died. The father, unstrung by his fate, threw his bow, arrows and assegai, broken to pieces, into the desert. The mother took her digging stick and her spoons and bowls and spoiled these things too. The next morning, after they had buried the child under the same tree where it had been born, without a single necessity of life they set out for another place, to begin again. Everyone who lived around them went away the same day, because these people never stay near a place where someone has died. Now, when they had all left, the old lady was indeed alone.

If there had been no foreigners in their midst, she would not have been left in this way. When a group is forced to move, as frequently happens when the seasons change and the foods each brings must be found in different places, the people cannot take those who are too old to walk, but they leave them food and water and put thorn branches over the entrance to their house, not to keep the old ones in but to keep the jackals and hyenas out. It is also told that these old people are hit on the head and then their houses are burned down on top of them. But no one could remember seeing this happen.

In the abandoned werf, as a collection of houses is called, not a sound could be heard except the drumming of the taut folding wings of dung beetles as they flung themselves on and off the ground in reckless flight. For several days there was nothing moving near the old lady except the beetles; even the camera was still. The beetles were clumsy, dogged and truculently unconcerned with anything but the ball of dung they grasped between their legs and seemed to roll forever in all directions. She wasted in the silence of abandonment, her inertia a concentrated mockery of the camera. What began with such certain promise came ineluctably to lose its certainty. She lay, and her incessant stillness made her more and more remote.

Apparently, film is at its best when it confronts motion and development. It should seek frenzy, not quiescence. This accounts perhaps for the extraordinary perfection of The Miracle of Flowers, in which, in seconds, a plant rises out of the ground, gives bud and blooms. Suppose one tried the same technique with the old lady. One turn one picture, one turn one picture, every ten seconds or every ten minutes, and she would have looked the same at the end of a day's turning as at the beginning. The time and the considerable amount of film that would have been used might be justified as a compromise between Léger's hope of making a twenty-four-hour document of a married couple and Jacquetta Hawkes' idea of making one that would cover the entire life span of a single human being. The absurd impracticality of both notions reinforced the dubiousness of my idea. Obviously, men and women are not going to permit a camera to see them as they see themselves, and men and women are not going to allow themselves to be forever shadowed by filmmakers. And if they will, who would want to see the results? Any idiot can take a picture, can sit with a camera on his knee or propped on the ground and wait for his subject to move. It doesn't matter what the subject is, either, because it's much easier to watch through a lens than through one's own eyes. The lens alienates and separates. The man with a camera sees with a different perspective, and most of the light that might have affected his own perception is mercifully intercepted by a moving band of light-absorbing silver particles that can be safely stored away.

But the old lady wasn't even moving anymore, except to eat the bowl of mealie meal brought to her every day since she had been left alone. She didn't like it very much but she ate it anyway, and her dark fingers would lighten as she dipped them with hot porridge into her mouth. By now every visible corner, wrinkle and crack of her being had been photographed and the camera was useless.

One day as she slept, so still was she, it seemed even her death would defy the camera. I realized it was for this I was waiting, for a sign of death, not life, a flower falling back into the earth, not opening out of it.

She lived, and in a short time her people came back to their old houses, and she went back to eating sand and smoking their tobacco. Though she still weakened in health, she gained in spirits because the terrible loneliness said to kill these people when they are not together no longer afflicted her.

At about this time, too, the expedition decided to move. We were leaving the desert to go home. For several months the lives of these people had been witnessed by cameras. Thousands of feet of film had been exposed and were already on the way to the processor. Every meaningful motion, glance, and detail to be discerned existed somewhere in approximately one hundred miles of unedited footage. There would be miles of the old lady, more miles of not so old and young women digging in the desert for their wild vegetables, playing with their children, cooking, eating, sleeping, arguing, doing everything they knew and wanted to do. There would be miles of men and boys, hunting, clowning, going into trance and coming out of trance, being erotic, being mean and being sad. There would be a body of film that contained the visible portion of an entire culture, its people and its things. The cameras had done everything they could, within the limitations of the people who used them. There were thousands upon thousands of fragments of a larger time and place being taken away, which belonged to the past of these people, and there was a problem, now, how some of those fragments might be fitted together to tell about their present and future.

> As you know my interest is focused on the Bushmen in their decline, in their death struggles, which I see as a sign both of demise and, perhaps, rebirth. The struggle in death is also the pang of new life. In my fascination I seized, somewhat ghoulishly, upon our dear old lady. She was a buoy of hope that these people were not just dead and dying. She was ironically and un-majestically an exemplar of a spurned and forgotten tradition, ironically because she might have been happier on the farm from which she was supposedly rescued; un-majestically because she played, as far as she could, the same games the others were playing. But still, she suited me and I loved her.
>
> RG [from a letter]

Since the trucks were going north and some of the people lived in that direction, as many as possible were given a ride. Among those who would come were the old lady and her recently returned relatives. She was now too weak even to crawl and too uncertain a bundle to be simply picked up. She was put into a blanket, which I carried, holding on to its four corners like some preposterous stork. Her relatives steadied her into a crevice on top of the truck and it started out for Tchum-Kwi, one of the central waterholes of Nyae Nyae. We were there by mid-afternoon. Some would stay and others would go farther east, probably immediately, because there was not enough food at this place for everyone.

Late that afternoon, just as we were setting forth again, the old lady lay on her side, still covered with the ashes that had blown over her from the fire she had slept by the night before. She was tasting a mouthful of sand that, in this place, is whiter and maybe saltier than elsewhere. There was a faint sign of satisfaction on her face, and I knew, as well as I knew that I would kill her when I cut the film, that she would die in Nyae Nyae.

F1

F2

dead birds

The following lines are taken from journals I kept, sometimes fitfully, during a lengthy stay in the highlands of what in 1961 was Netherlands New Guinea. I was invited by the Dutch Government to take a party of interested friends to a remote corner of the Grand Valley of the Baliem River, home to the last practicing stone-age society on the planet. We were to document its authentic but threatened warrior/farmer culture.

Inevitable circumstances of change were altering the behavior and values of a few tens of thousands of naked agriculturalists who spoke a language called Dani and practiced ritual warfare. Our purpose was to witness and take down in motion pictures, still photographs and words what we saw. With me were sometimes as many as four or five others including Peter Matthiessen, invited for his accomplishments in natural history and for his nonfiction and fiction writing, Karl Heider for his ethnographic abilities gained from his study of anthropology at Harvard, Michael Rockefeller and Samuel Putnam, recent graduates of Harvard whose interests and capabilities were in still photography and sound recording, and Jan Broekhuyse for his competence in the local languages and sociology of highland New Guinea. My own purposes lay largely in filmmaking and occasional writing.

These efforts resulted in my first nonfiction feature, *Dead Birds*, in 1964. The journal writing, done while I made the images, can be thought of as a filmmaker's chronicle, presented here in the hope it has meaning for those interested in human beings and their cultures, especially those at the margins of this complex world.

Netherlands New Guinea, February 16th 1961

Hollandia is a curious place. On a public monument I read: "Hollandia 1910-1960." The sign, which almost says everything, is a kind of gravestone, since no one sees any future for this island, certainly none for the Dutch as masters.

The absurdity of Hollandia is really no one's fault, unless that of the Americans who came in the 1940s to create a military base to battle the Japanese. Even the American nomenclature survives: "Base G, Dock I." Starker reminders of Hollandia's origins are the rusting hulls of landing craft that clutter its harbor. Everywhere along the American-made roads are dumps of derelict equip-

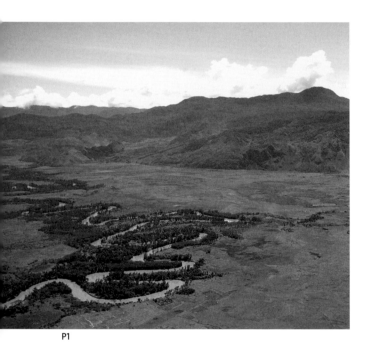

P1

ment. By the end of the war the American Air Force had abandoned hundreds of bombers and interceptors on Biak, the offshore island air base.

Today the only Americans in New Guinea are missionaries, usually of a Protestant fringe manifestation. I have met few but, judging from their literature, they are a doctrinally narrow-minded group free to go wherever they wish. They often pick the more remote parts of the highland valleys where the culture is the most vigorous and where, usually within a short time, there is an exchange of values with terrible consequences for the local population.

A word that expresses my initial impression of Hollandia is provisionality. A makeshift quality pervades everything except the beautiful if unpromising land on which the city rests. Instead of tables, there are giant wooden spools empty of telephone wire. Fences are made from barbed wire or perforated metal planking once used for improvising airstrips. Everywhere metal is rusting, and there is so much it will take a long time to disappear. Ironically, Japanese merchants will come next week to pick up all the scrap that's fit to reuse. One of the grimmer aspects of Hollandia is the uniformity of its architecture. Being a government encampment both in its American and Dutch phases, there are few if any privately conceived houses.

Overlooking Lake Sentani, a lovely inland sea about twenty miles from Hollandia and noted for its rare freshwater swordfish, stood General Douglas MacArthur's wartime headquarters. The site has a view of the lake and valley to the south where the airstrips were located, and of the terrain leading up to the Central Highlands.

February 28th – March 1st 1961

I planned to leave Tuesday morning by the regular Krooduif flight to Wamena, the administrative outpost in the Grand Valley of the Baliem. On Monday I arranged the shifting of our crates from the customs shed at the harbor to the government stores in town. The film and packages of batteries were put in cold storage so as to last through my stay with the Dani.

On Tuesday morning at the airstrip, twenty-five miles out of Hollandia by the only road in New Guinea, the plane to Wamena remained on the ground with engine trouble. Without a way to arrange other transportation, I returned to

Hollandia with the only surgeon in New Guinea. On Wednesday the plane to Wamena was due to leave at 8:30 a.m., but at 7:30 a.m. the flight was again canceled because of rain (33mm) in the Baliem Valley the night before. Fortunately, I had made arrangements with MAF (Missionary Aviation Fellowship) to take me in their single-engine Cessna in case this happened. By eight o'clock, I was beside Mr. Johnson (lately of the Moody Bible Institute) at 12,000 feet heading northeast for the Wolo Gap. The weather was fine and included the usual assortment of cumulus clouds. Mr. Johnson decided on the Gap entry to the Baliem Valley due to restricted visibility. Once through it, we could make out some familiar features. The best landmark is the ridge where a DC-3 crashed during the Second World War, a spot that another pilot for the MAF had shown me the previous week. Beyond that ridge is the Grand Valley.

We landed at Wamena at about 9:30 a.m. I was met by Jan Broekhuyse, the Dutch patrol officer who had been assigned to us. By ten, we were traveling north on the Baliem River expecting to arrive at a village called Tulem a little after noon. There we hoped to find carriers who would come with us to an area named after its most famous warrior, Kurelu. The river was high due to heavy rains in February, progress was slow, and the boat landing at Tulem was completely submerged, making docking difficult at best.

No carriers from among the Wittaia Dani living nearby could be persuaded to accompany us as far as Kurelu, it being the home territory of their traditional enemies. We asked to be taken out

P2

9

P3

along a ridge that points like a giant forefinger toward the foothills about a mile from the frontier dividing these two groups. With an unimpeded view in every direction, we spent the night high above the flood plain and close to the geographic center of the Valley.

March 2nd 1961

Early the next morning, thick fog covered the ridge until the sun began to burn it off. Except for a few patches in small ravines still shaded by the steeper hills, the fog was gone in an hour. At 9 a.m., the search for carriers began again. At the start there were only three. All the others were too afraid, saying, "They will kill us because we have killed so many of them." We tried to persuade potential carriers that we would deter their enemies, that they would be safe with us, and that if they helped us they would be given some of the small cowrie shells I had brought with me. These are prized possessions in Dani communities. The men might also demonstrate their courage by coming, and even achieve some renown by doing so. Many admitted their cowardice and consequent low social status. Apparently life is preferable to death, even though they might risk it in ritual wars and fights among themselves. Finally, about twenty agreed to help carry our many boxes from Tulem to Kurelu.

At first the ground was dry and made for easy walking, but soon the ridge ended in a slope that ran down to marshy ground lying between the Wittaia and Kurelu territories. At the watchtowers along the frontier, there was considerable activity. Men were seated in the tops of their towers, and groups of warriors were standing or sitting beneath them. It was obvious that they had seen us for the last hour and were following our progress with intense interest.

We entered the marsh that lay between us and the gardens under the mountain wall. The mud was extremely heavy and it took almost as long to cross 1500 feet of marsh as it had a mile or so of high ground. At the farther edge of the marsh stood a throng of warriors. They greeted us in a cautious but friendly way. Abututi, our Dani interpreter, persuaded them of our peaceful intentions. Their weapons looked appropriately menacing, the spears being ten or more feet long and the bows three or four. The weapons are designed for killing

P4

both people and pigs, the only animals living in sizable numbers in this valley.

An initial group of a half dozen Dani warriors grew to twenty and, before long, there may have been fifty, most of them unarmed, following us to a village where one of the headmen had agreed to take us. We spent fifteen or twenty minutes in the *honai* (the Dani word for a men's house) of this village still feeling that, although no spears had been hurled and no bows drawn, things could take a different turn. The assembled headmen went on at some length about who among them would provide the pig that we would share as a gesture of welcome and willingness to live together.

March 3rd 1961

A day has passed, and in the intervening twenty-four hours no further mention has been made of sacrificial pigs. The afternoon of the first day was one in which the people of the villages near us displayed immense curiosity, even disbelief, concerning everything about us: our clothes, our shoes, our skin, our hair, and especially the way we ate food. Most of these Dani had never seen white-skinned people in such close proximity. A few might have glimpsed them from afar, and undoubtedly they had all heard of their presence in the Grand Valley, but to sit with us, touch us, smell us, and hear us talk was a wildly new set of experiences.

P5

F4

We tried to explain that our intentions were completely unrelated to any government or religion. We told them they were entirely free to do as they wished and that we hoped they would. This included conducting their wars or stealing enemy pigs and women. They were relieved to hear this because these activities have central meaning in the Dani scheme of things. Without war they would cease being the kind of men they were supposed to be, according to the precepts of their culture. Much of their system of values is built on issues of renown that are connected with ferocity and prowess in warfare. If their lives did not permit them to pursue such aims, their system would crumble and the economic structure, which articulates with status and rank, would also collapse. Undoubtedly some among the warriors who met us at the frontier had killed five or even fifty men, women or children. I shall not soon forget the look of fright in the eyes of the Wittaia carriers who had been led by us into the heart of their enemy's territory. Seeing the homes and gardens of the people whose warriors had killed their friends and family members was an enormous occasion.

March 4th 1961

Rain began at 3 a.m. and continued at a gentle rate well into the daylight hours. A few of the nearly one hundred people (almost all men) who came to visit us yesterday have returned to greet us again. This is hopeful since there is always, in my mind at least, the possibility of a radical change in mood. Leaving the dry comfort of their houses to visit our wet camp was an encouraging sign. Why am I such a pessimist? Has reading missionaries' reports of the perfidy of the Dani put me in an anxious mood?

By noon the rain had stopped and the sun again shone in Kurelu. I wanted to explore the immediate surroundings in order to find a better place to stay. Where we are now it is dry and, being some distance from their villages, perhaps preferable to the Dani. On the other hand, I do not feel our situation is what I want. At the edge of the territory regarded as belonging to the Kurelu confederacy to the north and the Wallalua confederacy to the south, we are a bit peripheral to both group's main villages. I feel we need to be closer to at least one village.

P6

Our movements are to an important extent influenced by the kind of arrangements we make with our new Dani acquaintances. The next few days should tell us more about our chances in this respect. For now it is probably possible to look around in ways that were unthinkable upon first coming to this extraordinary place. So, during the afternoon, we visited many of the villages within a half-hour walk.

We hoped to find a place to live that was near but not inside a village, dry without being on top of too high a hill, shaded but not in an impenetrable forest, and, most importantly, near good water. I had almost despaired of finding such a place when, on our way back to our temporary home, I walked up a shallow rivulet, marveling at its freshness and clarity. In the midst of a stand of monumental araucarias, piney and strangely prehistoric, I found where the water sprang from an underground source, the only such spring I have seen so far. Innumerable brooks run down the hill that rises behind us, but most of the water draining the high ridge behind it passes by or even through several villages, bringing waste and debris on its way to the valley floor. Above and around the spring I found two or three small but level clearings that with some work should make adequate terraces for tents. Hopefully, we will have no problem staying there, and that will put us close to the village of Wuperainma where we have spent most of our time so far. This evening the man who owns these woods came to ask if we would eat a pig with him in his village tomorrow. As it happens, we shall not only have to eat a pig with him but also with another more important headman.

The large Cymbium shells I bought from a shell collector/dealer in Newton Upper Falls, Massachusetts, are proving to be worth an enormous amount in rapport. To eat a pig with someone of importance is probably the best insurance against being eaten. I have heard it has taken missionaries months or even years to get this amount of goodwill. The past two days have been more successful than I had expected.

March 5th 1961

The morning began late, owing to the dreariness of the weather. However, by mid-morning, Wali, one of the headmen who had offered us a pig, came to say we should go to his village and attend the preparations for the feast. On the way, I was struck by the thought of how incomprehensible any explanation would be of why we had come and of the vast amount of money and effort involved in doing so. The gesture they had made to share one of their valuable pigs seemed to justify everything.

We entered Wali's village, Wuperainma, carrying the coveted Cymbium shells, which the Dani call *mikak*, and a canteen of tea, which we supposed would be useful in our efforts to do justice to steamed pig. We sat with the important men of the immediate surroundings (news of a pig to be eaten no doubt spreads quickly and widely), enjoying the cool silence of their darkened *honai*. They smoked and spoke infrequently. The atmosphere was tense for reasons I had difficulty understanding. We knew from many accounts both spoken and written that these people have been accused of treachery arising from violent swings of mood. Up to the moment we entered the *honai*, they appeared to be acting warily. They were the ones on their guard. We were unarmed and they, who were armed, should have been the confident ones.

The death of a pig, a necessary prelude to its ritual eating, could become an occasion for killing us. As we tried to change the mood from suspicion to congeniality, there might be moments when one could not be sure of how to behave. The Dani may fear the shotgun we had brought to vary our diet, but they could also resent our presence, if only for the reason that we might interfere with their secret and sacred lives. They are warriors who, without war, are not men. Some

must have thought that the best thing would be to kill us and gain not only their privacy but also the acclaim such deeds confer.

The pigs were caught, held at both ends by their feet and shot in the heart with pig-killing arrows. Next, a fire was lit to burn off the bristles. The pigs were rapidly and expertly butchered by a bamboo knife and opened out flat. Soon everything was prepared for cooking, which would be done in an earthen hole lined with long grass and hot stones. Portions to be eaten by those of us luxuriating in the *honai* were lightly broiled on the fire that had heated the stones. In no time, several pounds of rare meat and thick slabs of fat were passed through the narrow entrance to the *honai* and we were told to begin.

In a few minutes, most of the food was gone and we said that in exchange for this gift of estimable pig meat, we wanted to give them a large Cymbium shell that they prize so greatly when made into a neck ornament. We told them we had come a long way and wanted to stay. We also told them our desire was to see how they lived and that we would not interfere as they went about their lives. We said we hoped that eating their pig meant we were already friends and that we would become better friends if we stayed with them. Finally, we said that, if they helped us, we had more Cymbium shells with which to make them rich and handsome.

It must have been clear to everyone that our methods amounted to the crudest bribery. Nevertheless, to all this fine and pointed talk, the assembled warrior dignitaries chanted in unison: "*Wa, Wa, Wa, Wa.*"

After more discussion about their need and desire to fight with their enemies, we left the *honai*

F5

P7

to accept the rest of the pig that had been cooking in the steam pit. By late evening, I sensed a prevailing mood of friendship and well-being. That, and not a little malaise from overeating or, perhaps, from the black magic they might have put in the pigs to make us die.

March 9th through Easter 1961
Broekhuyse, Abututi, and I returned to Wamena as I made my way to a region called The Asmat in order to be certain which of my two opportunities to work in New Guinea was most compelling, the Grand Valley of the Baliem in the highlands or The Asmat on the southern coast. I was eventually convinced that our best prospects lay in the highlands.

April 4th 1961
Yesterday Broekhuyse and I set out for the second time from Wamena to the araucaria forest where we chose to live several weeks ago. It was early afternoon when we arrived at the navigable end of the Aikhé River. Actually, the Aikhé isn't very navigable anywhere because of the large number of tree stumps and other obstructions along its course. Several times we were thwarted by half-submerged trees and had to apply full power to ram the boat over them. They could be cut but it would take a long time and people who live along the river's edge sometimes fell them to use as bridges. From Wamena it is not far to our forest home, less than

ten miles, but it takes a long time in an overloaded boat that is moving against the current and in the face of many obstacles.

A few hours after we arrived, Michael Rockefeller appeared with Abututi and his wife. They had walked from Wamena along the Baliem River. Abututi is a Dani policeman from Wamena, but his importance to our enterprise is as a translator of the Dani language.

Broekhuyse went back to Wamena hoping for enough light to see his way. His wife and new son are there and he is worried that his child is not well. In the morning he will come back with Karl Heider and more of the baggage from which we will try to make a tolerable life.

The people living nearby have not ceased being friendly and helpful. This morning before the others arrived, it was important to find a place for each of our tents. The forest, which is large but not flat anywhere for long stretches, stands below and grows part way up an enormous hill, which in turn foots the high escarpment that is the eastern wall of the Grand Valley. The choice of the site depended on several considerations: first, that we be close to but not on top of the Dani; second, that we be in a position to observe the open space used by everyone for gardening, warfare and anything else of a public nature; third, that there be good water near at hand; fourth, that there be some refuge from the heat of the flat valley floor; and, finally, that there be some serenity, even beauty, upon which to repose.

These requirements seem to have been met in the choice of a stand of the extraordinary araucaria tree. Among the few drawbacks are insects. I am not sure there are any more than elsewhere, especially anywhere near pigs that are herded into their pens every night. Dani housing has solved insect problems with the smoke from their continuous fires, an option not available to us.

Almost simultaneous with our arrival in the forest, an enormous roar came from a great distance. The thought that this might be a prelude to war went through everyone's mind, I am sure. The sound was full of exultation, preempting all other sounds normal to an afternoon in the valley. Climbing to a place on the hill behind our camp, I saw out on the valley floor an immense cluster of dark motion—waves of bodies running in the shad-

P8

ows of a setting sun. We discovered it to be the start of a victory celebration. Recently, possibly on Easter, a Wittaia warrior had been killed by one of the Willigiman Wallalua, the clan name of the Dani group on our side of the frontier. His Wittaia kin burned his body yesterday and today, after the death was disclosed, the Willigiman Wallalua responsible for the killing began to celebrate. Broekhuyse and I went to see what was happening out beyond the gardens in front of our forest. Soon we were not far from platoons of warriors surging back and forth on the same field on which we had first met our future hosts.

Hundreds of warriors were outlined on the horizon. They all had brought their weapons, either spears or bows and arrows, and they had dressed as they would had they been going to battle. Many carried wands or whisks decorated with bits of fur. Some important-looking persons wore magnificent headdresses topped with the plumage of birds of paradise. Many wore carefully painted white and yellow faces. Two bits of red cloth were the only evidence of modernity in the entire assembly of 250 dead-serious fighting men.

The extraordinary theatricality and raw energy of this spectacle was difficult to absorb. The warriors danced on a vast valley floor against a backdrop of 10,000-foot peaks. The sky lightened and darkened at intervals linked to the rhythm of their celebration, as though a gigantic stage had been set for an illuminated performance.

April 9th 1961
Tomorrow we will have spent a week in our forest home and our reception has been almost too good to believe. I have just finished a dinner of duck, shot on the Aikhé and shared with several of the younger warriors. When these men kill an enemy, they take his ornaments, feathers, weapons and any other possessions the victim may be carrying. These are called *suwarek*, or dead birds, a term that refers, almost interchangeably, to dead men. I am astonished by the stories I'm hearing about all the things they call dead birds. The Dani are equally astonished at the ease with which we can kill creatures and they crave the meat we bring in, especially that of dead birds.

Almost everything that has happened until now must have been as amazing to the Dani as to us. How long this fascination with each other will last, or how much time we have to enjoy our welcome, is unclear. Nor can it be predicted what will happen if the enchantment wears off. Will we be thought responsible if pigs die or do not grow fat? I am quite astounded by the totality of their desire to please us and to be helpful but I am still apprehensive all might suddenly and inexplicably change. For now, I am content to learn as much about them as I can.

I am also struck by some initial impressions I have of appearances: the physicality of the men, their penetrating eyes, the subtle and somewhat apprehensive smile at the corners of their mouths. The women, on the other hand, are neither pretty nor particularly graceful. They are designed for work and that is what they are perpetually doing, pursuing their endless chores with amazing diligence and obedience. The men hold their heads up and walk straight as columns. The women are bent and amble under heavy loads with a look of resignation. The men frolic, apparently unconcerned about wasting either time or energy, and the little boys are utterly free to look for pleasure in everything. They play well together but appear to do so without much pattern or organization. I have not yet seen toys or games, but this could change when the novelty of our visit wears off. We are their entertainment at the moment.

The little girls are more serious and extremely shy. The smallest of them perch on their mothers' shoulders and concentrate on whatever women do. The bigger ones give serious help to their elders who need all the assistance they can get. Tiny and

timid, dressed in the grass skirts of maidenhood, they often have a frightened look. Perhaps they are already aware of the burdens they will carry through life, of the likely absence of much joy in the years ahead. Clearly, pleasure is a reward reserved in large part for the males in this society.

April 10th 1961

Today there was war. By dawn many people were singing in Wuperainma, the village a few hundred feet from where I sleep. The Dani are sometimes given to singing, especially at night, in order to quiet their fears of ghosts, or of the enemy, or of anything else that is dangerous. Once up, I could see on the Warabara, the long rocky ridge on the fertile plain lying to our west, many warriors had already gathered and it was clear they were there to fight sometime later in the morning. Apparently, the Wittaia, who live in an area about as large as that of the Willigiman Wallalua but centering on Tulem where we first landed, had asked for war. The *etai*, which is what the Dani call a victory celebration, of two days ago was celebrated because two, not just one, of the Wittaia warriors had been slain. Apparently, they now wanted to even the score. War for the Dani is a central element of their culture. It is what men are required to do. A political mechanism for maintaining boundaries, war is also, and above all else, an almost religious duty and way of expressing one's manhood. An enemy is killed to placate the ghosts of one's own slain warriors. Great men must be great warriors if they are also to be rich and important. After watching them fight, it is clear to me that everyone involved is also enjoying himself. War is exhilarating in the way certain spectacular and dangerous sports are in other parts of the world. There is huge pleasure in plotting to kill, in dodging arrows and spears, and in attempting glory in the company of 500 comrades in arms.

The war began in earnest early in the morning and the first wounded were on their way home to their villages soon after the two sides engaged. We heard but could not know for certain that the Wittaia had laid a successful ambush. Watching from the hill behind our forest camp, four or five hundred feet above the valley floor, I could see only that large contingents from both sides were rushing from hillside to hillside. The movements

F6

F7

appeared to be orchestrated by much shouting and a terrifying realization took hold that less than a mile away several hundred expert warriors were intent on killing each other.

At noon, Broekhuyse and I climbed down from our vantage point to draw as close as possible to the fighting. When we arrived near the place they were doing battle, we assumed we would enjoy the same friendliness and amused tolerance so far shown us. On the way to the fighting ground, it is necessary to pass several of the many watchtowers that warring groups put up to guard against surprise attack. Under each of these is a little house built for shelter from the sun or rain. Innumerable paths lead wherever people need to go and, as we ventured along them hoping some combination would take us to our destination, we encountered many women working, as they always do, gathering potatoes, weeding, and tending the ditches that irrigate the gardens. Their husbands, fathers, brothers and sons were all at war within earshot of their drudgery. The women were curiously unconcerned with what was happening, as if this was nothing new or particularly exciting. Some, though, must have been wondering who might be hurt or even killed.

P9

P10

We stopped at one of the watchtower shelters and talked with the men who had stayed behind to watch over the women and their sweet potato fields. They joked and laughed about the war. They thought that after they had eaten a little they would go to the front lines and possibly fight themselves. We moved on, and in the course of half an hour passed several such groups. In the distance, the warriors at the front could be seen sitting or standing in little knots along a ridge that stretches westward from the no-man's-land between the Willigiman Wallalua and the Wittaia. The warriors were groups of friends or kin who had fought together, but were now resting and enjoying the spectacle of others moving out to join those who were doing the shouting and shooting the arrows.

As we climbed the slope leading up to the ridge above the fighting ground, a man came past us on his way home, holding up an arm in which the broken-off shaft of an arrow was embedded. Only a little blood was flowing and scarcely any fright showed on his face. I wondered how he would get this arrow out.

Farther on we saw some men who had come often to our camp. They were happy about the way the battle was going. On top of the ridge itself, we were met by the din of battle. The noise came from the shouting of men fighting and of men watching. From the earth itself came a sort of rumbling, made by hundreds of bare feet hitting the hard ground as warriors ran in all directions. As one cluster of fighting men came off the flat terrain and made its way up onto the ridge, another moved down onto the level field of battle.

From time to time, and especially after a particularly severe clash, a man who had been badly wounded would pass me on the shoulders of a companion. One was carried in such a way that his body almost floated above the ground. Doing this avoided the possibility of any pain that might be caused by the frequent turns and twists along the pathways home. One of the younger men who had sat by me at dinnertime the night before came toward me in this way, his whole lower body red with blood from a spear that had struck him in the upper leg. He greeted me wanly, and continued on.

We were too far away to see how many were returning in similar fashion to their homes on the enemy side, but there must have been several, because the battle was fierce. At least, that was how it was when they were actually engaged. At other times, as if on a signal given and acknowledged by both sides, the fighting would subside; both groups would retire and the struggle would end. Then, with much shouting and perhaps other signals, it would begin again.

By late afternoon, as rain clouds filled the eastern sky, the war ended and the warriors started along the paths leading back to their houses as far as three or four miles away. Neither side had won. The war was over by mutual agreement, stemming from an act of God that had sent clouds full of rain and discomfort for those who were far from home. The contest was left in suspense, unless later some warrior was badly enough wounded to die and cause there to be a funeral at which many women would mourn and be unable to work in their gardens. Then the enemy side would celebrate on seeing gardens untended or seeing the smoke rising from a funeral pyre, giving proof that they were indeed great warriors and should dance the *etai*, their victory celebration.

April 12th 1961

It is the tenth day with the Dani and still shocking to walk through the great trees in our encampment encountering virtually naked men smiling or grasping an arm in greeting and saying, "*Nyak! Halaok!* (Friend, I eat your feces)."

Even after this long a time, we are a continuing source of astonishment for the *akhuni*, as the Willigiman Wallalua refer to themselves. I suspect I may have been over-generous, even obsequious, in my demeanor toward our new acquaintances. The temptation is great to use our riches to dazzle them and transport their mostly innocent desires into a sort of rapturous loyalty. They want our shells with a craving bordering on desperation. We may be here only because, on our first meeting that tense afternoon a month ago, we showed them the large shells we knew they loved.

Today three important men have come into our forest, principally, I believe, to further their chances of getting such a gift. One of them was Kurelu, a famous warrior for whom the local area

is named and a man commanding the unhesitating respect and admiration of everyone living in this part of the Grand Valley. Like many men of authority, he has a deceptively modest demeanor. About him there is a quiet dignity that is backed, I'm sure, by a stern will and possibly violent resolve, leaving me no doubt about his ability to lead. He came at midday, naked and unadorned except for a simple headdress of fur and a relatively modest-sized *horim*, which is what the Dani call the hollow gourd they wear covering their penis and tied by string to their waist. I have seen him twice before, once on our first trip to this area and again two days ago on the battlefield. Both times he impressed me with his subdued, even aloof manner. A distinct aura of respect is obvious among those who find themselves in his company.

We were eating ducks I had again shot on the Aikhé River. Kurelu said they were creatures from enemy territory and therefore unfit to eat. He took a cigarette though, as much perhaps from politesse as desire.

P11

Everyone enjoys the fruits of this land's abundance. Here there is tobacco and all manner of things to eat. Even in such a land, however, some things are not easy to come by, such as the large Cymbium shells and the smaller cowrie and snail shells that hang around their necks. The *mikak* that are made from Cymbium shells are especially scarce and must be paid for dearly. Kurelu knows and accepts this, and so he will bargain in order to obtain them.

After lunch he came to my tent where there is a small, locked wooden box containing three enormous specimens in my larger hoard of Cymbium shells. When he saw them, Kurelu could hardly restrain his interest in possessing such marvels. I had the feeling he would do whatever he must in order to acquire even one of them. My conviction also grew that Kurelu was an important key to unlocking a wider Dani world, and I intended to be mercilessly pragmatic in my use of the shells to encourage his complicity.

Two other headmen came to see me while Kurelu was here. They also wanted a shell and they too would go to great lengths to get one. With the men was Husuk, the son of an important leader of the Kossi Alua, a different Dani group living to the north. Husuk was even less adorned than Kurelu, being entirely naked except for tan-colored mud he had smeared on his arms and sprinkled in his hair. Husuk talked for a long time about the war the day before yesterday. He spoke of how the enemy had asked for it before sunrise by shouting challenges across the frontier. He also spoke of how the leaders had gathered their men and their arms and of how the medicine men had come with their sacred green stones to sit immobile by a ceremonial fire as the battle was fought. He mentioned the superior numbers of the enemy and of how his own side had been afraid they might be overrun. He observed how poorly his own outnumbered side had fought and that, despite this, they should have killed at least one of the enemy. Husuk would like one of the shells. He knows about them because he followed Kurelu to the tent; he even gave into his lust by asking to see them. Because he had not been asked to come in, however, he sat outside, quietly. There is no doubt he heard the sound of the shells clinking together as they were put away and that Kurelu would probably tell him more in due time.

F8

F9

Besides Husuk and Kurelu, there was another headman named Wereklowé, to whom belonged much of the bitterness resulting from the recent war for the reason that it was he who had asked for it. Had things gone differently much of the sweetness of any success would have been his. In asking for war, he had not challenged the enemy but had requested that he be permitted to accept the challenge they had given, and so to him belonged the responsibilities such acceptance entails. He is a large and powerful man whose face is animated by a succession of changing and no doubt conflicting emotions. His mouth moves in concert with his thoughts, as do his eyes that appear to behold and reveal everything and nothing at the same time. He was not at all dismayed by the outcome of the war in which he had fought hard and bravely. It was an undertaking he will no doubt repeat. Meanwhile, Wereklowé would like another Cymbium shell, bigger than the one we gave him when we first arrived.

April 13th 1961

The realization has finally come that the sort of community we are trying to make here in the Grand Valley means that both permanent dwellers and impermanent visitors learn from each other. This process involves, most importantly, learning a new language, if for no other reason than to make a workable relationship with the hundreds of strangers who form the largest part of our new world. In terms of the patience required, the Dani have shown as much or more than we have. I am in fact distressed by the barrier to deeper understanding caused by my halting progress in their language. On the other hand, language has not prevented anyone from expressing endless curiosity about the other. I am amazed by the Dani fascination with the smallest detail of the lives unfolding in front of them. Binoculars, tins of food, mirrors, and plastic bags remain part of a different world, strange but for some reason unthreatening.

Yet they must be at least as anxious about where all these curiosities will lead as I am about whether our welcome will continue. They have as much to be explained to them as we have to us. How is it, for example, that we are so much better equipped to deal with common misfortune? Perhaps they know we can depart on a moment's notice, leaving them to fathom why we ever came. As long as we are here, they must reckon not only with the problems stemming from the cumulative, daily effect of our presence, but also with the difficulties in a future when we are no longer here. Between now and then, they may stand to gain little beyond diversion and much to lose through being distracted from the settled traditions that have given meaning to their lives until now.

The women are far less easily diverted than the men. Yesterday, at the salt wells high above the valley floor, women had come many miles to soak banana plants and certain grasses that grow in their garden ditches. These women showed none of their usual fright. They did not hide or even turn their heads, but instead went on industriously with the work they had come such a long way to do.

The salt well is at the end of a long and arduous climb. For what must now be centuries, people from the northern part of this valley and even far away to the east have climbed this hill, moving along the same path to the only salt for miles around. The stones on which so many people have walked for such a long time are worn smooth by this endless parade of bare feet. The rocks glow with a patina one sees when the Japanese rub stones by hand for a lifetime. The trees lining the trail and the roots that cross it also shine from being grasped by countless hands and feet. The path is full of the mystery of every forest.

After climbing for nearly an hour to a place 1000 feet above the opening into the wooded hillside where the trail begins, one comes upon a sudden clearing where light pours down on a small multitude of men, women and children going about the gathering of salt. They attend mostly to the leaves and grasses they have put into the huge basins formed by boulders set in the course of a salty stream, but the chatter of many women gossiping and exchanging news creates a marketplace mood. The understanding is that the task at hand is something of a fulfillment, where the object is at once both reward and prize. The body needs salt, and to get it people sometimes must risk their lives passing through the territory of the enemy carrying large burdens up and down a mountainside. The salt trek is not without its lessons in human tenacity.

F10

F11

P12

F12

April 15th 1961

Dawn came with mist still covering the gaps between the ridges above the slopes that connect them to the valley floor. Soon, singing began as men got themselves ready for a day at a war that had been planned the night before. Sweet potatoes, steaming in the hot ashes of their fires, will quicken everyone's interest in the wetter world outside their comfortable houses. Each village proceeded with arrangements customary on days of battle. Certain men would go to the gardens and stand watch while women worked. Younger men, older boys and all experienced warriors collect their arrows, bows and spears to do battle. Everyone who owns them puts on his best feathers and furs. Those so inclined also whiten their legs and shoulders with clay. The occasion calls for a man to look his best and everyone prepares himself according to both custom and personal taste.

The enemy was again the Wittaia, the group that lives on the western and southwestern edge of the Kurelu confederacy. The Willigiman Wallalua asked for this war and agreement to have it was given the evening before by several Wittaia leaders.

P13

Because the war was to take place on the Tokolik frontier, near the Warabara and the other traditional fighting grounds, it fell to a local leader, Wereklowé, to manage its conduct. I understand now that several fighting grounds exist in this area — the Warabara, Tokolik, and the Siobara ridge. Each is part of a no-man's land, or frontier, between Dani groups that make war with one another.

At first, it seemed there might be no contest at all. Hundreds of enemy warriors clustered at the southwestern end of a long strip of uncultivated ground upon which the war was to be fought, but few were present from the side that had made the challenge. The sun was already high above the ridgeline to the east and the low clouds that had covered the higher ground out on the valley floor had burned away. The day was bright with a promise of heat, enough to encourage one of the sudden rainstorms that keep this land so green.

It was early in the day, and every man and boy in this masculine world knew what to do. Short of some calamity such as rain, there would be time in which to do it. The sort of war these people wage involves formal elements apart from dressing well and appearing brave. First of all, there is an arrangement as to the place where the fighting is to be done and, second, there is a time when the fighting is meant to subside and finally to end. Very little strategy exists for mounting a surprise attack, though the older men do take it upon themselves to guard the fields where women are working in case an ambush has been laid. On the field of battle where the warriors gathered, all would happen according to a relatively predictable pattern.

Later, large knots of enemy that had been collecting since daybreak had grown to several hundred. Behind and to the side of the main bodies of warriors were other clusters, grouped according to their village or fighting affiliation. These, too, were being slowly augmented by bands of five to ten men arriving all morning from sometimes great distances.

Today's field of battle, the Tokolik, is 1000 yards long by about 100 wide. It was dry and open on one side to a copse of small trees and high grass and on the other to an area of thick brush and swamp. Here men would fight within 150 feet of each other. On the harder, middle ground where one's enemy was always visible, the distance separating the front lines might narrow to sixty or seventy feet.

F13

F14

P14

F15

At about one o'clock, the calling and shouting between the warring groups grew in intensity
until, at a moment both sides must have agreed
was appropriate, two relatively small contingents
of opposing warriors began to engage. The initial
skirmish resulted in several arrow wounds on
both sides. In this first flurry, lasting less than
twenty minutes, fewer than ten were spent in
actual combat.

The wounded came back alone, if they were
able to walk, or were carried on the shoulders of a
comrade, if they could not. Under trees in a shaded
glen, a man with an arrow embedded in his thigh
was held by companions who worked it free. Often
a bright green dressing of large wet leaves is put
over the place where an arrow has been extracted
with the front teeth of an experienced surgeon.
Other times, when the wound was not particularly
serious, a man would take up his arrows and bow
or his spear and hasten back to the front.

Between the first and next engagement was
an interval of perhaps one-half or three-quarters
of an hour. The front remained stable until one
side or the other decided to renew the battle; in
the meantime, men talked with each other or
shouted at the enemy warriors, who were doing
the same thing. Occasionally, whole cohorts of
fighting men, numbering fifty to a hundred, would
shift from an area behind the lines to a position
closer to the front. This change was often a prelude to a renewal of battle, which is what happened early in the afternoon.

The Wittaia, who had responded affirmatively
to the request for war, seemed the more eager of
the two sides to engage in fighting. One particularly well-decorated warrior, wearing a bark crown
with a train of long white feathers, leaped and
danced with great spirit mere yards from the
Willigiman Wallalua's most forward position. In an
utterly tireless fashion, he moved from one end of
the skirmish line to the other, teasing and taunting
his opponents by darting forward, stopping, lurching sideways, prancing forward, and then once
again back.

The effect on his opponents was to stir them
into retaliatory gestures of their own. Among our
friends who replied to these theatrics was Jegé
Asuk, the small, clownish, bowlegged younger
brother of Wali, the village headman of our local-

F16

P15

F17

F18

F19

ity. Asuk, Weyak and Aloro, a fearless and tireless man with a crippled leg, were three of a band of maybe thirty men who began to stalk their enemy across the broad Tokolik frontier connecting Wittaia and Willigiman Wallalua territory. Jegé Asuk, whose name means dog's ear, sprang forward and backward on his elastic, bandy legs, feinting with his bow and arrow. Occasionally snapping his rattan bowstring and, though probably no match for the feathered marvel on the other side, he nevertheless was an effective counterirritant and heightened the mood for greater violence.

A climax came in mid-afternoon as a huge cluster of warriors, hitherto quietly seated on a small rise 1500 feet from the battlefield, swarmed past their comrades on their way to the front, feet pummeling the ground. They went into action all across the flatter ground, just behind Jegé Asuk and his little band of provocateurs, but close enough to shoot and be shot at. As this group charged forward, the Wittaia made a countermove. It seemed almost as if both sides had told their opponents what they were going to do, so evenly matched were the newly committed groups in size and so coordinated was their arrival at the front. For perhaps fifteen or twenty minutes, as the two sides increased in numbers and as new groups of warriors moved forward, the battle increased in severity.

Wounded men were being carried to the rear by twos and threes, while others with more superficial wounds were treated nearer the conflict. From time to time, one side or the other would stage a particularly determined assault. There may have been no intention of overrunning the opponent's position, only of pressing them back and together so that arrows would have a greater chance of finding their mark. When warriors are scattered thinly across open terrain, an arrow, as long as it is seen, can be easily dodged. The men at the front enjoy near misses for it means they have the additional pleasure of firing arrows back at their owners. The arrows carry for perhaps a 100 yards. At that distance, their accuracy is minimal, especially because they are not feathered.

Often warriors depend on stealth to release an arrow into a knot of men from some more or less hidden position. Anyone hiding himself along the edges of the Tokolik frontier, either in the tall grass or in the swampy bush, stood the chance of being speared by patrolling warriors whose job it was to protect and clear the flanks. Despite these dangers, as many as seventy-five or a hundred men, on both sides, played on at this deadly game.

For anyone watching near the front lines, the sight of an enemy armed and eager to kill, tempting his opponent to come closer and present a vulnerable target, brings home the deadly facts of this intricately ritualized form of human combat. In agreeing to engage in these events, both sides accept the consequences of their decision. The object is not only to wound as many opponents as possible but, more importantly, to achieve a killing. Because everything happens inside a formal structure of conventions does not mean the fighting is mere sport. Elements of play are involved, but this may also be true of our own culture's use of deadly force. To explain what the Dani are doing as being mere recreation would be entirely insufficient. What is clear is that this is a phenomenon of enormous complexity central to their larger scheme of life. Fighting is what men do, even what they must do in order to be men, in the same way toiling in the gardens is what women must do to be women. If there were no wars, the shape of Dani society would surely change, if not cease to exist.

Today no such threat to the status quo seemed likely and, judging by the tender age of many who fought the good fight, the future looks assured. Small boys, no older than nine or ten, ones who come into our camp early in the morning and watch us with their arms clasped about their necks for warmth, were armed and ready to join the seasoned warriors. One of the twenty-year-olds, Hanomoak, who had been brought back from the battlefield with an arrow in his lung five days ago, was present again today, armed and ready, though still too frail to participate.

By three o'clock the tide of battle that had gone first one way, and then another, slackened almost to the point of rest. Perhaps it was an interval for reassessing the day's events. Would the rain, which was hanging close to the eastern ridge, arrive to spoil the afternoon's exploits? For twenty or thirty minutes both sides were relatively still and then a few rose to start for home, which for some meant several hours of steady walking; no one wanted to travel in the dark, especially if there was rain along the way.

P16

An hour later, it seemed quite certain that the war, after two or three major clashes, was over. No men were killed, but a dozen or more on both sides were wounded. Soon, only a few Willigiman Wallalua were left near the battlefield. Several large contingents of them remained seated half a mile or so from the now quiet front, watching carefully to be sure there was no risk of a sudden attack. Late in the afternoon, while the remaining Willigiman Wallalua warriors still at the front made fun of their enemies by telling them to go home to their wives and sweet potatoes, a large cohort of Wittaia unexpectedly advanced, inviting their deriders to demonstrate their valor.

In an instant, the sudden shift in tactics was communicated to the many Willigiman Wallalua who had been moving away, and they all ran back in time to meet the assault. As the battle grew in ferocity and weight of arms, more and more of those who had left came back, streaming along the major paths through the surrounding gardens. For another thirty minutes arrows flew and everyone seemed bent on causing at least a death that had so far eluded both sides. But it was not to be and, to the accompaniment of mutual catcalls and much derisive posturing, both sides withdrew. Finally, at the end of the afternoon, everyone was homeward bound, confident no more fighting was required.

In the evening I learned this war was not asked for by the Willigiman Wallalua but by the Wittaia. This explains the unusually large numbers of Wittaia who were first on the battlefield early in the morning.

April 18th 1961

The last twenty-four hours have been full of both large and small events, all having an influence on our situation as visitors to this remote corner of the world. For days there has been vindictiveness on the part of several in Wali's group. Jegé Asuk and Hanomoak have been especially active, kibitzing about who should get big shells, how people should behave toward us, where we should and should not go, and so on. Our having things they want has set in motion an internecine struggle. They hardly understand we have no special preference for one village or one set of friends over others. The idea that we will make gifts to whoever helps us does not fit well with their desire to have an exclusive arrangement. Many have set their hearts on what they regard as great riches, which means competing for a limited supply. Only Wali and Wereklowé have been given a large Cymbium

P17

shell. Kurelu is promised one, and Wali a second one, in expectation of their continued friendship in the days ahead. They already know which shell is theirs and they come often to admire it, offering the thinnest imaginable excuse for happening by.

Kurelu tells me, "*An eleken Holitia* (I have seen Hollandia)," which is a claim few of these mountain people can make. In response to his journey into the heart of Dutch colonial life, Kurelu is said to have derisively observed that not even the most important white man had more than one wife. Furthermore, the climate was intolerable and, as far as he could see, there were no big shells anywhere. About the only remarkable feature of this other world for Kurelu was the great salt pond, the Pacific Ocean, which was much bigger than the well in his own domain in the Grand Valley. As far as he could see though, this pond didn't even belong to anyone in Hollandia.

Since first seeing and talking with us, Kurelu has shown how deeply committed he is to the values of his own world. He is a man of unequaled importance in this part of the valley. His primacy was achieved by skill in war, in politics, and in the application of economic pressure wherever possible. Within the system of opportunities provided by his own culture, he was a master player. Nothing we could tell or teach him would improve his standing in his own society. The only objects we had that he wanted, and which might enhance his prestige, were our large shells. His desire to own one of them was transparent from the start.

Last night, almost on the stroke of midnight, when I had been asleep for an hour, a voice came through the netting: "*Pom—Pom—Pom*," my name in Dani. I was unprepared for this visitation. No one of Kurelu's stature had ever come after dark but he had walked for an hour and a half this moonless night from his village to talk with me about shells. Oddly, before going to bed, I had for the first time loaded the shotgun. I am not sure why except that I have recently felt a vague sense of disquiet. Everyone has undoubtedly talked for long hours about us as they sat in their *honai* waiting three days for the rain to stop. I know that many of these people regard us privately as snake-people, with white skins and strange ways. It is not our material possessions like knives, tents, and clothes, but our wealth in shells that gives them pause.

F20

F21

Kurelu must have been talking to Wali about our being here and why we had come. Wali feels possessive toward us and wants what we can provide in shells of all kinds. He points out that when Broekhuyse and I came the first time across the swamp to the dance ground in front of the Warabara, everyone went away except for him and Wereklowé. The others did not like us to be there and went home. Wali said we were human beings too and that we should be allowed to stay, if that is what we wanted to do. Now many others, despite the conflict between their twin emotions of greed and contempt, are in competition with Wali for what they worry are big shells in limited numbers.

Kurelu had come in the middle of the night to look again at the one he had seen the day before. He has been told that when there is a *mauwé* it would be his. A *mauwé* is an enormous celebration at which there is an extravagant exchange of gifts, especially pigs and shells.

Today, when I had returned from a walk in the gardens that stretch out toward the frontier to the west, about twenty small boys began performing an exact pantomime of their older brothers and fathers at war. They sang and charged, pranced and challenged, ducked and feinted, all of them bursting with proud energy, exactly as they have seen in the adult world. I was able to film them and I realized later how unique is this opportunity to make a film and how arresting is the physicality of this culture's expressive life. Its abundance and perfection are a little terrifying and so is the apparent ease with which we have been accepted. Perhaps I should say tolerated.

April 22nd 1961

This week has brought more rain than all the rest of the time I have been in the Grand Valley. If this wetness continues, we will not soon dry out. For the moment, the paths are channels for water to run in all directions. A walk is impossible without getting soaked, especially if you lose your balance on a pole laid across a ditch as a makeshift bridge. The only other event with remotely the same regularity as rain is warfare, which has occurred twice since I arrived. For the Willigiman Wallalua there was also a war involving many local warriors along the Kossi Alua frontier on April 20th, two hours away. The Kossi Alua are a confederation of clans living to the north and northwest of the Willigiman Wallalua. They form one of several groups conducting war against similar groups of Wittaia. Their villages are scattered across the vast garden areas between the territory of the Willigiman Wallalua and the high walls at the northern end of the valley. These villages are more difficult to see than hill villages because they are often hidden in the shade of the occasional groves of beech remaining despite years of gathering wood and clearing for new gardens. The inhabitants often can be seen walking great distances with heavy loads of firewood so necessary for daily life.

Tonight, as we were beginning to eat, two young men came to tell us that in the morning there would be war on the Tokolik frontier between the Willigiman Wallalua and the Wittaia. Apparently, our connection with these people is friendly enough so that they are ready to include us in their most solemn affairs, but we have yet to make real headway in their sacred world.

P18

In some ways I am not convinced we are enjoying their complete confidence and trust. I cannot help feeling some of the same skepticism with which I began this adventure, though now I am wholly relaxed in their company. The opportunity to be at ease tends to disarm us all. We can pursue our obsessive curiosity about almost anything they do and maintain our abiding disinterest in persuading them to adopt anything foreign to them, including Christ. Our only persuading has been that they go about their lives as though we had never come. Curiously, I feel that if there was to be a war tomorrow, I might experience some reluctance about going. Now that I know many of them, I am involved in their fates and it would be quite terrible to see one of them killed or even badly hurt.

April 24th 1961
Yesterday, following lunch, a strange hush fell over our forest. On looking up, I saw four or five boys of eight or ten years standing politely not far away. They were with an older and darker-skinned person dressed in blue trousers, sneakers, shirt and a baseball cap. He was a teacher, from the coast, and the boys were from his mission somewhere to the north, enticed there by the steel machetes they now carried and by the clothes, now rags, which they wore. They were students in a religious school. Three months ago, a Roman Catholic missionary had come to start this school in the northern part of Kurelu, the last large area in the Grand Valley that has until now escaped the reach of proselytizing missionaries. The boys of our neigh-

borhood stood in silent wonder of their contemporaries who looked so different from themselves. They were perhaps wondering when they too would have clothes and machetes.

I told the teacher he should not come again because we didn't want Christianity or any other doctrine confounding the people we were with. Soon the ragged band moved on, wondering themselves, perhaps, which distraction was more appealing, the missionaries or us.

This moment in the Grand Valley may not be so unlike the last years of the 18th century on the Great Plains of America. Here, now, is a culture that lives according to the customs and codes of preceding centuries. Until now, change has not been a factor in the living out of their lives because influences that might have engendered change have been thwarted by isolation. The discovery of this valley by Richard Archbold in the late 1930s, and the entry of missionaries beginning soon after the Second World War, were the origins of considerable blight for some. But in Kurelu, until a scant few weeks ago, most of those who dwell here had scarcely seen white skins and had no familiarity with foreign languages. Now they can listen to Dutch, Malay, English and an assortment of other strange tongues on the four or five transistor radios that have accompanied the missionaries and ourselves.

So far, the Dani have shown that the spirit need not break when curiosity is aroused, nor when the wealth we bring is more than they ever dreamt existed. Their culture is sufficiently vital and coherent to survive the distress and commotion we cause by being here, at least for the moment. I am certain though that new circumstances are beginning to alter what was here. Before, ignorance of other customs and ideas prevailed, but now the Dani can never return to innocence about others unlike themselves. Our behavior and our inventions must now enter into their calculations and nothing they can think of doing can prevent the inevitable alteration, even collapse, of the culture they have maintained alone and unmolested for unknown years. The boys of the mission school are merely the vanguard of a bleak army of once-upon-a-time warriors that will eventually be defeated by cheap cotton, metal axes, machetes, and suspect values.

P19

The war, which had been planned yesterday, did not materialize. Apparently, when people awoke they decided the certainty of the night before was not so certain after all. We waited in vain for the shouts and cries that pass from village to village on the brink of war. Yesterday's prediction of a battle may have been a rumor circulated by unreliable women working in the gardens north of us, or so I am told.

April 25th 1961

The rains have been so heavy that no DC-3 has been able to land at Wamena for three weeks. Four inches have fallen in the past three days. In midmorning a badly wounded man was carried, first by one and then by a second comrade, from the region of the upper Aikhé River to a Kossi Alua village about three miles away. He had been speared in the leg, arm, side, stomach and head by two men, both of them frequent visitors in our midst. Tegé Arek and Jegé Asuk were the assailants. The name of the wounded man is unknown to me at this time. The story of how the spearing came to pass was related as follows: The victim had had a quarrel with his wife; in a moment of thoughtless rage he had told her he was sick of the very sight of her and that she might as well leave his presence. She did so, rather unexpectedly, and when the man in question realized his loss, he sought her out. He assumed that she had gone to Tegé Arek's village for reasons that are not entirely clear. The husband went there to fetch her but was met by rebuffs. He persisted on three or four further occasions and, in doing so, made Tegé Arek extremely angry, because it was his village and he was the person blamed for what was happening.

The aggrieved husband was eventually persuaded to look elsewhere for his wife and so he set out with two friends to help him. Walking near the Aikhé, he met Tegé Arek and Jegé Asuk, who had gone to collect the fruit of their pandanus trees. They all fell to arguing while the husband's two friends moved on toward another village to inquire about the runaway wife.

In a fit of anger, Tegé Arek pricked the Kossi Alua husband in the shoulder, side and leg. Jegé Asuk, thinking of the time when the same individual had accosted someone else's wife, thought to do the same but his spear caught the man in his midsection and pierced the stomach wall. Grasping the spear from Jegé Asuk, the husband removed it from his own body and brandished it at its owner. Tegé and Jegé sprang upon the man, beat him to the ground, and left for a mountain village belonging to Wali. When the victim's friends returned, they found a badly wounded man. It was that man, wifeless and soon perhaps, lifeless, who was being carried home on the shoulders of his two comrades across the potato fields.

The sudden and pointless bloodiness of this affair reminded me that for nearly a week I have been awaiting the next war. I do this knowing that in the two battles I have seen, four warriors on the Wittaia side have perished. I do so also knowing that the chances are good that some men from the villages close to where I am living will also die. I even wonder, if it may not be true, that to take a life is the most intense, possibly ultimate, human experience there is.

April 27th 1961

On the tenth of April, after a particularly heavy assault by the Wittaia, a young and handsome warrior from the Kossi Alua was hit above the heart by an arrow shot at close range. Before he was lifted onto the shoulders of a comrade, the wounded man's legs were bent, and apart, and his shoulders were hunched slightly forward, as if he had fallen into some vile substance and was wondering how to rid himself of as much of it as he could as quickly as possible. When he glided by on the conscientious shoulders of his friend, I thought I could see more than fear in his eyes – anger perhaps, or disgust at the folly of risking so much so early in life. Yesterday, after sixteen days of pain and waning hope, he died. Today he was burned and tomorrow his ghost will accompany his living comrades in their next battle with the Wittaia.

On the morning of the funeral, men of different lineages met in their home villages to decide what shell goods they would bring to the funeral in celebration of the dead warrior. Aloro, Wali, Asuk and several other important members of the Willigiman group came mid-morning to the village of Abulapak. They sat in the men's house, discussing the long woven fiber bands, with their gleaming snail shells attached every three or four

P20

F22

inches, that had been collected for the occasion. The bands are about seven feet long and colored yellow, buff, and red in segments of unequal width. When it had been decided which bands should be distributed, and after the men had talked about their merits and values (all goods are given in the near certain expectation of reciprocity), each band was rolled into a ball and wrapped in straw. Aloro carrying one and Asuk another, the men emerged from the *honai* and set out for the funeral village.

Everyone who was going to the funeral had taken pains to appear as inconspicuously dressed as possible. Few shells were worn and only one or two men had their weapons. Some wore a few feathers, and nearly all carried a roll of tobacco looking like a book of common prayer as they held it in a casual manner. The little procession moved off past groups of women waiting for it to pass by.

In no time, the men were close to their destination and everyone stopped by a small river where there was shade and a place to rest. Along its farther bank, a large number of women were putting on bright orange and buff-colored clay they found just below thick layers of loose soil. This body painting was done without any particular regard for design or texture, but the effect was distinctly ceremonial. Whereas the men had reversed their usual practice of dressing up and had come largely unadorned, the women took the opportunity to add some color to their characteristically drab appearance. Instead of shell goods, they brought, besides their babies, gifts of the largest and finest sweet potatoes they could find.

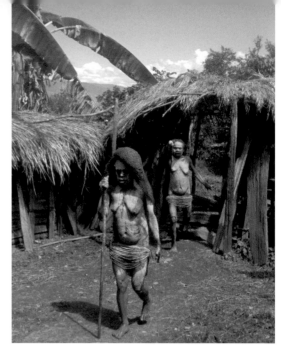

P22

By noon two hundred people had gathered in separate groups of men and women and were sitting off to the side of a crudely made wooden chair in which the dead warrior was tied. A congregation of women stretched back toward the village entrance and a small number of those most closely related were crouched at the corpse's feet, where a few children quietly played. On both sides and in back of the chair stood the principal female mourners: a mother, a sister, and a wife. From time to time, each languidly waved a bough of wilted leaves at the flies that swarmed around the dead man's still-festering wounds.

The sun circled the seated corpse and its heat drew forth putrid fluids even as it dried the tears of his women. For another hour or two, groups of men and women climbed through the village gate. Some had walked a great distance. Others were less closely connected and came mainly out of courtesy. The women set down their burdens of sweet potatoes, putting them into a pile of other nets full of similar potatoes. The women would find their empty nets when they were ready to go, as easily as if their names were written across them. Hanging from the women's heads was at least one other net containing tobacco, cooked foods, or even a sleeping baby. Sitting down with their friends wherever they found room, the females all the while kept up a sorrowful dirge with occasional solo parts punctuating a continuous chorus of lament. A woman would chant a line and the others would answer with liturgical precision. The unmistakable presence of grief filled the midday air.

P21

36

P23

P24

April 29th 1961

I filmed some birds on the Aikhé, including baby cormorants squawking in their nest. Adult birds were in the tree and circling above it. Nearby was Weyak's watchtower that had been knocked down by the Wittaia, who were angry because a few of their women had run away. The warriors had first laid an ambush for Weyak, but he had miraculously avoided it and certain death by spending the afternoon with us. I shot several rolls of film about rebuilding the watchtower. Weyak ended this tabooed work by cleaning everyone's hands with the feather of a parrot. The work needed the right magic in order to strengthen the tower.

May 7th 1961

Early this morning a man and two small boys came to my tent to tell me that one of Wali's wives was having her baby and that I should come quickly. This announcement came as the result of an agreement with Wali that, if he would allow me to film the birth, I would provide him with a large shell and a pig. His cupidity being what it is, there was at first no question this was an excellent bargain. Since the agreement involved more than Wali's bottomless greed, the assurance that it would be kept was fraught with several uncertainties. The affairs of women belong to a separate realm. Though women would appear to have little authority and are continually bent down by the long and difficult labors assigned them, they constitute a powerful and coherent force. Men have been thrashed by angry women who, however, will pay more for their impetuosity than men, had they done the same. Keeping women in an inferior status requires as much diplomacy as harsh repression. Though there are some signs of male weakness, men manage to protect their privileges

P25

38

P26

through astute management of delicate and economically promising day-to-day transactions.

Lokoparek is the village Wali established for the wife who was delivering. She was unable to live in the same village as his three other wives through want of mutual affection. It is less than two miles from our forest and 1000 or more feet higher in the eastern hills. We started off a little after dawn with Jegé Asuk to help carry our things. As yet, the sun had not come through the inevitable cloudbank above the eastern mountain wall. Climbing through the bogs and wet clay with thirty pounds of equipment soon wore me out. Knowing babies are not particular about when they are born, I made what haste I could.

We went through the village entrance straight to Wali's *honai*. He had heard us coming for some minutes and, when he saw us in his doorway, he began the traditional chant of affirmation: "*Wa, Wa, Wa.*" Clearly his thoughts were on the shell that he rightly supposed I had with me and of the pig which he looked forward to eating. Almost immediately, I surmised from his demeanor that the child, a girl, had already arrived. It is difficult to say just when she had been born but probably the night before. When I looked at her and at her mother I was certain her arrival was not a recent event. The child was washed and dry. The mother showed no evidence of labor and was fully recovered, smoking a cigarette as she rocked the newborn in her lap.

Wali's predicament was plain. He wanted the shell and pig despite the fact the baby had already arrived, which meant his bargain had not been kept. By arranging for me to come after the baby was born, he must have hoped to avoid the problem of his wife's and her female friends' disapproval of the agreement he and I had made. Coming such a long way expecting to film childbirth, only to discover it was over, put me in an even darker mood. I understand how lucky we have been in our first three weeks. But in recent days, two wars have aborted and today a birth came too soon to be seen.

Wali does not get his shell or his pig and I do not film a birth. We both are disappointed. I think my ardor, if it can last, and his greed, if it can be controlled, will mean we will both have more chances of the kind I missed this morning. Wali claims he is afraid of my anger. I think that he is only afraid that the shell is beyond his reach. He also told me that he was afraid to come down from his village of Lokoparek in the darkness. He certainly was afraid to face his women with me there to attend the birth.

May 8th 1961

In the early morning I set out for Homaklep, Weyak's village, to spend as much of the day as possible with him. Weyak was not in his *honai* when I arrived, but his close relations were and they made a place for me on the clean straw. I had come before they had begun to eat and, soon after I was seated, a small girl, barely able to walk, came with four enormous and very hot potatoes. As a rule females are forbidden to enter a *honai*, but among certain groups young girls not yet married can come and go, especially when they are doing chores for the men. Weyak's is such a group, and though it may have been this way before he had become important, his nature is such as to allow the little girls to mingle with the men.

Weyak cuts a formidable figure, with his powerful and athletic physique. He moves with great economy and grace, while still holding in reserve what must be large amounts of energy and strength. He is not especially tall, perhaps 5'-8" and maybe 150 pounds, yet his frame has the musculature that gives the impression of his being taller and heavier than he really is. With his physicality

F23

F24

goes a genial disposition. He thinks quickly but deeply, speaks clearly but not sharply, and is firm and thoughtful. Taken altogether he comes close to being admirable. I sometimes regard him, however, with an uneasiness that his apparent good nature might not prevent him from taking the lives of enemy women and children, should they stray across his path.

In a few moments, Weyak came back to the village and into his *honai*. As usual he offered me some of his breakfast and I accepted half of a peeled potato. Other men of his immediate circle came by to chat. One was a shy boy of nineteen or twenty whose foot still festers from an arrow wound he suffered nearly three weeks ago. The others were older or much younger. After two enormous potatoes and a cigarette, Weyak was ready to leave for his watchtower. He took his bow and a handful of arrows and started out. Unless he is very sick or there is a war, he does this every morning. It takes only fifteen minutes to go from his *honai* to his watchtower, stopping along the way to scan the expanse of gardens and intersecting paths for evidence of an enemy warrior who might have come in the night, possibly to lay an ambush.

Where the rain last night had smoothed the sand along part of the path he took, Weyak stopped to draw with an arrow the outline of a man and a large shell, a gentle reminder of the gift he felt was his due. He was amused at what he had done and did it again farther on. Near the Aikhé, which forms the southern boundary of his people's territory, Weyak took the arrow that he had been holding in his right hand and put it against his bowstring as if to shoot. After looking for a moment or two in the direction of the river, he took the path leading to his watchtower, which is built on a rise above the gardens situated around it on the valley floor.

Immediately on arriving, he put down his weapons and climbed to the perch atop the watchtower. For perhaps ten or fifteen minutes he carefully studied the countryside stretching out before him. When he came down he started a fire in the small shelter built beside all watchtowers as protection against rain and sun. He made another cigarette and then went off to his garden, where he would work until mid-afternoon. Before going, he

F25

changed his long, almost chin-high penis gourd for a short one that he had tucked away in the grass roof of the shelter. With his weapons in hand and his large bib of snail shells turned around to his back to be out of the way, he began at once the heavy work of turning the earth for new sweet potato vines.

May 9th 1961

Today I have been busy thinking of how to balance and adjust the factors contributing to our welcome and those prevailing against it. The evidence of trouble became obvious around noon yesterday. Despair over my abortive journey to Lokoparek was assuaged neither by the beautiful scenery on the way back, nor by the discovery of human bones in a shallow cave near an unknown and picturesque village up against the cliff's face. And later that afternoon, when Jegé Asuk decided to resist my efforts to film him in a minor sequence, the frustration and wasted efforts of the early morning took their toll. During my four or more hours trying to make a sequence with Jegé, I came close to hitting him.

Jegé Asuk knew exactly how to bring this on and I went off without finishing what I had started or resolving the conflict. That night he wanted a flashlight to light his way home to his village and, when refused, he used the refusal as an excuse to be vindictive. He is far too clever to not know we require his good will and he is too ambitious to allow his own wrath to spoil his chances for wealth or reflected glory in an association with us. He is manipulative and clever in his use of people, especially the young warriors from Wuperainma. Jegé is also an amusing person, tremendously alert, cunning and capable of a great variety of moods. He is among the most interesting subjects for film-making; much of the problem is that he is fully aware of my need of his help and involvement.

During the morning I had another serious talk with Wali, our inventive and exquisitely immoral host. It is easy for him to control his younger brother, Jegé Asuk, but difficult for him to keep his relationship with him untroubled. Our talk was meant to serve the need of airing our grievances, both Wali's and my own. The men in this culture talk a great deal, sometimes the truth, sometimes not. At other times they want to learn something or they just make conversational smoke in order to conceal their true feelings.

In the midst of this verbal confusion, helped not at all by my lack of fluency in the Dani language, Wali and I discussed giving Wereklowé a big shell. Wereklowé is one of the two men who originally got one, the other being Wali himself. Wereklowé is a man of greater stature than Wali. He may not know how to apply the same degree of craft to profit most from the snake-people, as we are sometimes called, but he can and did say of himself, "I am man enough to settle my own affairs and so do not listen to stories that people who claim they are headmen tell about me." This remark was in reference to a story we had heard that he was displeased with us for shooting ducks on the Aikhé and for offering them to Wali and to others who ate them and used the feathers for ornaments. Wereklowé had said he was indeed displeased about the ducks but only because people ate them. He said if people ate them they would not be able to see the enemy coming into the gardens, nor would they be able to dodge the enemy's arrows. He explained that the ducks came from the Wittaia region and so must certainly contain magic that would blind those who did eat them.

It was decided that Wereklowé should be given another big shell, as a gesture of goodwill to everyone in his sphere of influence, as a means of repairing the damage caused by eating taboo birds, as a way of patching up the supposed differences between him and Wali, and to gain back whatever good will we may have forfeited by being such inquisitive onlookers at all times of the day and night. Wereklowé accepted gracefully and without a hint of unction. He then left, asking me to keep the shell until some later time, as if to say that as much as he liked it, he did not in the least need it.

May 10th 1961

This morning some warriors were saying that Husuk was going to lead an ambush against the Wittaia with the singular intent of killing a man. The motivation was to avenge the death of Husuk's kin, killed by an arrow he received on April 10th. The camp was ominously silent throughout the morning, it having been said the ambush would take place at midday. In the early afternoon, we were still pacing our forest home, waiting for a sign that the raid was taking place. I was quite prepared for nothing to happen, having already seen two announced wars fail to materialize.

I was in the midst of an attempt to repair the broken iris in my 300mm lens when an enormous shout broke like thunder on the stillness of this expectant morning. The cry was the unmistakable signal of war. Obviously, the ambush had taken place and provoked a battle. The Warabara frontier was covered with knots of warriors dispersed along the entire length of this much used fighting ground. The Wittaia had assembled at least a hundred men who were engaged in a verbal skirmish with the larger Willigiman Wallalua forces. From the information we received at the front lines, no one was yet sure whether the man ambushed and speared in his garden was indeed dead. The mood among the attackers was solemn. This may be partly explained by the fact that during Husuk's raid, one of his fellow attackers was speared and another was hit in the belly by an arrow. The man wounded by the arrow was being carried on the shoulders of a companion along the narrow ridge atop the Warabara. When this sad spectacle came closer, I saw it was Tuesiké being carried by Sioba. When they were within a yard of me, Sioba bent down to rest a little for the long journey ahead and to allow Tuesiké to bathe his feet in a little pool of rainwater.

Tuesiké was rigid with pain and fright. His arms and legs were cocked in an attitude frozen by restraint, as if he might be trying to assume the pose of death in order to escape its grasp. I searched for the place where the arrow had entered his belly and saw a hole the diameter of a pencil, reddened but not bleeding, which could easily have been mistaken for his navel. The arrow had broken off and he must have felt it as he breathed, which would be another reason for keeping as still as possible. Sioba lifted him once again to his shoulders and left, while I continued on to the place where the Warabara falls away into a little valley in front of a higher hill to the west.

As I reached the front, the two sides broke off their shouting and retired to positions behind their skirmish lines. I went to talk with some from our neighborhood while waiting to see if there would or would not be a war. Wali asked for and received one of my cigarettes. We waited in this way for about twenty minutes, until there was a sudden move that I took to be a signal the war was about to start in earnest. Everyone leapt to their feet and ran forward, shouting. As soon as the surge reached the end of the Warabara I realized, from the inaction of the Wittaia and the elation of the Willigiman Wallalua, that news had come confirming the death of the man speared in his garden. At this point the Willigiman Wallalua would ordinarily be satisfied and start celebrating their victory while the Wittaia would simply go home and there would be no war. As the Willigiman Wallalua moved back in separate cohorts shouting their victory songs, grass was set afire along the top and sides of the fighting ground. Slowly and deliberately, the entire army of Willigiman Wallalua moved to its northeastern slope, and there conducted a preliminary celebration.

When I reached the main body of warriors and the few women who had heard the news, I noticed a quiet but anxious group of men at the edge of the swamp between the Warabara and the gardens. Tuesiké was there with Jegé Asuk and Sioba, as well as others who were making a stretcher on which they would bring the wounded Tuesiké to the *honai* in Wuperainma. He was in greater pain and more profound shock than when I had first seen him. His eyes were tightly closed and he drew his breath in a cautious manner. The men making the stretcher were concerned and their task was not simple, since there was little available except grass and a few rotting tree branches. When they thought the litter ready, Tuesiké was lifted up and put on it, rigid with pain and fear. Once on the bed of grass and leafy vines, he was covered so no part of him could be seen by the ghosts and so that the shape he made in his improvised cocoon did not at all resemble that of a man.

P27

P28

The last I saw was his stretcher being borne off in silence by four comrades, up to their knees in the swamp that borders this no-man's land. He will live or die depending on where the arrow lodged when it penetrated the wall of his belly, whether the surgeons who will treat him are successful in removing the point, and how resistant he will be to infection. He will not soon be fit for battle.

May 11th 1961

The graphic and defining moment making known the fact that the raid had been successful was when a fire was lit to burn the blood of the ambushed Wittaia farmer. Only then did everyone take up the shouts and songs of celebration. Even though today was to be the formal festivity, the dancing began yesterday on the eastern slope above the Warabara, and the sounds of celebrants from late yesterday until the middle of this afternoon have grown in volume.

Today in every Willigiman Wallalua village, people gathered from dawn until dark to sing and cheer. All the warriors took scrupulous pains to look their best before joining their respective fighting groups gathering at their customary watchtowers. Hanomoak took hours looking into some water held by a banana leaf to arrange his hair underneath an opulent headpiece of fur and bird of paradise plumes. Jegé Asuk, having little hair, took similar pains to paint his face.

The whole valley must have heard the exaltations that rang from hilltop to hilltop. The mood was one of high festivity despite the cowardly manner in which the enemy was slain, and the taste of victory was enjoyed by men, women and children alike. To successfully cross the frontier and penetrate enemy territory requires much stealth and guile. That there were enough of both may be the reason for so much jubilation. Yesterday's midday was strange; in the camp, usually full of visitors, there was no one except a few young boys and three or four idle women. The men were waiting for an announcement of war or at least the start of some kind of hostility. Thousands of Willigiman Wallalua were waiting to take part either in a fight or a celebration. Today they celebrated and women were the first on the field of victory, which they call the Liberek.

F26

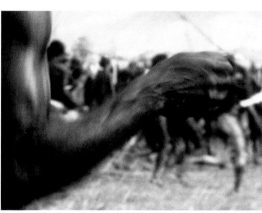
F27

Small groups of about fifty comrades danced first at their watchtowers and then across the gardens to the women who sang them a welcome by encircling the men with churning arms and legs. The celebration today belonged to the father of the victim, who was memorializing both his son's death and the retributory slaying of the Wittaia man yesterday. Hundreds came and participated with huge enthusiasm, but the mixture of people was more than the occasion could unify. At several points tempers flared over old grudges and unsettled disputes between warriors who were technically but not warmly connected. Wali created a scene when he saw a Kossi Alua who once had stolen one of his wives. The other man was chased off by the father of the victim, who wanted no unseemliness to mar the dignity of his son's memorial.

Men wept for the dead son, and women ran and jumped for joy over another lady's man being burned. Children watched and sang. The spectacle was vivid and affecting, seeming almost to justify war.

May 16th 1961

Since the visit five days ago by the police inspector and his squad of armed men, all aggressiveness seems to have fled the Williigiman Wallalua. They are still manning their watchtowers and are still afraid of the ghosts of slain enemy warriors, but I detect an apathetic population. It may be a long wait until the next war.

May 17th 1961

A young warrior has come to me with an arrow wound in his foot. He wanted it to heal and asked me to bandage it. My wish was to decline by saying I was not a doctor, but his request came at a time when I could not refuse. I finished putting ointment on the young warrior's wound and another man arrived, telling my patient there was war. Without a moment's hesitation he took his spear, saying he was going to the fighting. He went off swiftly so that he would miss as little of the battle as possible. Just before dusk I saw him talking with his friends about how they had surprised a Wittaia, weaponless, high in his watchtower and about how they had speared him all over, killing him with a thrust under the chin.

F28

Today I also saw a mother tempted to beat her little son with her digging stick for crying at having to watch pigs for such a long time in the rain, alone. The little boy, Pua, is very small and very quiet. If he is not alert, some day the Wittaia might find him and kill him, even steal his mother's pigs.

May 24th 1961

The last several days have passed amid hope, despair and finally certainty that normal life would resume among the Williigiman Wallalua. At times it has seemed as though we would not be able to stay on at Homoak, the name given to our place in the forest; at other times that, if we did stay, we would never see another war. On the 11th of May a police patrol made a visit to our neighborhood. On several subsequent days, patrols were sent to warn warriors that if they fought any more they would be taken off to jail in Wamena.

For days the effect was dramatic. Fearless warriors came to ask me if they were going to be put in chains. I thought not but said I did not know for certain. When I went to Wamena on Friday, I met with Broekhuyse, who had gone there to visit his wife and child prior to their departure for The Netherlands. He told me he had been called to Hollandia to answer charges based on fictitious accounts of his activities put out by both Protestant and Roman Catholic missionaries.

I decided to go to Hollandia myself to try and straighten the matter out. Of course, there was no certainty a good result could be obtained or even that there would be a plane to fly me out of this valley. For three weeks the runway has been useless owing to the endless rains. I went to Wamena and settled into the guesthouse for what I hoped would be a short wait. Early Monday morning, a DC-3 arrived and took Broekhuyse's wife, child and myself over the range and down the highland slopes to Hollandia.

Once there, I discovered it was a holiday, the second day of Pentecost, meaning among other things that the annual auto race was in full swing, having begun at 3 a.m. in the morning. At the airport there was very little transportation, since all offices and shops, except those run by the Chinese, were closed for the day. Finally, I was able to get a taxi. I knew the only way to see anyone was to go into Hollandia and say I had come with urgency all the way from the Grand Valley.

My thinking on the problem confronting us dwelled mostly on ways to restore our independence. A number of factors had to be taken into consideration. Above all were the verbal guarantees by the Dutch that we would be unmolested by police or other visitors. On the other hand, an allegation had been put forward by the local government in Wamena that our toleration of warfare was leading to new outbreaks of violence in the valley. This accusation was concocted from rumors circulated by missionaries and from gossip emanating from a variety of other equally unreliable sources.

One finds here in New Guinea plain but honest men thinking in relatively small ways and maybe not at all about their responsibilities as part of an historic process. The whole question of cultural disintegration is buried in the conflict over the goals of colonialism vs. self-determination. The most important issues have less to do with the destinies of the indigenous peoples of New Guinea than with the disappearing colonists of Europe. The problems stirred by our not entirely dispassionate study of Dani culture, including of course their ritual warfare, tend to heighten the basic anxiety of officialdom that the internal situation might not appear to the outside world as entirely settled and humane. That there is ritual war in the Baliem Valley is something all people who have lived in that valley know for a certainty; but what no one has bothered to find out is what warfare means to those who make it or what it could mean to deprive them of it.

Following discussions with various government figures in Hollandia, I returned to the Baliem Valley where another conference took place between the local authorities. In that discussion they talked about missionary activities, relations between the various religious sects, and about violence in other parts of the Highlands, such as in the south valley where CAMA (Christian and

Missionary Alliance) missionaries held a day of wholesale fetish burning with disastrous results. Apparently, a group of Dani was persuaded by a CAMA missionary to burn all its possessions, including weapons and holy objects. On the day when this mountain of goods was to be consigned to flames, a neighboring group appeared, angry that any Dani would do such a thing, and began to fight them. The toll of this battle was five Dani dead and many wounded. Three of the dead were from the attacking party and two from among those who had agreed to burn their goods. The missionaries later complained to officials in Wamena about being insufficiently protected from the nefarious natives.

May 26th 1961

On returning from a trip down river to see off a visitor, photographer Eliot Elisofon, I was surprised to see no one in the watchtowers and alarmed that no one was at the landing on the Aikhé. I knew something was happening because, when they heard the sound of our engine, people always came to greet us. As soon as I reached the little ridge above the river, I could see that no one was working in the fields which, unless there was a war, would never happen. Either there was a war or a funeral I had not been told about.

A glance in the direction of the Warabara confirmed the first possibility. Hundreds of men were grouped along its near slope and hundreds of the enemy were visible beyond them. I took my camera and with Broekhuyse quickly crossed gardens and swamps to the fighting ground. When we neared the frontier, we met Karl Heider, who had been stopped by dire warnings about black magic activities on the Warabara. Karl told us what had happened: the day had begun with a victory celebration for a warrior killed several days before, but was interrupted by Wittaia who had come asking for war. Reluctantly, our friends agreed to do battle. When we had arrived, things were very much at a standstill. The older men who had stayed behind decided there should be no war and that everyone should resume the interrupted victory celebration.

By mid-afternoon it looked as if the old men were right, but I could see Peter Matthiessen on top of the Warabara waving frantically. It had to be a

signal to either come because there was something
to see, or because there was trouble.

In a few minutes, Jan, Karl and I reached the
near slope of the Warabara and started the steep
ascent to the ridge on which Peter was standing.
The feeling in the air was one of greatly intensified
activity. Both large and small groups of men were
moving from place to place along the ridge, and I
could easily make out the sound of warriors taunting and calling to each other across the fifty or so
yards that separated the two armies. At the top of
the ridge, Jan, Peter, Karl and I retired behind a
clump of bamboo to rest and watch.

For ten minutes small groups of five to ten
warriors ran toward the enemy and then retreated.
These little forays were occurring with increasing
energy and frequency. Suddenly, a sizable assault
took place on the Warabara, involving perhaps one
hundred men from both sides. Hanomoak, Weyak
and Aloro, despite his recently healed spear wound,
were in the front ranks. In my experience there had
never been so many and such determined enemy
warriors. They had a grimness and concentration
that, though never before entirely lacking, seemed
to greatly enliven their ranks.

For two or more hours the battle was fully
engaged with few and very short interludes
between encounters. It was the first time I was able
to photograph fighting with spears at close quarters. On several occasions both spears and arrows
were sailing back and forth at a furious rate. Once,
a Wittaia charge carried the Willigiman Wallalua
completely off the Warabara. Regaining their position required tremendous courage and considerable
effort, because the way back was uphill. But the
Willigiman Wallalua recovered their lost ground
and the battle ended near the point where it began.

Several men were wounded during one of the
many sallies made by both sides: Jegé Asuk was
hit by an arrow in the small of his back; Siba was
hit above his heart; Hanomoak was hit in the left
hip by an arrow; another man was wounded by a
spear in his left thigh. No one was killed outright.
Siba is no doubt the worst off but he is famously
strong and, unless overwhelmed by an infection,
will probably survive. The victory celebration,
which had been momentarily suspended, would
start again the next day.

F29

F30

F31

F32

F33

May 27th 1961

The most recent victory celebration must be the seventh or eighth since we arrived. The first two or three were such novelties I was unable to comprehend much of what was happening. As spectacles, they are simply overwhelming. In these recent festivities, I have discerned something in the way of a structure. What appears to happen is that the name of the newly dead enemy is shouted across the no-man's land between the two warring sides. On the day the name becomes known, there is a preliminary celebration involving small, informal groups of men and women who gather to sing an exultant chorus or two. Usually, when one group does this, another will take up the chant at some other place, and so there is a chain reaction of singing all afternoon and well into the night, spreading the news up and down the valley.

On the day of a formal victory celebration, everyone is enormously excited and great pains are taken, especially by the men, to look one's best. The women also dress up. Often they will wear either the *mikak* or the snail-shell neck ornaments of their husbands and put red or yellow clay on their faces, arms and legs. In the late morning, following a few hours of gardening that cannot be suspended entirely for any reason, cohorts of warriors assemble at one of the main gathering points along the frontier. For about an hour, those belonging to a particular fighting unit, and associated with one or another watchtower, will dance as a separate group.

At a certain moment, they decide the time has come to be at the Liberek, the celebratory dance ground, and they start toward it, dancing as they go. Groups that have assembled at other points between the main garden area in front of our araucaria forest gather to dance at a midpoint watchtower a little back from the frontier. They wait there for some minutes until other groups join them. When this happens, they charge off, alternately halting and resuming their running dance.

On reaching the Liberek, an enormous shout arises and everyone merges with the new arrivals in a counterclockwise maelstrom of frenzied running and chanting. After several minutes of this, some of the men break off and start a running dance up and down the length of the dance ground. Separately or in small numbers, they savor

F34

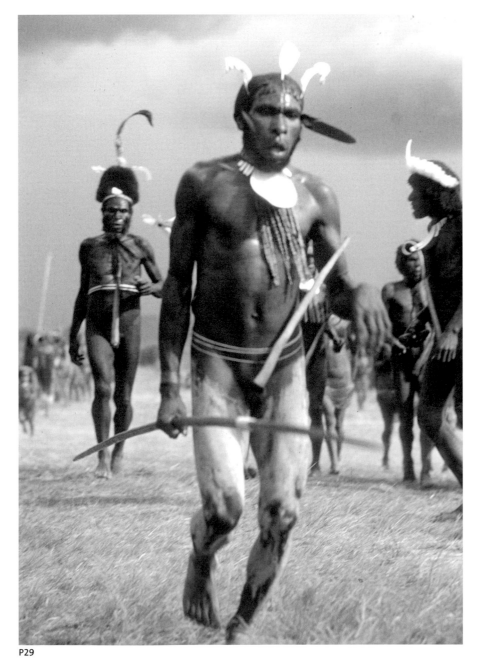

P29

the pleasure of their recent killing of an enemy. From time to time a group sits down, or another gets up to begin again to dance. Only when an entirely new group arrives does everyone fold together in a massive, counterclockwise spinning.

These victory dances involve all who belong to a certain confederacy of allied groups. The Liberek is used by those who live within that larger neighborhood. Other such places relate to other neighborhoods, both on our own and on the enemy side. The sentiment that characterizes the celebration is felt over an intense twenty-four-hour period in an area of no more than a few square miles. Each watchtower and gathering point on the way to the Liberek is a focal point for the singing and dancing that renews and sanctifies all the significant landmarks in a particular locale.

On the occasion of today's celebration, I chose to make the steep climb up the hill behind our forest camp. While remote from any dancing or villages, this is a place where all the different dance grounds can be seen in relation to each other. I spent most of the day in the company of a few children who helped carry my equipment. No adult Dani would have enjoyed this lonely vantage point so far from the joyful activity out on the valley floor 200 yards below.

Today's festivity was also an occasion for Wali to vent his anxieties. A concern is growing among important men about who will get a big shell. They cannot, of course, believe that we have many to give. They only can think of such a valuable object being extremely rare. We have given away only five: one to Wali, two to Wereklowé, one to Kurelu, and today one to Husuk, a grave and helpful man. Broekhuyse and I thought he should have it for all the answers he has given to our endless questions. Because he is not Willigiman and because he does not live in the immediate surroundings, he was not considered a serious candidate by our local friends.

Late in the afternoon when it had turned quite dark, Husuk came into my tent with Broekhuyse and Abututi, our Dani interpreter. Husuk was given his shell and a towel to conceal it when he passed through Willigiman territory on the way to his own village a long way off. As we walked contentedly toward some food, Husuk made his furtive way home through the deepening shadows. When I had gotten within a few feet of where we eat, I was

grabbed urgently from behind. Turning around, I saw Wali, who loudly hissed in my ear that Husuk should not have a shell and that he, Wali, was going to go away. This outcry only partly relieved his anger, and he kept shouting at everyone to stay away from us. He went off after saying again that he was very angry.

His rage will undoubtedly subside and the people he chased away will come back, but this episode exposed with clarity the tension our presence has created. The Dani we are living among have learned to tolerate and even help us, but what they see and learn from our presence has resulted in a number of conflicts in their minds. What has been important to them is now changing and they are entering a phase of waning innocence about another kind of world than their own. They are diverted but also disoriented and disturbed. The big shells from Massachusetts are important reasons why we can stay yet they also account for much of the friction and jealousy among those with whom we want to live and work. Still, I believe that along with the brittleness of some of our attachments there are meaningful and profound bonds connecting all of us individually and as groups.

May 29th 1961

Broekhuyse and I went early this morning to Weyak's *honai*. He had invited us to come to be with him before the victory celebration that starts later in the day. Weyak is a quiet and considerate man who, though he is without great wealth, commands respect. His age is difficult to guess but I think he is about thirty-five. Perhaps we were born in the same year. He is the most important man in Homaklep, a beautifully situated if not especially populous or important village. He has two or three wives, one of them extremely friendly and attractive. In his *honai* with us were several men. We spent half an hour talking and smoking while others were eating their morning sweet potatoes. Weyak blew off the ashes and scraped away the charred outer skin of a potato but then thought to give it to us, assuming we were as hungry as he was. One of the regular nine-year-olds had come to carry a bag and was very hungry, but because it was not his *honai* he did not ask for food.

We had brought a Coleman lamp so I decided to film this quiet interlude. Weyak is utterly con-

siderate, friendly, and maybe most amenable of all
the Dani men to the requirements of cinema. He
never tires of doing as I ask and I never have to
tell him to disregard the camera. I decided today
that Homaklep would be a good place to stay a
while. Our camp and its routines are confining and
too much time is taken up going there for meals,
listening to the radio for telegrams, and writing
notes at night. Such things should be done, but I
also must have the experience of living in direct
contact over a period of time with people in their
own surroundings.

After spending much of the morning in the
honai, we set out for the Tokolik frontier where
the Wittaia were said to be coming in order to
reveal the name of their most recently slain warrior. Once the name was known, the large victory
celebration could begin. Unfortunately we arrived
too late to witness the exchange of shouts giving
the victim's name.

When I arrived on the Liberek, I noticed
clumps of men breaking away and running off in
the direction of the Kossi Alua. In fact, most of the
warriors who had gathered there only thirty minutes
earlier were leaving. For ten or fifteen minutes, a
small group of women danced desultorily by themselves. Otherwise everyone's attention was fixed on
a group of older men seated near a fire. They said
prayers, held hands above the fire and made a path
from the fire in the direction of the place where the
Willigiman Wallalua warriors had gone to fight in a
war which had just begun on another frontier.

May 30th 1961

The rhythm of this place has returned to normal, or
at least it has returned to what it was when we
first arrived. Yesterday's victory festivities were
interrupted by a raid, hastily undertaken by the
Wittaia along the Kossi Alua front, so today the
interrupted celebration was held in earnest. Many
people came and the whole day was filled with
singing and dancing, which had actually begun
late the night before. Afraid of ghosts on his way
home, one of the young boys who visits us regularly slept under our cots. He listened to the
singing of joy that an enemy was dead, and to a
typewriter as Peter Matthiessen wrote about it.

P30

```
EC/400/28    (31/V/61)
    150'---Gaio game cont.-toy gaio against Warabara-light ext emely var-
iable-Uwar knocks man from gaio-sequence of boys going off from
Anelerak tried 3-4 times (Uwar puts seed in gaio and the gang goes off
toward the gardens///gut bird in distance (90mm)--3 shots women coming
home (75mm, 90mm)--Pans of Sokolik and Warabara-Mapiliama-Black hawk
faraway (90mm)-single women going home with big loads-Polik walking
in ds-with pan to Warabara Sokolik-Polik walking in ds with pan to
Warabara ((75mm F4)

EC/400/29    xx   (2/VI/61)
    Rufous hawk above Wuperainma (about 5 shots)camera off tripod
part of time--WEAKLEKEK SEQUENCE  goes high into mountains for 'lysanika'
leaves (for wrapping tobacco into cigs)--behind Homaklep,through fields,
up trail, view of valley past Weaklekek, cu Weaklekek, wife (Laholokleg)
joins Weaklekek, they climb through scrub, 15-20 shots gathering leaves,
cu's gathering (150mm)--Weaklekek's cayou (150mm) and man going to garden
from it-150mm of Homaklep- 150mm dead tree behind Homaklep- 150mm Okili b
in garden behind Homaklep-walking shots coming down to Wuperainma- (about
20' lost because of jam due to battery failure)
```

D1

F35

F36

May 31st 1961

Many people came by today including a large contingent from the Kossi Alua. Word of how to get a shell is spreading and there is a definite upturn in numbers of candidates willing to accept us. (I sometimes feel I talk like a missionary and maybe I am one.) Largely, however, I think the good relations we presently enjoy have to do with the rapport built by us as people who are at bottom generally nice but do strange work.

Wali and Wereklowé were particularly amused by the fact that a Wittaia woman had fallen into the Baliem and drowned. No celebration would be held for her death, since it is accidental, but everyone is nevertheless pleased.

This evening a young boy was speared by a branch on a fence he was climbing and a long splinter was pulled from his thigh by someone's teeth. He was then carried home like a warrior.

June 2nd 1961

Jan and Karl went down a very low Aikhé River to get the mail and I climbed far up the mountain wall with Weyak, who asked me to come while he and his favorite wife collected leaves to wrap cigarettes. Were it not for the spectacular views of the valley west and north, and the marvel of this man peacefully gathering leaves, I would feel more troubled than I do.

June 3rd 1961

Apparently the Wittaia wanted war today, or so a Dani with Kurelu connections said to us when he stopped by on his way to visit some Kossi Alua. The Wittaia wanted a war but decided not to ask for it. The decision may have been wise because rain started in the mid-afternoon and has continued late into the evening. I spent the morning in a cave near Lokoparek doing an experimental film sequence of a young man dreaming. It is the first completely fanciful roll I have shot so far and may easily have no merit.

June 4th 1961

I began the day sleeping late, then walked a mile or so to a secondary rain forest filled with orchids and ferns. I saw my first bird of paradise, which is something of a crow to listen to and to look at, except for a wonderfully iridescent blue collar that fluffs out when it cries. When I returned, and while Wali was visiting me, a great crying for war was let forth. Wali burst out of my tent, looked to see where the trouble was, and ran off to his watchtower where some Wittaia lying unsuccessfully in ambush since noon decided to set a fire. A small battle began and three men were wounded, including Jegé Asuk.

June 5th 1961

Today Jan, Peter and I moved to Homaklep to be closer to village life. While talking to Weyak, word was shouted that the Wittaia were once again asking for war. Weyak ran to the front and I tried to follow. The war never developed beyond the release of a dozen arrows and everyone stopped when it began to rain. The night was spent at Homaklep and a wretched night it was, full of mosquitoes, mice, rats, bats and clammy air. I was able to do no more than some still photography with flash which no one seemed to mind too much.

June 6th 1961

I was late waking after a night with rats and mosquitoes and got up well after dawn enveloped in tremendous clouds of smoke created when Weyak's wife began a fire for the morning meal. Later, Jan and I watched Weyak working in the gardens until midday. No woman would think of going to the fields until after some men had gone ahead; in this and other ways a woman's rhythm is subsidiary to a man's, a sort of female harmonic. Weyak later killed a pig for us and we ate it with him and his family. Peter stayed on but I returned to Homoak extremely tired. This visit to Homaklep has been worthwhile because without it I'd have no sense of the mundane in Dani life. I must do this more.

June 7th 1961

Peter has come back from Homaklep and I have sat at length looking at the valley through binoculars. Suddenly, as if a movie had suddenly begun, a whole community came to life as war erupted on the Tokolik. Instantly, Peter and I ran through the swamps and climbed an araucaria tree. It turned out to be much too hot for the heavy kind of fighting taking place and gradually all action came to an end.

P31

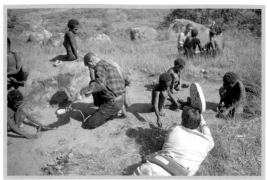

P32

June 8th 1961

Today was quiet, though there was talk of a Wittaia ambush and a Willigiman Wallalua counterambush near the Aikhé. In the afternoon along with Pua and a few of his friends, I watched emerge from the innocent imagination of the boys a village made from araucaria seeds. They had created detailed models of all the different structures essential to village life.

There has been talk of our Indonesian cook having a heart attack, but I think it is more likely stomach trouble caused by a bottle of Dutch gin I gave him.

June 9th 1961

Karl and Mike made an early start for Wamena and Peter accompanied me to see an old man with a withered hand. He was in the *honai* with his son who was terribly infected by an arrow in his left shoulder, inches from his backbone. He had also been hit in the leg. I dressed both wounds after milking several ounces of pus from his shoulder, and I gave him some penicillin I carry when making these visits. Now he may not die, though more than half the deaths in wars must be from infection.

June 10th 1961

From dawn until evening there was a *wam kanekhé*, a ceremony to renew the holy stones meant to give warriors strength in battle and others uplifted hearts. The awful irony was the murder, in the midst of this ceremony, of a small boy named Weaké, which means "wrong path." Wittaia warriors had crept close to the gardens next to Weyak's watchtower and speared him from an ambush as he went down to the Aikhé for a drink. Tomorrow, mice and birds will be caught, killed and eaten to lift the magic spell put on everyone from eating, or just having, so much pig meat.

June 11th 1961

The funeral for the murdered Weaké was today and we went early to the *honai* of his forsaken father. In the dark I did not at first see the dead boy, who was propped against the wall just behind me. When his funeral chair was finished, he was taken outside and carried to it, at which time his penis sheath was changed. Women began coming into the village with nets of sweet potatoes while men came carrying nothing, but in many cases wearing the much beloved snail-shell neck ornaments. Many pigs were killed, the steam pit was made ready for cooking sweet potatoes, and wood was gathered for the funeral pyre. In important ways it was a boy's ceremony, with the young prominent in all its aspects. The village was filled with mourners and the collective mood was one of profound sorrow.

The boy had lost his fine looks from a prominent lump on his head where he had either been hit or had fallen. His was a most misshapen and abused corpse showing the evidence of multiple spearings. Eventually he was taken from his chair and placed on the funeral pyre late in the afternoon at the same moment I was buried in a film-changing bag and unable to film his final journey.

June 12th 1961

Today Weaké's funeral continued as did the *wam kanekhé* but we arrived too late to see the holy stones cleaned and put in their shrine in the back of the men's house. Mice were hunted, ritually purified and eaten by the boys and a few of the men. At the funeral, women had a subdued feast of sweet potatoes and their mood swung almost to jocularity. Weaké's mother, though, spent more than an hour fishing her child's bones from the ashes.

As custom has it when someone is killed, a few of the victim's relatives are mutilated. Several joints of the fingers of three girls and part of an ear of a young boy were cut off. To accept my offering of a shell, one of the little girls extended a bloody hand she had used to cup the elbow of her wounded limb. She and the others were wide-eyed but not undone by pain or grief over their recent losses. We, on the other hand, are more prosaically exhausted by the week just ended.

P33

F37

June 13th 1961

Today was one of the last in a sequence given to observances connected with Weaké's funeral. While the women had another feast, Weyak and close relatives caught more mice and rats to lift a magic spell attending the death brought about by the enemy's treachery. In Weyak's *honai*, several headmen had a long discussion about the division of funeral shell bands brought by Weaké's kin, the organization of their defenses against such attack and the strategy to adopt in reply to the death. I was able to spend a relatively quiet day but Jan is apprehensive about what is to happen to him when we leave.

June 14th 1961

Midway through the afternoon, word reached us that some Wittaia were in the woods near Lokoparek. Every man burst from the village, ran to Homaklep and then up the steep garden slope rising behind the village. I followed, legs failing from fatigue and, on reaching Lokoparek, learned that the alarm was false. We spent part of the day getting ready for the trip tomorrow to take Mike and his friend Sam Putnam to Wamena to begin their journey to the Asmat. Jan will go with them as far as Wamena.

June 15th 1961

I was told early this morning there would be war, but the description of what would happen and where suggested a raid more than a formal battle.

P34

P35

Many strangers came by on their way to the front. Clearly, they all expected an engagement. Weaké's uncle, who would lead the raid, came trailing his spear through the bushes on his way to the fighting ground. He would try hard to kill someone if he was given the chance. Toward the end of the afternoon all the warriors were drifting home. The raid was not a success and it would have to be tried again, or maybe the Willigiman Wallalua will ask for war as a way to avenge Weaké's murder. Wali came tonight to ask for another shell he described as being "big as the end of your bed."

June 16th 1961

Willigiman Wallalua strategies appear to be developing since the discussion a few days ago. Many strangers appeared in camp yesterday and today, and with each warrior there has been a larger than usual bundle of arrows. Jan has come back on a very low Aikhé River and I have spent the morning with Pua on the hill behind Homaklep while he tended his pigs. Midday was a low period for me. I tried to be alone, but with little success. Solitude is a condition contrary to the Dani sense of rightness in human society.

June 17th 1961

I tried to do a little early morning filming on the hill behind Homaklep, but the work lacked inspiration. The people have slowed their pace and the raid planned for Thursday and Friday has run into police patrol activities. Still, a war is expected today on the Willigiman Wallalua front.

The film report I got yesterday in the mail is entirely inadequate and I think seriously of going to Tokyo to have a look at the rushes. Might I also be thinking of finding relief from the discomforts and frustrations of my Highland Dani life?

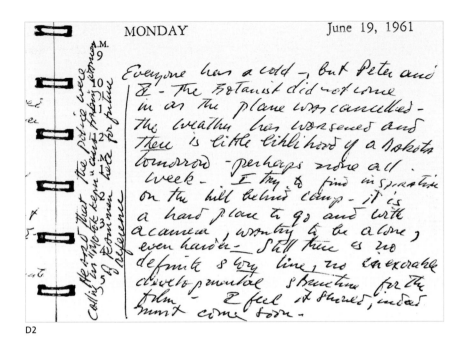

MONDAY   June 19, 1961

D2

June 18th 1961

An earthquake last night went on for what felt like
minutes. Today, however, has been quiet. Since the
week of June 7-15, life has definitely slowed. We
think this is due to nearby patrol activities by the
Wamena police. Tomorrow, if I go to fetch the
Dutch botanist I have invited, I shall want to discuss these matters with the authorities. The police
have been telling the Dani we are people of no
importance and they also have been saying certain
Dani men will go to jail should they make war.
Such news is dispiriting and, if true, means the
agreement I made with the Netherlands government may have been broken.

Pua tells me again his father was burned. I'm
not certain what he means but assume it is a way
of saying he died.

June 19th 1961

The botanist did not come because the plane was
canceled once again owing to weather. I look for
inspiration on the hill behind our magical araucaria grove. Getting there with a camera is hard
and trying to be alone is harder. As yet I have no
storyline for the film, and no clear developmental
structure either, only some motifs and a few thematic notions like the bird/man business. I feel an
approach should, indeed must, come together in
my mind before too long.

June 20th 1961

The tempo of recent days has slowed dramatically.
The wife of our policeman-translator ran off today,
pursued by her husband. He found her after she
had gone a fair distance into Wittaia territory.
Apparently, last night he wanted to shave and she
wanted the light out. She hit him and he hit her.
She left, slept at Wuperainma, and then made off,
pregnant, across country.

June 21st 1961

The rain continues and so there are no flights. I
used the day trying to sketch the film. The cover-
age seems vast and sometimes the scale feels
appropriately epic. But more material with a little
humor and common appeal would help to balance
the spectacular. Pua looms more and more important as a sympathetic figure and counterweight to
the heaviness of death and misfortune. I want to
do closer work with pigs, holy stones and sacred
practice of all kinds. Everything is tied together
somehow.

June 22nd 1961

At first light, I climbed the hill behind us, hoping
to film an especially dramatic morning with mist
hanging above the Warabara frontier and the
Baliem River. For almost an hour, as the mist
slowly dissolved, I single-framed the scene from

P36

my perch on the hill until I was engulfed in the cloud, which would not lift but instead enveloped me and our forest home. Later I went to Wuperainma to see Pua take his pigs out for their daily rooting about in the fallow gardens. He exits the pig stalls three times trying to get it right (for me), crosses a little bridge, looks at himself in a rain puddle and then goes past what I call the bee tree, owing to the hives in its upper branches.

As Pua climbed over a fence to get into the gardens, the Wittaia shouted for war, which quickly followed. It happened that the Wittaia were routed by an army in ambuscade. I started to film them in retreat following the ambush, but the battery cable shorted and the opportunity was lost. I was myself in a kind of retreat until the needed repair was made. I later spent a long time filming a man while an arrow was extracted from his chest and while holes were made in his belly by a surgeon comrade to release the bad blood caused by his wounding. Kneeling down to shoot, I managed to get a long thorn in my knee. It was removed with ease.

June 23rd 1961

I went with Peter to Wamena on a river high from the relentless rains of these weeks. We found the Javanese botanist Versteegh and gathered our supplies. I also managed to have an amiable talk with the Dutch officials who promised to give the patrols stricter orders about staying out of our way. The official is a friendly and sincere man who is being assailed on all sides for our being here. Things will hopefully improve even if the critics grow louder.

June 24th 1961

I spent much of the morning in the gardens with our botanist and while not especially fruitful for filming, the experience was useful in that his expertise was filling an immense hole in our knowledge of our surroundings. This quiet Javanese, who first came here with the Archbold Expedition in 1938, had to be one of the first from the outside world to enter the Grand Valley.

I would like to have someone providing the same kind of understanding of our geological surroundings. When I was thinking a year ago about who should come on this endeavor, every possibility was considered, including a painter. It seemed then and now that the points of view, and the ways for expressing those views, should be as many and different as possible.

June 25th 1961

With Peter and the botanist, I climbed almost to Lokoparek and looked hard at many plants and trees, including numerous gardenias, fragrant rhododendrons, yellow and red orchids, and even pure white orchids as if for the first time. Much of the local flora is in flower and so I filmed a few of the most arresting specimens. I hope to see in bloom the orchid that grows on the Tokolik frontier; it is tall and said to be yellow.

June 26th 1961

Shouts of war this morning announced that in the region of the northern Willigiman Wallalua there was to be a battle. Few from here went that way. I spent the morning thinking again about film continuity while the others kept on botanizing. No gunfire has been heard since my talk with the officials in Wamena, but I learned today the Catholics would soon build a schoolhouse almost in our front yard. The date for this is not known, but the end for these Dani as themselves is now a certainty.

June 27th 1961

Today, behind Homaklep, I filmed the preparation of materials used to gather salt. Pua watched from his pig place behind and up the hill. Jan is distressed about the future, as is natural for a man with so many bureaucratic enemies. He wants to continue working in anthropology and hopes to redeem himself when he shows what he has done here and when he is asked why he ever came.

June 28th 1961

At daybreak, a number of us started out for the salt wells. The day turned out to be as physically hard as any I can remember. On our return, we learned that a man named Alum had planned with others to ambush us, but they appeared to have scattered when we drew near.

June 29th 1961

The abandoned ambush turns out to have been the brainchild of one Amouli and not Alum, though Alum is probably in the background. Wereklowé went to tell them both, neither of whom I know except in passing, they should not try to hurt us or anyone working with us. Otherwise, jail will be the consequence.

June 30th 1961

Weyak has told me of a Kossi Alua killed by the Wittaia quite far away. He is said to have been burned today but no one went from here. Wereklowé had a pig feast to inaugurate the new *honai* in his village near the trail to the salt wells. It was strictly a clan affair. Karl has learned some Roman Catholic schools were burned because promised shells never materialized. I have no idea which schools or where they used to be, but I will be even more careful to make no promises about shells we don't possess.

July 1st 1961

Late yesterday we were told the police shot and killed a Dani who gave them trouble when a patrol went to investigate a private war. The funeral for the incredibly old and decrepit man whom I have had my eye on since coming here was held today. I compare him in my mind to the old lady I knew and filmed at length in the Kalahari and who was the subject of one of my infrequent essays. The man's name meant "child" and, when first told about this death, I thought it might be a child. Still thinking this I went into the *honai* where the corpse was propped against a wall. As I grew accustomed to the darkness, I saw the long finger-nails and the torn dry skin of the old man. The funeral was the smallest I have yet seen.

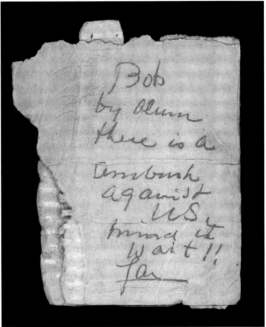

D3

F38

July 2nd 1961

Word spread early this morning that a headman from the village of Abukulmo was dead but when I went to greet his family, I found that he was not dead at all but what is called "dead sick." A rancorous fight ensued over where he should be burned, even before he was dead. Early this evening he was carried past our forest home, wrapped in grass, on a litter bound for another village. If he dies, he will be burned there. If not, they will carry him back to Abukulmo.

July 3rd 1961

The weather has been wet from the rain and raw from the cold for nearly two weeks and I have decided to take the first day off since February 11th.

F37

July 4th 1961

At Wuperainma on this warm and beautiful morning, I filmed a sequence of Pua taking pigs out of the pigsty and out of his village as is his duty and his destiny as a Dani boy. In Homaklep the salt-soaked banana leaves were put out to dry. Concern is growing over the still unavenged murder of Weaké. Today I heard for the first time the story of how he had gone to the Aikhé to get some things belonging to us and was killed doing so. I hope it is not supposed that this is true because it is not. We may have had things there, but no one was asked to go and get them.

July 5th 1961

I sat with Weyak at his watchtower until he left with a war party at midday. Later Peter and I crossed the Aikhé and hid in the high grass, watching warriors move toward the fighting ground farther to the south. Shouting began late in the day because the Wittaia had begun a victory celebration for having killed young Yonokma, one of the local youths of fighting age. Our Willigiman Wallalua friends were stunned and disbelieving. This occurrence was a complete reversal of the fortunes expected when our side planned this unfortunate raid to avenge Weaké's death many days ago.

F39

Just as the sun began to set, the Wittaia brought Yonokma's body to a place where it could be claimed. The blood of a newly slaughtered pig was smeared on the corpse and four arrow-like twigs were shot in an arc over it. This raid is a disaster. It was meant as revenge and has ended in yet greater imbalance between these warring groups. The father of the boy who was killed today belongs to a *honai* that has just cleansed and renewed its holy stones. What dark inferences should be drawn from such misfortune?

F40

July 6th 1961

The funeral for Yonokma was spectacular. Eleven pigs and twenty-five shell neck ornaments, amongst many other goods, were exchanged. Hundreds came and feelings ran high throughout the day. Yesterday's raid was a great blow; the men are angry and the women forlorn. I felt more weary today than at any other funeral, perhaps because there is so little I feel I am able to do. As soon as the funeral pyre was half consumed, the

P38

headmen could afford. Does this mean that the ritual significance of little girls' fingers is less important than conserving pigs?

This morning was a high point in recent inclemency. The rain began before dawn and did not end until mid-afternoon. Late in the day I filmed several boys chasing ghosts, something they are able to do without the anxiety that fills the adult mind agitated by the mere thought of ghosts.

July 9th 1961

I was awakened several times last night by our recently acquired puppy. Dani purebreds do not bark but they do moan, especially in a new and unfamiliar place. Today I have arranged with one of the children from a nearby village to take the puppy at night and bring it back in the morning.

For the second day I was able to film boys chasing ghosts out of Wuperainma under the instructions of Wali who is more or less in charge of magical practices. I also worked with Pua on two sequences which may or may not be of any use or interest. One concerns his walk home past Homoak, in which he imagines ghosts and the other in which he stubs his toe by the bee tree. What I saw in the viewfinder held little promise for the reason that asking people to do something they do convincingly on their own seldom looks right.

July 10th 1961

The man from Abukulmo has in fact now died. I was told this by Weyak, after he had seen certain individuals carrying a particular kind of wood down from the hills behind Homaklep. The man has been declared dead on three different occasions. How people knew he was about to die eludes me. His is the third funeral in ten days. Everyone is exhausted by them and the bloodiness of it all is beginning to cloud my mind.

July 11th 1961

Cables have arrived about the processed film and they need immediate replies, so Jan and I made a trip to Wamena on a very low Aikhé. Thanks to a submerged tree, Jan had an accident that nearly cost him his life and sent both boat and motor to the bottom of the river. We had to walk back through thick grass and swamp to our home in the araucarias. I had been able to save the engine but

mood swung toward nervous relief, though the women fell into even deeper despair.

July 7th 1961

We rose early waiting for the finger amputating we were expecting to happen but never did, at least not where I had been told it would take place. I am not sure I am sorry. I wish some things were not part of this culture and cutting off joints of a little girl's fingers with a stone ax is one of them. I am unsure though if I would object enough to try and change the perpetrators' minds. Has anyone filmed such an event and, if not, has it some irresistible cinematographic allure?

July 8th 1961

We had arranged to go again to where the little girls whose fingers would be cut off were meant to be waiting. However, a message came that no fingers would be sacrificed. To do so would, it was said, involve an expense in pigs which none of the

the boat remained submerged. Tomorrow we will go back to try and retrieve it. My patience is not as ample as it has been. This whole endeavor is providing diminishing satisfaction, explicable in part at least for being told by the laboratory I'm getting problematical results.

July 12th 1961

Peter, Karl, Abututi and a small party of Willigiman Wallalua youths went with me to salvage the boat. We found a way to refloat it and I paddled eight hours to Wamena, only to discover the government radio transmitter was being moved and there would be no service for two days.

July 13th 1961

I worked all morning on the boat's motor, changing the head gasket, cleaning the carburetor and fuel pump. Finally, it started.

July 14th 1961

Radio contact with Hollandia was too poor to send cables but a DC-3 flew into Wamena with Michael and Sam and then left with someone who will take our cables to Hollandia for transmittal. Michael is extremely happy with his trip to the Asmat and speaks of returning to give it a closer look after I've left the valley. On the Warabara fighting ground there was a flurry of activity, but the raid failed because no Wittaia were in their gardens. Something will happen soon, I feel sure.

July 15th 1961

I am more and more certain we have begun the corruption of the Willigiman Wallalua; they long for things that are only emblematic of our world. They crave many of our belongings and appurtenances and then give vent to their craving by begging and even stealing. We are really not so different from the missionaries in long-term effect on the Dani. We cannot leave with clean hands. Ours is, by contrast with the missionaries' holy undertakings, an unholy enterprise in which the Dani have begun to lose their way as they learn about ours. I've come to see that the young boy named Uwar is among the brightest and the most corrupt(ible). He is frighteningly adept at getting himself the little things he wants. An inevitable result of lost innocence may be humiliation. Many have not reached this point yet, but are we gentle enough to preserve their dignity as we undo their culture?

P39

P40

July 16th 1961

It has rained almost all last night and today continues in concert with a plague of termites. I suppose they have been washed out of their nests and have found our tents their next best refuge. They were several inches deep inside and outside our quarters. Today, though torpid and decimated, they hopefully have enough will or instinct to move on. Time weighs on our affairs more heavily and none of us has the same enthusiasm as when all this began. No doubt there is more to do, but until I see some processed and printed film, it will be hard to proceed with any semblance of confidence.

July 17th 1961

The day was dull at first, but gradually became brighter. I was able to shoot what I hope can be the final sequence of a film. The Aikhé may be too unfamiliar to carry all the intended meaning of ending images, but it might suggest at least a frontier, a place where fresh water is abundant, and where Weaké was killed.

Peter and Karl went to a cave where there are some quite beautifully conceived charcoal drawings on the walls. Evidently the images are by some young men whose names I do not know.

July 18th 1961

I was in the Elokhera River valley with Weyak, Pua and Peter today for many hours. I had had the idea to try and film a hunting sequence. The terrain was wet, even away from the river, and birds of any kind were scarce. The day was one of the longest and hardest so far. At the end of it, Peter complained about our light being on at 10 p.m. when I had awoken from two hours of after-dinner sleep. He thought it should be out because he had not slept and because I had "snoozed around."

July 19th 1961

I went with Pua far out on the Kossi Alua flats beyond the Elokhera River to a new garden where he is expected to work. On the way, slapping at mosquitoes, sliding on the mud borne down by the ponderous weight of my craft, I had a sudden revulsion for nearly everything I was doing. My former tolerance of the small frustrations and annoyances of five months was giving way to a despair that it all must continue for another six weeks. For a moment, I tried resting by the river, but people and a parade of other pests drove me on.

Tonight, after heavy afternoon sleep, I recognized an essential pitifulness about the Dani, who think everything about themselves – their skin color, their hair, their culture – is weak or bad. They are seduced by any novelty, including the cheapest trinket. I have a horror of the pain they will someday know.

July 20th 1961

If a boy lives to be twenty-five, his chances for old age are good. The crucial years are between fifteen and twenty-five, when he is exposed to the enemy in wars and when he must accompany his comrades on dangerous raids. Women's lives are unenviable, but as a rule they do not meet with violent ends or, if they do, it is sometimes at their own hands.

The day was cloudy, and somber, with dull light from morning until night. Mike and Jan went to Wamena for mail and to see a dentist who is meant to show up tomorrow. The camp is wet and spirits are depressed. Much of our work is done and many of us are anxious to be finished as soon as possible. I dread the thought of leaving these people to the un-tender mercies of government officials who will replace us when we depart. I don't yet know how to tell the Dani their fate.

July 21st 1961

I started early with Pua to film more of his morning activity, which consists almost exclusively in his alliance with pigs. A sunny day seemed possible, but at midday clouds settled back over Kurelu and the rain started once again. While with Pua, I witnessed another of his mood swings, from pure delight and warmth to silent resentment. I mistakenly laughed at one of his small follies. He had slightly scorched his hand when, from a small fire we built before the rain came, he picked up a still-smoking piece of grass turf of the kind children sometimes use to sit on. When he held it up, it burst into flames. He had miscalculated as usual, but I should not have laughed. He returned gradually to a fonder mood.

July 22nd 1961

Heavy rain lasted the entire night. Nothing is dry. Jegé Asuk says that we have brought the rain from America, since he cannot otherwise account for it. Wali has given us his beautiful big stone adze in exchange for a steel one. Weyak has given us a small one that will have to be given back because he needs it. The Willigiman Wallalua are mired in inactivity. It is wet but there are two deaths to avenge. When the sun comes out to stay, something will be done about it, I am sure.

July 24th 1961

Today was warm and bright, a great relief from the discomfort of so many cold weeks. There was war, or at least hostilities, far to the west this afternoon. Vast clouds of smoke hung in the sky for several hours suggesting a village may have been burned.

July 25th 1961

Today was brilliant, the second in two weeks. Jan has brought up another in a series of irrational problems. He thinks Peter's nearly finished book, because it is full of facts, will prevent him from writing his own. We had a long discussion in which he would not budge from this belief. Peter is despondent because he thinks he may have exploited Jan. Actually, he may have given him as much as he has taken.

July 27th 1961

Peter, Karl and I went again to Wamena. On our way we were intercepted by a father whose little girl of less than a year had rolled into a fire and burned her upper back. We took the child and her parents with us so a doctor could treat the frightful burns. She hardly complained at all.

August 1st 1961

Upon our return, we were greeted by a huge number of Willigiman Wallalua, who seemed genuinely glad to see us. A war on Friday was broken up by a gun-firing patrol.

August 2nd 1961

A battle on the field southwest of the Warabara was not especially fierce, due to the lack of enemy numbers. It had something to do with Wereklowé stealing a Wittaia pig yesterday, hoping to ambush the owners when they came to retrieve it.

A man has asked me to buy one of his holy stones this afternoon, just as the Willigiman Wallalua were going out to the end of the Warabara to make their final stand. A curious ordering of priorities, or is it?

August 3rd 1961

Pua's threat yesterday morning to run away may only be temporarily blunted by my offer of a machete. He is very independent, stubbornly so, and filled with mercurial reactions. He was recently beaten by his stepfather for letting one of his pigs wander too close to the Aikhé. I have now been told the story of Weyak's name, which means "wrong." He is said to have hit his wife hard enough to kill her when he found she had deceived him.

August 4th 1961

Wali wants some small cowrie shells. He gave one of his *mikak* away at the funeral for Yonokma, which in truth means he has really invested his shell in a system that will return it, or some equally valuable object, with interest at an appropriate moment or ceremony. Pua is still sulking, but a shell and machete have subdued his combativeness. I sense an undercurrent of gladness that the police will eventually come to our forest of Homoak. The thinking goes that it will mean clothes for everyone. Is their pride stained by thoughts about their nakedness, or do they see some practical advantages in being dressed? The tragedy I foresee but which they cannot yet appreciate, is the sudden unraveling of traditional patterns. The Dani, on the other hand, imagine their stolen pigs returned, their wives fetched back from the enemy, and so on through a long list of grievances.

August 5th 1961

Abututi's wife has run off again and Mike has an infected arm that is swelling prodigiously. It started as an insect bite ten days ago. I have started him on Declomycin and he will see the doctor on Tuesday when he goes to Wamena with Peter, who is leaving for Hollandia and onward. Karl's collecting means nearly every day as many as a dozen stone axes are brought in for trading. Soon steel will outweigh stone.

August 6th 1961

War began on the Warabara, and grew into a peculiar contest, fitful and inconclusive. Very few were wounded despite one or two intense forays and skirmish lines that drew dangerously close to each other. Mike's infection is bad but not such that he cannot work. Today's war made for a dramatic finale on Peter's last full day.

August 7th 1961

Last night's party has destroyed everyone's resolve. Peter left in the middle of the day, sadly for all, including himself I think. However, the only Dani who expressed any visible sorrow over Peter's departure was Weyak.

Karl tags his collection of material objects; and I have a faint heart about these people's future.

August 9th 1961

The Willigiman Wallalua continue their acquisitiveness. If they had planned to drive me out, no more effective persuasion could have been devised than the one they are employing, unconsciously or otherwise. They are on top of me, asking for everything in and out of sight. Do they smell the end of our visit? Filmmaking is now doubly hard because everyone has suddenly become curious about the camera. If there is ever a film, it will be a miracle.

P41

August 10th 1961

Today was one of a recent series in which the light has been uninteresting and the pace slow. One of Wereklowé's men stole a woman from across the Elokhera and everyone expects an armed raid to get her back, but it has not come yet.

August 11th 1961

I took Wali to Wamena on a journey that should be a short story. I'll call it "Down the River," to imply that his proud moment is also the tragic deception by me of him, his people and their traditions. He was at once brazenly aloof, haughtily proud, childishly amused, and genuinely awed by what he saw. Unable to button the shirt I loaned him, but seeing the enemy through dark glasses I had also given him, he became both disgusted and terrified but wanted most to remain above it all.

August 12th 1961

Another war erupted at a distant battlefield and almost everyone went except Weyak and a few others, who are either more afraid of the police than of the Wittaia or unenthusiastic about the long walk.

August 13th 1961

One of the local headmen, Maikmo, decided it was time to do something about the weather. For days it has been sunless and gloomy. The Dani do not like too much rain or the mud that comes with it. Maikmo chose an auspicious day to do his magic, bright sun and clear skies from dawn until dusk. It was the absence of women in the fields that told me he had started. Apparently, it is bad luck to be gardening until the magic has been performed. I have been told more than once that we are connected to the prevailing inclemency and so the magic may be intended to dispel more than just bad weather.

August 15th 1961

I have had success where I never thought I would. Finally I managed to film a bird identified by Peter as Rosenberg's Myzomela, the little bird of death according to the Dani imagination.

Maikmo's efforts to discourage rain have been effective through most of today and I managed to work all morning with Pua. Later, several of us drifted down the Aikhé to shoot some birds. Weyak and Jegé Asuk tried to propel the boat by pulling

P42

on the gunwales. They were unbelievably bad hunters, seeing birds long after I did.

August 16th 1961

There was a war on the southwest end of the Tokolik frontier. The two armies were large and eager but, except for one savage skirmish at mid-morning, there was little action. The Willigiman Wallalua inspired and directed the war, which was meant as a surprise but was discovered by the Wittaia too early to be successful. Anyway it ceased as the rain began, one of the major reasons for wars ending.

August 18th 1961

Karl brought Jan back from Wamena with a telegram saying the last film shipment had an intermittent processing fault, an announcement that put me in a state of helpless anxiety. Broekhuyse has learned that when we leave he will be sent as an information officer to Biak, the bleak island airport created by the U.S. during WWII. This punishment is for his un-governmental attitudes and behavior.

Our time draws to a close. Given the problem in the last shipment of film, I sometimes wish it all had never begun. In that shipment were the death of Yonokma, the *wam kanekhé,* and much else. Woe is being a filmmaker.

August 19th 1961

It started to rain early last night and it has not stopped. I think mud especially in quantity is among the most fiendish of all nature's offerings.

Pua has shown a rare independence these past few days and only tonight has put in a brief appearance. He may sense our impending leave taking.

F41

August 20th 1961

Many returned early from still another distant war, which suggests rain may have interfered again. Wali said, "*etai lek weem weragat*," meaning roughly, "war as usual, no victory." The rain resumed at noon and lasted most of the afternoon. Nevertheless I was able to film Weyak emasculating a pig and to enjoy the unlikely delicacy of roasted pig testicles. If the weather stays as bad as this, I will not finish satisfactorily, but how can it last? It is hard to believe only a week is left to me in this still astounding place.

August 21st 1961

Maikmo has been shamed as a magician and my temper shortens along with the time remaining. I know how unreasonable I must seem to people whom I badger all day long. My perversity can only be explained as a way of making the separation inevitable. Soon they will be glad to see me gone. Because of the weather and my own considerable indisposition, the filmmaking is proceeding badly. I honestly do not know what I need at this point, other than a few good ideas.

August 22nd 1961

It rained most of the night and Wali, for some reason, has put a thoroughgoing taboo on our forest home so no women can now come to it, not even small girls. Wali claims to have done this because so much *mikak* dust is in the air; we are giving away many shells for trading purposes and they are being cut and ground into ornaments. I feel the reasons are much deeper and have to do with the rain and un-avenged death.

August 23rd 1961

Jan is black with gloom and anger. The strain caused by our presence is beginning to tell on us all, especially on me and through me on those I work with most intensively. Pua cries, Wali is in a frenzy of nervous laughter and Weyak merely looks harried. The knowledge that we are going and the police will be coming is sinking in. We all are living with a deadline and that is affecting everyone.

August 24th 1961

Today had a strange calm about it until noontime, when a plan to kill a runaway Wittaia woman was plotted and then prevented by me from happening. Every man and boy was distressed to see the idea thwarted, yet too timid to say so. It was to have been the answer to the male population's determination to avenge the deaths of Yonokma and Weaké. But I could not be a witness to such an event, despite what some might think its cinematic value.

The spirit of these people, their *etai eken* (Dani for "seeds of singing"), the imagined personification of their very soul, is still in dreadful shape. The sight of women forever smeared with clay is hurting the men's pride. In mid-afternoon there was a move to engage the Wittaia on the Warabara. For two hours there was a shouting match between a small band of the Willigiman Wallalua and an equally small and far more reluctant band of Wittaia. It was a young person's war. Today may be these young men's last appearance on a ritual battleground.

August 25th 1961

Tonight I wanted to film Pua eating a pretty yellow-faced honeyeater bird. Instead a man was killed, and Pua put his little spear into his lifeless body just the way some others did, symbolically sharing in the homicide. The man had come with a friend to kill someone. He was discovered and speared to death, while his friend escaped. He had made his way close to Wereklowé's *honai*, or so the story goes. I saw him in his final twitches outside the village from where he was dragged by exulting young warriors to the Liberek and where, under a full moon, a victory dance began. Husuk held up his head by his hair to see who it was. Jegé Arek picked up the body like a butchered hog and threw

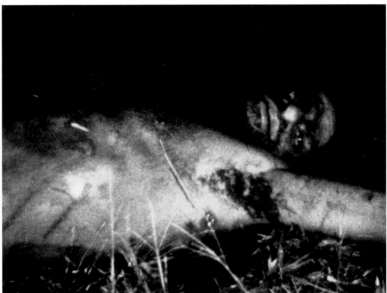

F42

it over a fence into a garden ditch. The Wittaia will come for it tomorrow and, also tomorrow, the killers and the killed will have their separate ceremonies. The valley rings with song already.

F43

August 26th 1961

The story of last evening's killing has changed. The victim was one not of two but of four men who came peacefully from their village near the Ibele River mouth. Two of them had relatives in the area.

This morning the Wittaia fished the body from the muddy ditch into which it had been tossed last night and dragged it away to Hulukluk, off beyond the salt wells, where it would be burned. The many macabre details of this last wanton nightmare act are fitfully present in my mind: the uncombed, muddied hair; eyes staring openly and piteously at me no matter where I stood; the steam of a warm body mingling with the night air; a moon like ripe fruit ready to fall from the sky; frightened men and women huddling in the shadows; Wali nervous and excited by the kill; the absolutely naked corpse; Husuk with his brand new steel ax (a gift from the Catholic priest) looking like an executioner as he held the victim's head by his hair and troubled the body with his foot; Jegé Arek maniacally pitching the corpse into the ditch.

August 27th 1961

The victory celebration today was immensely sincere and the tribute to the dead man was vast, though unremorseful. When I asked Weyak why the man was killed, he responded with a torrent of words that told about the murders of Weaké and Yonokma, of how the women had to wear mud for so long and how badly the men felt to see them this way. He asked me at the end if it was bad or good, and I said that it was good that he and his women felt better but that to kill a man who made a peaceful visit was bad. They should have done such a deed in war and not in treachery. He understood and said, "Yes, we should give visitors sweet potatoes and let them sleep."

August 28th 1961

All day I could hear the shouts of war on a southerly wind coming through the valley. There was a particular cry or set of cries that I could not

distinguish from the rest, but which told everyone
around me there would be a second victory celebration. Yet another man had been killed. Weyak
would not have gone to it if I had detained him,
but he clearly wanted badly to be there, as did
Wali and many others, and so they had gone. Some
feared that the nearer Wittaia would stage a raid
while so many men from our villages were far
away, but like others of their fears these were
groundless. A teenager named Aikpon and I went
hunting down the river. He asked for my lighter to
set fire to an enemy outpost and I told him he
could come there tomorrow by himself.

August 31st 1961
To Wamena and beyond for us all.

P43

P1

a kind of sacrifice

My first impression of Michael Rockefeller was of a slightly scattered but immensely polite young man whose inner and outer drives had achieved a semblance of chaotic truce. He seemed almost to ricochet through the world with what I took at first to be a combination of poor eyesight and boundless curiosity but I soon learned that he made imaginative use of his immense physical energy to live very much his own life.

We first met when he was a college senior beset by the usual academic deadlines made even more vexing owing to an abundance of competing youthful enthusiasms. I, on the other hand, was a lapsed graduate student trying to invent an anthropology that used film and photography instead of words, an endeavor in which Michael one day would become an important collaborator. Though the last thing in the world I can imagine Michael ever allowing in himself was any kind of lapse (he was too filled with a sense of obligation put there by schoolmasters, right-minded relatives and his own abundant conscience), it happened that an interest in a larger geography than even his precocious travels had already revealed drew him into a conspiracy that would soon fill his head with undreamt wonder. In fact, his response to the world into which we all fell like so many Alices in Wonderland one fateful year was so rapt, so earnest and wide-eyed that I sometimes marveled at the extent of his amazement. I still hear him saying, over and over again, "I don't believe it."

In the many hours of sounds recorded by Michael during those months we lived in a stone-age valley high in the central mountains of West Papua, there is a moment when an old man tells him that a young boy has just been "eaten" by the enemy. This was the Dani way of saying there had been a ritual killing, that a life had been taken to restore a disharmony among the ghosts caused by an imbalance of deaths between two warring groups. The dead boy was one that Michael knew and, if you listen carefully to his recording, you can hear him saying, "Oh, Oh, Oh," as he responded in stunned disbelief.

When, not many months later, Michael was himself eaten by the unforgiving Arafoera Sea, he too became a kind of sacrifice. At least, this possibility persuades me to believe that such an abruptly ended life can still be full of promise.

P2

P1

creatures of pain

There is in Nigeria an annual event called *sharo* in which young men invite one another to trade blows using a long and menacing herding stave. I knew of this spectacle only from spotty reading but hoped to find where it could still be seen. I was told the season for it was really October and November but that it might also be occurring in the Sokoto region in the North during February. Certain preoccupations of mind concerning human addiction to hurting one another powerfully disposed me to seek out and witness this curious ritual of pain.

I was also drawn at the time to the idea of visiting in the same region a small nomadic group called Uda Fulani who were said to be exclusively devoted to their flocks. This by itself was a matter of intense interest and worth almost any effort to explore further, or so I thought. I pictured a people who had elected to devote their lives to sheep-fancying in a place notorious for its spare beauty, the Sahel of Equatorial Africa. Here I hoped to find a set of circumstances sufficiently reduced in complexity to permit a quite particular way of life to flourish on its own terms. I didn't care if Uda lives were rudimentary as long as I could flesh out these people's peculiar love for their animals.

February 10th 1965

At about 8:30 this morning Umaru Dikko, a young Nigerian acquaintance studying mathematics at London University, and I set out for Hadejia reportedly some thirty miles northeast of Kano. Umaru was born in this part of northern Nigeria and was fluent in Fulani, a language essential to my purposes. Umaru was hopeful of being a teacher following his training in mathematics but it was easy to tell he also had a deep interest in both the past and future of his young country.

With a side trip to Tarbu and relying on some sketchy maps, the journey up and back was both fruitless and tiring. I had wanted to go to Hadejia to make contact with Uda who were said to be there in these days. In fact, they are said to be in two areas, to the northeast and to the northwest, around Bornu and around Sokoto.

In Suru last night the scribe, a literate man who writes letters for the illiterate, encouraged me by saying there was *sharo* in Gurja not far away. Much of the day was spent finding a way across the Sokoto River in order to reach a place called Dakingari. It is there too that the Fulani hereabouts had told us we would find *sharo*. They should know because *sharo* is a Fulani specialty practiced by men fifteen to twenty-five years old.

P2

Unable to cross the Sokoto, we returned to Suru and discovered some musicians, indispensable to *sharo*, still there waiting to follow others who had gone off to the south. Those who had stayed in Suru agreed to come with us to augment the ones who had already departed.

We started for Gurja in the late afternoon in a Jeep with a broken spring and a punctured radiator. I worried it would fail us on the way. There was no road to speak of and little likelihood of another vehicle should we have a breakdown. But we made it to Gurja arriving just as the sun was setting. *Sharo* was ending but a boisterous group of enthusiasts was still celebrating. The excitement was due partly to our appearance and partly to the intensity of the *sharo* that had just ended.

I have come to realize that my bewildering whiteness and the exotic Jeep are potent stimulants in these remote villages. Europeans come only on the rarest errand having usually to do with human or animal health. Of course, the camera absolutely transfixes everyone.

The village head in Gurja is a man with outrageous pretensions and worse manners. Umaru and I lay on the ground too tired to ask for food but we did drink another Fanta which, with a few crackers, is about all that was left of our provisions.

February 17th 1965

Sharo began early in the morning under an already blazing sun. There were hundreds of people crowded into the headman's cramped compound making it almost impossible to film. The *sharo* was at times awesome and terrible. The ceremony began with musicians playing flutes and establishing a tempo with a dried-out gourd containing a handful of seeds. They played an eerie, teasing melody meant as an invitation to the ordeal to come. Many eligible young men had come in order to demonstrate their manliness and all of them appeared impatient to seize that opportunity.

The music prepares the adepts by putting them in a kind of trance. At the very least, their minds are focused and their nerves steeled for what they know will be a painful experience. At a certain moment, in a mounting passion for the contest, a challenger began an elaborate testimonial to his strength, courage and fortitude. It went something like this:

F1

I don't listen to anyone unless I've been hit. How did you get so lazy? Was your father like this? Rather than lose your good name, you should lose your life. If you have no magic for fighting, ask me and I will give you some. Better you lose a lot of money than fail in what you are doing. Why don't you take medicine before you come to fight? Who is going to come and show he is greater than I? Why do you act like people who are falling into the deep river?

And the musicians sing a response like this:
Don't behave like a big man, if you don't mean it. If you don't act when your name is called, it is better for you to die.

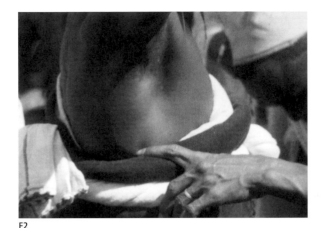

F2

Thus pressure is put on the young men through the shaming done in the songs which speak of important Fulani values and also by the boys when they say the things they do about themselves and their opponents. Being Fulani, as it is expressed in such rituals as *sharo*, is not a gentle way of life.

The contestants assume poses that are full of boastful pride. Their bodies are held rigidly vertical and turn hieratically sideways in relation to feet that are fixed to the ground. One arm is stretched upward and outward toward their adversary and their head is pitched backward, eyes glazed with disdain. In this attitude, they continue singing their own praises for four or five minutes at a time. Friends act as seconds and, as in some 18th-century duel, provide a measure of calm and assurance. Then they sit down and wait for some provoked youth to accept the proffered challenge by going through a recital of essentially the same self-adulation and dismissive rhetoric.

One said:
If you come to fight, fight. If you come to see the ladies, see the ladies. Hold your arm properly.

And another said:
I am like corn in the mortar. No matter how much you beat me I will never become flour.

A great man will never tire. It takes a lot of time to become tired.

I am black and born of black men. So I am stronger.
(The challenger of the boy who said this had considerably lighter skin.)

A contesting pair thus forms, always under the oversight of a few older veterans of this brutal business.

The challenger is bound with long cotton scarves, nipple-high across his chest. They are pulled tightly and tied so as to leave a patch of flesh under the armpit as a target for the one swinging his stave. The wrapped one plants his feet wide apart, cocks his head and lifts his arm straight up. He has iron rings he shakes like a tambourine to make a sound said to be protective and sustaining.

F3

Next, the one holding his long herding stick asks his opponent if he is ready. This he might do more than once. Then he walks off a short distance, turns and comes striding back raising his long cudgel preparatory to letting it loose. The music skirls and, in what feels like slowed motion, the stick is swung with ferocious accuracy. Immediately after the sickening impact, there is a momentary hush followed by an intense exclamation of flutes saluting the reckless disdain of the one struck.

Onlookers surge forward, dance him around for a few triumphant moments and deliver him up to be hit again. No mark is at first visible where the blow was struck but, in the time it takes for the second blow to land, an immense welt appears where the skin has been torn and gives unmistakable evidence of the effect of this mad contest.

Sharo ended by noon owing to the great heat of midday. We could not stay to see more. Maybe there will be another opportunity when we next encounter these self-adoring Fulani herdsmen.

N.B. This account of my odd questing in Nigeria in 1965 ends abruptly with a February 28th entry. I can report at this clarifying distance in time that I abandoned the Uda sheepherding idea for a number of reasons. Among them was the rapid onset of the civil war that devastated Nigeria both north and south. Just as importantly, I was never able to find Uda in the state of simple innocence I had allowed myself to imagine them. My present view of those days is that I wandered too mindlessly in that particular desert, trusting that luck would prevail and that I would be able to attach myself to these astonishing examples of the husbanding life. In the end, the very elusiveness of the Uda that first caught my fancy was what defeated my best intentions. Nearly all that I harvested in imagery came from those hours I spent transfixed by the triumph of will over pain shown me by those who practiced *sharo*.

F4

P3

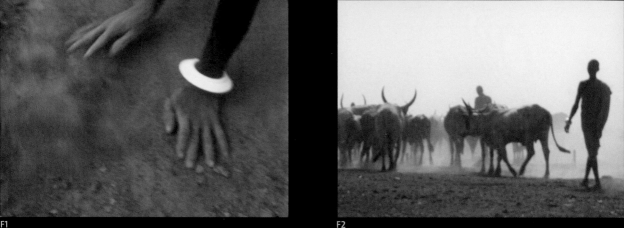

F1

F2

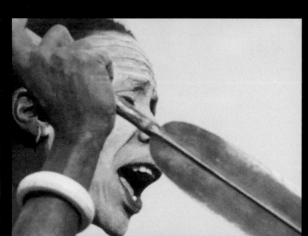

F3

the nuer

P1

P2

Ethiopia, February 1968

Last year I asked Hilary Harris to join me in Africa, convinced that filming the Nuer would be an inspired use of his enormous talents as an image-maker. The Nuer were a group with arresting cultural expressiveness and were famous in anthropological literature but virtually unknown beyond those confines. They had to be seen to be known.

Hilary's deepest concerns were with what he calls kinesics and he had told me he wanted to keep working with dancers to illustrate his ideas about movement. The Nuer were known to have an important place for dance in their lives and so it has happened that we are now together in Africa.

The Nuer are only one of several ethnic populations in a large area in this part of Africa that is suffering from hostilities between the largely pagan Sudan of the south and the Arab north. The hostilities originate from an ancient antagonism between Islamic and Christian sentiments. The Nuer are, or were until recently, animists with Christian tendencies owing to a long history of missionary contact. So, as enemies of Islam they are being slowly dispossessed of their homelands along with their cultures. The end of this sad and sometimes violent tale is not yet in sight.

Though most Nuer live in the Sudan, several thousand have also lived just across Sudan's frontier with Ethiopia, and their numbers have grown steadily owing to the civil war.

February 19th 1968

From Gambela, Hilary and I set out at midday for Ciengach, the Nuer village in which we will stay during the days ahead. The distance is a bit more than sixty miles and the journey lasted 6½ hours along a track following the Baro, a tributary to the Blue Nile. The terrain, undulating toward distant horizons in all directions, suggests as much an ocean as the Earth. I'm not sure what geological or meteorological events account for this geography but I suspect much of what is dry now will be under water soon after the rains arrive. The approach to the village was at the end of the day and the sun, setting behind it, was an enormous globe of light falling rapidly toward the horizon, reddened by the dust and smoke of dung fires.

P4

P5

Inside, where the floor is packed mud, the Nuer house is cool, swept, and mostly free of insects.

Our own housing is more provisional and, despite advances in tent technology, there is little room for living, either horizontally or vertically, and what there is affords no privacy whatever. The tents are brightly colored and so it has been decided to keep them as hidden as possible, even if it means being a bit removed from the people we have come to visit and try to know.

February 20th 1968
Our meal tonight was a scrawny chicken cooked on a campfire by two youthful Nuer. Hilary tried to explain that we would like some peace and quiet, but I'm not sure this new regime is going to work. People come all the time to visit and make demands, a chronic and historic Nuer trait. They are mostly young and unmarried men with little to do. Women do far more than men as so frequently happens in traditional societies. The compounds would not be clean or the food cooked, were it not for the young girls and women. Of course, children are the sole responsibility of women since men take little apparent interest in them. Men are responsible for the cattle and spend virtually all their time and energy ensuring the well-being of the herd. There is nothing in the world of greater importance to a Nuer male than his bulls.

Ciengach has a perfection made especially memorable by its look in the magical evening light. Nuer houses, round and made from sun-baked clay, are built wattle-and-daub style up to shoulder height where a conical framework of branches rests on a kind of ledge. Bundles of heavy grass are held in place on top of this structure, forming a steeply slanting roof. A low opening in the outer wall provides an entrance through which one can go in and out, bent over at the waist.

P6

84

P7

P8

P9

P10

P11

In my visit during the day to some houses nearby, I was struck by the prevalence of smallpox. Probably there is little we can do to help, but tomorrow I will try to alleviate some of the misery of those suffering the most. We have vaccine so perhaps we should be doing inoculations. But I do not know to what effect because I am too medically unschooled. The night air is mercifully cool and it is only 10 p.m.

February 21st 1968
From dawn until dusk I closely watched the movement of the cattle. It is a cycle of progression and regression, out of and then back into the village, repeated invariably every day. There can never be any interruption of this cycle as long as there are cattle. They must go to pasture in the morning and they must return to be milked and tethered next to their dung fires at night. They are hapless slaves to the bucolic tide of this dusty ocean plain.

Early in the morning, the bellowing begins punctually with one or two animals and then becomes a grand chorus of insistent others impatient to be released and given their temporary freedom. Young men hasten them out of the village that is soon emptied and strangely quiet. It will remain this way until the tide turns and the cattle flow back in the evening.

During the late afternoon, dung, which has been gathered and dried during the day, is piled up at dozens of little fireplaces and lit as the cattle make their way homeward. As soon as the cattle are where they belong, they are sometimes fed a little and brushed with ashes to keep away flies and other insects. The cows complain loudly until they have been milked as do the heifers that sometimes spend the day tethered to a stake, waiting for the moment when they are allowed their mother's teat. The Nuer deeply love their herds and the village is an embodiment of this emotion and exists for the animals as much as for the human beings who anyway cannot conceive of life without them.

F4

F5

F6

P12

P13

P16

During the hottest part of the day, the smallest boys, ones who were not engaged in watching the cattle or other chores, came by with a collection of miniature cattle they had fashioned from clay. They were sometimes well done, even quite beautifully done especially in the attention given to horns and coloring. These are important distinguishing features, especially of bulls, and so to see this reflected in the children's play is hardly remarkable. What is quite wonderful is the care and attention given to expressing these ideas by using charcoal for black skin patches, ash for white and both red and orange found in plants or fruits. These toy animals have stylized udders and genitals as well as decorations hanging from their necks or horns as routinely happens in the grown-up cattle world.

I was looking through a remarkable window into this culture seeing these exquisite replicas of the Nuer's beloved animals. The boys probably play with them and I hope to find them again tomorrow to see what this is like.

The incident called to mind *Homo Ludens,* which I remember being a book about play as a mirror or indicator of life. I never finished reading it but always thought I should and so I have pretended I did. Learning from children is certainly not a recent discovery. Margaret Mead told me she was never psychoanalyzed because she observed children and so didn't need to be. This is a compelling idea. Most often we are told children learn from adults but what about the other way around?

In the midst of the lesson I was learning from the toy bulls, a mother and father came by with their sick child. It was clear it had smallpox but the child was suffering in other ways too, convulsing

P14

P15

90

P17

and wasting away before my eyes. I hydrated it with the rubber syringe I use to blow air at the gate of my camera and tried to get sugar and salt into its mouth with a spoon. The shaking and convulsing subsided momentarily and I gave it a shot of penicillin knowing the child was coughing badly and, with its high fever on top of everything else, might have pneumonia.

At the end of an hour or two of bathing and trying to calm the child, I gave it back to its mother and she went off to her house. Tonight I went looking for her to see how the child was doing and found her by her fire stirring a pot with another, smaller child in her arms. With one look, I understood that the sick child had died and was already in the ground.

There was no recrimination or even overt sadness, only a sort of resignation over what had to be. The child may not have reached its tenth year and is only one of many millions in Africa who will not reach their tenth year. Maybe I should come tomorrow and inoculate the other children and, maybe, I should not. What do I know?

P18

F7

February 22nd 1968

What we are looking for is a moment or two of privacy. Its near absence is a prevailing condition in our lives out on this vast plain. There is no place to be alone, no place even to shit without walking to a vanishing point on the encircling horizon. Of course, the Nuer shit too and with inimitable circumspection. The little ones do it wherever they are moved to but grown people stroll out and away from the houses into the surrounding countryside to a dip in the terrain where they drop down and, with no clothing to adjust, invisibly relieve themselves. We are far less transparent and can almost never find a way to not be seen.

The Nuer obsession with cattle of all sizes, shapes and colors is entirely fascinating. I watch the Nuer world and conclude that it comes close to being completely harmonious, in that these animals are everyone's unquestioned focus. This life is neither simple nor automatic but unambiguously devoted to fanatic husbandry. I wonder if the Nuer are alone in their obsessions, or if what I see around me in Ciengach might be the modern expression of a deep prehistoric tradition.

Keeping animals, cows, camels, goats and sheep has been a modus vivendi for a very long time. Sheepherders, reindeer herders, and all other such specialized economies have their own obsessions, I am sure, but the Nuer have brought to theirs an astonishing ardor.

It seems not to matter that this village is temporary, annually subject to disappearing under a flood when the rains arrive. Ciengach and its sister locations are submerged until the water recedes and they reappear. To me this means the Nuer care less about where they live than that their locality is suited to the well-being of their only true interest, cattle.

I cannot imagine what happens to the one hundred or so houses sheltering the inhabitants of Ciengach when the floodwaters arrive, but by then the Nuer would have moved to rainy season locales taking what they needed with them. I also do not know if some of what they leave behind is reclaimable when the dry season returns. Apart from a few old rifles and bits of tattered clothing, their only possessions are cooking utensils, baskets, pots, and a few wooden stools.

Today I saw women pouring water down the throats of young cows. They are said to do this because they, the women, like to. I suspect they enjoy the maternal nature of the act. Only women do this work because, as is said, they have softer hands. Another woman was sitting near her house making a pot. Her technique was intriguing because it was of the simplest and crudest kind owing to there being no wheel on which to work. She rolled long strings of clay on her thigh just the way we did as children on a tabletop. She then coiled the strings together to make the bottom and sides. All the while, she wet her hands and smoothed the clay in a kneading motion.

It took more than an hour to make a pot about nine inches high and four inches wide. When finished, she rubbed it with butter and then, for decoration, impressed the damp clay an inch down from the top with a bit of rope. I recalled my encounter with corded ware during a brief encounter with European archaeology and realized a woman was doing right in front of me what I once thought was such an ancient thing. She then took the rope and brushed the sides of the pot from the rim down to where she had made the cord impressions, creating a textured band of decoration. She finished by roughening the rim itself.

I got much of this on film for reasons that are not entirely clear to me. Sometimes I do this for its restorative effect on a weary psyche. Such tasks are not at all challenging and they have a purposefulness that is pleasing to a troubled mind. Surely my effort is the same as recreational therapy in institutions for the mad. I do have the feeling though of having preserved a fragment of reality, trivial as it may be. She has a useful pot and I have made a simulacrum of it. Larkin, the English poet, speaks of such undertakings as being "at the bottom of all art." I wonder if this could not but be true.

P19

In this otherwise idyll of pastoral harmony, there is much that is distressing: infections, malaria, tuberculosis, venereal disease and especially smallpox, which is so disfiguring to these glorious looking people. At the swamp where everyone goes for drinking water and to wash, there were several beautiful young women filling large jars and at the same time washing away the ooze from their sores. Through its use by a smallpox-ravaged village whose inhabitants and occasional visitors such as ourselves find their only solace bathing in its suspect waters, this pond must be one of the most poisonous on the planet.

The young women, once they had filled their water jars, draped themselves with a foul sheet of brown cloth and huddled beneath it to protect not their modesty but their running sores. Returning to the village I feel a great lust for these girls who I imagine rid of their horrifying pox.

F8

P20

94

February 23rd 1968

In the evening I sit looking at the smoke-shrouded village unable to make out the houses; only their vague shapes remind me of where they are situated. This transfiguring smoke is absolutely wonderful in the way it makes everything both more mysterious and more real. I'm reminded of fog along the Maine coast and times when I had no idea where I was, even though I knew I was in a place known by me since childhood. I remember a friend saying years ago on his way to San Francisco that he wanted to make a film about fog. At the time I did not know what he could possibly mean, but now I do.

Nuer smoke is made foggier by the sea-like land we are on, land that becomes a sea when the river rises and spills over its banks flooding everything for miles.

Today was especially hot and bright, causing dazzling mirage effects that lifted up the few trees and hills floating off in the distance. The nearer Itang Hills and the further Gambela Hills were on a cushion of vaporous air. There is no thermometer but it must be over 100 degrees Fahrenheit, memorable but not at all as hot as I have known it in the Afar desert.

We try to make life tolerable spending our limited energy boiling the water, putting it in bottles, getting something to eat, arranging for firewood, and washing utensils. When such things are not done, we will be on our way to desperation; but I must stop hectoring Hilary who has lived here longer than I and will be here when I have left. He must establish whatever style suits his purposes. But the battle with insects, heat, and the discomfort of no chair, no table, and no way to take care of my camera take their toll. I look at the orderliness of the Nuer world and find mine wanting.

I have only a week or so left, and I should get busy with what interests me and do all I can before the opportunity is gone.

I'm tempted by the idea of entering the realm of sickness that has been the cause of so much despair. Supposedly this outbreak is the first in a generation. I wonder why it has come now. It stands in such contrast with what otherwise is a perfected though curious life. Of course, I am not thinking about the large political issues that hang over these people. The Nuer are refugees from Sudanese tyrants and from modernity itself. Maybe I, too, am a refugee.

P22

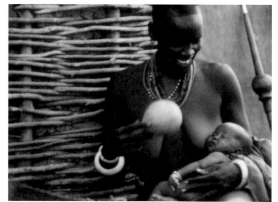

F9

February 24th 1968

It has only just become dark and the night air, already cold, is our best defense against insects. Earlier I watched the animals return to their tethers and dung fires.

In the heat of midday, young boys and the oldest men collect dung in stiff goatskin trays and carry it to the edge of the village where it is spread out on smooth earthen floors to dry. When sun dried, the dung is gathered up again to be brought to where the nighttime fires burn. Here it is heaped up into little mounds and lit just as the cattle are coming back into the village.

I am very fond of these fires that protect the animals and give the village a look and smell unlike any other in my experience. The flames produce a fine white ash that has its own importance. Men use it to dust, really bless, their favorite animals, and I have seen it used by many to clean their teeth. They take it on a forefinger and rub it on their teeth and gums. White teeth are common among the Nuer so there may be unknown benefits to the ash of their dung fires.

Everything pivots around cattle. A Nuer feels privileged to be alive as long as he lives with his herd. God, he argues, has given cattle to the Nuer and, since they are his greatest gift, every Nuer should be happy. Without them they would not have a life worth living. This deep and complicated bond between people and animals interests me.

F10

February 25th 1968

Smallpox still stalks Ciengach and makes it unlikely there will be any dancing or singing at least for now. A few victims have survived the disease but been badly disfigured in the process and today another little girl has died despite our efforts to prolong her life with injections and forced fluids. Much sadness pervades the village, and I understand the reluctance to celebrate. What surprises me is how genial and lighthearted people can be despite the grimness of their circumstances.

Late in the afternoon a man began singing to his bull and I immediately began filming. His response was to stop and say that, if I was going to make pictures, he wanted to wear clothes. So he went off and found a pair of pants and a blue plastic belt. Returning half-clothed and white-faced from dung fire ashes, he resumed adoring his bull.

F11

At first, I was distressed by his apparent surrender to modernity, but then I wondered what I would do if I was told I could not take my clothes off. This man grew up not wanting or needing clothes, but who is to tell him now he can't wear them?

February 27th 1968

I am in awe of the Nuer capacity for self-regard. They show this in many large and small ways. They set a high value on themselves, on their possessions, and on things they want belonging to others like myself. In the Asmat (New Guinea), I recall villagers relinquishing anything they had, art or artifact, for the merest token: a fishhook, a few cigarettes, an article of cast-off clothing. The Nuer make known what price they think is just and bargaining is not allowed, only consummation or nonconsummation and always on their terms. My admiration begins to waver when Nuer attitudes concerning their wants and deservedness are translated into demands like "Give it to me," or, "I want that flashlight." They never ask for a cigarette, they demand one, frequently and despite being told "No" over and over again.

Hilary and I have tried to promote the idea of dancing and we may yet succeed. But it may also be possible that, even if we are successful, it won't

F12

F13

P23

98

look right. What we are experiencing has been rich enough without music and dance and so I'm not disappointed. Dancing and music is the way French films about Africa begin and end. It can be a fatal cliché.

February 28th 1968

I wondered for a long time whether there would ever be a dance but, at a certain moment, the village prophet said there would be dancing, if everyone could go to the river and bathe. So we jumped into the Landrover and sped off to the Baro. When everyone had washed and come back, the singing started and men began to dance. A few young women did erotic turns in front of them. I was aware of the artificial nature of the occasion, but I think the dancing itself was entirely genuine. The men had gotten into their best short pants, there was marvelous leaping, and I worked hard at close range. I was happy that Hilary's hope to witness dance had been realized. The singing was especially superb, but all was over before darkness arrived.

February 29th 1968

It is Leap Day and my last in Ciengach. It is not different from any other, including yesterday, which was Ash Wednesday. I sense a slow resurgence of vitality in the village, although a full measure of misery still lingers on. I don't think anything has so saddened me as watching small children in their pox-encrusted rags walking from their houses out onto the empty plain to relieve themselves. They look to be in a trance as they move slowly in their pain toward privacy.

March 1st 1968

I left Ciengach at midday after I had spent a morning making some final images. They were of men early in the morning attending to their cattle. I also filmed a conversation with an old man who has no wife and whose son lives he knows not where. He is alone except for his animals with which he has achieved an astonishing rapport. He sat absorbed in his fire as we asked him questions to which he tried hard to respond. A few of his answers I found quite profound.

I also filmed music made by a six-stringed lute I had heard earlier in the week. It should look and sound quite beautiful. So much in these people's lives is worth noting, worth attention. I could stay actively employed at this for many weeks but the time has come to go.

> Time of movement.
>
> My big bull will be the only one that will remain alone,
> like somebody without a friend.
>
> Look at our convincing behavior.
> We are the ones who let it be hidden.
>
> But now I say it.
>
> My favorite bull, we make the life of other people very difficult.
>
> I burn other people like fire when I sing.
>
> [Nuer song]

F14

F15

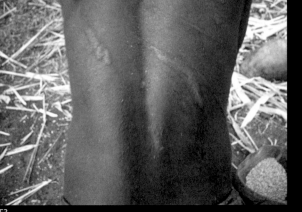

F3

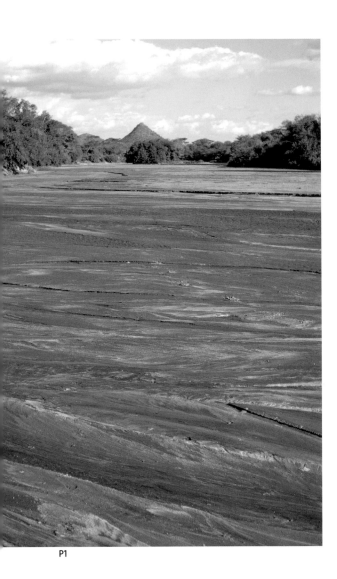

P1

Ethiopia, June 1968

By the mid-1960s whatever fuss was made over the release of my film *Dead Birds* had largely subsided and I was thinking of what next to do. I had a scheme of sorts to make a film about pastoralists, preferably with a nomadic bent, to complete a trio of films that had begun with *The Hunters* (in which I had a minor role collaborating with John Marshall) and *Dead Birds,* a film about warrior farmers.

Beginning in 1965 I looked for a subject in a number of African countries including Nigeria (nomadic Fulani sheep herders), The Sudan (nomadic Arab cattle herders), and Mauritania (nomadic Peul camel herders). I settled on the Afar, a formidably xenophobic society of cattle keepers in the Danakil desert of northeastern Ethiopia.

My idea was to start working with the Afar in late 1967 using a generous foundation grant and, simultaneously, to film the Nuer along the Baro River near the Sudan border. For the film on the Nuer, my friend Hilary Harris agreed to assume the major responsibility. In the Danakil desert I had the company of Clark Worswick who did sound recording and photography, Abdullah Kaloita, an Afar interpreter who spoke almost incomprehensible English, and Joan Mitchell who helped with photography and in the maintenance of civility under difficult circumstances.

It was not long before I realized Afar misanthropy would not yield to my attempts at rapport and I moved to southwest Ethiopia to spend time with Hilary and to search for a group that might serve to engage me in my notions about the pastoralist life.

The Hamar, in a thorn jungle in Gamo Gofa Province, became my subjects and after the work I did among them in 1968 I arranged to return in 1971. It was more or less this combination of times and purposes that resulted in the film *Rivers of Sand* in the early 1970's.

The words that follow are from the journals I kept during those two visits.

June 8th 1968

Despite a mountain of unfinished business, we have finally departed Addis Ababa. The little things are the hardest to manage in a country that moves as ponderously as Ethiopia. Also hard is abandon-

P2

ing this city's considerable charms. I am quite devoted to its beautiful people and glorious food.

We are now only three: my son Stewart, Clark Worswick, and myself. Joan Mitchell must stay behind to see if her eye that threatens to ulcerate will heal under the care of specialists. She allowed someone to look through her camera viewfinder who must have had an infection, and now she has it too. She will join us when she improves.

We drove 150 miles to Shashamane in less than five hours, thanks to Mussolini's 1930's adventures in Ethiopia that bequeathed little other than misery and a few fine roads. Tomorrow I want to get to Arba Minch, another 150 miles.

Arba Minch is pivotal geographically because just beyond are substantial rivers that could be high enough to give us serious trouble. The rainy season is beginning, and we won't know if that has made a difference until we get to these waterways. All I know is that we must get to the other side of the rivers and out onto the plateau that leads south to Konso, the name of a people, a region, and also a village. Konso is where I want to be. Nothing of great interest is on this side as far as I know.

Going to the Konso was a decision made while I struggled with the Afar people earlier this year. The Afar are the classic nomads in the northeastern deserts of this country of manifold terrains. The Konso people are reputed to be interesting on several grounds. They keep animals but they are also, unlike the Afar, agriculturalists. Most importantly, the Konso are said to be musicians and artists. Musicians I can believe, but the artist part seems less likely. East Africa has never been noted for its artistry, although Konso grave figures are a specialty esteemed by players in the

international tribal art market. Before too long, I should know more about their expressive lives. Although there is still a long way to go, I have a decent supply of film and a great desire to do something with it.

Shashamane is a pleasant little town inhabited by Galla-speaking people. I think it is in Arussi Province but I am not sure. Arussi maidens crop up on postcards from time to time in Addis, owing to their perceived pulchritude and seminudity. They have a delicate look and wear scanty clothing made of skins (in the postcards) that are decorated with colored beads. We have seen some young women who fit this description, though we are by no means in the heart of the province. Of course, nothing along any road is in the heart of anything except the commerce taking place along it.

June 9th 1968

The sky is very dark this evening, boding badly for river height south of us. By early afternoon, after driving five hours on a comparatively good road, we reached Arba Minch, the capital of Gamo Gofa Province. The town sits on the crest of a hill and has a look of considerable shabbiness. Not much happens here as far as I can tell. We are in the only hotel, which once served as the governor's palace. Not at all palatial, it has no running water and only the most modest arrangements for eating. If the beds are not too uncomfortable, the hotel will have served its purpose and we will be able to leave in the morning more or less rested.

P3

The trip from Shashamane led through a green but puzzlingly infertile landscape. I saw no cotton or coffee, though I would expect both at this altitude. We stopped only once in a place called Buge, where people dwell in large circular houses with sloping roofs reaching up to a central pole that supports the entire structure and protrudes two or three feet through the roof. We went into the compound of a cluster of these dwellings and asked if we could look inside. I was told, "Yes, of course," though the question appeared to cause some embarrassment. We went inside and were met by almost pitch-blackness, owing to the absence of any windows and the fact that our eyes were adjusted to the bright exterior. The interior is divided into two halves by a curtain of reeds that reaches twelve or fifteen feet above the floor. Where the center pole goes through the roof, the height must be twenty feet. The house, which from the outside had the look and feel of a barn, is remarkably ample. The inside looked even more barn-like, with a donkey tethered in the doorway and several cows on a lower level eating from the earth floor. A woman in the house was wearing a silver cross of the kind I have seen in Tigre Province. She was wonderfully kind, though not at all as gracefully made or winning in looks as many of the inhabitants of this land of beautiful people. I will be happy if the gentle natures we have found here are also to be found where we are going. With luck, we should be in Konso tomorrow.

I asked a Peace Corps volunteer, who had been a short distance south of Arba Minch, what he knew of road conditions. He thought that we would have no trouble, especially with vehicles that are in reasonable condition. Only serious rain, more than I see in the clouds now gathering above our heads, could make a difference.

June 10th 1968

My prediction about rain last night was not correct for at 2 a.m. I was awakened by an immense thunderstorm. Visions of flooding rivers agitated my brain and I wondered what excitements lay in wait. We had to cross two more rivers in order to reach the Konso. On our way by late dawn, we were soon at the first river fifteen miles from Arba Minch. I went into the deeper part to a point well above my knees and looked down at a fast moving stream. While strong enough to carry the smaller stones in its path, it appeared low enough to cross. What must not happen is for our cars' electric circuits to get submerged and then short out. As long as the engines kept running, I was not worried.

I got in my car and made it across with no trouble, at which point the second car then crossed just as easily. After traveling a good part of the morning, we reached Gidole, a principally Galla-speaking village lacking any discernible charm. The inhabitants were friendly and the wildlife nearby supplied us with as many guinea hens as we could eat. I also saw wart hogs and a huge black snake left under a tree that someone had had the nerve to kill.

The road beyond Gidole was uneven and twisting, and therefore tiring for the driver, but I will always prefer driving to being a passenger. We reached the village of Konso in mid-afternoon and my first thought was to find the Icelander I had been told works for the Norwegian Mission. I spent an hour talking to him without learning much. I don't think I communicate well with missionaries. Either that or missionaries sense in me someone less than enthusiastic about their calling.

Konso is more an administrative outpost than a traditional village. It is in the Konso area but is not particularly representative of Konso culture.

I went in search of a man named Aferwork, the son of an ex-governor and one of many traders and businessmen who own and operate farms in the area. I have been told he is familiar with these regions, and I hoped he would tell me something of what he knew. When I found him, he sounded full of knowledge and willing to help.

On my way back from talking to Aferwork, I encountered a vehicle with a few policemen who stepped out to question me. I was not at all surprised. I thought it would happen long before now, in Arba Minch or Gidole. I presented many documents but they were not enough, or maybe they were too many. They told me I would have to see their lieutenant and brought me to his house.

Not unexpectedly, he was asleep, wrapped in his *shamma*, the fine cotton shawl everyone uses to keep out the highland cold. Flies buzzed everywhere as he slept away on a bench in front of his house. I was required to sit and wait, all the time hoping that the flies and the fleas were doing him as much injury as possible. He woke in about twenty minutes and looked through the same papers I had shown his underlings. Saying that he had had no word of my coming, he announced that this was nomadic country and therefore dangerous. His last thought was that I should return to Arba Minch and petition the governor for a pass to undertake the journey I was proposing.

I explained that I had been traveling everywhere in the country quite freely and that I had assumed I would be able to do it in this province as well. He said I should go back to Arba Minch and I said I would not. We both were angry and I left. I wonder if it will be possible to settle things in a friendlier manner tomorrow.

June 11th 1968

My situation vis-à-vis the police lieutenant is very much a standoff. My new friend, Aferwork, has gone to him pleading my case, saying that surely this *ferengi* – their word for any foreigner — has all the necessary papers. Aferwork even informed the lieutenant that I carried the personal recommendation of his Highness the Crown Prince. I decided to get this document before leaving Addis, and it was procured with the help of Mr. Pankhurst, Director of the Institute for Ethiopian Studies, who knows the Prince personally. I even had photographs taken of the Prince and me in friendly conversation. Of course, some risk was involved in this strategy inasmuch as Ethiopia is undergoing rapid and irreversible political change. Emperor Haile Selassie, for all his durability, cannot last forever. I might gaily wave a glossy portrait of the Crown Prince, by no means a popular favorite, only to discover that a revolution had taken place toppling the regime and taking me with it. For this reason I listen frequently to the BBC on a portable radio.

Aferwork's intercessions with the lieutenant have brought about no change in my situation or in the status of my mission. I am not talking to the lieutenant and he is not talking to me. What is clear is only that he feels he should have been apprised of my visit. I am not asking for help from the police and that is what this lieutenant cannot understand. He is unable to provide assistance, if he hasn't been notified of my coming, but reading the Crown Prince's pleadings on my behalf, he thinks he is supposed to be helping. I am not sure how this peculiar impasse will be resolved. For now I am going about my business pretty much as usual. I have the feeling that the status quo could last as long as the monarchy and I could stay here for months or even years, without anything being done.

Today I visited a village near Konso where there was a cleared space described to me as an area for play, which I understand is the word (translated from Amharic into English) for the singing and dancing that happens in the dark at this season. This special site seemed to suggest something beyond play and even to enter the sphere of religion. While definitely a place where people go for dancing and singing, in it are also impressive carved stone and wood figures. The stone blocks are about four or five feet high and a bit less than a foot wide. They remind me of megalithic objects I have seen in images made in islands in the Mediterranean.

P4

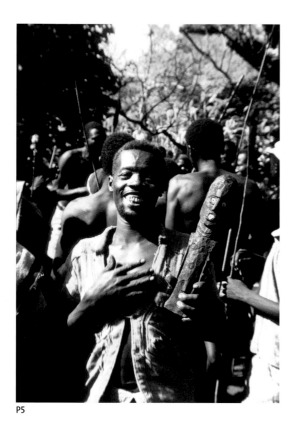

P5

At the entrance and exit of this village stood wooden effigy figures. These are the famous Konso funeral figures that are carved from wood and planted in the ground to commemorate departed souls. I believe the social status of the deceased may have some minimal importance, but the practice might also be more democratic than I'm supposing.

These figures, which occasionally qualify as high art, show considerable strength and character. Sacred, but not enfolded in any solemnity or awe, they were shown to us with considerable enthusiasm and more than a hint of entrepreneurship.

This afternoon we walked to another village thirty minutes from Konso town. Aferwork had said we should visit there because it was not only large but also uninfluenced by local mission activities. Aferwork is very genial, but his information on these matters is seldom accurate. In fact the village had a school and a mission where preachers warned those listening not to drink the locally brewed beer. The locals may have heard the sermons but when we arrived they were well along in the enjoyment of their beer. Many men, even a few of the adolescent boys, were very drunk.

With fine compounds and entryways, the village looks in every way like the one we were in this morning. I'm impressed by the attention the Konso people give to their immediate surroundings in an effort to achieve order and even beauty.

June 12th 1968

With its terraced gardens, women bent over cultivating the fields, a pervasive greenness, and rain-filled skies, Konso puts me in mind of New Guinea. Much care is put into making such things as gateways and doorways. Even houses are built following a tradition of shared features, such as sleeping platforms and central fires. I would like to have been here a generation or more sooner to see this culture living under its own rules and less heavily influenced by borrowing.

I look everywhere for an element that gives coherence and strength to the Konso way of life, something akin to the ceremonial war of the Dani in New Guinea or to cattle for the Nuer. Perhaps that element is the corn these people grow with such care and industry. Corn might be central in some way, but the Konso also put much effort into weaving, pottery, woodworking, music and dance.

Their life is not pale or shallow, but finding anything of surpassing interest is hard.

I may be talking myself out of staying here to embrace something, somewhere, more compelling. With the Nuer, obsession with their herds was enough reason to stay and see what in the world that meant. In New Guinea, once I saw the importance of ritual warfare, I was completely absorbed in watching how this investment in violence gave meaning to their lives. On the other hand and despite its many appealing details, the Konso world feels to me somehow unfocused. Maybe I will retrace my steps and return to Arba Minch, speak to the governor, and then proceed toward people called Arbore. There is no guarantee they will provide what is missing here, but I think it might be worth taking that risk.

June 13th 1968

On the way home yesterday we heard singing for an old man who had died. When this happens, the Konso immediately begin celebrating with dance and song. A young man who spoke both Konso and Amharic was able to tell us that in a village not far away there would be serious singing and dancing, at least until the market started. So we made plans to go by foot. Once there, we found a large number of people dancing in enormous clouds of dust. It was very spirited, with many enjoying the occasion. After we arrived, many more people came and took part in this spirit of fun that is so prevalent in Konso.

We arrived early and although the dancers had planned to stop in order to go to the market, I coaxed them to continue which they did for another hour and a half. I had a feeling the energy was in recognition as much of my camera and sound recorder as of the person who had died but this did not matter to me as long as what was happening had sufficient sincerity.

A few men were dancing with a carved ancestor figure which I thought might have something to do with the death that had brought on the celebration. Later I discovered that at least one of these men had wanted to sell it to me. Had I known this at the time, I would most certainly have done as he wished.

A little later I decided to take the long way back to our compound. I wanted to think about what we had seen, not just this morning but in the few days we had been here. Could we perhaps find a more remote Konso village and work there, or should we double back to Arba Minch and go in a different direction to find the Arbore?

I decided to turn around and head back to Arba Minch, but I was conflicted about leaving. Going back will mean spending far too much time in transit and far too much effort finding the perfect location. For me, this problem is an old one — the turmoil of travel that does not allow for real engagement.

June 15th 1968

We rose early to put things in order before starting the journey to Arba Minch. I worried about the rain and wondered whether we would get through. A detail that delayed our departure was the need to pay some furtive men who had come in the night with effigy grave marker figures, like the ones they had danced with and that are called *gattos*. Having heard I was interested, they obligingly found them for me and were intent on getting full value for their efforts. I had guessed something was afoot in the night because the dogs were barking at these grave robbers, who could not have wanted to be seen at their nefarious business. The *gattos* were not spectacular but their authenticity was confirmed by the dirt sticking to their bottom ends. They clearly had recently been standing in the ground.

At around 9 a.m. we set out with rain already falling heavily. By the time we had moved through the valley and started up toward Gidole, the showers had stopped and the appearance of the sun meant the road might be dry enough to let us make decent time. Then came a hill with a road the rain had turned to a mixture of rocks and mud. Only by pushing one car a few yards, anchoring it and winching the other car forward, were we able to reach Gidole.

Once in Gidole, I decided to keep going, not knowing how difficult the road ahead had been made by recent rains. What we found was that the first river between us and Arba Minch was too high to cross. We stopped in the hope it would subside and allow us to get across it in the morning.

June 16th 1968

The river that was so full last night was easily crossed this morning. I assumed we would be in Arba Minch in time to meet the flight bringing Joan Mitchell, whose eye problems have kept her from being with us until now. Because of localized rain that has fallen in this area, however, we had a hard time on the same road we had traveled with such ease not many days ago.

We were too late to meet the plane but found Joan as she was making her way from the airfield to the hotel. She appeared to have no ill effects from her eye problems and was happy to be back at work. I needed to find the governor of Gamo Gofa Province and ask him to authorize my entry. His Landrover had been seen leaving town, but I should be able to see him tomorrow. It means a comfortable night in the hotel which, after all the car wrestling, might be a good thing. If the meeting with the governor tomorrow goes well, we can start the next leg of this speculative journey.

We will be hindered not only by the rains, but also because I have such flimsy information about where to go. I did what little research I could in Addis, consulting people and libraries, but neither of these resources was particularly helpful. I am looking for a group, the Arbore, that is not well known but that have caught my fancy. What I have been told about these people is little more than travelers' tales and not very thoughtful ones at that.

June 17th 1968

At about 9 a.m. I was able to speak to the governor but through an interpreter, since I am as lacking in Amharic as he is in English. I explained why I was in his province and what I hoped to do. As I spoke, I was forced to explain some things to myself as well. What, really, am I doing in Gamo Gofa Province?

I was disingenuous enough with the governor to shamelessly imply that if I was able to make the pictures I wanted to make, they might encourage tourism. I hope the impression was not that I wanted to see holiday seekers tripping through Gamo Gofa, but that this beautiful country had possibilities still largely unknown to any but the most intrepid travelers.

After lengthy and irrelevant conversation, I asked if I would need more documents than the ones I already had in order to travel to Soddu, beyond that to Baco, and eventually to Amar Coche. The governor said he would give me a letter and within the hour his word was made good by the delivery of what I was told is all I needed to keep going.

We were quickly on our way and arrived in Soddu by the middle of the day. From here it will be new for everyone, since none of us has been this way before, not Tecle our cook/helper and not Abdullah, our other helper who also assists with the language. We managed to find gasoline and took on as much as we could carry for the journey ahead. While this was happening, I tried to find someone who knew the road to Baco.

This quest was frustrating, but I found a man in the local bar who, though Italian, spoke little of that language and only bad Amharic. He came into the bar seeming to know about the route to Baco, including the correct turn at various forks, what state the rivers were in and where to cross them. He inspired me to set out in the direction of Baco.

D1

P6

My attempts to find directions were frequently frustrated because there are often two or more names for the same place. Sometimes the same name can refer to different geographic entities, such as the town and the district, but sometimes one entity can have two names. Baco is also Jinka, I think.

It is evening and the stars are bright, suggesting that tomorrow we might be able to cross a river fifty miles from where we sleep tonight.

June 18th 1968

We left early this morning for Baco and ultimately Amar Coche, but were soon stopped by a pretty river that is nameless, according to my entirely inadequate map. We have come thirty miles in nine-and-a-half hours. The slow pace is the result of many hours spent hauling cars through deep mud. We are able to pull ourselves along foot by foot only because of an immense winch with a long cable we attach to a rock or tree stump out in front of a mired vehicle. We are making spectacular time, even though our average speed over the ground is three miles an hour. Three miles an hour in glue is not bad. At this rate we will reach Amar Coche in four record-breaking days.

June 19th 1968

The day was laborious, though not as bad as I had anticipated when the skies opened last night to lash us with yet more rain. As things turned out, we were on the edge of last night's downpour and the road ahead was spared. We were stuck only two or three times, not the ten of yesterday.

We made excellent time to the Masi River which is considered a definitive boundary hereabouts. If it is flooding, you sit down and wait for it to become shallow. I found the deepest part of the Masi to be mid-thigh in height, the upper limit of our vehicles' river-crossing capabilities. We tried and succeeded and are now another forty miles closer to where we want to be. I estimate forty-five to Baco and another sixty or thereabouts to Amar Coche. It is athletic, this sport of bush driving.

P7

109

June 20th 1968

Each new setting-forth seems harder to manage. While our journey is not quite a film, I have sometimes thought it should be. Maybe what we are doing to get there is as important as anything we do when we arrive.

The journey is made more difficult because we are seriously overloaded with gasoline, water, food, camera equipment, camp gear and personal belongings. We even have the wooden effigy figures from Konso. It was inevitable that our luck would run out at some point, which it did mid-morning when gasoline began leaking from the main fuel tank of my Toyota. The hole was not a puncture but a rent caused by the chassis twisting as it goes over this impossible terrain. I was able to rescue what gas remained by transferring it to an empty jerry can and, luckily, we can fuel the engine with an extra tank installed a long time ago in Addis. At a certain point, I saw no sign of Clark, and, on going back, found him with a very long face. The left front spring of his car had just snapped at the U-bolt shackle that holds it to the axle. We couldn't continue without improvising something. Working for what remained of the daylight, we made modest progress in pretty outrageous ways drilling new holes and taking bolts from other parts of the car deemed less crucial. All the time we were inventing ways to make the vehicle roadworthy again. Finally, darkness came and it was impossible to carry on.

We have come too far never to reach Baco, where there is an airport and a telephone. If we have to, one of us can fly to Addis for what we need. We are extremely unlikely to find spare parts anywhere else in Ethiopia. We know this because twenty-five miles behind us on the so-called road there is an American vehicle belonging to the U.S. Mapping Mission that is sunk in six feet of the blackest mire, abandoned except for a single, frightened sentinel left by the Americans to stand guard over a phantom vehicle.

I felt badly taking C-rations of which there were mountains. The poor man guarding this cache of edibles begged me to not take anything, as he would be held responsible when the *ferengi* returned. I was sure the *ferengi* would never return and certainly would never care about a few missing rations, but I gave him a long letter explaining that it was I who had lifted the rations and that their guard had been stalwart in the face of my craving. I only hope he, too, will help consume them.

The frogs tonight have begun a concert of what sounds like miniature bells. It is really very beautiful. I think of *Henderson the Rain King* and cannot help smiling.

June 21st-23rd 1968

Almost a week ago, we left Arba Minch full of enthusiasm, thinking we might get to Baco in three or four days. Instead it has been a continuing nightmare of mishaps and accidents on top of an already impossible set of other circumstances. In the span of three days not much more can happen, having had one car overturn and another lose its muffler and springs. Getting the upset car righted was easy compared to fixing springs without tools or spares. Bullying our way up and down impossible inclines slick with mud, we advanced only ten miles yesterday. On one steep hill, four wheels seldom touched the ground at the same time, so large were the rocks and so uneven the ground. Going over the road's edge would have meant rolling 1000 feet into the ravines below.

Reversing direction might have been an option, but we could not and pressed on. Progress today amounted to half a mile and only because we were overtaken by a monster truck that threw us a cable and towed us like a toy boat through a sea of mud to dry land. We stopped for the night where we had been let go by the truck, but ahead was another impassable mud hole. The driver told us another truck was on its way and could give us a tow through the next sinkhole, which is the only way we will make progress in this season of rain, of that I'm convinced.

Within an hour, five lorries coming from the opposite direction pulled up at the brink of the vast mud hole where we were stranded. They told us they would be coming back this way the next day and that, if we were interested, they would pull us all the way to Baco.

Baco is not far and, once there, we will refit and continue on to Amar Coche. No one wants to retreat, especially since local information has it that the road beyond Baco is far better. As we are only three hours walking to Baco, I sent Joan Mitchell and Abdullah ahead so that Joan could take one of two scheduled flights to Addis, where she could try to get the parts we need to resurrect the cars.

These semi-highlands are not especially interesting to the eye, and the population is denser than I would have expected. I suppose it is agriculture at this elevation that accounts for the numbers. Girls and women are dressed in grass skirts and striped cotton shirts, which shows, sartorially speaking at least, one of the several dualities in their lives. It is not an appealing sight, this look of poverty. No doubt to study this population would furnish anthropology of merit, but I am not interested in it pictorially. Is this way I have of viewing appearances a result of being a purist? I expect we will have to get well beyond Baco before I find anything else. This particular stretch is strewn with mica, which glints in the sun when it is picked up by the wind or scuffed by feet. A road of fool's gold is, I hope, no more than an ironic comment on our present circumstances.

It is extremely cold tonight and I look forward to our descent to lower ground tomorrow.

June 24th 1968
Our arrival in Baco now guaranteed in some way or other, we rose this morning in a more leisurely way, washed clothes and ate chickens bought from people walking back from a market somewhere near the bottom of these hills. Soon we heard the lorries snarling their way toward us.

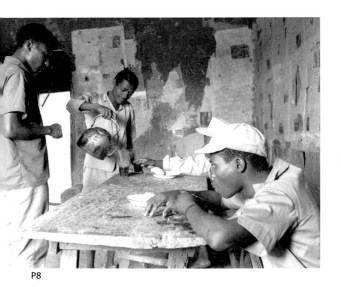

P8

Lorry people are friendly, buccaneer types who drive and do other work like sailors on a merchantman. Each lorry has a captain, a crew of mates, and a small band of menials who wield the shovels, poles, and other implements of their trade.

A huge truck with immense tires fitted with chains dove into the mud and churned its way to the far side. There it stopped and waited while the smaller trucks tried it on their own. Some made it; those that did not were heaved an enormous cable with which the larger truck winched them to the other side. We were the last to get this service.

The trucks were loaded with tons of *teff*, the fine Ethiopian wheat taken overland to be sold in places like Baco. When a truck gets mired, the crew jumps off the sacks of wheat and down into the muck. There they make channels to divert water and arrange rocks and tree stumps to provide the stranded truck with sufficient footing to be towed or, more rarely, to use its own power to move on. It was necessary only to pull us quickly enough so that we did not sink and become engulfed.

At sunset we entered Baco in the jubilant company of our road companions. They had more or less dragged us the last ten or eleven miles of the journey. Tonight there will be some very drunken lorry drivers.

Baco resembles a forbidden city after our weeklong ordeal in which only 187 miles were registered by odometer. Everyone is relieved and tired. None of us is much impressed by Baco. Other than its name, which means "compact," there is little to say about this typical mid-highlands village. Its only interest might be when it functions as a weekly marketplace.

We learned that Joan had made the flight to Addis, meaning we may get our vehicles repaired by Wednesday. We also learned that Abdullah had been arrested by the local police on suspicion of being an agent who had slipped across the border with Somaliland. He looks like a Somali, as might be expected with his Afar parentage. Somalis and Afar are almost indistinguishable. I went to extract him from jail so he could help find us a place to stay, which he did, although it was one dedicated mainly to fleas and cockroaches.

June 25th 1968

Eight days of travel on these roads have created an urgent need for washing both bodies and clothes. I must also see the local governor, as each new town we come to means submitting to the formality of presenting ourselves and requesting imperial permission for further travel. I realized, as I thought about what I might say to this man, that traveling in his province is all we can do now anyway. To escape its boundaries in the next three months is impossible. We are trapped in Gamo Gofa until the rains have stopped and the roads have dried. Only the great blue Fiat lorries are equal to this landscape in this season. Had they not arrived at the precise moment we ourselves did, we would still be on the road, possibly for weeks, in vehicles fast becoming derelicts. We have one broken shovel left; one front spring assembly is flattened, and both mufflers are gone.

I have extracted some letters from the governor's office and will pick them up tomorrow. I am also looking for a person with local knowledge, which I think is always the best to have, but have found no one.

Hearing myself recording these thoughts at the end of the day, I'm struck by how little is described beyond the struggle to reach an obscure destination. The cameras stay packed and there is no strength left from the ongoing battle with cars to do anything anyway. I have begun to think the film to make should be about this struggle, not my own necessarily but that of those who drive the Fiats. The story, if one were to join them and see what happens, is about tearing up the countryside hauling freight from one market town to the next. Formally speaking, all the necessary narrative elements exist, including a cast of characters and an element of the chase for tension and suspense. Will the *teff* get through? When will the lorry sink to its windows next? Here might be the ultimate road film. Besides, going with them would mean never having to haul one's own vehicle out of another quagmire.

Instead, I keep chasing the chimera of isolated people offering metaphors for pondering not only their isolation but my own. As a graduate student, I remember repeating to incredulous professors that what I liked about anthropology was that it would help me understand myself in more ways than the people I observed. About this I have not changed my mind.

P9

June 26th 1968

The governor, actually sub-governor, is still unavailable but I managed to get clearances from a surprisingly dim colonel of the police. His rank seems rather high for him to be dim-witted or to be stationed in Baco. Maybe these two things are connected somehow. He has told me the way to Amar Coche is open.

Joan came today on a charter flight, bringing most of the parts we had asked her to find. Getting on scheduled flights is very hard because of too many passengers and too much cargo for the few regular flights.

With this in mind, I asked the local Ethiopian Airways officials to reserve seats for our return to Addis. The rainy season has come, which means there is only one way, by air, to leave Baco. The lorry drivers are adamant that this is their last visit until November. If they can't get through, we never will. Our intrepidity has conjured a dilemma. In getting here against all odds, we have arrived at imprisonment.

We began readying ourselves for the next stage by replacing vehicle parts that had failed, taking on gasoline, filling water containers, and getting food. We will spend one more night in our makeshift camp, having abandoned the hotel to its insect clientele. Baco will not be missed.

June 27th 1968

By the end of the day we managed to get fifty-five miles south and west of Baco. We played tag with overloaded government trucks moving soldiers and supplies. First they would get stuck and we would pass, then we would get stuck and they would get by us, and then something would happen to them, and on it went.

I despair at the way the calendar is mocking our progress. I had believed that at least a week ago we would be where we could start film work. The drive to Baco was meant to take only two-and-a-half days.

I now know there are at least three groups of pastoralist/agriculturalists living in this region: the Hamar, who give or take their name from Amar Coche; the Bana, who are a little intimidating owing to their penchant for emasculating their foes and using the trophies to purchase brides; and the Arbore, about whom until now I have learned little or nothing. I welcome the sight of any of these three unsuspecting groups.

June 28th 1968

The car is becoming more odious with every mile. I long to step on the gas and put it into an accommodating ditch. The act of driving is depriving me of all thought and curiosity. I'm a slave to the car's least whim or summons. It is not the way to make film. I am unsure where to go and what I will find. I'm location hunting without any clear intentions. The landscape and whatever people may inhabit it are writing the script as I stumble on.

We are impeded by officialdom too. Today we were questioned first at a place called Gayasu and again at Turmi. Gayasu was not so bad. I presented a copy of the governor's letter and we were on our way in no time. At Turmi, the police were more suspicious and it took nearly two hours to convince them we were not a threat to imperial security.

Later this afternoon, not far from Turmi, I decided to stop in the bed of a sand river. I was attracted to its peacefulness knowing nothing yet of the habits of sand fleas that also find these dry rivers to their liking. As we were getting our little camp ready, I heard foreign voices and looked up to see some young men carrying wooden stools and walking sticks. They lived nearby and were bringing lumps of white clay back to their village. Their bodies were covered with zigzag and curvi-linear designs they had made by drawing with wet fingers in the white clay smeared on their skin.

The person I brought from Baco as an interim guide was a Mohammedan trader named Kadir, who speaks Hamar and Bana. Between him and Abdullah, I was able to learn a little about these passersby, who are Hamar. Someone is being married tonight and they are on their way to the celebration. I asked them to stay with us for the night so that we could go together in the morning. They said that they had first to find their cattle, which they would bring this way in the morning, and then take us to the village. I hope they will keep their word. This encounter could be the beginning of something long overdue. Here are some people who suddenly materialize looking as if the world of lorries, governor's offices, and fleabag hotels were of no concern to them whatever.

F4

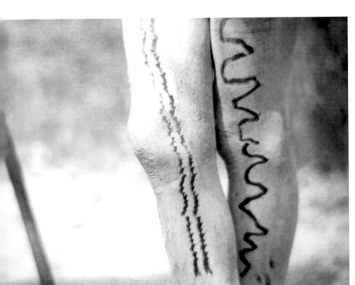

P10

June 29th 1968

This morning one of last evening's visitors came by our camp with cattle he was leading to a nearby watering place. Nothing flows in these rivers but, if one digs in the middle of the dry bed, water will appear at about ten or more feet. Made from dried and hollowed gourds, calabashes are used to gather the water, which is then passed along to a trough that has been set up nearby. Our new friend's clay markings are smudged from dancing last night. He said only young men are dancing and that although the real rains haven't come, people are quite happy and willing to have a good time.

Because arrangements have been made to fly out of Baco on July 7th, we are pressed for time and we head immediately for this person's village, going back five miles to take a path he had described to us. Then we walked for fifteen minutes through an endless thicket of thorns. The path was clear enough to follow and we soon came to a small Hamar village of three or four compounds, each containing about the same number of houses. As far as I could tell, most of the inhabitants had left to do their daily work. The women were probably gardening and the boys and men looking after the animals. Only a few people had stayed back and they slowly began to come out of their houses.

All of them were shy and reticent, having had no warning of our sudden entry into their quiet world. A few children darted out, only to dash back into their house as soon as they got a look at us. Finally, a man appeared who must have been asleep. With the help of Kadir, I explained that we had come simply to see them going about their lives and that it was our wish to begin by setting

F5

up our own little compound close to theirs. None of this was easy for me to formulate or for the man to comprehend, but he said he supposed that would be all right and why didn't we go get our things and come back later. He also said the village leader was off doing something somewhere else but would be returning later. I asked about dancing, saying I was interested in seeing that as well. He said there might be some tonight and supposed it would be fine if we were there.

After chatting for about an hour, we set off to get our things and bring them back along a wide path used when cattle are herded to the riverbed for watering. The round trip was quite easy and we were back in the Hamar village by mid-afternoon. We then began making arrangements for a stay of as many days as possible.

Dancing did not begin until well after sunset but we went to it early, taking with us cameras and lights. The scene was extraordinary. Women and girls were dancing in large numbers to the beat of ankle irons clanging together rhythmically. The occasion was unmistakably joyous; men leapt and women clashed their leg irons with a scuffling step just out of range of the men who periodically danced up to them only to retreat. Sometimes a small phalanx of men would dance in unison and a few young women would move quickly toward the men's space in a teasing, seductive way.

Women screamed with fright and surprise when my portable light went on. It made them nervous and afraid to keep dancing. What they were doing clearly requires a degree of obscurity, so it was not a good idea to reveal too much of what was going on. Persisting, I managed to expose some film at the probable cost of dampening their spirits and ending the dancing about an hour after it had started.

At least we are here and have foisted ourselves upon them. What they think of this intrusion into their lives may be a little clearer tomorrow.

June 30th 1968

Our camp is near the Hamar houses and under some low trees I hoped would provide shelter from the sun at midday. In the early morning, several people came to see us out of curiosity and need. In places like this, people are often ill and have

F6

P11

P12

enough acquaintance with the larger world to know that powerful medicine and the *ferengi* go together.

I am not yet sure how vital this little group is. They don't appear to have an overabundance of energy, but I cannot be sure of anything on the basis of such short acquaintance. I keep comparing them with the Nuer who are an immediately more compelling people. I will have to be patient with the Hamar. I'm all too ready to dismiss them as inexpressive, despite the dancing we saw last night. I am also too ready to condemn the landscape, which can anyway hardly be seen owing to the thorn growth that precludes the possibility of even an horizon.

Are the Hamar just another exhausted group of indigenes forced onto the geographic margins? The question arises in part because of my discussions with some men who have visited our little camp. They are unanimously interested in, even obsessed by, clothing. Somehow, what is worn is of paramount importance. Dressing sets one apart from everyone else, meaning everyone has sloughed off the coils of cultural identity and put on machine-made garments. Among their proudest possessions are scraps of Western clothing. A man wearing a tattered T-shirt, or soiled and torn trousers, is raised in his own and other's estimation to a higher social plane.

Despite these urges to be different, many in this community retain their Hamar identity and so look no different than they might have fifty years ago. Appearances are more important in filmmaking than they are in life, which forces one to wonder how much filmmaking has to do with life. What is clear to me is that the less the group I choose to film is influenced by modernity, the greater will be my freedom from having to explain such matters. I have always thought populations undergoing change were the business of sociologists and of those anthropologists interested in change for its own sake. My own interests are to look for that which is an apt symbol or sign and, at the same time, is distinctive in and of itself.

My initial response to the Hamar is not especially enthusiastic. I tend to see them as yet another example of waning traditional life. It may be too short a time to make any sensible judgment about them and it may also be that, because of the colossal effort to get here, I have expected a larger reward than what I see in front of me. So I will give the Hamar more time and hope they do not dance and milk their animals only in the dark.

I will also resist falling into the same torpor I see them succumbing to as the day wears on and the sun climbs higher. I asked a man to show me how he and his friends and relatives live, but he said they felt ill and tired. I pointed out that I was leaving soon. He said he had diarrhea and couldn't do anything until I gave him pills. I said, "All right, here you are. What can you show me?" Now I have fallen prey, with no shame and little hope of success, to the same engine of change that I condemn.

F7

July 1st 1968

More dancing took place last night, though I am told it will not be at its best until and unless real rains arrive. From the look of the skies this morning, that moment cannot be far off. As encouragement, I have made it known that I would happily provide a bull, if that would improve their mood for dancing. I am unsure whether it would or not, but it seemed a good idea just the same. I was told the killing of this bull should not happen in the absence of their leader who is still far away. I suggested a goat and they all agreed that could happen.

The animal was brought later in the day and was so large the owner was asking more than the agreed-upon price, about one U.S. dollar. What he was asking was already twice what goats cost among the Afar, but it was a lot of meat for not that much money. My intention was to film its slaughtering and eating, although the scene probably has nothing to recommend it cinematically.

The Hamar have little experience around cameras or *ferengi* with cameras. One man, who has been the most outspoken critic of our presence, said he would not eat the goat because the cameras had been pointed at it and he might get sick. This phobia was one of the most developed I have yet encountered in regard to the meaning and effect of image making. I tried to illustrate what I was doing by making a Polaroid. Everyone looked at the picture and was hugely amused, but the man who first objected was more convincing, so the others said they would not eat the goat and that I could have it back. I said I did not want it back but, if they would not kill and eat it, they must give me back my money. I also said I wanted the screw with

which I had fixed a man's rifle in the morning. Thinking long and carefully, they said they would kill the goat but they would not eat it. I said I didn't care if they killed it or not. I wanted my money back, not the dead goat. I had shot an antelope and it was enough for me to eat for a long time.

They thought and thought and finally said, "All right, we will kill the goat and we shall eat it too." I said, "Fine, but I want you to understand that I am going to photograph you while you do those things." I then asked if we were still friends and whether they would be dancing tonight. They said we were all friends and that they would play tonight.

Another crisis has passed involving their concern with what we are doing here and what effect it might have on their lives. These worries are certainly not without foundation since anything we do is bound to have some effect. For all their interest in such things as Western clothes, they have very little understanding of what else we carry around with us in the way of technology or ideas. They are marginalized well beyond my initial impression of their place in this rapidly changing world.

The man entrusted with the goat's execution punctured its neck with his spear and three young men began to drink from the blood provided by the goat's still pounding heart. About thirty men and boys had gathered for this occasion and all of them smeared the contents of the goat's intestines on their legs and chests. When I asked why this was done, I was told that God liked to see it and that it made everyone equal, poor men and rich men.

P13

P14

While the goat was dealt with, a man was getting his hair dressed. It was an elaborate undertaking having spectacular results that I wanted to see from beginning to the end. On asking if I might photograph this long and exacting procedure, I was told, "yes," if there was anyone who wanted it done. A man said he was interested, but then decided against it because of an infestation of lice. A new hair dressing would be pointless if he spent the day scratching his head. I told the man I might be able with some powerful medicine to cure his problem. He was, of course, interested and so I took some Shelltox and wetted his entire scalp. As I was treating the man, I thought that with enough Shelltox I might win over the entire Hamar nation. When I had finished, the man was extremely grateful and stopped poking his head with twigs to dislodge his lice. They were either dead or sufficiently stunned to stop whatever they had been doing. Inevitably, this detoxing became a service everyone wanted.

This afternoon I filmed a relatively active scene: men eating goat while one of them paced nearby, saying that God was watching and wondering if the person who had provided the goat was good or bad. I hope to convince God of my goodness before we leave.

July 2nd 1968
Electing to live as the Hamar do in this infelicitous place had to have taken both determination and ingenuity. Cruel and unwelcoming, to say the least, this location is flat tableland covered with thorns of many shapes and sizes lying in wait wherever one turns. Even the most seasoned Hamar herdsman comes home from a day in the surrounding countryside covered with the tracings of thorns that have torn at his arms and legs. Men use a *burkoto* – the word for their wooden stools – in order to put their rear ends out of reach of thorns. They, the men that is, also carry elaborate walking sticks to keep thorn branches at bay. Some men have little loops of hide, almost like boxing gloves, to cover their knuckles. I'm told they also sometimes fight with them. Stools are indispensable for the Hamar and for me, too. It would be impossible to shoot film my way without something near at hand to perch on. The women are not permitted stools, but must sit in their skin skirts directly on the ground.

118

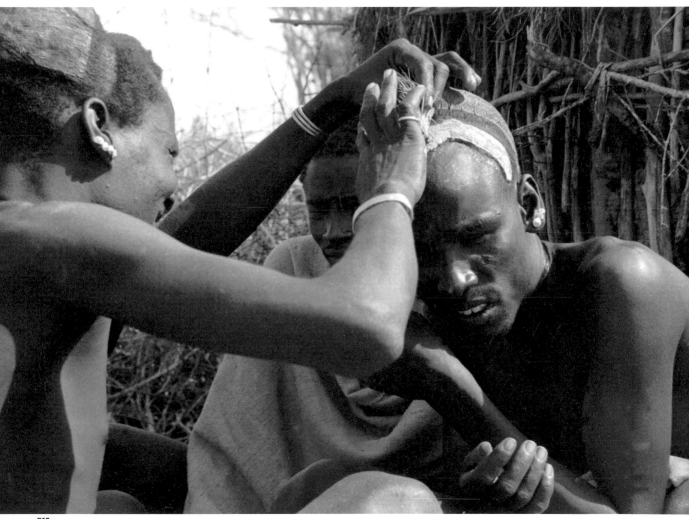

P15

F8

The dancing last night was somewhat diminished in vigor and splendor. I have been trying with one naked, very bright light to illuminate this activity, but it is not at all satisfactory. I am still hopeful the Hamar also dance in the daylight hours.

I filmed more of the man getting his hair done. What was left was to create two red bands of clay over the crown of his head. He now looks quite stunning.

The women and girls leave early and return late from their gardens with heavy containers of water filled at nearby wells. The village is lifeless during the day. Thorn bushes block entrances to the houses and there is only the buzzing of flies over spilled milk or scraps of garbage. In the river beds you see best, since there are no thorn trees to block the view, and the rivers are where everyone must come to reach the fields, refresh the cattle, and fill water vessels at the end of the day.

For a time this afternoon, I sat under some rare trees that must owe their size to roots reaching far down into the riverbed. I watched women using vines to fashion harnesses to carry the enormous gourds used to transport water from the wells to the village. The scene was very peaceful and I intend to return tomorrow.

July 3rd 1968

I think we are becoming as interesting to the Hamar as they are to us. In the mornings now, several women and men come to watch us rise and ready ourselves for the day. Women leave earlier than the men for the reason they have less leisure and are the ones who do the steady laboring in this and so many other societies.

My intention was to return to the little sand river where I was yesterday, but none of the women I have come to know dropped by and so I went alone and found several of them threshing sorghum. The scene was lively, with many ladies engaged in a variety of harvest-time jobs. Some

threshed, others winnowed, and still others swept up the grain and filled huge skins for still others to carry away to a storage place. Those working also live here in a temporary encampment they use until the harvest is over.

I had no difficulty at all filming what was happening in and around the harvest activity, young women playing their maidenly flutes and older women repairing the threshing floor with fresh cow dung. It was an exclusively female world, though occasionally a stray male would come by, put his stool under his arse, and clean his teeth with a twig used only for that purpose.

I filmed women dressing their hair by rubbing in clarified butter and a red powder, while others were grinding sorghum close by. There were numbers of boys decorated with white clay in imitation of their older brothers and nearby wandered a few dogs that had been painted with yellow clay. In the background there were cows with neck bells made from tortoise shells and iron and not so far away baboons ventured out to the shallower wells for a drink. The banks of the river were very alive today and I tried hard to sort things out visually.

Only by leaving the village did any of this activity become apparent, which is a lesson I am continually taught here and everywhere else. Nothing happens without moving, without sallying forth somewhere, anywhere.

I did not go to watch the dancing last night. I have worked hard but have exposed only 7000 feet, a mere three-and-a-half hours on the screen. I still must establish some things before I leave, including the thorn jungle, various aspects of the men's world, and the role of animals, which is quite unlike that of the Nuer or even the Afar. But a start has been made that I sense has promise.

July 4th 1968

Red ticks are making a hard life unbearable. I find ten or fifteen on me every day. They announce themselves with telltale tickling as they set forth in search of I'm not sure what human delicacy.

Still, the Hamar have grown steadily more cordial and, in a few cases, even affectionate. My feelings toward them are filled with warmth and a desire to know more and understand better what is behind the coherence I am beginning to see in their lives. More time is needed to come away with

F9

P16

F10

P17

any understanding, so I will have to come back. All I can do now is respond intuitively to what I see, hoping the images I make are ones I need when I start to edit.

What I sense is that men are cruel to women, whom they regard almost as slaves. The men do little now that they are deprived of cattle raiding, owing to the advent of police and the disappearance of game. Despite their inferiority, women are the ones who appear to be happiest, who laugh and are playful. Work is an apparent tonic for them and a lack of employment makes these men's lives heavy with regret.

Today is our last day, since we must set out tomorrow for Baco to be in time for the plane early on Sunday morning. I was able to take a longer than usual walk out by the little sand river where I am most happy and where, yesterday, I encountered my first Hamar policeman. The man had left his tribal setting to learn about the outside world in Baco, but was sent back to his kinsmen as a sort of stooge to report wrongdoing.

We look ahead to our last evening of dancing, thinking of it more as entertainment than subject matter for film. I have no way to adequately illuminate the event, so I will content myself with a few still photographs.

July 5th 1968

Last night the dancing was different and better than it has been all this time. Younger people were dancing and a new energy and playfulness were evident. The play is obviously a teasing, provocative game between girls and boys. I stayed until midnight and the dancing was still strong when I left. I am struck by the energy of these people who play all night.

At dawn the man who had told me he would draw blood came for me. Stewart and I went to watch him at his work. He took a small bow and sent an arrow into the neck of a cow that seemed not in the least put out. A large amount of blood was collected from the puncture and I tried, futilely I suspect, to film the procedure at a time when the sun had scarcely begun to rise above the nonexistent horizon. The scene had its pictorial interest and so I kept shooting despite the darkness. Many people were nearby in the compound getting started on a long day of labor. Our own work is over, except for the journey to Baco.

We are tired but content. After a brief rest in Addis, I will return to our little Hamar village near Turmi, feeling fairly certain a film is waiting there to be made.

July 11th 1968

Yesterday I put Stewart on the plane to Madrid to join his mother. This leaves four of us: Clark Worswick, Joan Mitchell, Leslie Shatto, and myself. Clark and Joan will do still photography and Leslie will manage the camp. Today we have come by Ethiopian Airways to Baco, the district capital. I think we are all feeling fatigued from our previous efforts and not overly eager for what lies ahead. We had to come to Baco, if only to retrieve the two Toyota Land Cruisers we will be using to take us to the Hamar. Today they have carried us only twelve miles, but we didn't leave until late in the afternoon so it hasn't taken long to get here, considering the same journey a week ago lasted all day.

Our new interpreter is Hassan and he reputedly speaks both Hamar and Galeb, the language of people a bit further south. He says he was in the group that took Marshall Tito on one of his infamous Ethiopian hunting trips. I have been told Tito had an insatiable appetite for wild animals, which may have given him his taste for other atrocities. He must not have been disappointed, because game here is quite prodigious.

July 12th 1968

We are back to where we were visiting a week ago, the small village that is about twelve miles beyond Turmi. Our friends among the Hamar appeared to be mildly pleased to see us, and I began immediately to think of what I might do. I am especially interested in getting information by using Hassan to frame my questions in Hamar. I feel I know nothing about these people and I can only get interested if I can form a better picture of what they want from life, beyond survival, in this bleak and forbidding landscape.

When we arrived, most of the villagers were out with their cattle or working in their gardens. Tomorrow I plan to be up early enough to surprise some unsuspecting milker of cows. I find this Hamar life somehow satisfying, though it is not lived on the same level of ecstatic bucolic pleasuring as that of the Nuer.

P18

July 13th 1968

The morning began so windy that our source of shade, a large piece of cloth, was quickly blown away. We are now thrice plagued: by wind, by dust, and by a blazing sun. Fortunately, sufficient distractions kept us from dwelling on these tribulations.

At dawn I was filming the milking and other early morning chores, most of which fall to women. Apart from giving children and women instructions as to what they should be doing, the men appear to be employed scarcely at all, at least not beyond drinking the coffee that is supplied in quantity by these same tireless females.

My own chores fall mostly under the heading of mechanics. I am once more replacing springs that had simply disintegrated from carrying excessive loads on impossible roads. This work is just a small part of what is a great expense of time and energy spent on keeping vehicles going. I am not sure what would have happened had they simply been abandoned, except that we would never have gotten to where we are. We might still be in Konso doing an entirely different, possibly more interesting film. I only know that when the time comes, I will gladly bid these Land Cruisers an eternal goodbye.

This afternoon, Clark and I managed to do some synchronous-sound filming of women at their habitual and unending labors. They were more active than usual because they were at home, instead of in the fields. They were at the same time grinding millet and dressing each other's hair. Their ubiquitous grindstones have an ever larger meaning for me as I watch the hunched figures of women and girls attending to this incessant and mesmerizing business. Through lifelong practice a wonderful rhythm is achieved, whereby the grain is reduced to flour with an economy and grace suggesting both ritual and dance.

Last night there was singing and dancing in the village to which we were too weary to go. I sense there will be more, perhaps tonight, but I am not privy to much good information. No one is able to tell me what to expect because no one can communicate my interests to those who might know. Hassan spends most of his time in small negotiations with Hamar men taking orders for such things as bullets, knives and clothing that he will someday bring here from Baco.

P19

July 14th 1968

In the Hamar households I have been frequenting these days, I have sensed a mood swing of some size. This morning I noted gloominess not apparent before. I wonder whether mood is determined by the course of the chronic malaria from which they suffer. Yesterday the village was animated in ways I had rarely seen. Today it was the opposite. No one wanted to do much, though in the afternoon a woman asked a friend sitting near her to make small incisions in her abdomen. Plenty of this kind of thing is done in a fairly impromptu manner. Many women have scars on their shoulders from cuts that get mildly infected and then heal into raised weals. These marks have both visual and tactile appeal for women and men alike. Most ladies choose to have them somewhere on their upper bodies. Today's volunteer was a young mother who underwent her cosmetic surgery with one arm lying across her face, no doubt as much to keep out the sun and flies as anything else.

The equipment was basic: a large thorn to grasp a small fold of skin that was then sliced by a sharpened piece of metal. The cuts were very short and were made every half-inch or so in several rows across her midsection. I was interested in the desire behind this woman's request to be marked in this way. The use of the thorn was ironic, given that it is so ubiquitous and emblematic of the harshness of her environment. As I was filming,

F11

P20

the thorn took on a significance beyond its botanical status, but I am not sure what that is, either for the Hamar or for me. The image had a weight of its own, connected somehow to my own interest in the infelicity of the thorn jungle in which we find ourselves here in Hamarland. How we think we should look, both to ourselves and to others, means something.

In the afternoon I went back to where I had seen water retrieved from the riverbed. I saw that many of the old holes had caved in from heavy use by innumerable animals. I could collect only one full jerry can, which we will not drink but use just for washing. Tomorrow we will get more water, unless baboons decide to use these stingy wells for their own baths. The water has little recommending it as a beverage, but there is nothing else. Once it is boiled and transformed into tea, the smell of cow urine and other less easily identified impurities are not too noticeable. The liquid is not so bad, at least not so bad as having nothing to drink at all.

Tonight I expect more dancing, having watched women getting their hair buttered and reddened and otherwise preparing themselves for the evening's entertainments. Tomorrow I think we will push on in search of the Bumi, another cattle-keeping group said to be fine dancers, despite our situation here improving as a richness of life begins to unfold. Still, I keep thinking that by getting farther from highland Ethiopian influence I will find what I am looking for. What, though, is it I am looking for? Sometimes I think I am only withdrawing from, and never venturing toward.

July 15th 1968

We left hurriedly in hopes of getting across the Omo River by the end of the day but the ferry across this formidable river is seven or eight miles down the road from where we have stopped for the night. When we left this morning, our Hamar hosts and hostesses showed more sadness on this departure than others. I will admit to having come to enjoy the company of a number of them, including several beguiling children.

Tonight, on the east bank of the Omo, the sky is clear except for squadrons of mosquitoes, and the sun has just descended in a blaze of glorious light. The scene is quite peaceful and promising, despite an earlier, bizarre encounter with two policemen who arrived in their boat from across the river. One was drunk and decent, the other was drunk and surly. The surly one demanded passports and papers, which he reviewed and gave back, satisfied that we were not aliens trying to overthrow his Majesty's government.

We ate *dikdik*, the tiny antelope that abounds hereabouts and makes delicious eating. I had shot it, which is quite against the law. However, this offense is minor compared to the worries the police have about Abdullah, who keeps getting us in trouble by looking so much like a Somali.

July 16th 1968

The prospect of being on the farther side of the Omo has faded gradually into obscurity. The ferry had no outboard and we have no time to find one if we are to depart Baco on the 30th for Addis. Baco is two or three days from where we are and further by another few days were we ever to reach the Bumi. I think I'm close to resignation, having

P21

hurled myself so many times against the walls of mindless authority, missionary indifference, and general incompetence. I am concerned about my hopes to find a film on the margins of these obscure provinces of Ethiopia. I am too tired to wander further and too ill-informed to have faith in my decisions about where to go. I am also, I fear, no longer feeling lucky. The time may have come to call things off.

July 17th 1968

Since we are so close to the edge of Lake Rudolf, Africa's great inland sea, I thought to look for some lake-adapted people before returning to the Hamar. We are near one of the most beautiful bodies of water in one of the world's most glorious countries and so why not look for someone who had chosen to live here?

I didn't get far with these thoughts owing to a problem that arose over my having shot a gazelle and being found out by some local people who wanted not only parts of the animal, but much more. They demanded sugar, tea, coffee and medicine. I said that since they were dancing, we would be interested in trying to help them. I would even buy a bull they could kill, eat, and use to regain their strength. They weren't as interested in this as in my shooting the lions and hyenas that were making off with their cattle and goats. I told them I couldn't shoot all the hyenas but that I would try to make them happy by killing a few.

Late in the afternoon I went to the edge of Lake Rudolf where everyone goes for water. At a distance of four miles, the lake is very far for the women to carry their enormous loads but the view at the water's edge was beautiful, with the sun falling in a cloudless sky behind trees and papyrus. Were I to linger, there would no doubt have been a procession of animals more various and wonderful than any I have seen. But I had to leave while there was still light and I feel disoriented, wandering mindlessly through this unfamiliar countryside. Returning to the Hamar and settling down long enough to learn more about them might be a better idea. In the short time left, I can do little other than gather a few impressions of the inscrutable group we are presently with.

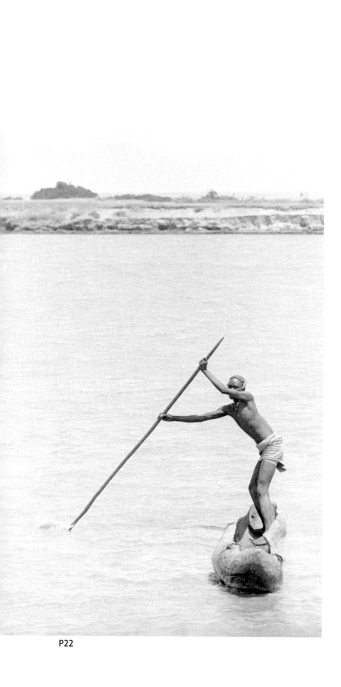

P22

July 18th 1968

I suppose we are about six miles east of the Omo and six north of Lake Rudolf. The region is called Naikaya and includes several Galla-speaking settlements we have come upon in the past few days.

The atmosphere is palpably contentious. The older men are angry with the youths for not going with the animals to graze and the older women berate the girls for failing to fetch such necessities as firewood and water. Everyone seems to have a reason for being angry. Mothers are scolding their children for minor infractions, which is not how African societies I have known socialize their young. A new dynamic, one of strife, has become a governing principle.

The old man with the milky eyes who had said he would sell me a bull brought it today and set about ending its life in a lackluster way. He tried to do the job himself but then gave the spear to a younger person who desultorily poked the animal between its ribs. A handsome bull should not have to die this way. I could not help contrasting this abject behavior with an Afar sacrifice where men leapt on their animals, snatched their heads back, and with one swift and ferocious stroke released a fountain of blood.

The sorry butchering I was witnessing led to further contention about who should cut it up, who should eat it, and who should dance. That had been the understanding of what would happen. I felt as though the animal's life had been sacrificed in vain, or at least in an inglorious cause. My naïveté had assumed there would be a mood shift once stomachs were filled. Instead, there was almost no change of heart that I could detect. People did start to eat and soon most of the animal was gone, with the result that those who had eaten the most were now the sleepiest and the least able to dance.

The dancing never did get properly underway. A few men looked as though they might do something, but nothing much came of it. Everyone said it was too hot and the best thing was to lie in the shade until it was cooler. I did that too. Later in the afternoon the old man with the milky eyes came again and asked for the rest of the money I had said would be his. I told him the agreement was not kept, that no one had danced. He said he

P23

had begged everyone to dance but they all had said it was too hot. It was indeed very hot and their reluctance was understandable. I was not sure what to do. What I wanted was to not be where I was, to be almost anywhere else in the world and so I decided to return in the morning to the Hamar. I long for tranquility of any kind.

July 19th 1968

We are back once again with the Hamar. The group we just left were simply too stricken by the heat to want anything other than to suspend further demonstration of their capacity for long suffering. My own capabilities in these regards fall far short of theirs and, possessing alternatives they can scarcely imagine, I am ready and able to concede defeat. Indeed, I have already subtracted sixty miles from the number remaining to be traveled between where we were this morning and Baco where we are scheduled to be in ten day's time.

Being with the Hamar again provides both pleasure and clear evidence that it was a mistake to try and enlarge the scope of this mission. The impulse to strike out for the elusive Bumi was in order to discover yet more interesting communities that would somehow fall prey to our nonfictional purposes. I expected these other peoples to disclose to my camera the fascinating details of a life hitherto scarcely imaginable and certainly not yet fixed in particles of silver nitrate. Instead, we found men, women, and children subdued by adversity. I could not keep my old illusions alive in the face of so much despair.

July 20th 1968

Last night I learned the Hamar were going to have a big celebration, including much dancing and other play. I am not yet sure what it is that is about to be celebrated, but I think its larger purpose has to do with coming of age or possibly with marriage. I know there will be a congregation of clans. With increased numbers will come the necessity for killing animals so that there will be enough to eat. I have also been told the event involves cow jumping, or bull jumping, which turned my mind to the Minoan world I remember from painted vases. The bulls here are formidable enough to provide exactly the excitement one might expect on an occasion of this kind. I wonder what it will be like. I also wonder why my thoughts turn to antiquity when I search for validation.

The practice that defines the life of Hamar men is drinking coffee. When they do this, they also utter blessings and beseech their Gods. A proper coffee blessing includes much drinking and spitting, which reminds me of the tales of Gilgamesh, the Mesopotamian figure. I recall descriptions of how his world was created with spit. While far-fetched as parallels, these tales do echo practices here, where creation and blessings are made palpable by expectorating coffee in the midst of prayer.

I talked this morning with one of my Hamar friends who claims to have something to do with the celebrations about to begin. I was told nothing would happen until tomorrow and that, if I wanted to come, it would be all right. I did not like the idea of having to travel between our place and where the festivities would be held, so we moved our little camp nearer to where the rituals would take place.

F12

F13

P24

I was shown the way by my friend's son, a child with malaria whom I was treating with heavy doses of chloroquine. He had never been in a car before and kept saying *nana*, which means mother in Hamar.

At the Tolta riverbed where we made camp, the water was less than three feet below the surface. Nearby were many animals: sheep, goats, donkeys, baboons, and cattle that I filmed in the business of being watered. The orchestration of the many elements involved is not without interest. The animals lust for liquid; the young men gather water in the wells to put into the drinking troughs; and the herdsmen direct the traffic. We should hear, if not see, some lions, along with hyenas, baboons, and other creatures that come down to these wells to drink. Speaking of animals, Abdullah, in a fit of uncharacteristic playfulness, threw me a baby cobra that landed on my shoe, but I was too tired to care.

July 21st 1968

At nightfall, the hyenas began to cry and laugh after we had eaten and were enjoying our recent successes in the art of nonfiction filmmaking. I cannot remember feeling better about a day's accomplishment since I began this quest in southwestern Ethiopia.

In the morning of this new day, I shot more sequences of watering the herds. Then Hailu, our Hamar friend from the nearby village, appeared wearing khaki pants five sizes larger than needed and a beautiful white ostrich feather stuck into his well-coiffed hair. He led us two or three miles down the riverbed to a path leading up and over a ridge and along a little plateau to an opening in the thorn jungle. Soon we were in the midst of a celebration of more than fifty women dancing in surprising unison, while at the same time singing an accompaniment to the clanging of their leg irons.

The sound and the visible energy of their dancing were both powerful and unexpected, given my brief experience with Hamar rhythms. An additional and more subtle sound was made by the multitude of bent nails fixed in the hems of women's leather skirts. The nails make a tinkling sound. I think each skirt might even be idiosyncratically distinguishable to those who hear it as the wearer makes her audible way through the

P25

thickets of thorn. Maybe musical skirts are worn so that men will know where their own and other men's women are.

Those who had gotten their hands on machine-made cloth were sometimes quite preposterously dressed. Sometimes what they had put on was no more than a discarded remnant of a worthless garment, something no one could have wanted in the land of such clothes but which here in the thorn jungle is desirable for its color and for its association with the *ferengi* world. Most of the males were in their traditional skirt-like lower garment, which is short and made of cotton. The men also had had their hair carefully plastered with clay painted red and white.

The women danced vigorously for about three hours in an open space and then several cows that had been lingering on the margins of the dance ground were brought into the clearing and encircled by dancers. Soon after, a young man was readied for what I was told would be the cow jumping.

I was told it was a bridegroom who was being celebrated, but I learned nothing in reliable detail, so I cannot say with confidence what it really was I was filming. But the ritual was wholly convincing and, though it was far tamer than a Spanish *corrida* or what might have happened in Minoan Crete, Hamar cow jumping was not without excitement. At the very least there was the tension of whether the boy was going to get over the cows lined up six or so deep. I would not say he jumped them so much as he leapt onto the back of the first one and then tried to keep his footing while he struggled to get over the others.

P26

F14

The young jumper was entirely naked and under the escort of what appeared to be priests, older boys whose bodies were blackened by charcoal and smeared with butter. Their faces were wonderfully painted and they carried handfuls of switches about four or five feet long. These they used to lash women and young girls across the back whenever they asked to be. This whipping was the most puzzling part of the ritual and what I paid the most attention to, trying to fathom the significance of what I was seeing.

Frequently, the whippers laid on with ferocity. Sometimes a woman whose flesh was nearly opened by the force of the blow would fling the perpetrator a scornful look and then dance off energized by her triumph over pain.

July 22nd 1968

We remain in our beloved shade by the Tolta. I am more and more grateful for a few huge trees that flourish from the moisture flowing beneath the sandy riverbed. We are a little apart from the Hamar, but it is here, really, that they lead much of their daily life. The village itself is empty during the day, except for the very sick or very old who are unable to leave their houses. By this riverbed comes almost everyone on the way to or from herding or farming. We can watch the activities or join in as we wish, while all the time staying far cooler than we would out in the midday village sun.

We went back to the continuation of yesterday's ceremony, which I have discovered is not a wedding but part of the preparations that boys of a certain age undertake to become marriageable. The rite is the Hamar version of the ubiquitous coming-of-age ceremony and we are fortunate to have been wandering in this particular season in this particular place. One might stay a long time by the Tolta without seeing anything like women being whipped and naked adolescents leaping cattle.

Today the whipping was particularly fierce, but the dancing was less animated, owing perhaps to the smaller number of women. Those who had come today were strangers for the most part and were as interested in us as in what they had come for.

The flies were ubiquitous. I am not sure why I fixated on them today, but I have been feeling particularly oppressed when they get behind my sunglasses as I try to frame a shot. I was also feeling

F15

burdened by the weight of my equipment, which with extra magazines and batteries must be nearly fifty pounds. All this I must carry myself since it has never occurred to the Hamar that they could help. A Hamar man is proud and will never compromise his lordliness doing menial tasks. How unlike the Dani they are and how convincingly this attitude signifies their lack of self-assurance. Male supremacy has little to validate it except the subjugation of others such as, in the Hamar case, their own women.

I am getting weary of thorns, flies, and domineering males but we will stay to see what develops in the ongoing coming-of-age ritual happening down river, or is it up?

July 23rd 1968

People have become increasingly friendly as we have lingered under our canopy of trees. Compared to the first days, when no one would make the slightest effort to be sociable, the change is dramatic. Although we are wearing clothes, they know now that we do not belong to the police and that instead of taking away their weapons, we are more likely to repair them.

I see these people as drastically marginalized by the choice they have made to live in this jungle of thorns. Little competition exists for this locale, owing to its spectacular infelicity. Here are only Hamar and no one else is going to take land from them, unless it is the missionaries. Hamar life has real shape and satisfaction, despite the physical circumstances they must endure. The more I have been able to experience it, the more interesting I find it. In these last days I hope to discover something more substantial than the few fragments I have so far gathered.

Today I talked with a man who had said he would answer my questions and he has told me more about the ceremony we have witnessed, which is called the *ukuli*. It is the preparation of young men for marriage and the entire process takes several weeks. I learn many details about the *ukuli*, such as the requirement that the initiate fast while the ceremony is in progress. The ones officiating must also fast, although they are allowed milk and honey.

I have now loaded my final magazine and, unless I go to Addis for more, this will be the last I expose.

July 24th 1968
The older man, with whom I had some conversations earlier, came this morning to tell me he would like us to come to his village where there would be more celebrations for one of the boys who had just, as he said, "jumped the bulls." I was interested in seeing where he lived and what would take place, so we set out to the southeast, traveling about ten miles through countryside that was open and full of game, including the little *dikdik* I am so fond of roasting on hot coals.

The village teemed with people who had come for a day of dancing and other celebrating but who, during the midday hours, were drinking coffee and lounging in whatever shade they could find. Temporary shelters had been put up to house many guests. The sun was high and very hot and I felt sorry only that I had not yet developed a taste for millet beer, which I know to be refreshing.

In one corner of the village an old man and a person who might easily have been his twin were playing crude harps made from a skin stretched over a large tortoise shell. They played a simple but haunting melody.

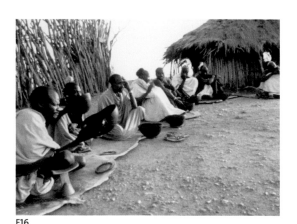

F16

At a certain point, women began to stir. Some started to clap and others to dance. The men were separate, perhaps talking with each other about the strange costumes they had put on for the occasion, castoff rags and tatters but also a few military tunics with braid and other ornamentation. I assume what the men had put on was the modern equivalent of lion and leopard skins of their father's generation. Many wore T-shirts in bright reds and yellows. I cannot blame them for wanting to look their best, but I know that when they are filmed in these outfits, the question hovering over the scenes will be "where did they get the clothes?" not "what is the significance of what they are doing?" We stayed all day and watched much excellent dancing. Both the women and the men performed with skill and vigor.

I am slowing down during these closing days in the hope of maintaining the tone of calm and mutual respect now established between the Hamar and myself. This rapport must be kept intact as long as we stay in their company and enjoy their hospitality. I think their dignity, like that of any people exposed to the scrutiny of others, must always be protected. I had not thought I would feel this way when I first encountered the Hamar, but I now think we are embarked on something meaningful.

By late afternoon the guests who had come twelve or more miles on foot were thinking about going home. We were thinking the same thing and managed to extricate ourselves in time to reach the Tolta shortly after dark. Tomorrow we will get ready to press on to Baco, picking up loose ends of filming while also packing for the journey. The sky was dark to the north, suggesting that the rains are on their way. I cannot help feeling pleased with what has been started. Now is the time to take advantage of this opening I have made and even to look for someone to come and do conventional fieldwork.

July 25th 1968
Everyone is tired, even though we have been at this for only a few weeks. It is the nature of the undertaking that is draining, especially the mechanical difficulties with cars, cameras, and tape recorders. Making *Dead Birds* in New Guinea was hard, but here it is harder because of the endless travel.

P27

I wonder what I will choose to do next, and whether it will have anything to do with the traditional world, or even with actuality. I think about *Cooper's Creek* and what it would be like making a narrative film. The little progress Ted Hughes and I have so far made writing a treatment may be enough to begin planning. I should go to Australia where the film will have to be made, if that is what will happen. I even fantasize about Peter Ustinov in the leading role.

I'm happy this particular African venture is at an end and that I have something about the Hamar with which to work. A film exists here somewhere and maybe the time will come when I won't have to go so far to see into my own heart.

F17

It was clear by the end of my filmmaking efforts in 1968 that I had made a start but needed to see and know more before there could be a film about the Hamar of southwestern Ethiopia. In 1970 I asked a German anthropologist, Ivo Strecker, to go to the Hamar and then act as an advisor and interpreter for me on a return journey I would make in 1971. On this second visit, I again had the company of my son Stewart, and also Michael Mathers, a young photographer at Harvard.

June 13th 1971

Addis looks and feels differently. Many new buildings, some with eight or ten stories, are strikingly evident. The Hilton hotel has finally been finished and, owing to a conference of the Organization for African Unity, it is full. Otherwise, I understand it's empty. Impending disaster is in the air. I sense it in the fact that many of the stores I knew three years ago have closed and "to let" signs are hanging on them. I suspect the owners foresaw upheaval. When the change will come, what it will bring, and what chaos it will entail is difficult to predict. The emperor will die before long or otherwise must surely go. He's almost eighty and there's a sense of doom about his reign that I didn't feel before.

I sent Stewart, Mike Mathers, and Ivo Strecker down to Baco ahead of me, while I searched for more supplies and someone to help with the cooking. Ivo's mother, wife, and children will fly down separately and stay in a village called Dambyti.

June 18th 1971

After collecting more supplies, I departed Addis Ababa, but in half an hour we were turning back owing to a vibration in the port engine that concerned the pilot. Following two hours of shifting the cargo to another DC-3, we were off again by mid-morning on one of the milk runs these dependable old aircraft make from town to town, taking a few passengers and urgent freight, like spare parts for stranded vehicles.

On the airplane with me was a young man wrapped in a full-length *shamma*. He was seated next to the policeman with a rifle on his lap. I noticed as I was deplaning that the policeman was taking a bullet out of the chamber of his gun and, when I looked out the opened door of the airplane, I saw an entire platoon of police meeting the aircraft.

The policeman got off first with his prisoner who, looking distressed and bewildered, was immediately surrounded and led slowly across the grassy ramp to a waiting truck. Hundreds of onlookers were watching. I was told the young man would be executed publicly in the Baco marketplace at 11 o'clock tomorrow morning. His gallows were already built.

The condemned was convicted of burning down a house and in doing so killing two people, the parents of his beloved. The act was terrible, if true, but to hang this young person and leave him dangling all day is hardly enlightened. I'm told a public whipping occurred here not many days ago and that several more hangings will take place in the next few weeks. Only clemency from his Imperial Majesty can save a person sentenced to die, sometimes for less than capital crimes. A grave respect for law and order pervades this country, with numerous public hangings, whippings, and the cutting off of hands. Surely, some day, there will be a great reaction to these kinds of punishment, or will they just be done in the name of another authority?

Baco has neither industry nor much of any agriculture. The available produce appears limited to potatoes, a few onions, and even fewer tomatoes. The fruit is unappetizing and consists mainly of bananas and some limes, lemons, and the rare orange. Everywhere inevitable Bougainvillea vines are flourishing, as well as a few other exotic looking flowers. In this unpromising countryside only a few unhealthy cows graze discontentedly.

Tomorrow the Strecker women and children, as well as our supplies and equipment, will go by chartered aircraft to a place called Dimeka. This will put everything closer to the little village near Turmi, where I want to begin work, and nearer to Dambyti, where all the Streckers will soon be living.

June 19th 1971

The young man with the very white *shamma* was hanged this morning, on market day, as an example for all to see. I watched, unable to close my eyes. I had to watch; not to do so seemed like putting my own feelings above the meaning of hangings to our collective humanity. He was docile and got up without a struggle from the bottom of the truck where he was kneeling, arms tied behind

P28

his back. Standing, he allowed the rope to be looped around his neck but said nothing, at least not as far as I could tell from my safely distant vantage point. Around him were police with guns and the false confidence of their uniforms. Perhaps the boy who was hanged had seen the same event as a child. If he had, the demonstration had not done what it was meant to do. This country, so full of beauty, is also full of futile cruelty.

We left Baco late in the day and stopped at the first main river. The road looked exactly as it did three years ago. Except for some holes that are full of water from the little rain that fell yesterday, the surface is firm. We went off in such a hurry nobody realized we had nothing to eat. We now expect to be on our way again early in the morning, after a night looking to be filled with stars.

June 20th 1971

We reached Dimeka at midday, having gotten on the road early this morning. Dawn is at 6:15 or 6:30 and we were up a little before that. Except for some stale rolls, tea, and an orange apiece that I'd brought from Addis, there was nothing to eat.

We came into the mission compound and were met by a Mr. Bonk, an affable gentleman of Polish-Canadian extraction. I think his parents were Polish and that he was born a Roman Catholic in Canada. He somehow became a Pentecostal missionary and is now in the uttermost parts of Ethiopia. His fervor is not overtly apparent and I doubt that I will stay long enough to discover what it is that animates this man beyond the desire to make an island of perfection in a most unpromising landscape.

Later in the afternoon, Ivo took our Landrover to Dambyti, the village in which he will put his things and in which Mesdames Strecker and the two babies will stay during the next few months. He will spend some time installing them in their new house and tomorrow will bring the Landrover back to make the first of two or three trips to wherever we are going to settle. We'll try first the village I knew near Turmi in 1968. Actually, Turmi proper is a police post and the name for an entire district but, fifteen or twenty miles beyond the police post, beside a modest hill, is a small Hamar village. I saw it first when I crept through the thorns in 1968 and met, almost eyeball to eyeball, a man coming the other way who was armed and as surprised as I was. That visit was full of unexpected pleasures and I hope this one will be too.

June 22nd 1971

Yesterday the Landrover was loaded by noon and ready to start down the main Turmi road, but our trip had hardly started when the main support for the rear spring broke, letting go of the spring itself. One must expect this to happen from time to time, but our situation is different because we do not have the parts to put the spring back in place. Our only choice was to return to Dimeka, hoping Mr. Bonk, who also has a Landrover, might have the needed spares.

Mike offered to walk the four miles to the mission to see what Bonk would say. Meanwhile, all I could do was to get the car ready to repair. In about three hours Mike came with the spares and, at exactly eight o'clock, the repair was made, using our one jack and almost no tools.

F18

F19

By late evening we'd driven back to the mission, where Mrs. Bonk took pity on us and set out tea, rolls, and jam. She even provided chocolate cake. This Bonkian world is getting more and more surreal. They can't give away everything they have, even to become exemplary Christians, but they are decidedly generous. We hope soon to reach the village near Turmi and begin doing more meaningful things.

June 23rd 1971

It's been dark for a little over an hour. Ivo Strecker and I are alone in a small temporary camp we've made by a river whose name for the moment eludes us both. When I speak of rivers, they are rivers only in the imagination. In reality, they are sandy riverbeds, would-be and once-upon-a-time rivers formed by the often prodigious rains of February and March when torrents of water appear almost magically and disappear in the same manner. Most of the year the only water to be found is at a depth of between three and ten or more feet. To these uncertain wells the Hamar go to get their water.

Walking in the bed of the nearby Kaska River, I was struck both by the profound motionlessness of these rivers and by how they contain the possibility of life, invisibly, beneath their surface. It occurred to me that the title of any film to come from the work done already, and of what I'm about to undertake, should be "The Rivers of Sand" or "River of Sand." Probably "rivers" in the plural is better because there are many little tributaries feeding into the larger courses running toward the Omo, the famous and substantial river that flows into Lake Rudolf.

For me, "The Rivers of Sand" suggests something both timely and timeless. The rivers themselves also serve as reminders of the many uncertainties of the world that have arisen near these curious formations.

We left yesterday at noon and went on beyond the Turmi police post to the site of the village in which I had worked three years ago, but the village was no longer there. It had moved a mile or so to the south, which meant that we were not able to find old Hailu who'd once been so helpful and welcoming.

F20

gembala!

gembala!!

(*Gembala* is a metaphor invoking fertility. The fruit of a tree called 'gembala' is hard and round like a fist and likened to the fetus in a pregnant woman.)

shati!

shati!

(*Shati* is a metaphor that invokes health. It is used to describe water said to be good tasting because it is healthy for the cattle that need the salts and minerals contained in brackish water.

[Hamar blessing]

We returned to the Landrover, a poor wreck I dare not take far into this trying countryside, not even down the track used by the infrequent official truck. In the dark of night we made a pathetic camp beside the road. We have one jerry can of water for washing, cooking, and drinking.

Today we began a search for Hailu, whom we eventually found. He invited us to come live in his village, but with no shade it would be far too hot and, with a plague of flies, quite unlivable. We decided to stay by the river, down near Hailu's field, where the harvest is about to start. We have even found a few authentic trees.

I asked how to get all of our things to our temporary home. Hailu said we could drive up the Kaska, go off on a road that meets another river of sand, and then go right and up the Kaska again. I had the feeling this was asking too much of our sorry vehicle, but because Hailu had been so kind and generous, I felt we should at least try. If we were successful, there would be some continuity with the work I'd done three years ago. Still, I was concerned that even though the same people would be nearby, the village had moved and things couldn't really look the same.

We started off and, after a few minutes laboring through deep sand, the engine began overheating and the clutch sticking. To use this vehicle meant we would have to lighten the load considerably and make many trips. Even if we made camp with Hailu, we'd be far from things we would like to be near. To get anywhere, just another village, would be problematic at best.

Ivo suggested we go further south of Turmi and look at some villages he knew that were close together and where we wouldn't have as great a risk of a breakdown. We would also have better access to the Omo and to mountains off to the east where large numbers of people are living. In any case, Hailu and his people were not a possibility. I reluctantly decided to try and find still other villages about which I've been told.

June 24th and 25th 1971

For now we are camped around a few large trees by a river's edge near a group of villages two miles north of the road that leads back to Baco. This cluster is known as Logera. I settled on this place after a sentimental journey back into the forest of thorns, the indispensable trees, and the great sandy river where I spent so much time three years ago. The wells were still good, with clear water and relatively few people using them, but poverty and deprivation have created an atmosphere of hopelessness.

At our Logera location, we drank coffee with people I did not know and then went with them along the river to look at their sorghum crop. I decided to do some work while the grain is ripening and people are in the fields chasing away birds. In anticipation of the harvest, and all the things that happen at harvest time, there's a discernible buzz of activity.

P29

F21

Tomorrow Michael and Stewart will go to Dimeka to fetch another load of supplies, including my camera. It's never taken me so long to get started, but I'm relaxed and still optimistic that the work ahead will be interesting.

June 26th 1971

By late afternoon, in the failing light, I took out the Bolex with the thought of making some shots of rain and sky effects. Rain is important. The last time I was here the sky was never as full of rain as it was today.

Our cook, Dejene, woke up complaining of a toothache and having not slept last night. Nevertheless, he is amiable and works hard all day making meals, gathering wood, and bantering with the Hamar, who often appear in outrageous shirts, some striped, some flowered, some simply dirty. I don't care when I'm not looking through a camera, but the moment I am, the colors assault my senses.

This morning I was beside the sorghum fields on one of the platforms that are put up to give a better view of what is happening in the gardens. They remind me a little of the watchtowers in New Guinea situated along the frontiers. The Hamar platforms, usually manned by boys but sometimes by girls or even older women, are the first line of defense against the cheeky, sparrow-like birds that steal the grain. These sentinels have slingshots and a pile of stones at their feet. Every five or so minutes, one is hurled with a slingshot into the rows of sorghum. The stones can be heard hitting the dry stalks and making a clatter as they skip through the plants, scaring off the avian intruders. The boys do a lot of yelling back and forth between the platforms. The scene was nice and I look forward to filming it.

The maiden's flutes are yet to be heard. Young women play them when the grain is ripening, as if their music is required to keep the sorghum healthy and abundant.

June 27th 1971

I went back to a field close by, trying with mixed success to make friends with a boy distressed by my camera. He was there to sling his little stones and mud balls at the birds. He seems a nice boy whose name is Aiki. I think he might be preparing

F22

for his *ukuli* ceremony and so the time I spend with him now might give me better access later.

I slowly adjust to the swarming flies and sand fleas. A woman has just walked into the riverbed with the leg of a cow. No doubt this leg is from the cow that was caught by a hyena last night. I learned about this from young Aiki when he was stewing on a little garden fire the meat he said was from an animal killed by a hyena. I remember hearing last night one crying close by. It may have been the one that found the unfortunate cow.

June 28th 1971

The stars are bright and the moon is on its way to its second quarter. Today I was told by one of the children in the fields that the sorghum would be cut at the time of the full moon, two weeks from now.

As I filmed in the fields this morning, I was again amazed by how much one sees on subsequent visits. Things get clearer and begin to fit together. I will go to different fields tomorrow and take coffee, hoping to make friends with some people who have been quite distant.

June 29th 1971

The coffee I've been drinking since early morning is made in a huge black pot, full of water smelling distinctly of cow urine and into which is put far too few beans. Lengthy boiling produces a tea-colored liquid tasting vaguely of cow that is served in what is called a *sherka,* an all-purpose dried and hollowed gourd. The morning coffee hour is more accurately hours, because it takes a long time to boil the water, more time to brew the coffee, and then even longer to consume the unpalatable results. Nonetheless, the occasion is special, with

P30

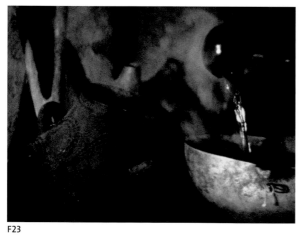

F23

people laughing just to be drinking coffee and wasting time. At least this is the impression I get from men who are the major participants.

Ivo Strecker and I went early to see one Owli, a curious, high-strung man of perhaps thirty-five who is married to an old wife with an immense tumor in her belly that she carries around like an unborn fetus. We went in order to discuss filming an activity that would involve her husband.

Owli is not an important person but he is Ivo's friend and when he's not depressed or excited, he's amiable and cooperative. He is also what is called a *koimo*, or specialist. A *koimo* is a practitioner of differing skills, such as curing the illnesses of animals or people, or for making various objects like tools or weapons. Owli is a *koimo* for making implements. This morning he was shaping an axe handle and I managed to shoot a little film as he worked. But the visit was mostly to fix in his mind that I had come in order to use my own tools. These include the Arriflex BL camera, a battery belt, and a light meter. I don't think there was much question about my specialization: I am a *koimo* for making pictures. We made clear that our collaboration would lead to his having coffee, soap, and matches, a prospect that quite appeals to him.

Later we came back to our camp and ate the kidneys and liver of a goat that had been freshly slaughtered for reasons I have already forgotten.

June 30th 1971
It has been arranged that Ivo and I would go with Owli, the neurotic *koimo*, to select a tree from which to cut the wood he would use to carve a *burkoto*. This ubiquitous object, a stool, is carried at all times and everywhere to be sat upon or just languidly held for display by all males old enough to have jumped cows in a coming-of-age ceremony.

In the morning, while it was still dark, we had tea and then climbed the little incline toward the Logera hamlets. The walk takes thirty minutes, except when there is a great amount to carry. We reached the summit when the sun was well into the sky, no longer dawn but morning. The villages were lit by a slanting, early light streaming across the riverbed, then over the fields and finally over the ridge itself. I haven't seen this scene in the evening light but that must also be nice.

P31

Several children were leading goats out of the village. The youngest boys and girls take the smallest animals, the slightly larger boys the slightly larger goats or sheep, and the biggest boys the young cows. Only men herd the important cows and bulls. Baby goats can be quite endearing and seeing small children in charge of them, in such a responsible way, is quite impressive.

Eventually Owli appeared. He had gone to a neighbor to have coffee, a perpetual activity as long as there is a single bean to boil. Owli took us briskly westward, down the other side of the Logera ridge. A friend of his who joined us ended up carrying a large piece of wood cut from a tree, chosen after looking at alternative possibilities for a long time.

Owli strikes me as quite unstable. His eyes dart about and he behaves as though he is under continuous but unnameable pressure. I see this as a condition in which many men in this society find themselves. The widespread insecurity that permeates their manners and gestures is clearest in their constant attention to their appearance and in a sense of self-importance that borders on narcissism. They are preoccupied with being handsome, winning, graceful and, most of all, the objects of female attention. I will work on this theme and on that of the contrasting female world, where I find considerable serenity and purposefulness.

The filming of the *burkoto* carving went well today, with Owli getting it close to completion. For the next three days, it will reside unfinished in old dung in order to harden and be ready for more of Owli's knife.

P32

P33

July lst and 2nd 1971

A filmmaking life consists of distinct peaks, plateaus, and valleys. Recently I have seen a few minor peaks and plateaus, but mostly valleys. The human subjects under present scrutiny are not yet regarding us with much warmth. A few have been gracious, while others are being nice because they feel they may have something to gain. For the most part the Hamar go about their business with a considerable lack of concern for us. They are more interested in clothes, coffee, sugar, and salt than the people in the village where I lived three years ago.

The wind has been deeply wearisome and I do not feel many good things are happening though at least the grain is finally ripening. One can see the heads of the sorghum changing color from day to day, meaning there will be a harvest and whatever else that entails. I long for the general lifting of spirits when the grain is cut, threshed, and packed into sacks. Beer will be made and the maiden's flutes played almost continuously. I have heard a few hesitant notes already, which I take as a promising sign.

Today a man washed himself in a nearby waterhole. He is said to have let himself down to an opening at the bottom a foot or two wide, where perhaps two inches of water accumulates very slowly. He is said to have also urinated. Urinating in these wells is done all the time, not just by humans but also by donkeys, sheep, goats, and baboons.

Ivo, Stewart, and I went today to a nearby village to film a girl known for her fine flute playing. I took the enormous Arriflex BL camera and Nagra recorder, but the girl was feeling too ill to do more than swallow chloroquine tablets. The other girls were friendly but unprepared for the onslaught of a Nagra and a BL. So big and so heavy are we in the way we move or simply sit that every attempt I made to film was cause for embarrassment.

July 3rd 1971

Early in the morning a young lady named Duka came to see me. She is an *anza*, the word used for a woman not yet living with her husband and not yet a mother. Only about twenty years old, she has a look of far greater age. Despite bearing marks of physical abuse, Duka is remarkably animated. She invited us in the Hamar fashion to come to her field and we followed her, wondering why we had been asked. We discovered that she was willing to play the flute one hears at this time of year. The instrument has just five or six stops and the girls who play it have only a limited repertoire of tunes. Still, the sound is sweet and the context in which it's played is one of thanksgiving for the harvest.

Duka's field was at a distance of a mile or so. Walking in the sand with our equipment was not easy, but it was a beautiful morning and our hopes were high. Duka and two other women stopped at some wells and filled their largest gourds with water. For half an hour they went about filling these delicate vessels while I tried to film what they were doing. Duka walked further down the river and I made traveling shots of her that felt fine while I was making them. She was casting a long shadow from the morning light that slanted across the river and she kept on walking through her neighbors' fields to her own, at which point other girls came with their flutes and they all climbed onto a platform next to the field. All morning, we were busy recording and filming the small marvels performed by these winning young women.

Later I walked back up the river to Owli's field that looks shabby compared with the well-kept gardens and crops in those of the flute players. Owli was finishing the *burkoto* he started a few days ago and I stayed until mid-afternoon filming him at work. He appeared to be losing interest in what he was doing, perhaps because I had asked him to do it and he was now bored, or because he was annoyed at being watched. I think I have done a half-hour just of him carving this stool. If it were not a *burkoto*, the quintessential male possession, such filmmaking would be a waste of time, but I think it is important for any film that might come of all this and also for cementing an alliance with Owli, who might be helpful to us some day.

Because I am starting to get around, I understand more about what I see, particularly the busyness of women's lives. I will go back to Duka's field in the morning and spend the day there making more images.

July 5th 1971

The *anza* women like Duka are more independent than the younger girls and the women who already have men living with them and children to look after. Duka has decided to be nice, in part knowing it will mean beads and other gifts. She again invited us to come early in the morning and I filmed her preparing sorghum porridge. She insisted that we eat it, which I did without enthusiasm. Hamar cuisine has to rank at or near the bottom of the world's manifold efforts in food preparation.

We sat around all day until early afternoon, by which time it had become extremely hot. The way back was difficult, since I was carrying the big camera and had put the battery belt around my neck. For some reason, I had brought no hat and when I got back I more or less passed out. On waking, it was time to leave for Gabo, the complex of villages south of here, where we'd heard that an old man was going to perform some kind of cleansing ceremony.

Soon I was sitting in a small house in the company of a multitude of flies, thanks no doubt to the surfeit of food being thrust upon us. To me everything tasted exactly the same as the porridge of this morning. In the evening, after some desultory filming of a young girl working in a garden, we made our way back, having seen nothing resembling a cleansing ceremony. My head aches from the sun and everything under it.

I've shot only 3000 of a total of 25,000 feet of raw stock, but in the next four to six weeks the film will almost certainly be used at a faster pace. Four-hundred feet a day, which is about ten minutes of screen time for every twenty-four hours of real time, is probably my average rate of use. I do not know if this amount is more or less than what my fellow filmmakers use, but it has usually been enough for me, sometimes too much when I see my results and wish I had used more restraint.

July 6th 1971

This morning began with a few unlikely raindrops. Rain has been a mostly distant phenomenon, evidenced by huge buildups of clouds and angry skies a long way off in the north and east. Sometimes, great sheets of it can be seen falling on the hills and mountains in the far distance.

Later in the day a man passing by our little establishment said a woman had died in the night in a village a short distance to the north. He said she had died in childbirth and would be buried today. She was the owner of the field next to where I did my first filming of the boy named Aiki. We got the equipment together and walked for an hour along the ridge to the dead woman's village, just in time to see the corpse taken from the house in which she had died. I began to film immediately, but not before I was presented to the woman's husband whose hand I raised in the air, the greeting for a bereaving spouse.

I kept threading up the camera in the hope of capturing a scene of women and men going about their grim business. The woman's eldest child, a boy, was in the village and looking nonplussed by the whole thing. He held in his arms a pure white, newly born lamb. I could tell the boy would become a central figure in the filming I was to do.

The body was laid on the ground and wrapped tightly in a cowhide shroud while women wailed and beat long sticks together. Someone shook a cowbell. I really don't remember everything that happened in those moments. No doubt the film rushes will tell me more.

Quite suddenly, everyone went through the village entrance and started on their way to the burying place. A gun went off as they left the village, swung around at a trot to the north and then to the east, while holding up a litter bearing the corpse. I put down the big Arriflex, picked up the Bolex and ran after the cortege.

The procession was a motley assortment of people, goats, cows, heifers, and a tall, white-skinned filmmaker loping eastward toward the

P34

146

F24

Kaska riverbed. The entourage of close relatives and neighbors of the deceased were arguing about how many goats would be killed and to whom the animals would belong. The little son was carrying fire and the brother of the husband the newborn lamb. Altogether the sight was remarkable. I filmed what I could as we hurried on. Mercifully, high clouds obscured the hot sun.

We reached the stony ground where the woman was to be buried. Several graves were nearby, but I don't remember filming them. I was too intent on filming a number of ritual sidelights and on trying to use the Bolex, a camera able to make shots no longer than twenty seconds without rewinding. I missed several things, including a scene in which the mourners stepped in the blood of the white lamb that was slaughtered next to the grave. The Bolex's limitations required making strict choices and finding visual strategies quite different from those possible with a motorized camera with large magazines. It was an exercise I quite enjoyed.

July 7th 1971
For the first time in my acquaintance with the Hamar, objects belonging to us are missing. Most of them are not important but, if something gets taken every day, we'll be in trouble.

Today I sent a note to Dimeka, the mission two hours away, saying we wanted a charter aircraft for July 27th. Going to Addis then will make it possible to send film off to the U.S. and will also give us time to rest and regroup for a return visit of a few more weeks. If I leave Ethiopia by the end of August, I would have time to see the painter Mark Tobey in Switzerland and to work on the *Cooper's*

Creek project with Hughes. Making plans to leave is a little bizarre at a time when the Hamar are more and more willing to accept us, although no less covetous of our clothes, coffee, and everything else. But they have become accustomed to us and we to them. I must get done as much as I can.

This afternoon I went for a walk in the *bino,* the Hamar word for river. More and more I think about these rivers as the central theme of a film I might someday make. These rivers have nothing much to do with rivers elsewhere. No boats or bridges exist in these arid waterways, but there is a conjuring of motion evoked by continual waves of cattle, sheep, goats, and people moving in them. They embody ebb and flow in their coming and going that suggests something to do with tidal repetition and dependability.

Later in the day, I filmed a young girl, perhaps twelve or a bit younger, grinding sorghum. Grinding is incessant and it perfectly embodies the essence of femininity in the Hamar firmament.

My old friend from three years ago, Hailu, has come to spend the night and we talked about the old days.

P35

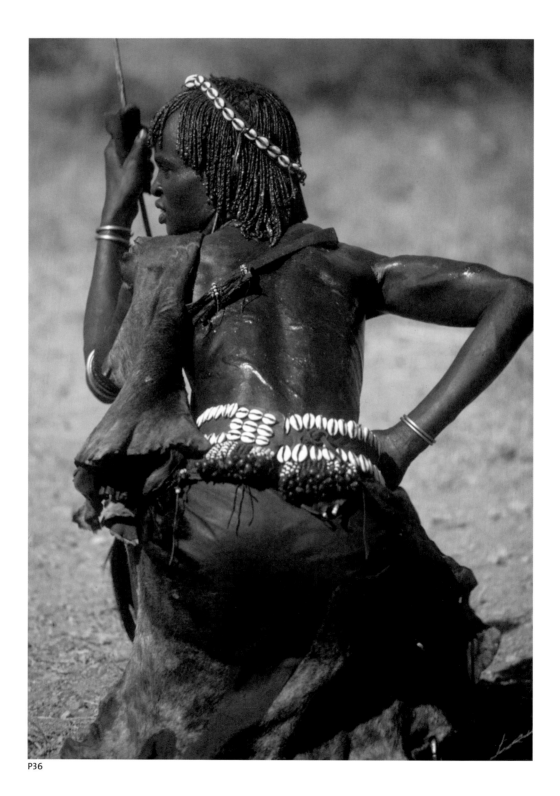

P36

July 8th 1971

We have reached a kind of plateau in our relations with the Hamar; now we wait for the harvest that should not be long in coming. I was told it would begin when the moon is full, which is imminent, but I have also heard the cutting may wait until the moon has gone, meaning perhaps another two weeks. Meanwhile we must get closer to these people in order to discover where and when something is about to happen. I am especially interested in knowing where and when any dancing is going to take place.

I still need many images, such as children at play, cattle at the water troughs, milking in the morning, wandering with one of the young herders and his goats or sheep, a hunting session, and also something about women's adornment, such as making skirts or scarification. I stumble on these things only rarely. If I knew people better, I would hear beforehand what was going to happen. After all the time I've been in Africa, it is saddening to feel so cut off. In years past, I thought I knew what images I wanted and how to get them, but I feel isolated here, what with Strecker's Prussian self-importance and his reluctance to share information.

July 11th 1971

Yesterday began gray and almost believably promising of rain. At a certain moment our highland helper, Dejene, announced that a great rain was imminent. People from the highlands know more about rain than almost anything else. Even to me the sky looked remarkably different. Rain and possibly something quite immense was on its way and quickly.

In moments, a curious misting began. It was so fine and the light was so dull I had difficulty getting an exposure. An hour later, the rain came, heavy and convincing. The wind rose and the sky darkened dramatically. Soon it was night-dark and unaccountably cold. I'd made a number of shots and decided to go inside to dry off.

In minutes it was obvious I should have stayed outside where the rain had become violent. I wanted badly to film this excess of Nature, but wondered what I could accomplish in the profound darkness that had descended.

P37

There was no way to stay dry and so I undressed and went out to what was becoming a biblical event. Water was running in substantial torrents along the cattle trails going down to the riverbed and I began to film what happens when rain gets serious. Water was flowing down our river of sand. I didn't hear the bang and roar of what I have been told is the unmistakable sound of a tidal bore. I saw only a sheet of water, which I filmed by running in front of it.

Our river, the Kaska, was now real and in full flood. The rain continued heavily for two hours and then steadily for the next four or five. The sandy riverbed, symbolically and functionally so important to life in this geography, was a flood, three or four feet deep, carrying all manner of debris on great foaming waves.

I crouched in the stream filming with one eye and watching for tree trunks with the other. Leaving occasionally in order to wipe off the lens, I would return to find the river still raging. The event was thoroughly transformative, something I could hardly imagine despite knowing there would be no riverbed without an occasional deluge.

For several days I have been thinking about making a traveling shot on the riverbed and now, with all the foot- and hoofprints erased by the recent flood, it is the right time to do it.

July 13th 1971

I ruefully contemplate the Landrover that has been a continuous problem despite our constant attentions. I thought we had cured its difficulties, but when we started for the Kaska to make my long-awaited traveling shot, the wretched vehicle failed before going a hundred yards.

P38

F25

July 14th 1971

Yesterday, I made a trip to the field of Ailu, who is a most remarkable woman. She's full of confidence and regards me with little or no apprehension. In this way she is quite different from nearly all the other women. Tall and middle-aged, she's in good health, except for a cough that is being treated with honey and tea we give her when she visits.

I filmed little things she was doing, like attaching a new end to the *roisha,* which is what she calls the object that serves both as a whip and a slingshot to scare away birds. She was quite happy, and I would have stayed, except that I heard the police lorry in the distance and had to run to stop it and ask for a tow. When the lorry had pulled the Landrover a few hundred yards, the engine cleared and, despite a dead battery, came back to life.

July 15th 1971

The Landrover has been running for twenty-four hours in the hope of restoring its battery. Everyone's fingers are crossed. We seldom speak of this vehicle, fearful it has a mind of its own that could change at any moment.

We think now we will be able to get to the road that branches off to cattle camps near the Omo. If we can, we will go hunting and stay to work near the camps. We won't leave for a few days because the harvesting will soon be starting. People are building platforms on which they pile the sorghum before it is threshed. Once begun, the cutting should take no more than two or three days. I don't want to have stayed this long and miss it all by being away on a hunt, so I will try to find out when the cutting will start. The people must already have begun in the north where the harvest is frequently earlier.

Yesterday I was finally able to make the traveling shots in the Kaska. If I had been able to go sooner, immediately after the great flood, the river bottom would have been a tabula rasa.

Today, under a dark sky, I shifted my attention to where a man was to have his hair redone. He has killed a buffalo, which is a large and important animal, and now he will have the front part of his head shaved and painted red.

F26

July 16th 1971

The harvest is underway. The first fields were cut this afternoon and everything will be done in the next four or five days. I keep thinking of what I need to film in order to flesh out some of the themes and topics in which I'm most interested: a little boy off alone with his goats; coffee blessing; hunting; women grinding sorghum; and of course, dancing.

I went with Ivo to find the girl who will do the special hairdressing for the man who killed the buffalo. The man's name is Dube. The girl needed the right ingredients, including red ochre, butter, and a special berry that is pulverized to make a black paste. I suggested we send somebody to get whatever was needed. All it meant was making a young boy happy with one Ethiopian dollar, about twenty-five American cents.

When the boy came back, the hairdressing started. The scene was interesting, but some persuading was necessary to complete the task. Sometimes things must be provoked in this fashion, but I don't worry about whether it will look the same or better for having been induced. Getting his hair prepared today didn't distress Dube at all. He might have had it done next week or the week after. It was the same to him. This kind of hairdressing is only done by a female. Most of the time, men do each other's hair. Dube is having his done for the first time. He's about twenty-five, a *gorumsa*, or unmarried man who has no children. The girl hairdresser was unmarried, or rather is married but not living with her husband. She's in her early twenties I would judge, competent and seeming to enjoy what she was doing.

I sat talking for much of the day in a little teepee of logs with some grass thrown on top. The Hamar sometimes sleep in them, but mostly they are used for shelter during the days of the harvest. The logs are full of termites building their own houses and so sawdust keeps raining down on one's sweating neck. The walls pitch in, making it impossible to sit straight and there are usually five or six people stretched out sleeping. Others come and go, shouting at friends and family in the fields. A fire fills the fetid air with smoke and frequently a sick person is coughing in your face. It is dismaying as housing but the kind of price you pay for filming scenes you think you should have.

July 17th 1971

The day began with the appearance of a man dressed in a cloak made from strips of goatskin, feathers, and even bells. I saw him yesterday and asked him to come this morning so I could film him. Incredible sounding and looking, his costume advertises the fact that he has killed somebody. The aura enveloping this person is quite sinister. He appears to inhabit a state of ritual impurity, though I may be imputing this from knowing what he has done. After all, he has taken the life of another man. Going about with bells and feathers identifies him the way a leper's bell does. His costume is a way of saying, "Look, here I am; I've done this immense thing so give me food or shells. Give me beads or tobacco or I will trouble you somehow or other." These individuals are outside of society, even though they've attained an exceptional, even elevated, status within it.

I told him that if he came to see me, I'd give him beads and ask him to put a band on my wrist made of hair from a giraffe's tail. I don't think there is much to commend in the filmmaking I did with this person, but it was interesting to see this unsettling fragment of Hamar culture.

The life pace of this community has greatly accelerated in the last twenty-four hours owing to the onset of harvesting. I noticed that the field next to us, the field of the woman who died, was being cut by her relatives. This afternoon I went to Ailu's field to see what was happening there. She and some of her close family members, a daughter and a few grandchildren, were cutting sorghum and making the platform on which it is stacked. She sorted the sorghum according to color and arranged it on the platform, red ones first. I am lying now in my shelter with a book, scratching insect bites and befriending a small lizard that has come to live with me.

July 18th 1971

It's almost midnight, after one of the grimmest days thus far. Early this afternoon, Ivo and I were in the Landrover when it stopped in the same place it did exactly one week ago. Not only will we be kept from going hunting, but now we have no way to get to Dimeka for the charter flight to Addis. I feel as though we should have used donkeys.

I cannot concentrate on filmmaking because of a fuel system that never works. In the midst of our torment this afternoon, it began to rain. Again the river flooded, though not as dramatically as it had earlier. If there was any brightness to the afternoon, it was the darkness of this storm and the fresh, clean water that came down our sandy riverbed once more. This time I was able to film the flood almost like an incoming tide.

I think we're closer to the Hamar every day, that it's easier to work with them and that I understand the pattern and the rhythm of their lives better than I did a week or two ago.

July 19th 1971

Despite my disquiet, I've spent a productive day filming the harvest. Everyone is anticipating a period of plenty, even though hungry visitors will start arriving from the south, where there has been no rain and where fields were scorched by the great winds and bright sun of the recent weeks. I've already seen some of them coming to their relatives here in the north and they are sad. The people here are sad too, because they're obliged to provide.

I spent the day in the field of an older man named Oita. He has a well-kept field and is one of the few Hamar men who make me think he enjoys

F27

the farming life. He is always on his platform shouting at the birds and hurling rocks and bits of mud, something that is not at all typical of grown men. At first, I thought it odd to see him performing these labors, odd in a way that made him look like an unfit Hamar male.

I have also been watching his wife, daughter, and some younger male relatives who are helping him. The atmosphere was relaxed, contrary to many days spent in other fields where there are palpable tensions. Could these moods be part of the balancing going on between the male and female domains of this society?

July 20th 1971

I was surprised when Michael returned from Dimeka and said Bonk had agreed immediately to come to help with the Landrover, even suggesting that he would have a little picnic with his family. The couple arrived in the early afternoon with their three children, some cupcakes, and an enormous thermos of hot tea. They joined us to consume the tea while we concentrated on the cupcakes. Then Bonk, saying he wanted "to get dirty," began working on the Landrover. Four hours later, after finding a faulty diaphragm and filter, he tightened some connections in the fuel line and stepped on the starter. The engine burst into life. At least his God is merciful.

Michael also said our air charter was scheduled and will be in Dimeka to pick us up as requested on the 27th. For the moment I have decided we should give up the camp here in a few days and move to Dambyti. I think by moving there I will have the opportunity to see things of a more intimate and personal nature. Here I've been getting a general view without ever really getting to know people. In Dambyti, I hope to know a few well enough to become a participant in their lives.

July 21st and 22nd 1971

I've been shooting Oita's harvesting activities and have come to know him better than when he came in the evening to stare at us with his wide, unbelieving eyes. He had a strange look about him, including sunken cheeks and a mouthful of bad teeth, which is not appreciated at all in the Hamar world.

The last two days I have been with Oita as he went methodically about his business, meaning I also participated in his family life, at least to the extent of getting to know his children and sharing his food. It's important to the Hamar that a guest eats with them. Remoteness and closeness are measured in mouthfuls. I may have spent more hours eating or drinking coffee in their houses than I have filming the Hamar.

July 24th 1971

Yesterday was uncommonly blustery, a day one would find at the New England seashore in early November. The air was raw and nobody wanted to do much of anything. We kept near the fire and were joined by a dozen young Hamar women. The men had not even bothered to get up. The women had had to because it is they who draw water and fetch whatever else is needed.

I realize that on Tuesday we will have been here exactly forty-five days with little opportunity to rest. I think Mike and Stewart are both ready to keep working, though I also think they may not be ready to come a second time.

July 25th 1971

Tonight is the last in our long stay in the Logera area. I think it was the 24th of June when we came along the road from Turmi. The moon is new again, the sky is clear, and the camp is quiet at the start of another African night. Stewart and Michael have gone to bed and so has Dejene. Nothing moves except my voice recorder and my companionable lizard.

Ultimate nights such as this are always troubling. During recent days I have felt little warmth either for or from the Hamar. I will even say I'm not sure they are particularly nice people. All of us are ready to say farewell, at least for now.

July 26th 1971

Dambyti is higher in elevation and in a much greener countryside that includes substantial trees and even what looks like grass. The fields I saw en route this afternoon are far more abundant than those in the Logera region, not to mention where I was three years ago. There the fields have turned yellow and even the birds can find no grain. I had

a feeling this afternoon, looking at enormous stacks of grain, that to be in Dambyti is to be extremely fortunate.

We came too late to do much except eat the goat that had been killed, I was told, in honor of our coming. Since the occasion was special, many people were present to drink coffee and eat meat late into the night.

Ivo and his wife live in a house the Hamar built for them, but which is not really a Hamar house. It is a compromise between what we might build for ourselves and what the Hamar have. The Strecker's house has a mud floor and a thatched roof but more space. One has room to stand up, if only where people eat and where Ivo and his wife sleep. At one end of it, in a small anteroom, are their two small children, a boy of two and a girl of a few months. Also with Ivo is his mother, who is staying until she returns Tuesday on the plane to Addis. I noticed the eyes of both children were swollen closed and running with pus. When adults are afflicted this way it is more serious and can end in the loss of sight. The children whimper continuously from the effect of what must be a combination of colic and diarrhea. The ticks and bedbugs cannot be helping and so Strecker's wife has her hands full. Ivo is often with me or with his Hamar male comrades doing what they do best, which is almost nothing at all. Maybe they are thinking up kinship systems, which is the way someone wryly described male behavior at the preliterate level.

The Strecker's house is on a ridge looking east over the Kaska valley. Beyond the valley is a backdrop of quite spectacular mountains that form part of the highlands of Gamo Gofa Province. The space between the Strecker's house and the Hamar dwellings creates a sort of stage on which one can be seen in silhouette in the afternoon light. What Ivo seems not to realize is that this stage is something he's acting on as much or more than the Hamar. The audience is not just the Streckers watching the Hamar, but the Hamar watching the Streckers. The Hamar will be here longer and it is they who will have the most tales to tell. It is total theater, in the sense that there are no players and no audience; each is both and all are engaged in the time-honored anthropological enterprise of participant observation.

July 27th – 30th 1971

These days were spent in Addis finding needed supplies, sending off Stewart and Michael, and welcoming Adele Pressman. She came to give me aid and comfort during the days ahead when I must be in close proximity to the remaining Streckers, staying in what must be understood as their village.

August 5th 1971

The other day while I was sitting in a room in the Strecker's house reserved for lounging, coffee drinking, and talk, I was struck by the enormous languor of middle-aged Hamar men stretched out with their heads propped up on their *burkotos*. Their togas were draped from their toes to their chins and sometimes over their heads. The scene reminded me of a tubercular ward in a Thomas Mann novel, filled with recumbent figures lined up saying and doing nothing. The coffee had been started, but for at least an hour the men simply lay there dozing.

As soon as the ladle was put into the coffee, they sat up in unison for their share to be handed to them. This sort of event can sometimes go on for several hours, repeating itself the next day and the day after. Any hope for sociability depends on an adequate supply of coffee beans as much as anything else.

Work has gone slowly since I returned six days ago. I've done a little shooting but far more thinking about why I am here and what I would like to be doing.

August 12th 1971

A few adult Hamar men will join in a hunting venture near the Omo River, said to be the place where we would likely find their favorite animals. The Omo plain is vast and beautiful, but lacks much of anything of a staple nature to eat and so we hunt with a purpose.

Hunting is a central feature of Hamar masculinity. The male ego is inextricably tied to guns, cartridge belts, even the noise a rifle makes when it is being fondled or cleaned. Aiming, pretending to fire, making the sound of the explosion, all such gestures contribute to being contentedly male.

At the moment, we number five. Ivo came on his motorbike in case the Landrover, which I drove

with three of the Hamar hunters, reverts to its former ways. The main hunter is Bordimba. This is his bull name, the name of the small cow that he jumped at his coming-of-age ceremony. The second is Karimba, and the third Kula. These three men have brought their guns and their spears, and tomorrow morning we will look for an antelope.

Four days ago Karimba and Bordimba met with a man who tells fortunes. He claps sandals together and throws them on the ground, reading a prophecy from the pattern in which the sandals come to rest. This soothsayer said the men should try to hunt an antelope first and then an ostrich, the animal we're in the greatest hope of killing.

August 14th 1971

The hunting is going poorly because the ostrich, a most elusive quarry, runs very fast and has fantastic vision. It has seen us first on every occasion. If a Hamar is not a keen hunter, he is an immense eater; whenever the opportunity arises to enjoy a dinner of game, he will certainly take it.

The only animal my companions have managed to kill is a hartebeest, which is a fat but not particularly large antelope. Bordimba's first bullet misfired, the second hit the animal in the rear and Karimba speared the creature to death as it lay down to die.

The three Hamar hunters have been eating this antelope since it was killed, breaking the bones and eating the marrow as well as biting off pieces of raw or scarcely cooked meat at all times during the day. The Landrover smells like an abattoir, engendering in me a great interest in being vegetarian.

I feel more like a zombie every day, every long and arduous day. I think I am tired of trying to be a filmmaker, anthropologist, and companion to a troubled person with a good mind plagued by enormous interior distress. Living and working with Strecker is a little like being with a lunatic, an experience I have learned from a few close friends to be singularly exhausting.

August 16th 1971

Saturday was a day of hairdressing and some desultory hunting. On Sunday morning, after spending the night on a hilltop, the hunters looked out over the ridge and decided to hunt in the forest to the west, off toward the Omo River. Managing to start by the breaking light, we made our way through thorn bush, scrub grass, and a plenitude of burrs.

Bordimba was in the lead. I was behind him with a camera and the rest were fanned out looking for the tracks of an elusive ostrich. After an hour of walking in the forest, Bordimba stopped and looked excitedly to his left at a beautiful waterbuck standing a mere forty yards away. The man looked at me as if to ask if he should fire. I indicated he certainly should. He took careful aim, fired one bullet and the buck stood as if he'd not even heard, much less felt it. Bordimba took up another position in an effort to get closer. He was about to fire again when Kula, the third hunter, indicated it was his turn and so he fired. The waterbuck still stood, absolutely unscathed. Following a discrete pause, it leapt into the brush.

This failure discouraged everybody. It meant that the hunters' guns were not shooting straight, that their eyes were not seeing clearly, and that luck had abandoned them. Swallowing all pride, we set off again walking another half-hour with Bordimba once more in the lead. Soon a much adored ostrich was in sight.

Karimba and Kula went after it while Ivo, Bordimba, and I sat in the shade to see what would happen. Waiting for perhaps an hour, we decided the ostrich must have escaped and that the hunters were on their way back to our camp.

Soon after leaving the forest, we heard a shot. Spirits soared, knowing that neither Karimba nor Kula would fire unless they had a decent chance. We quickened our walk in the direction of the gunshot and in a few moments I knew that luck had befallen the hunters. Unhappily my camera had no film in it when we arrived to see a wounded male ostrich lying on the ground, expiring. Both Kula and Karimba were ecstatic, talking furiously and gathering up feathers. Karimba hit it from about 100 yards, a respectable shot, particularly in that one bullet had done the job.

By the time I had put film in the camera, the ostrich was almost dead. What followed was a frenzy of butchery, mutual admiration, and evident joy on the part of the hunters. They'd finally done what the sandal oracle had predicted: Bordimba would shoot an antelope and Karimba would shoot an ostrich, both events taking place in the sequence foreseen by the prophet.

P39

F28

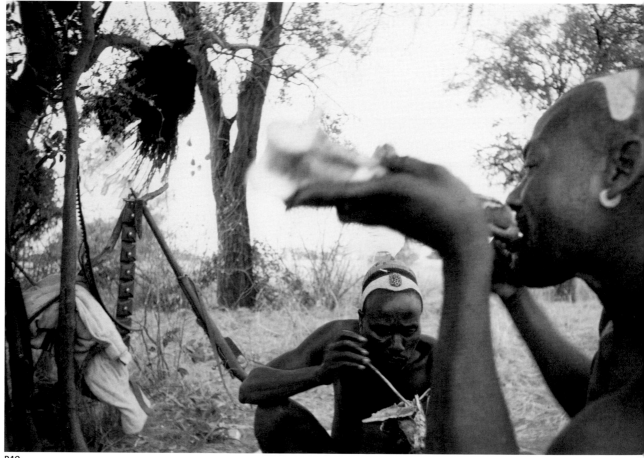

P40

The ostrich made interesting filming because it is such a fabulous animal, prehistoric in its scaliness, length of legs, span of wings, blueness of skin, and beadiness of eye. We began almost immediately to eat the creature. The meat is as red as beef, but also fat, goose fat, with a taste not unlike turkey. We began by eating the marrow from the leg bones. The hunters chopped the legs off at the hip, cut them in half at the knee and put both halves of both legs on a lively fire. They then cracked open the legs with a rock to get at a column of greasy, yellow marrow.

Later, back in a small riverbed near Bordimba's sorghum field, the hunters were able to tell my camera the story of the last three or four days of hunting. They all had ostrich plumes in their hair and delighted in reminiscing about the hunt. I did the filming in one uninterrupted take of about eight minutes.

From now on feathers will be everywhere in Dambyti. They are loved as hair ornaments both by men and women. More than any other animal, the ostrich provides the Hamar with finery.

F29

August 17th 1971

It is early evening, and I'm sitting on the dance ground behind the Dambyti village looking toward the eastern range, which is where the Hamar believe they originated. The night is beautiful and the sunset pink, glowing and utterly African. I have pursued the feather motif. They have drifted about the whole region. It's rare to see a man passing by without part of the ostrich sticking out of his hair or carrying some plumes back to his own village to give away.

F30

The light was clear but my feelings about the Hamar male were not. I find little that is admirable in their character. Much of the time they seem exclusively absorbed in themselves as members of a dominant gender. On the other hand, I have noticed that when two of them are talking, they project a sense of themselves as almost free spirits. I don't know what I'll do with these undigested thoughts when I set about editing a film. I am sure I will not romanticize these men, or portray them as stubborn individualists eking out a meager livelihood in a jungle of thorns.

Hamar men appear to be trapped in a system of values that does damage to their own spirits, while also giving women a life not too different from slavery. Women speak of themselves as resembling dogs, living on scraps for which they have had to beg. To know their story better, I need to hear in greater detail from a woman I have found who was willing to answer many questions I put to her about her life as a female in this society. My thoughts at the moment are based on rough translations of what she was saying as I filmed her and what I have gleaned from conversations with other individuals.

Men clearly have mostly themselves on their minds and are forever concerned about their looks and standing among their fellows. This is something I'm trying to reveal. At the same time, I'm trying to include women and the evidence of their purposefulness to illustrate the contrast between the sexes. The men are limp, smooth, and sometimes cruel. Their manner partakes of social and domestic fascism. As the film slowly takes shape in my mind, I see it as an opportunity to relate some rude facts about a traditional society.

> *Editing the* Rivers of Sand *imagery made a huge impression on me. I kept being reminded that I especially disliked Hamar men and I don't think I would have felt differently had there been no Women's Movement. I don't see how anyone can escape feeling the same way once they see the film. It was a painful life for both sexes. So why not say so? I don't think anthropology is doing its job by being value free. I do think it should accept its responsibility to look for larger truths.*
>
> RG [from an interview]

F31

You are worn in like the grinding stone.

August 19th 1971

The day has been long and arduous, less so physically than emotionally. This morning I was talking to Ivo again about how little time was left to do the things I'd planned, such as the filming of a young woman having a leg iron put on. To me, this piece of imagery is important. Later in the afternoon I was filming a few Hamar men reinforcing a house that had fallen into near ruin. It is the house I hope to use for interior photography. The way they set about doing the work was almost hilarious. Woodworms and termites will no doubt continue to infest the structure, but the holes the men dug for the uprights were barely scratches in the ground. No attempt at anything enduring was even considered. Surely the fact that they do not bother to do something in a way that is going to be more durable is of some interest. It may fit with the worried and apprehensive quality in Hamar men's outlook on life in general.

N.B. This account of my days with the Hamar ends here, approximately two weeks before I returned for the last time to Addis Ababa. I can find no more recordings or other notations made after the 19th of August. They may never have existed or they may turn up in an overlooked corner of the remains of those days. I know only that I was losing my patience. I also recall a comforting feeling that I might already have the material in both words and images to say what I knew and felt about my experiences among the Hamar to whom I had first come, unbidden, in 1968.

P41

P1

the hanging (lines from a filmmaker's journal)

Baco, Gamo Gofa Province, Ethiopia, 1971

Today is the Saturday market in a provincial capital and many have come from the surrounding countryside to sell their surplus staples and to buy extravagances like batteries, matches, and salt.

It is quieter than usual and, at the top of a little rise in the middle of the market square, there is something I have never seen before, a crude scaffold about fifteen feet high constructed of two vertical posts and a horizontal member connecting them. A loop of heavy rope hangs down from where it is attached to the crosspiece. I'm told it will be used for a hanging later in the day.

I buy a little sugar and am kicked by a donkey for standing too close. Trading is frenzied, as though time will run out and the day's business will not get done. An occasional look is thrown in the direction of some soldiers who stand where the condemned will make his entrance.

The mayor and other figures of authority take their places near an army truck whose engine is started with a collective push from the guard of honor. It sputters into life with a solitary passenger, kneeling on its open bed. A goat skitters quizzically out of the way.

Lurching spasmodically, the truck's engine dies and it comes to a stop between the newly planted uprights. There is a soldier on each side of the silent prisoner whom they ask to stand while they tie his arms behind his back. He's dressed in a white shawl, dark tunic, and trousers. His head and feet are bare but his appearance is formal. The crowd arranges itself, languidly, in a semicircle facing the unfolding spectacle.

On a vague signal from the mayor, the truck is heaved forward by brute strength through the uprights and the boy is swept from his feet by the rope that was put around his neck. He dangles and then throttles to death with a slight jerk of his legs. It is said that men who are hung ejaculate exactly when the rope grasps their neck.

Ululation bursts forth but only momentarily and the sound of interrupted commerce begins again. The body will hang from its hasty gibbet until sunset so that everyone will be instructed in its meaning.

Had all my sallying forth to make a film resulted in completed works, I would have a far lengthier list of credits. There were many attempts: the aborted first feature of my extreme youth about the Kwakiutl nation; the documentary of a farmer who with his horse and cart were engulfed by the tides of Newfoundland when they lost their way in the fog; the narrative feature based on Alan Moorehead's *Cooper's Creek* that I developed with Ted Hughes; a documentary about obsessed sheepherders in the north of Nigeria; the narrative feature called *Isle of Dogs* about a beheading on a French outpost in the North Atlantic; the last moment demise of a feature based on J. M. Coetzee's *Waiting for the Barbarians*; and many more examples including the work noted in the journal that follows. I have in mind to some day gather the bits and pieces of my abandoned and peripatetic filmmaking and to give them a shape that I think of as an unintended road trip. I even have a title: *Roads End*.

July 5th 1978

I am in Sonamarg, Kashmir, in a tourist bungalow of recent construction that is part of a dubious scheme to encourage and facilitate travel in these relatively remote regions of northwestern India. The city is in a valley whose quaintness is a little too reminiscent of the Alps. My eyes register meadows, lusty streams, cows and wildflowers, and I have difficulty remembering this is Asia, not Central Europe.

I am with a woman I have recently come to know named Helena Norberg-Hodge. We joined company at the Delhi airport this morning and have traveled together all day. She is writing letters in the dining room and I have come upstairs hoping to find a place to rest.

P3

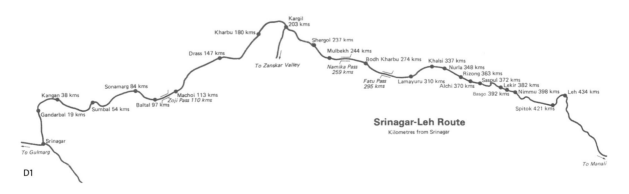

D1

Srinagar-Leh Route
Kilometres from Srinagar

Helena is an occasional student at the School of Oriental and African Studies, a refugee from uncomfortable marital relations, and a wanderer in a variety of emotional and topological geographies. She appears to care deeply about Ladakh, speaks some Ladakhi and has decided to come with me while I explore the idea of doing a film about shamanic practices, something I have wanted to do for a long time.

The flight from Delhi to Srinagar, the main city of Kashmir, took only an hour and we arrived around midnight at the Hotel Broadway, which is managed by a friend of the father of an ex-student whom I have just visited in Bombay. My idea was to stay in Srinagar long enough to arrange transportation tomorrow to Leh, the capital. Instead we found a Jeep which, for $100 a day, would take us there immediately. A great desire to escape a noisy city overcame any interest in saving a few rupees.

Now we are already 100 kilometers up the road from Srinagar spending the night in Sonamarg; the $2 cost of a room in our country inn is almost nothing compared to most other Hotel Broadways of the world. It is 10 p.m. and silence reigns for a handful of guests including a few French climbers and Indian police officers. The rooms are without electricity so I write with a small flashlight perched on my shoulder.

July 6th 1978

We have been up since 5 a.m. having been roused by a sleepy porter who coughed and sputtered outside the door for several minutes. Helena had bolted it shut for reasons I cannot fathom. He was swathed in a cape and blanket and looked as if he had simply stood up in his bedclothes. Nevertheless, he carried a tray with tea and two cups. It was welcome after a night of wakefulness owing to the unmistakable scent of vomit and the steady drumming of rain on the roof and windows.

Clouds filled every recess of the valley and a solid pall of yet more clouds hung above the escarpment. We were late getting started, having planned to be on our way by 4 a.m. so as to reach Leh before dark.

I packed the Jeep and discovered there was no fuel. The promised 200-liter drum had not been delivered. There wasn't much to do except wait. Finally, around 7 a.m., the drum arrived on a truck that had had a very bad time of it in the rainstorms last night. We loaded the drum and set out for Leh.

Hardly past the bridge in Sonamarg there is a sign reading "Drive Carefree" and a police checkpoint where everyone was stopped. There would be a considerable wait because a convoy of vehicles had just been cleared in the opposite direction and the road accommodates one-way travel only. These roadblocks are common owing to the increasing violence of Kashmiri politics. This is not at all the tranquil land of lakes and lotus plants it was before Partition.

The convoy was on its way by noon but our driver had not positioned himself well and so we were obliged to inhale clouds of diesel fumes as we edged past lorries and buses. We did not stop for nine hours. During that time my patience with the driving wore thin. There is a Muslim machismo that turns mountain roads in Kashmir into fields of combat. I have had many occasions to observe drivers of this faith and can say with certainty that far too much trust is put in Allah. For these reasons, I decided to go no further. We were still three or four hours from Leh, it was dark and we had been going since 5 a.m.

At Khalsi, where we find ourselves, there was a guesthouse but we were told it was fully booked. There isn't really much booking done in India. You can have a room if someone is not already in it and often when someone is. As it happened, the guesthouse did have someone in each room but after Helena's guileful pleading in Ladakhi, a room was suddenly empty. It was empty even of a bed, which apparently departed with whoever had been in the room first. The night was filled with opaque dreams and barking dogs.

July 7th 1978

By mid-morning we were in Leh and lodged in a Ladakhi-owned hotel on the outskirts of the city. Leh is burdened with a heavy army presence owing to India's fear of its Chinese neighbors. Ladakh is sometimes called Western Tibet and its destiny is thought to be inextricably linked to that of its Chinese larger half. For now it serves India's purpose of letting the world know it is a major power and will not be intimidated by China.

P4

July 8th 1978

It was late when we got back to the hotel following a recital last night by the Tibetan National Dance Troupe. The company is in exile living in Dharamshala where their culture may be better remembered than lived. I have hesitated going there despite urging by friends. My worry has been finding an atmosphere of yearning for the old days of an independent Tibet guided by authentic Buddhist traditions. I might add that the performance I just witnessed was not one that will hasten my visit. I can remember few times being more bored. I think it was due mostly to my ignorance of the theatrical forms but some of my dismay came from the sheer ponderousness of it all. In the end I could not summon the courage to simply walk out on so much national pride.

Early this morning we hired a local Jeep and went to a small village called Nang that a self-described expert had said would hold interest for the student of traditional Ladakhi life. It is two hours from Leh to the east and, like all the villages I have seen, situated in the valley of a small tributary to the Indus. The hills on all sides and the mountains lying in the distance lack visible vegetation. All is boulders, rocks, gravel and, finally, sand: a vast sloping desert of stone. But the villages nestle comfortably amid the ultra green fields of barley in the folds between hills climbing up from the small rivers next to which everything is built.

The houses, often connected by common walls, are two or three stories high. Around them are groves of what must be poplars and they command a view of the wheat and barley fields that lie terraced below them. The sound of running water dominates as it falls down the steep riverbeds over gravel and rocks. The less audible gurgle of innumerable canals flowing around and sometimes through the houses brings the water where it is needed for an intricate system of garden beds laid out close to the houses.

Nang was enjoyable to explore even though it lacked any magic of situation. There were many indications of disarray amidst a general orderliness. Worn-out sneakers, bits of corrugated roofing, discarded tin cans and broken windowpanes gave an air of neglect to a landscape of formidable purity. It reminded me that the Himalayas as a mountain system are said to be suffering commodity pollution from gum wrappers, dead batteries, bottle caps, and worn out garments pitched out by trekkers. The contrast with the well-kept gardens and cleansing streams is dramatic.

There was not a great deal of activity because it is the growing season. The barley and turnips need only occasional weeding. The hard work of planting is over and the harder work of reaping is still to come.

I walked a fair distance in this nearly vertical oasis of greenness cradled in the rocky hills and gentled by the astute hydraulics of a very old civilization. The blight of alien debris was troubling but somehow the hoboesque look of both adults and children was not. Ladakhis seem not to be at all clothes conscious. They wear what it takes to stay warm and as bits wear out they more or less slough them off, like old skins. Dirty Ladakhi clothes, in fact, have integrity in the way they hang loosely but fittingly on the wearer.

It is tempting to think that life in a place like Nang has an indigenous coherence and integrity, that the influence of the West on local culture has not yet altered too radically the long-established patterns of village life. From my own brief and superficial observations, I feel I could make a film in which the narrative was situated in an entirely Ladakhi way of life and that the realities of change would not be overwhelming.

My thoughts as to how to proceed now focus on a shaman/farmer who lives in Tikshay and who we will visit tomorrow.

July 9th 1978

Helena thinks I should guarantee her a role in the editing of anything that comes of what we are doing. These thoughts come up in the context of a busy and productive day spent with a Ladakhi shaman, not really a shaman as much as healer/magician. Helena wants to know that whatever she is contributing will be safeguarded by her having something to say about how it will be used. We agreed it was best to simply keep going.

Tomorrow we rendezvous with the Laba (healer/magician) from Tikshay. I want to take him to another village to treat a patient who has called him. I watched him perform this morning and have a good idea of his technique. When we went for a taxi to go to Tikshay, we found the Laba had already come to Leh, perhaps to hear Morarji Desai who was on a political stopover. Desai's speech was pretty dispirited and people barely responded. He went off in a cloud of Wagoneer dust and we went to find our Laba. He was staying at a modest house in the middle of Leh where he had come to perform a healing ritual.

The Laba is a bit over sixty and radiates immense mischief with his intricately lined and animated face. His hair is white and clipped in front and on top. He is shorter than most already short Ladakhis and moves with the restlessness of a hyperactive child.

The healing ritual took place in a multipurpose eating, sleeping, and living room where twenty of us were crowded together. Quickly the Laba set about his business. He sat in such a way as to be backlit by a window whose curtains he partially closed before starting. The rest of us, including several people who had come in search of his attentions, were seated across from him against a wall. He began by setting out the paraphernalia of his calling including small copper dishes, barley flour, uncooked rice, a saucer of oil with a wick, a gobbet of butter for the barley flour and more of it in a dish of what looked like ghee. After immense hiccoughing, bell ringing, and drumming, he entered trance.

P5

P6

167

The transition from awareness to trance was accompanied by much shivering and shaking. It was not until one, final convulsive shudder shook him from head to foot that his body fell into repose as he entered the realm of what I took to be an altered state of mind.

Speaking in falsetto he dealt one at a time with his supplicants. His manner was quick, definite, even admonishing, and his subjects were in turn docile, respectful, and grateful. A sense of awe hung over the proceedings and I felt like a witness to a religious drama.

The Laba had different ways of treating the complaints at hand but he held all of his patients by their wrists for several moments. In Tibetan medicine the pulse is a primary indicator of one's state of health. I have been told that experienced Tibetan practitioners make complex diagnoses with nothing more than the pulse. A few of the Laba's patients were treated to a divinatory exercise in which kernels of rice scattered on the skin of a small drum were read like tea leaves at the bottom of a cup. One patient was given classic sucking treatment for a stomach ailment. The Laba took a copper tube perhaps ten inches in length and put one end in his mouth and the other against a lady's midsection. In this way he produced some dark fluid and, after some especially intense sucking, what looked like a small ball of black fur.

In an hour everyone had been treated and the Laba emerged from his trance in more or less the reverse order of the steps he had taken to attain it. I have no idea what the clinical nature of this trance is but maybe more opportunities to watch it will shed some light.

Around 3 p.m. we took the Laba home and stayed with him a few more hours. It was agreed that we would return tomorrow and go to Sakti where he has an apprentice whom he wants to visit.

July 10th 1978

The Laba was waiting for us when we arrived around 9 a.m. We would have been earlier except our driver had drunk too much *chang*, or barley beer, at the archery festival in his village.

The road to Sakti goes east beyond Karu. This journey was the Laba's idea. I am merely a willing participant not even knowing what we will do. I am quite under the spell of this man's energy and do not care at all where it takes me.

There were some pretty meadows and little brooks to cross on foot before we reached our destination. Once there we found not the apprentice but his wife and two small children. His father was also there and very genial. Someone went to find the person we had come to see and for the next hour and a half the father and the Laba consumed a great amount of *chang*. I decided against the *chang* and tried instead to make a few still photographs of these two old men and the interior of the house. It was small, largely undecorated but neatly kept and comfortable. The father has another house that is larger but he uses this one because it is close to his cows and gardens.

The apprentice finally appeared a bit out of breath and perspiring heavily. He was immensely friendly and eager to join the Laba in trance.

In no time the preliminaries were over, perhaps more hastily than befitted the occasion and before long both men were deep in trance. I tried to film the proceedings in the tiny kitchen in which everything was happening. Only one person presented herself for treatment, a young woman to whom the Laba paid scant attention. He was coaching the younger sorcerer who spoke in a voice that did not change in tone as it did with the Laba. I was struck by how easy it was for the Laba to exist in what seemed to be two states of consciousness at the same time. While he was healing and supposedly in trance he would occasionally ask me if I had been able to make enough pictures. I would say I wanted to keep on doing what I was doing and he would then say that he needed to consult the spirits. This he did by asking me to place on the membrane of his small drum a kernel of rice which he then animated with the vibrations of his high-pitched singing. I presume doing this provided him with answers to any questions he might have had about what he should or should not do about me.

The spirits must have agreed to what I requested because the Laba continued divining and treating the apprentice's father before finally abandoning his trance. I think these hours have helped me make a stronger connection with the Laba as I begin my own slow apprenticeship in the mysteries of Tibetan healing.

P7

July 11th 1978

We have known for a few days that we would go with the Laba to the archery festival in Tikshay. I was not hopeful of finding anything of cinematic interest in that event but there was at least the promise of a congenial outing.

I left the Laba last evening at his house worried about his wife's health. She was complaining of nausea and looked very ill. I cannot explain, nor perhaps can she, why her husband is so conspicuously healthy while she is a heap of rags and bones. I left distressed and was happy to find her this morning not only vertical but able to tell us she had been attended by the *amchi,* or Tibetan doctor, who had treated her with apparent success. Nausea must be a constant fact of life in Western Tibet.

I managed to arrive early hoping to catch the Laba before he had gotten too poised in preparation for our meeting. I asked if he would sit in his kitchen and open his shaman's bag. I had the idea that this ubiquitous carryall might be a useful prop, even a major motif were I to pursue serious film-making. It is an undistinguished piece of luggage made from an old carpet and full of his equipment, his tricks, the tools of his trade. Everything he needs is rolled up or folded away in this bag. I tried shooting a sequence where he opened the bag and disclosed its contents by removing them one by one. Because it was my idea, the motivation was wrong and I could feel things stiffen as he acted out this little piece of business. Still, the bag is getting established and the more important items in it are becoming familiar.

P8

She said she had experienced possession by the spirits at twenty-nine when she was giving birth to her second child, a girl who, now a mother herself, was in the house with her own child.

We were led back down a second ladder to another side of the house that looked south onto many small gardens and orchards of apricots and apples. We were asked to wait there for the Lamu while she got ready by washing and dressing properly for the spirits. I was also told by her daughter to eat the peas that were growing at one end of the garden. The peas were extremely small but the most delicious I have ever tasted. They made me think again about experiences of scale in Ladakh where, in this immense landscape, familiar things are made strange by their diminutiveness: horses, vegetables, houses, and even people themselves.

It took a long time for the Lamu to get ready but when she appeared she was in vivid contrast to our friend the Laba. Where he is playful and assertive, she is demure and modest.

We were told a spirit would enter her while she was in the *gompa,* or holy place, and around 2 p.m. we went there to be with her when that happened. The *gompa* is at the top of the older part of her house and consists of a small room filled with articles of her faith. The same neatness seen in the kitchen was also evident in the *gompa,* a space that offered stark contrast with the Laba's dwelling.

Soon we went off to the archery contest in progress not far from his house. It was a small gathering when we arrived, only a handful of men and women who were preparing for a busier time later in the day. It had a troublingly folkloric look about it and I had no interest in staying longer than necessary to humor our Laba. I only wanted a brief moment to film the Laba releasing an arrow, some *chennai* (flute) playing, and a little drumming.

We left before long and I spent the afternoon in Leh being a tourist in search of souvenirs. I would like to have found something interesting like the wondrously blue, lazuli head coverings worn by a few of the women but the best of such things were more expensive here than in New York or London.

July 12th 1978

On this second of the two days devoted to the archery festival in Tikshay, the Laba is not available. I am not fond of festivals of this kind so I decided to visit another healer, a Buddhist nun living near the township of Skara where I am staying. We arranged to come to her late in the morning. She said she felt unwell but this might have been her way of forestalling a visit.

Her house seemed old compared to most I have seen and has two entrances on the ground level. Just inside was a wooden stairway of uncertain construction leading up to the nun's quarters on the second story. Here there was a small kitchen kept very neat and lit by only one window and a small opening in the roof to let out smoke. Our hostess, the Lamu (*la* for spirit and *mu* for woman), is a serene and dignified lady of sixty-four.

P10

171

The Lamu was seated in the near absence of light at what must be her customary place. I had the fast Zeiss lenses and went ahead hoping for the best in this profoundly darkened sanctuary. She began with a long incantation that sounded more scriptural than spontaneous and lasted three or four minutes. It was a low key but compelling expression of her devotion. Suddenly she sneezed just as the Laba had hiccoughed and I took this to be the sign that a spirit had entered. Later I was told not one but five spirits had made their entrance.

She began to speak in a different tone of voice and to use her bell and drum. I could think of nothing but to keep the camera running for the next eight or nine minutes. Other than her daughter, her granddaughter, Helena and myself, there was no audience. When I left to change the magazine, I heard her coming out of trance and wondered if she did because I had left the room.

I am impressed by this woman and hope to spend more time with her. My two practitioners have a common purpose but approach their calling quite differently. Where the Laba is theatrical, the Lamu is refined and spiritual. Both, though, are unmistakably adepts.

July 13th 1978

I have been wondering what the cause might be of a curious rash covering me from head to toe. Helena has experienced many of the same symptoms though her rash is not as widespread. What is our skin telling us? Can the Laba or the Lamu help?

Today it had been arranged to see the Laba early, not to look after our ailments but to keep going with the work, both his and mine. To be with him at 7 a.m. means rising no later than 5 a.m. This we managed without great difficulty but the Laba had already left when we reached his house thinking we had said 6 and not 7 a.m. We found him later at the house of a person to whom he had been summoned. He was just leaving as we arrived, looking like any other physician on his rounds.

We decided to take him to a village west of Leh called Peh. He was not very interested in this excursion but finally agreed to it. In Peh we entered a fine old mansion where he almost immediately began his customary routine of healing. It happened that this performance would be the most

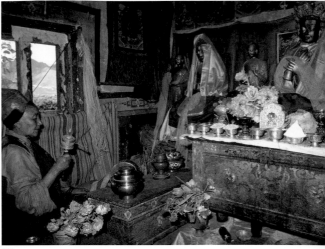

P11

powerful to date. Many people were awaiting his attentions and the Laba was in excellent form. His last appointment was with a middle-aged woman who had a menacing look about her. When she approached the Laba, I was sure we would see something new.

When she was close to the Laba, she fell into an immediate, convulsive, and convincing trance. Her behavior became progressively wilder and more uncontrolled. I had just begun shooting when two men in Western clothes stepped in front of the camera and forbade me to continue. They were her relatives and wanted no record of what was happening. I had watched both of them being treated earlier, perhaps in the hope of it having a sympathetic effect on their sicker female relation. There was nothing I could do. They were adamant. I was furious but helpless. Had I thought more cynically, I might have tried to bribe them but instead I simply watched as her madness unfolded.

I left Peh disheartened but found my way to Tikshay where I worked with the Laba and his crone of a wife.

July 14th 1978

In Nang, a village in the hills northeast of Tikshay, the Laba had friends with whom he was going on pilgrimage and they had asked for his ministrations before setting out.

The house was up-valley a short distance and nice in an antique way. Unhappily though, the interiors were extremely dark and I had no lights. It was stupid to have left them when I packed for this journey. I could have brought something simple which would have meant not having to shoot everything in silhouette. In the end, I was able to

P12

> *The world is apparent through our experience of it which we endow with meaning. When we do this, are we not creating fictions be they memories or images on rolls of film, and are we not also making something not only new but altogether real?*
>
> RG [from a letter]

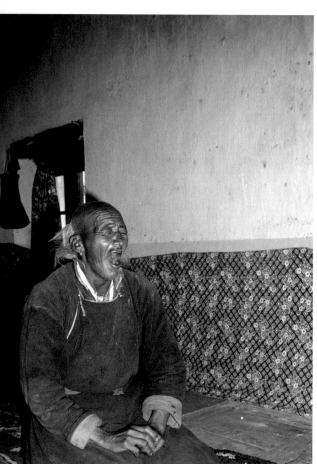

P13

move everyone outside to the terrace where light was no longer the problem, just the absence of energy or excitement. It was a routine day for the Laba containing no surprises, happy or unhappy.

We went again to Tikshay to work a little with the Laba and returned once again to Leh. This routine is hardly a structure for a film: a Tibetan faith healer making house calls. We'll come back tomorrow anyway. I have no other plan.

July 15th 1978

I have spent another day at Tikshay with the Laba who is willing, as usual, to allow the spirits to enter. I have not yet seen any spirit enter unbidden and this may be one of the distinctions between being mad and a medium. Lunatics do not decide when they will be possessed. Mediums do and our Laba is a finely tuned instrument in this regard. He is very much in command of his psychic state, almost to the point where there is little or no suspense in the practice of his mediumhood. Of course, he also has technique and a body of knowledge that confirm his status. Priests would not be priests without their grip on ritual secrets and practices.

Each performance has some freshness in that the subjects have individuality and the Laba uses his gifts for extemporaneity much in the manner of a trained actor. His asides, jokes, and abjurations are changed in response to new settings and new subjects. Like any magician, he makes sure his tricks work while doing them differently enough to seem unique to each occasion. The Laba is both an actor and a clinician and his success or failure as a healer depends on playing both roles. I don't think I will be in Ladakh long enough to investigate these things in a serious way, which is sad since it had been my hope to learn as much as possible about such practices. I would do this even knowing the Laba and the Lamu are not shamans in the strictest sense. But I am still unsure what a shaman, in the strictest sense, really is.

I suspect there is little or no psychic stress in going in and out of trance several times a day. In fact I have seen how these performances actually invigorate the Laba. It might be different for the Lamu. She practices austerities like dieting and prolonged prayer before letting the spirits take over. She also washes elaborately for an hour or two before each session. I know this only from being told by her daughter. I have not yet been present while she prepares. In any case, the Lamu and the Laba differ importantly in matters of style. The Lamu is deliberate and solemn and the Laba is almost irreverent and playful.

When the Lamu is on the brink of trance, she gives a dainty sneeze in the midst of some mild twitching and then is discretely possessed. The Laba is more boisterous and there is little doubt about when he crosses the threshold into trance. The filming should show this clearly just as it will show that in both cases the psychic states they achieve by whatever means they use do not approach the crazed heights reached by !Kung Bushmen in their healing ceremonies. When I watched the !Kung perform, I was not only awed by their extravagance, I was amazed by the unstinting abandon of those who ventured into such profound and lasting abandonment of their senses. The Laba and the Lamu do things quite differently.

P14

P15

P16

In Tikshay today the Laba was pleased to once again display his prowess as a healer. For the first time he worked at his own house under the baleful regard of his uncongenial spouse.

July 16th 1978
I had an arrangement to be with the Laba today for a ceremony involving his grandchild but my mysterious rash and attending nausea made me think twice about another day drinking *chang*, salted tea, and other such refreshments. Western Tibetan cuisine has to be near the bottom of any culinary hierarchy.

I spent the day lamenting the transformation of Leh from a deeply religious, high-altitude agricultural society into an Indian Defense Department outpost with a growing fascination with modernity. In Leh one can still see the dying embers of Tibetan Buddhism but it is unlikely much will rise from the ashes except trekking and tourism.

I also regret discovering that Helena was not up to the things I had planned – traversing a few major passes on ponies and finding a village where life could be seen with most of its traditions intact. But I am also aware of the mixed feelings I have regarding such undertakings. In some ways I am relieved not to be doing this. I realize I am less prepared mentally to engage in a major film enterprise than I was twenty years ago. Is it that so much else in life is losing its allure? Or, am I disappointed with the way my life never changed after *Dead Birds* and *Rivers of Sand*? What is the point, I ask, if satisfaction eludes me so completely?

There is less and less to show for my exertions. At the end of this adventure I will have some footage about healing according to Buddhist traditions that at best compares the styles of two different practitioners. Nothing more will come of it unless something remarkable happens in the space of the next few days.

This afternoon I was able to film the Lamu for the second time. Again her miniscule sanctuary was impossibly dark and it is likely that little of what I did will be properly exposed. I am really not well prepared and can only suppose it has to do with my ambivalence about doing what I'm doing.

At a certain moment, the Lamu announced the arrival of a second spirit; something, or someone, who has not appeared before. Its advent was entirely convincing, putting the Lamu into an ecstatic delirium. She stood up and swayed sensuously against the dark wall of her *gompa*.

The Lamu has said again she is not feeling well, especially now that her daughter has gone away. I also detect no interest on her part in what I am doing. I don't know how long I will pursue her.

The Laba has said he is going on a series of pilgrimages and I have no way to follow him.

July 17th 1978
The Laba came to Leh this morning to meet those who will go with him to various monasteries and shrines as they make their pilgrimage. He put on a perfunctory performance for the assembled pilgrims whose journeying I deeply regret being unable to join. Undoubtedly I would see a more interesting side of him, if it was possible to go with him. The pilgrim might be the original road warrior and the pilgrimage the archetypal road film. It is something I have wanted to do for a long time, hopefully with a proper Sadhu. Ever since my first visit to India preparing for the filming of *Altar of Fire*, I have nursed the idea of finding a subject from the ranks of ascetics like the Sadhu I met on the way to Baidrinath walking naked in the snow. I saw the man as I was coming up the road and I thought nothing could be more socially defiant. In Baidrinath, I saw him in a shop having a cup of tea and warming himself like anyone else, but still naked.

July 18th 1978
Yesterday it was arranged for me to meet the Laba at the Leh bus depot and to take him to Likir after first stopping at Peh. I had hopes we might revisit the madwoman of Peh who had been so deranged the day I was asked by her relatives to stop filming. Maybe they wouldn't be there and I could do what I had tried and failed to do the first time.

We waited for the Laba but he was nowhere to be seen. Like bus depots everywhere, the one in Leh has its own representative collection of bedraggled travelers burdened by the material contents of their lives. People like this are everywhere on the move, exposed and vulnerable, sleepy,

P17

unwashed, and buffeted by swarming others as they try to make a temporary accommodation to their circumstances. Maybe this is the film I should be making in Ladakh.

The Laba did not keep his appointment and at 8 a.m. we left by Jeep to go to Likir where we found him around midday. I made a small sequence of him circumambulating the *gompa* and then he disappeared into a tent with a horde of pilgrims being harangued by a bullhorn.

July 19th 1978

With the Laba out of reach, I fell back upon the Lamu whom we visited today and who repeated her earlier complaints about her health. It was clear that as a fly on her wall I would not see much were I to stay. I sense this whole enterprise diminishing in pace and intensity. I feel more like a tourist who has stayed longer than his travel consultant advised and wishes he was booked on an earlier flight.

July 20th 1978

The Lamu complains of *tiksha,* a common malady of this region that includes nausea and fatigue, classic symptoms of life at higher altitudes. But why would native Ladakhis be subject to this after generations of adaptation? Could these symptoms have more to do with the absence of sanitation and good water? There are almost a hundred hotels in Leh and most of them have flush toilets but the flushing is done into a sewer

of small brooks and streams all flowing down an open valley.

I am also unable to account for my own complaints. A rash has transformed into swollen glands, which is curious but not incapacitating. I crave a sea-level experience that I am sure would dispel at least the ringing in my ears. Mountains do not belong in my mystique of place.

July 21st 1978

The weather has been unsettled for days and has recently turned decisively worse. The higher mountains to the east, usually visible through a pall of haze, are wreathed in dark clouds. My efforts these days are directed at extracting some vitality from the Lamu but she feels feeble, as do I and many others who I meet here and there in the town.

The hotel is momentarily inhabited by a new contingent of tourists, this time from Zurich. It is a dour lot that sits impassively, listening to their leader's lectures.

July 22nd 1978

Word has come that rain and subsequent flooding have cut the road to Srinagar just as I was savoring a departure tomorrow for lower altitudes. Buddhist teaching must now prevail in the midst of rain and rock slides. It happens that I will, after all and as I promised, go with the flow. I only hope its direction is downhill.

Helena and I made off across the meadows of Skana to see the Lamu whom we found at home. She mostly eats and prays, always with beads in hand.

She shows me again her standard prelude of washing and recitation leading to entrancement. I have removed one of the two windows in the *gompa,* which might bring the illumination up to threshold levels. The early afternoon séance was different in that several spirits entered, each with its own distinctive characteristics.

July 23rd 1978

I heard that the road to Srinagar had been reopened so there is a chance of making my flight to Delhi on the 25th. At 7 a.m. I was in a Jeep driven by a sturdy Sikh and pounding down the road of that once fabled vale of Kashmir. This has not been a happy time owing to many near and distant distractions. I will have time to think more clearly when I am back in Cambridge. For now, I just want my own culture back.

N.B. I have transcribed the last of these notes in the Hotel Prinsengracht in Amsterdam where I have been invited to a retrospective of my films. I am struck by the similarity of feelings I had in Ladakh, particularly in the latter stages of that journey, and my feelings now of wanting to be on my way almost from the moment I arrived. I think it is a reluctance to engage, as Camus would say, that prevents me from having deeper layers of experience. New Guinea may have been a time when I was able to put aside urges to disengage, but even then I can remember moments when my craw was so full of spilled blood and the smell of death, I wanted badly to be elsewhere.

F1

F2

F3

The year 1978 was one in which my thoughts and energy were spread far too thinly, even recklessly. I assumed a state of pseudonomadism in the hope of escaping the rigors of a settled life. I went off, serially, to Ladakh in pursuit of an old dream of making a film on shamanism, to Korea to live with naked fisherwomen who used bare teeth to catch their prey, and to the Niger Republic to see what real nomads were about.

That experience, which I shared with my close friend and frequent helper Robert Fulton, resulted in the film *Deep Hearts*.

We began in Paris so as to fly Air Afrique to Niamey and there, almost immediately, set out for the Sahel where we eventually found an astonishing group of Wodaabe Fulani also known as Borroro. I learned something about them but more about myself as I watched the common human curse of envy uncommonly resolved by their invention of the Deep Heart.

What follows are the journals I wrote during that period of work.

P1

The Niger, August 17th 1978

I am once again in Birni Nkonni where I came twelve years ago in search of the Uda Fulani, sheepherders extraordinary. We traveled a straight and level road all night having started from Niamey last evening. We drove in a Landrover that has been rented at exorbitant cost and is dangerously, irresponsibly overloaded but we were on decent roads and the driver is experienced, or so he says. Our party includes three *Nazaras* (Songhay for people from Nazareth) — myself, our scholar/interpreter Patrick Paris, and Bob Fulton, my comrade in many adventures. Our Niger driver is Gerba. He is strong and seems able. He is also, so far at least, amiable, which helps a lot. Last night he avoided an enormous disaster swerving at the last second around an invisible cow standing in the middle of the road enveloped by the blackest of nights. We headed for Tahoua where we left some of our things with Catholic Sisters because the road from Tahoua to Abalak, ninety miles to the north, is not a road at all. We left everything we could with the Sisters but still our Landrover sounds fatigued.

Things have gone fairly well considering we are not particularly well provisioned. Water will be the biggest problem.

F4

F5

August 18th 1978

Three hours of driving yesterday and about the same today have put us in Abalak, the administrative post of the region in which we expect to be working. It's a landscape of rolling dunes colored green with seasonal grass and infrequent trees. Half shutting my eyes, I could mistake it for a golf resort but I know better and the illusion doesn't last.

We waited in the office of the *Chef de Post* whom we must properly greet before we can be on our way. I asked Gerba to return to Tahoua for the remaining baggage and provisions. He will come back here tomorrow afternoon. This can be done barring the kind of rain that interferes with travel on these so-called improved roads. He is meant to bring fifty gallons of gasoline in a drum that I bought yesterday for safekeeping here in Abalak. With this we can range more widely in our search for the Borroro. It is certain that the fuel will be needed because this is the time when they go great distances to join with other clans in celebrations. Finding the Borroro is the reason I have come so far.

The outlook is promising. First, the rains have started early and continue to be copious. Second,

P2

although the seasonal beauty contests (*gerewol*) among the young men have yet to begin, they will start soon and there is much purchasing in the markets of grain, sugar, and salt that is always a prelude to these occasions. Third, traders in the markets have told us that many lineages have gathered not far to the north (thirty to sixty miles) and are making contracts with each other. These contracts are agreements between opposing lineages to engage each other in *gerewol*. *Gerewol* is the singing and dancing that culminates in the selection of a young male who personifies in moral and physical terms what can be thought of as Borroro perfection. He is called the bull. *Gerewol* is an aspect of a larger activity called *gaynka* which is something like a ritual war without any killing. One lineage attacks another, which must defend. The former is guest and the latter is host. Both lineages dance but the attacking lineage has the last night to itself and the dancing ends at dawn.

The *Chef de Post* finally came but then went behind a closed door keeping us waiting. Was he sleeping? Like so much in Africa, particularly at midday, there is a general horizontality to everything. Many are sick, poor, hungry, and bored. It is hot and people, if they move at all, do so in a daze, stupefied by the sun.

I was drowsing when Patrick came to say that he had seen the *Chef* and we were free to move on. This I would do most happily were it not for the fact that Gerba had gone to Tahoua to retrieve our belongings and to get the drive shaft repaired. It clangs most ominously. The Landrover is patently too small to accommodate all of us and our manifold accoutrements.

August 19th 1978

We wait for the Landrover's return, which is still expected before sundown. Last night was cool enough to allow sleep until the sun rose with its customary exactitude. Here we have water we must boil, rice provided by the owner of the establishment we are occupying and a few of our own provisions such as dates, nuts and, while they last, limes. Fulton is doing reasonably well considering his fragile mind/body situation. It is not that he is especially delicate but that his nervous system is tuned to such an exquisite pitch. The slightest jarring can have catastrophic consequences. All of what is happening now will at least provide us with hardening for things to come.

I have been thinking of asking Fulton to film me in debate with myself as we wait in this halfway house on the road to the Borroro. I have never subscribed to self-reflexive cinema, and all the times I might have put on record in film what I was doing or thinking in various far-flung enterprises, I did not. But now I feel a little differently and wonder if it might not be the time to document some of the thoughts I am having about what I am doing here in Niger. I suppose the personal agitation over marital and extramarital matters of recent weeks has played a part in calling other aspects of my life into question. Why am I a filmmaker and, if I am one, what kind am I? Can this be of the slightest interest to anyone other than myself? Realist, actuality, documentary, even lyric, poetical or metaphysical film has large ambition but modest audiences.

At midday, Fulton got out the camera and I tried to unburden myself of a few of the thoughts that have crowded my mind these past days. When I am alone and experimenting with words, it seems easy and natural. I think the camera can be turned on and I will just utter words that will come forth effortlessly. What happened was I could scarcely murmur my name much less speak of what being a filmmaker means. So we abandoned this idea amid promises to try again another time.

Later we walked in the market trying to find some sardines, sugar, tea, a mosquito net. The merchants are half asleep and indifferent to all transactions. At some point I saw the Landrover hurtling into the marketplace past rickety stalls and coming to a stop amid clouds of dust. The vehicle contained everything we had abandoned in Tahoua. Gerba had done the round-trip in minimum time and so we should be able to reload and move on tomorrow morning.

By evening an immense wind blew fine sand into everything and spectacular flashes of lightning appeared to the west and north, the direction in which I mean to go.

August 20th 1978

A raucous muezzin broke the morning silence with his call to prayer amid praises of Allah. It was still dark and dawn would not arrive for at least two hours. When it did I started to load the Landrover, our pathetic tents came down, plastic jugs were filled with suspect water, bread for the day was purchased in the market and after some coffee we set off.

Thirty miles in three hours was slow travel but not slow enough for our ailing Landrover, which now has a broken leaf in its right rear springs. I actually heard it snap as we tilted to the right shortly after leaving Abalak. It's like hearing someone's leg break. There is no question what the sound means for anyone who hears it. I rest now under the welcome branches of an acacia tree and scribble these random thoughts.

Driving in a desert encourages conversation since there is little else to do. I have taken the opportunity to get from Patrick a better idea of both the Borroro and himself. It has been instructive on both scores. He told me the story of his love for a Borroro girl and how they had lived together in a climate of growing uneasiness for months until, one day, she came to where he was typing and said, "It is me or the typewriter." He may have said nothing or not known what to say but she took the calabash of milk she was carrying and poured it into the typewriter. Then she disappeared into the desert and Patrick has not seen her since.

My interest in the Borroro is long-standing, having begun almost twenty years ago when I saw Henri Brandt's film, *Les Nomades de Soleil*. It impressed me with its vivid depiction of these astonishing-looking people. The film was made with simple means, a Bolex I think and mostly from the back of a camel. Brandt was Swiss and offended that no one took his work seriously. It most certainly was not commercial.

P3

P4

P5

Soon afterward, I met a woman named Sophie Wenek. She was a close friend of Jane Rouch, wife of Jean Rouch, whom I had met in Prague in 1957. Sophie was a romantic figure in the 1950's African subculture of Paris. She was an American of Polish parentage who had moved as a young woman from upstate New York to France. She lived in a garret in the Sixième from which she made periodic visits to her much loved Niger Sahel, the stretch of semidesert below the Sahara. The Rouchs told me she had a husband who was a Borroro herdsman of immensely good looks. Sophie dreamed of making her own film about the Borroro even though she had no means or experience for doing so. She often asked me and I am sure others, too, if I would help her but I was always doing something else or prudently staying out of a situation that would be unlikely to end well. Sophie died in a plane crash in the Canaries before she could do her film. She was on her way home from a visit to her adored Borroro.

Patrick, to whom I was introduced by Jean Rouch, told me more in a week about the Borroro than I have learned in years reading about them in the anthropological literature. Marguerite Dupire is the main academic source of information and I have done what I could to learn something from her. I have even tried to see her to discuss my project, but without success. I'm told she has no interest in film.

Patrick is passionate about the Borroro for more than academic reasons. He still regards himself as married to a Borroro woman even though he is not presently living with her. The union has apparently dissolved over his decision to live in France and hers to remain in Niger. They are both too much what they were born and bred. In a few hours he may come to know how her relatives have resolved his case. They are the ones who must deal with the fact of her having left Patrick, if they still regard the couple as having been joined in a real Borroro marriage. Sooner or later we will catch up with the lineage segment that includes his disputed wife. It might be interesting to film a confrontation between them. Patrick is making an appearance after an absence of a year and a half, an interval that may or may not be a critical factor in the love affairs of the Borroro. I really do not know. In any case, I suspect his wife will have

moved on in her connubial history. I wonder what difficulties this will entail for us. At the moment, I sense that Patrick has never before felt quite this kind of distress.

During our discussions, I have been struck by what I am told about the Borroro version of a theme of universal importance: tension between behavior controlled by values, rules, conventions, even complex taboos and behavior exempt from such constraints. Here, as elsewhere, it will be instructive to see what happens to the will when it is in conflict with a value system.

A Borroro does not appear to desire power unless it is sexual mastery nor does the society recognize differences in status except that between the young and the old. At least in the masculine world, one man is as good as another. All have the same amount of power and are equally Borroro. Being Borroro is what is important. That and, above all else, attaining what might be called Borroroness, a state that is measured in beauty, grace, and sexual fulfillment.

We covered another twenty miles by midday despite the broken leaf in the spring that Gerba is now trying to repair. Had we not had to stop, we might have reached the *groupement* we were pursuing.

Late in the day we paused again having seen some cattle and a few Borroro herdsmen in the distance. Earlier we had stopped for me to make some shots of rain I wanted in case there is none in the days and weeks ahead. I feel I need rain scenes such as drops hitting the dry earth, trite though the image might be. As it happened, the showers turned into a proper downpour and then into torrential sheets. All the rain scenes I could ever desire happened in a matter of minutes.

Patrick went ahead to speak with the people we had seen from a distance and came back with members of his family when the rain abated. He and they were delighted by the auspiciousness of the conditions under which we were meeting, the land reviving under prodigious rain.

Only five minutes later, Patrick's best friend, a man named Neli, stopped by. He had intended to be miles away but some sign or other had told him not to leave. Patrick and Neli had an intense greeting in which both were wreathed in smiles.

F6

F7

We went on and the rain stopped only to begin again. Everyone at the little Borroro camp came to greet us, having unpacked beds which is a large gesture of welcome. They also intend to kill a goat, if the rain will cooperate for its cooking. We will not stay here because this is not where the gathering, called a *warsau*, is to take place. But it will not be too far to the west and everyone will be there tomorrow. Patrick will spend the evening with his old friends and family and tell them his work is now with me and that he cannot go with them. This may be a good solution to some complex matters regarding feelings and relations between Patrick and his family. It might also help these same people in their relations with the larger group that they seem not to really want to join. I cannot quite make out what is happening but it is clear Patrick is in an ambiguous position with regard to his erstwhile kin.

The thunder rolls mightily in the west but the rain here is quite soft as the wind subsides and twilight fades rapidly in a turbulent sky. This land is extremely flat and the sun plummets beneath the encircling horizon with astonishing speed. I have never seen the sun move this fast in any other sky. Here sunsets are fleeting in their glory.

LOCALISATION

D1

F8

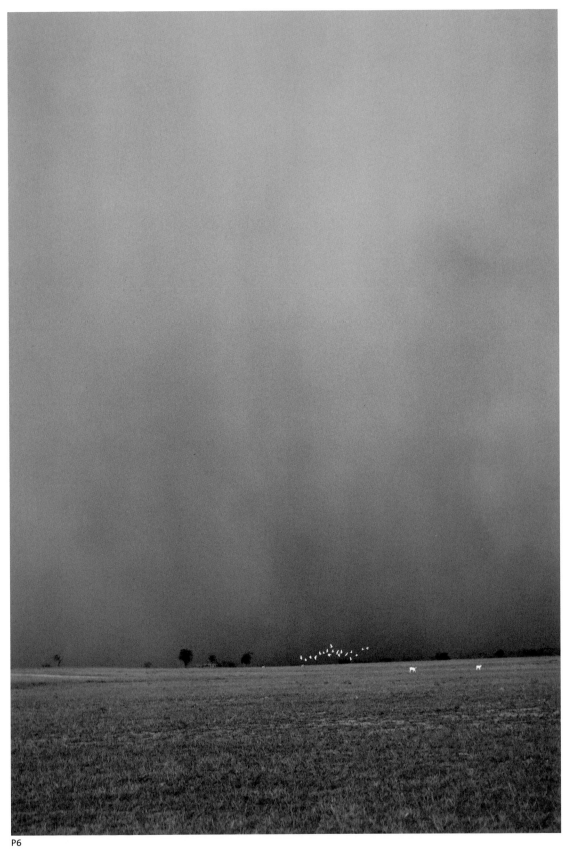

P6

August 21st 1978

It is late on a day in which we have moved only a few miles but during which our circumstances have undergone radical change. Yesterday we reached the small cattle camp of Patrick's in-laws. Today we have found the *warsau* of perhaps a thousand or more individuals belonging to related lineages. All of these people, together with many times that number of camels, cattle, sheep, and goats, are strung out in a north-south line. This arrangement has the surreal look of a small city without houses and only one street going nowhere. People walk on both the west and the east side of this line of temporary shelters and tethered beasts making gifts of meat that is being butchered up and down the line every hundred or so feet. The meat is for baptisms and weddings. This is the only time of the year when such celebrations are possible because it is only during the rains that this many people and their herds can coexist in such a limited space. Without the water that has collected in nearby basins, there would be no way for such numbers to stay together.

Everything must happen in the space of a few days before the *groupement* divides into small bands that then disperse throughout the countryside for another year.

P7

P8

190

P9

P10

P11

It is dark in my miniature tent owing to a faulty candle that has melted before it could be burned. Insects attack from the earth and sky and I am still removing hundreds of tiny burrs that are almost alive in their capacity to leap into promising openings. They are particularly fond of the insides of my pants.

Earlier, it was necessary to reerect my tent owing to a tempest that sprang up without warning in the middle of the afternoon. The little aluminum anchors tethering me to the earth were no match for the torrential rains. I long for release from this hideous confinement in which I feel so solitary and absurd. I am hobbled hand, foot, and mind. All activity is wearisome and possibly pointless. I say this as I listen to polyphonic singing accompanied by the intricate handclapping of the young who are impatient to begin the songs and dances of these long awaited days. In the background is the interminable groaning of animals.

I think about the problems ahead filming these Borroro who are smitten by modernity while still observing tradition. They wear cheap and gaudy rags, sporty sunglasses, costume jewelry, faceless wristwatches, and a tawdry collection of other cast-off junk. At the same time, they are extremely conservative followers of tribal truths and willing participants in a remarkably unenlightened social contract. I wish I could disregard the lurid clothing and trinkets that distract me. I wonder how important all this really is and whether or not I may just be wishing for a vanished state of being.

P12

P13

P14

P15

the impulse to preserve

August 22nd 1978

Almost simultaneously, my recently acquired Arri SR, with which I had hoped to film the Borroro, and Fulton's Bolex failed. The SR is beyond repair but the Bolex will survive. The SR's motor has apparently seized owing to some as yet undetermined electrical fault and the Bolex has a broken rewind handle. I am now obliged to use Fulton's NPR, a backup camera with which I have almost no experience. The few times I have used one, I felt awkward and unsteady, as though I was falling forward into a chasm that kept opening in front of me. I hope I can get on better terms with it soon enough to do the filmmaking I had in mind. I am not ready to let Fulton take on the major image making because I would not know what to do myself and because I am sure I would be telling him what he should be doing, which is not what camera people want to hear.

The *warsau* gathering of many clans seems to be dragging a bit with people arriving and leaving somewhat chaotically. There may be an orderliness I have no way of discerning. I am reminded of an enormous terminal where hundreds of passengers have come with all their belongings and are waiting for the next bus. But here there are not just throngs of people but also thousands of animals including a few rare horses belonging to the richer elders.

Late this afternoon some young men and women went to what is called the *daddo* which is, I think, both a place and an idea. The place is a convenient dance ground and the idea is of a social group composed of unmarried youth. Today the *daddo* is nearby and what they are doing is dancing and singing. They do more but I have yet to learn precisely what that might be. The sky has been threatening all day. Usually it is mid-afternoon when the rainstorm arrives. Today one came in the form of fine dust blown by impressive gales. This is a formidably inclement place.

August 23rd 1978

We stopped momentarily this afternoon to discuss in which direction to go. We were trying to find the camp of a man who is presently accompanying us. His family went off without him and no one is sure where they have gone. What we did know was

P16

that we had gotten to a place called Tadabuk where the camp existed earlier and where we were ourselves three days ago but now no one wants to remain. There is only some smoke from recent fires, not a single person.

A camel with an injured foot is here and the thinking is its owners would not have gone too far away. The man who came with us, who is something of a headman, has been sleeping happily in the Landrover but now has left it to look for signs that could tell him where his subjects might have gone.

The day has been extremely hot and oppressive. There was a little dancing in the morning but virtually none last night. All I have done is to make a few Polaroid SX-70 portraits of the younger males. A Polaroid made is most likely a photograph lost, so intent are the subjects on possessing them. I had the idea of doing a series on the male dancers to see if there was any agreement about what set of facial features defined the ideal Borroro. But I have been unable to keep more than a few of the many I have made. Doing this has also created a sideshow that is hard to manage and doesn't make for much good will. After a few hours, I was worn down by hundreds of pushing and shoving Borroro egotists entreating me to take their picture. I also realized I had not eaten for a long time. It sometimes feels as though I have not eaten since I left Cambridge.

P17

P19

P18

P20

P21

P23

P22

P24

P25

August 24th 1978

Around noontime yesterday I decided to return to 'Nwagga about thirty miles to the south where there is a water pump and an Arab who sells sugar, salt, and even sardines. The Landrover will continue south to Abalak and retrieve our off-loaded baggage along with the drum of gasoline.

The Borroro are now hiving off from the *warsau*. By midday yesterday there were hardly any remaining. They drifted away all afternoon in all directions. We may meet some of them again at other gatherings including the *gerewol* that I'm told has already started. Where it is to take place is the subject of endless discussions between lineage heads, four of whom are still in what is called the "big house." They are likely deciding matters such as which lineage is needed to support the one challenged, or the one attacked. The attacked lineage is responsible for the provisioning of the attackers. Here it has occurred to me are some echoes of Northwest Coast potlatching where hosts outdo guests with displays of largesse.

At 'Nwagga the idea is to refit ourselves to the extent possible and to keep watch as things develop. We will wash clothes, fill jerry cans with potable water, and find the man we had with us yesterday and make him a hostage in our intentions to attend the *gerewol*. Despite the tragedy of the Arri camera, I mean to do my best with what we have. There is also a question of how much energy remains. Maybe this brief respite will help.

All day we have been luxuriating in an abundance of decent water and have managed to put away gallons of it, mostly as tea and coffee. We have also been busy with household matters like washing clothes, cleaning equipment, boiling water, and buying sugar.

I have wondered about survival in a place like the Sahel where heat, dust, insects, thorns, burrs, and a thousand other noxious elements give no quarter. My remedy is to seek rest and quiet, even sleep. But whenever I lie down it becomes progressively more difficult to become active once again. The will is sapped and the mind begins to wander. I find that I am hungry without knowing it, dirty without caring. Even the Borroro say you have to be crazy to live in this landscape of agonies.

We stopped again at the campground where we have already been, lucky to be here before darkness descends. The tents went up, the cooking gear was brought out and our few belongings were mobilized for the night. We hope to leave tomorrow with our new friend who prefers the Landrover to his injured camel for getting to the *gerewol* where he believes his lineage will be found.

August 25th 1978

Sleeping was fitful on hard ground radiating yesterday's solar energy through a thin straw mat. It is three hours since my eyes first opened. We wait disconsolate about almost everything including a breakfast of hard bread from Abalak, a boiled egg from 'Nwagga, and Nescafé made with milk donated by the Borroro camped nearby. We are waiting for our lineage elder who has taken enthusiastically to the world of instant coffee and lumps of sugar. We hope he will guide us to the *gerewol* but no one knows where it is. Vague indications suggest the event may be within thirty miles of our present position but I sense there are other possibilities and that there is no fixed location for this occasion in which so much depends on sufficient water and grazing.

Our own situation in these respects looks bleaker all the time. We have already consumed one of four jerry cans of drinkable water. Gerba, our driver, whom I have converted into a cook, is unable to think ahead. He reasons that we are rich in water because one day is the longest span of time he can imagine. Often he calculates in units no longer than afternoons or mornings. If we stay much longer, we will stop all washing, curtail drinking, and start using the nearby, knee-deep and pestilential pond as a source.

P26

P27

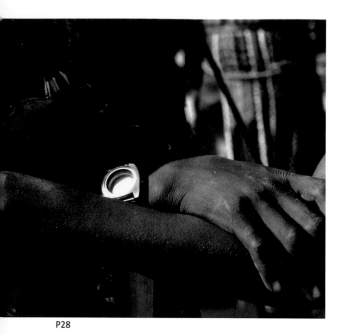

P28

He began to ask more and more frequently what we saw in the ever-enlarging landscape of our widening search. It took until mid-afternoon to finally glimpse across this vast and featureless plain the camels and small houses of the attacking group. We had found the *gerewol* which, it turned out, was already in its fifth day.

Since arriving at this event, I have been thinking of myself as part of a primordial play that is taking place in the largest and most desolate theater in the world. In fact, I am but one organism among a multitude of creatures sleeping, eating, shitting, drinking, dancing, fornicating, and singing here on the desert's implacable floor. It is a spectacular assembly, a congregation of the faithful sparing nothing as they celebrate their self-regard. Last night singing filled the cathedral of cooling stars as I drifted from sleep to astonished waking and back again to sleep on successive waves of dirging male voices.

During the day I grope among thorns, scorpions, ants, beetles, and biting flies for drink or food or a place to rest. I am oppressed by the weight of my equipment and my ignorance. The Borroro sing and dance all day, all night. Inexhaustible squads of young men and women seem never to falter. All participate and are impassioned, even exalted. They wear watches with hands that literally do not move; all is suspended while this spectacle unfolds.

Gerba, the driver, is starting to crack amid what to him is simply primitive madness. He is huge, soft, and very black. He craves the Fulani girls and is crazed by desire. They are repulsed by his attentions and flaunt their abhorrence. He blames us for his loss of charm and wonders what could have persuaded him to participate in such an undertaking in the first place. The Sahel enrages him and he quakes with anger and fear. He also refuses to do what he is asked and threatens to set out for Niamey. I think he is close to panic. Maybe I should send him to 'Ngall, thirty miles to the north and east. We badly need water, sugar, and tinned fruit, but especially water for which there is a pump at 'Ngall. The water there is salty but not diluted mud as it is here at the place where "camels wallow."

August 26th 1978

Following considerable wandering, we arrived at the *gerewol* location, Talmazaalam, around noon yesterday. We struck our camp at Tadabuk early in the morning but then waited at least an hour for our Borroro elder to ready himself for departure on what became the hottest day so far. When our guide/companion of the lame camel and attacked lineage took his accustomed seat in the Landrover, we hoped he knew in what direction to go. He pointed north and we set out.

When we reached the indicated destination, where the *gerewol* was meant to be, we found only the most convincing emptiness consisting of an immensity of heat and silence. There were not even the flies that follow the herds so ardently, or the ticks that feast on the camels. So we left to look elsewhere and before long detected a lone man walking in the distance. Our elegant guide could not see him but we came closer and asked this solitary traveler where we should go.

Of course, the stranger knew nothing and I began to suspect our traveling companion of ulterior motives though none of us could think what they could possibly be. Might he be hiding the fact that he could not see or that he was doing what he could to keep us at a distance from Borroro ceremonies?

August 27th 1978

More than one dance style is performed during the daylight hours. I have seen mostly what is called *rumi*, a circle of men maintaining a regular beat for great lengths of time while clapping and singing as they shuffle forward and backward. I have not learned the significance of this dance but mean to find it out whenever I can. Patrick is more and more isolated and subdued. I am afraid he has been drinking too much unboiled water in his efforts to deny he is not a Borroro.

There is another dance called *yaki* but I have not seen it because the *rumi* is getting almost all the performance time. The *gerewol*, which includes the dancing of aspiring young men who perform in a sort of contest, is supposed to turn so that the attacking lineage that has been dancing during the day facing the sun gives way to the defending lineage that dances at night looking toward the moon. There is a certain amount of malice and much mischief on the minds of the attackers. Of all this, I remain in considerable ignorance and it is hard to get any information owing to general confusion and to Patrick's unresolved role in what is happening.

P29

P30

P32

P31

F8

Gerba has gone to 'Ngall with Patrick for the supplies we so badly need. He is getting more and more irrational and I am not sure what the result will be of them both away. I hope I have persuaded Gerba to bring the bag of millet, so much needed by the Borroro. They, too, are almost out of food and a *gerewol* cannot proceed on empty stomachs. Gerba said at first he would not do this because he did not intend to do anything for the unappreciative Borroro. The Landrover should be back by nightfall and, if it is not, we can make do with our remaining three gallons of water for another twenty-four hours.

Fulton and I were on our way to the *daddo* (the site of the *gerewol*) at a moment when an exceptional light was illuminating an extraordinary scene. I wanted to film the dancing but felt unequal to the task partly through a continuing awkwardness using a strange camera and partly because of the enormity of the splendor of what I was watching. As the light died, the film in the camera expired. The dancing ended with a young girl pointing to the chosen male, called the bull. There were only one or two feet of film, a few seconds worth, remaining when I stopped just as the maiden reached her arm toward the winner. I can only hope there is to be another *gerewol*.

We are plagued by various system failures. Yesterday it was one of the two Nikons, which now will operate using only one shutter speed. I can't remember ever having quite so much technical difficulty.

The Landrover is back.

August 28th 1978

It is mid-morning and all of us, indigenes and interlopers, are recovering from a tempest that struck last night. My pathetic tent is presently perched on the lip of the small pond to which everyone comes for water or to bathe and that with this storm has grown much larger and come much closer. Storms of the kind that fell on us last night are frequent and are usually preceded by gathering winds and spectacular lightning. Last night everything came with such sudden fury that we could scarcely respond. I managed to get inside the tent as the first drops were falling but there was no time to see if it was fastened to the ground. It may not have mattered since the ground quickly turned to mud causing one end of the tent to collapse on my face. The night was long and noisy with men and beasts all seeking shelter from the wind and rain.

Today there has been talk of a sacrifice, a bull I would suppose. If this occurs, the *gerewol* will turn and the attackers will dance all night. It may all be over more quickly than I had thought. If it is, we will go sooner than planned to 'Nwagga for the rest we need before the next *gerewol* reportedly set to begin Friday.

August 29th 1978

A few hours following my last entry in this disjointed account of life among the Borroro, another storm began. It soon became a deluge that nearly drowned us all. My perch on the edge of the watering hole was close to the center of it by mid-afternoon and the entire inventory of my belongings was afloat. There is a special misery in wetness of this kind.

It is also taxing to find oneself submerged in excrement, an inevitability given so much shitting in one place by so many animals for such a long time. An additional menace was the innumerable insects and other beasts caught unprepared for the inundation. Suddenly at sea, they jumped on us hoping we could save them from a watery end. I did not care as much about hopping and spidery things as I did about anything swimming or crawling as I went, barefooted, looking for my clothes, food, film, and cameras.

We had to move and doing so caused us to expend what little energy we had husbanded for last night's final ceremony. But we managed to relocate out on the open plain where there are no trees and therefore no shade. What trees there might once have been were long ago gnawed to the ground by those in need of firewood.

I was up early hoping to rouse Fulton and film the transition to dawn. The undertaking actually went better than last night's turning of the dance from sun to moon, from west to east. The sun rose with conviction and the dancing was powerful. I was beginning to sense what would happen next and was able to get there in time to film it. This particular *gaynka*, as the whole event is called, has begun to accelerate or maybe to collapse in on itself. There is some talk of the attacking lineage not acquitting itself particularly well, not enough good dancers or good dancing, too much lying around to please the elders. The present phase was meant to end on Wednesday but will wind up today following some farewell ceremonies. It was as hot as I remember Africa getting, even in the Dallol Depression in northeastern Ethiopia where travelers have claimed to endure more than 150 degrees Fahrenheit, and by late afternoon I had lost all will to act. What is next is all I could think to ask.

I tried to write to combat the feeling that everything had become meaningless. Around sunset I looked at the northern horizon and watched as blackness once more filled the sky and wondered if we would have another African tempest. The answer was not long in coming. High winds soon were dismantling our living arrangements. The Sahel was on a rampage and for two hours we were punished by dust, dirt, wind, and rain. In the end, I could do nothing except lie back and ponder my insignificance.

August 30th 1978

The night has ended but not its sequelae of disarray and defeat. Black flies are swarming in unnatural abundance and the Borroro wander listlessly through our camp asking for medicine, clothes, and food. The absurd elder who has been with us all this time slurps coffee at my elbow and I want to hammer him into silence. The sun grows hotter by the instant and I have an awful feeling we are trapped forever in this encampment of despair.

P33

P34

I reel from thorn bush to thorn bush, plucking off burrs and burrowing insects. I marvel at the abundance of infelicity at every turn. But the Borroro are unfazed and quite able to keep dancing, singing, and talking as if it is their last chance before beginning another season of lonely wandering in the desert. They also are full of fears and anxieties that must surely have to do with the complex rules governing their conduct. Taboos, strictures, and sanctions abound and narrowly limit their choices. Personal liberty can find few avenues for expression under such circumstances.

Patrick has spoken about a variety of customs regarding sexual matters. When he had a Borroro wife, for example, he had to accept the requirement of sharing access to her with others. The rule is that a man must allow other men of a particular age to enjoy his wife as a sexual partner. This conduct may be as much about privilege as anything else. What is important are not erotic achievements but the abject submission of women to men. Patrick's wife was required by custom to enter into an unwritten contract of sexual service at least until the birth of her first child, a child that would begin life with ambiguous paternity.

August 31st 1978

We have returned to 'Nwagga, having left the *gerewol* encampment yesterday afternoon. All of our defender acquaintances were themselves leaving for their own camps to attend a gathering arranged by the government or to attend another attack in the northeast, closer to 'Ngall.

I am not at all sorry to have left the tempest, torment, and festivity of the *gerewol* site. While the event had its high and low moments, nothing was deficient in intensity. I had thought a week ago this would have been an appropriate warm-up for a proper *gaynka* but I am no longer so sure I want to participate in another such experience anytime soon.

A week or more has passed since we were last at this little oasis where there are no palm trees but permanent water, which means a few thorn trees have grown tall enough to provide shade. 'Nwagga is quiet for the reason there is no market, only one trader who has nothing more than *pain de sucre*, some dates and, occasionally, rice. As it is the rainy season, there are no visiting herds looking for water. They are out on the plain drinking at the many ponds that dot the landscape.

We are able to bathe, eat eggs and even an emaciated chicken while a few Tuareg children make tips by washing our clothes. From here we will go south on the theory that our dwindling supplies, particularly of gasoline, can do us more good there than in the north where there is no gasoline except what we take with us. Going south will provide an operating radius of about 300 miles. I did remember to leave fifteen gallons in Abalak which guarantees our reaching Tahoua, if things are tight.

In Abalak we can get adequate water and even some acceptable bread. From Abalak we will be able to range 250 miles in search of a rainy-season camp where I hope to start filming the nonceremonial part of Borroro life. What I have done so far may easily be enough to cover the celebratory aspect of the rainy season but I have gotten almost nowhere with quotidian life.

I plan to leave in the early morning so as to reach Abalak by noon when there will be a market to which, I am hoping, some Borroro will come and tell us where to find what we are looking for.

September 1st 1978

For hours during the night, insects tried to reach me through my less than impervious tent. They tugged at the netting, burrowed from beneath the nylon flooring and wiggled through any crack they could find. They easily succeeded in waking me from troubled dreaming.

We arrived in Abalak at midday, and it has the same flat emptiness I remember from our previous visits. There is the drone of countless cicadas, women slamming huge pestles into wooden mortars and, in the air, endless dust. The single eating place has little to offer except the occasional Niger soda. We will stay as long as it takes to find someone who can lead us to a rainy-season camp. I keep thinking of the more memorable images from the ceremonial life we have left behind, such as dancers' tied-together legs and other expressive gestures. I long to see something other than ritual.

P35

P36

Many rules govern Borroro lives but maybe it's the same everywhere. The regulations just aren't as vividly expressed as they are here. I'm struck by the ambiguity in the notion of nomad as a prisoner of conventions and strictures. I have always been taken by ideas that arise from conceptual pairings: individual and society, will and custom, freedom and constraint. The Borroro have shown me how much of their behavior is controlled by rules and how their private thoughts are filled with feelings of ambition, self-regard, and especially envy.

We will remain tonight on the north side of the town. The Borroro have demonstrated what it means to be a practicing nomad but I am not hopeful a constant change of address will provide any benefit whatever to my state of mind.

September 2nd 1978

We departed Abalak in the late morning in hopes of finding the camps of the Gojankoi clan off to the north between Alambaton and Bonkar. After scouring the intervening plain, we eventually reached the camp of an important leader of this lineage. What greeted the eye was a dismaying confection of cultural materials starting with Tuareg tents and ending with heaps of castaway Western apparel and other miscellaneous merchandise. I can't remember ever seeing so squalid an assortment of material objects.

What we have come upon is the handwriting of change written large, but I find myself not even interested enough in it as phenomenon to get out a camera. If this is the ordinary life I am searching for, it is one that leaves me in irremediably dismal spirits. In the face of this kind of change, I can think of no response other than retreat.

September 3rd 1978

Before beginning another day, I tried to record on camera how I felt about what I stumbled across yesterday. Fulton did his best to capture my indignation and sadness at finding the Borroro in their present state. No doubt what I said was put in too lofty language and betrayed my selfish indignation at having been beguiled into coming all this way to experience melancholy. It was an attempt though and I may try again before leaving for good.

We have come to the desolation of a place called Chintabaradan to gather information about the Borroro of this more southern region. The area is new to Patrick and this tends to deepen his already depressed mood. Each day he withdraws a little more, undertakes a little less and sleeps a little longer. To all questions he now answers, "*Je ne sais pas.*" I left him for the afternoon and evening in the town while Fulton and I retreated to its edge where there is a tree to sit under and where we could think and talk.

We are two days from Niamey, perhaps three. Three more days to clear Niamey for Paris or the U.S. and I could be home by the middle of the month. It remains to be seen what I can accomplish by remaining in the Sahel.

September 4th 1978

Patrick has been asked to find what information he can about any *gerewol* activity in our vicinity. He can do this quite easily by frequenting places where the Borroro come to transact their business in the market. I have decided to abandon the idea of finding a rainy-season camp and, instead, to look for yet more ceremonial life and make that the focus of our attention.

The Landrover has gone to Tahoua for fuel that will be needed should we learn of a place where there is *gerewol*.

Patrick, Fulton, and I are the only ones in a small mud house we have found to protect us from further ravages of Nature. More will be known in forty-eight or seventy-two hours. Meanwhile, a kingdom of flies, filth, heat, and frustration reigns triumphant.

P37

September 5th 1978

Some curious muscular collapse last evening has nearly made an invalid of me so the urge to urinate led to an almost unmanageable task. It had to be done under a brutal sun some place where I could squat in deference to local assumptions that only beasts stand to pee.

I hoped that by surviving the afternoon and night, things might change, that I would be better or worse, stronger or weaker. It is morning now and the pain has departed.

The Landrover by now is hopefully in Tahoua getting what we need to resume work. Meanwhile, we remain in Chintabaradan to enjoy our isolation from everything but the elements. I am waiting for news of the Borroro. The Gojankoi and Japtui are two lineages well represented hereabouts and their leaders are keeping Patrick informed, or so I'm led to believe. It appears that one of these groups will attack and thereby precipitate a new round of *gaynka*.

September 6th 1978

With a shift of the wind from the northeast, we who have remained inside the walls of our house of mud have been treated to a peculiarly African smell. It happens when locusts have leapt across the continent from somewhere in the Horn and landed ecstatically in the shallow ponds left by recent rains in this and countless other neighborhoods. In no time, the locusts drown, corrupt, and then offend the surrounding air.

P38

Nothing has been heard of a *gerewol* but I mean to be patient a few more days.

September 7th 1978

Frustration mounts in the prolonged absence of news that might improve our circumstances. I feel trapped once again but realize it is by choice. I consider this forsaken outpost of nowhere and see that everyone else is trapped too and I wonder what it really means to be free. It may mean no more than having the choice of imprisonments.

I have sent Patrick in the Landrover to look around to the northeast in hopes of discovering a Borroro gathering. He departed without much enthusiasm this morning and will return either tonight or tomorrow morning. Fulton and I grow extremely weary of our four walls, the blowing dust, and the buzzing flies. Our intention is to abandon this site, especially if Patrick comes back with a promising lead.

Our spirits are severely eroded by circumstances that have been anything but cooperative. I realize that Patrick, who was to be our bridge to the Borroro, has been shaky from the start. The issue is his health, both physical and mental, I am afraid. Our own bodies have fared better than his only because we have not pretended to be natives. Patrick has not really known who or where he is but has mistakenly assumed he could exist in two worlds simultaneously. Telling moments are when he is listening to Bob Dylan as he drinks unboiled water in the shade of the Landrover.

My thoughts occasionally turn to the meaning of what I am trying to get from this experience. There appears to be less and less possibility of finding a transfiguring metaphor to redeem what I think is so deplorable not just about local circumstances but those of a struggling continent. I also question whether there is any reason to make a film in the manner I have made them until now.

September 8th 1978

We have waited all day for the Landrover that should have returned by now. Could Patrick have found a *gerewol*? This is one of the two likely explanations for the delay in his return. The other is a mechanical problem, something that would not in the least surprise me.

P39

September 9th 1978

The Landrover and the news of a relatively nearby *gerewol* arrived in the late morning. I feel we must seize this opportunity. Our seven-day purgatory was meant to end in being awarded another chance and that is what seems to have happened. Although we are weaker and more dispirited, even Fulton agrees we should try again. The prospect of being able to board the Air Afrique flight from Niamey only ten days hence plays a part in my willingness to return to the fray.

Patrick rested while Fulton and I pulled things together in order to leave as soon as possible. As a parting shot, the weather demons arranged a brutal sandstorm in the midst of our preparations bringing this wretched place to its knees. We have finished the token whiskey and Perrier so long husbanded and now contemplate a future seriously devoid of provisions beyond our regular fare of sardines, condensed milk, Nescafé, and noodles. We will set forth in an hour for another spate of thorn-strewn days at the mercy of whatever gods punish filmmakers.

Fulton's camera is still running but is being powered by the last of our batteries, two of which I have linked in series for lack of sufficient power in one to drive our dwindling supply of raw stock. I am happy to be at last moving, though I wonder what impels me onward other than fatal restlessness.

September 10th 1978

We are in the camp of a leader of a Degerewol lineage that is under *gaynka* attack by a Gojankoi clan. It is the forenoon and we are waiting to hear where the busier aspects of the ceremony just starting will be located. We are fortunate to be here this early. We left Chintabaradan mid-afternoon yesterday right after the dust and sandstorm that swept through as we were preparing to depart. We made slow progress eastward along a track soaked by rain falling behind a curtain of sand. At the place where we left the track to cross the dunes, it was already growing dark. Between the low dunes ran shallow corridors of sand and sometimes deep mud formed by the water that has not yet seeped into the ground.

In an incautious attempt to cross one of these *couloirs*, the Landrover groaned wearily and sank to its springs in the soft terrain. Everything had to be removed before the digging could begin. But the digging and the pushing were to no avail. So we ate and slept fitfully through a night of light rain and steady wind.

At daybreak, I was up encouraging a reluctant fire, rousing the others and pondering how to extricate ourselves. By late afternoon we were finally able to free the vehicle and leave for the place where our little adopted group had decided they would wait for us. We followed them in a westerly direction to the edge of a large pond near which I suspect the *gerewol* will be located. Numerous herds of cattle, sheep, and goats have converged from every quarter indicating word had been passed to all concerned, both attackers and defenders.

P40

September 11th 1978

It is mid-morning and we have yet to recover from another storm. Shortly after midnight the heavens cracked and gave vent to a rage I never imagined possible, though there was some meager warning in yesterday's afternoon sky where, off to the east, vast cumuli were building on a blackening horizon. Later, when the heralding wind began, there was no question about the intensity of what would follow.

Long after darkness had fallen, the Gojankoi attackers were at the dance ground as expected, even with a sky at its most menacing. There were eighteen dancers by then, which is a respectable number on the first night and in light of what was about to descend upon us all. I went despite knowing the dancing would be abbreviated owing to the fact no one wants to perform in the rain.

The dancing lasted almost two hours under a three-quarter moon and in front of an immense fire. The spectators were not great in numbers but they were full of enthusiasm. At one point, an elder asked that the maidens who choose the bull be summoned so the ceremony could be completed while everyone was dry. An old lady, privileged by age, told him she thought there might be a wild pig dancing, which is a terrible insult, and that the best thing was to keep going and everyone should just be quiet. Around midnight the girls did come and one of them made her shy choice with a graceful, upward swing of an arm that off-handedly indicated the bull, chosen I suspect, not by the young maiden, but by old men who determine such matters.

The *gerewol* dancing was over and I got back to my little tent and was asleep moments before the wind shook me awake. I had to shade my eyes from the flashes of continuous lightning. Before long the wind had toppled the tent and threatened to hurl me across the dunes. Instead, I was plastered to the muck forming around me on all sides. The storm was over in a few hours and, content to be soaked by the first clean water I have tasted in days, I regained sleep.

September 12th 1978

I think often about being hobbled because it is a condition I see on all sides, not just of animals but humans as well, myself included. Restraints are everywhere in the form of ropes tying together forelegs of camels and belts tied around dancers' legs just above their knees. Then also there are the rules of conduct dictating what can be said, or done, or eaten, and almost everything else. We all are imprisoned by culture, one way or another.

I think, too, about the loss on the first day of my camera. I am not yet, nor will I ever be, comfortable with Fulton's. It is not a part of me in the way my Arriflex cameras were in New Guinea or in Ethiopia. I continue to trip and stumble instead of gliding quietly and smoothly in pursuit of elusive images. It has also not been possible to use Fulton as a surrogate operator. Although he knows his Eclair intimately, he cannot be inside my head. He has the Bolex, though, and there have been times when I was sure he was getting what I wanted. I keep hoping to persuade him to look for the meaning in gestures and not be content with optical allure alone.

September 13th 1978

It is the fourth day and I cannot help wondering why I feel so besieged. How often is there an opportunity to witness a spectacle like *gerewol* against a backdrop of elemental nature such as at this moment in this place hundreds of miles from anywhere? Almost never, I would think. So my disquiet may demonstrate that ordinary expectations limit one's wider prospects.

Last night the Japtoen lineage was to dance its first *gerewol* of this *gaynka*. I sat in the moonlight until the dancing began at midnight. From time to time, I wandered about to watch the dancers putting on elaborate makeup by the light of the moon. Despite a great weariness from endless spectacle, what I saw got my full attention: accomplished males applying rouge and lipstick under a full moon in preparation for a contest to decide which of them was perfect, the bull of choice.

The dancing was strong and disciplined. I stayed until early morning with the idea of returning later to film more with two small lights I had brought for such purposes. Unhappily, there is as yet no color film sensitive enough to expose properly with the light available from the moon and a fire in front of dancers.

It looks now as though this *gaynka* will continue through Sunday. Can I?

P41

P42

P43

P44

September 14th 1978

The *gaynka*, presently unfolding, is growing rapidly in numbers and energy. Although the defenders seem not to have been well supported by members of their own lineages, the attackers have been generously augmented by theirs. So many, in fact, have arrived that the attackers have fielded up to thirty superb performers just for the afternoon dances. At this point it is clear the right decision was made to wait out those limbo-like days in Chintabaradan. The filming is far more productive here than it has been up until now, partly perhaps for the reason that I know a little better what will happen next. I also have developed a few thematic ideas that might give this work some coherence. I find myself thinking about specific forms and of an overall shape those forms might take. Maybe it is not impossible to make this film after all.

The idea of a "deep heart" has been intriguing me since I first heard of it from Patrick. As far as I can tell, the construct is of central importance in that it makes possible for Borroro males to hide their deepest and most private feelings from each other and from public scrutiny. (I have not yet learned whether women have their own deep hearts.) Males appear to live in such an exaggerated state of mutual envy and suspicion that, were they to reveal their true feelings to each other, there might be violent consequences. By hiding their feelings within deep hearts, the Borroro can at least pretend not to harbor them at all. Of course, they would be doing this knowing that everyone else was doing it too.

Much of Borroro interpersonal life is likely contained in words chosen to keep others from knowing what lies at the bottom of one's heart. Mistrust and suspicion must be inevitable in a compact of this kind in which no one takes other persons at their literal word.

Whatever else human nature might be, it will surely include some tendency to hide strong and troubling feelings. What interests me about the Borroro is that envy has such a grip on their psychic makeup. Still, it is said there are relationships based on trust and forthrightness. They appear to be most common between members of the opposite sex where kinship forbids any element of sexuality. I have heard that these pairings often have a great beauty and depth of sincerity.

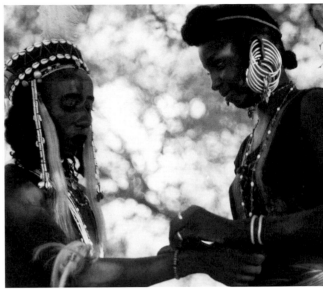

P45

The Borroro fear others' eyes and mouth. The mouth because it can impart malediction as well as benediction. They say, "the mouth can eat you," whereas eyes are instruments of envy. Flocks and whole herds can be spoiled by looks but mouths are still more dangerous. Greetings, which are ritually extended, are really incantations that nullify the potential dangers of mouths. The maidens who choose the bulls are fearful of eyes, of the looks of other girls whom they say "eat or suck" them with their eyes. The one who is the best liar is the one who wins. The best liar is said to chase the other person away.

In the *gerewol* there is no room for personal or romantic notions; it is principally social in significance. No connection exists between virility and being a bull, although women sometimes come to one for a child. Between men who know they might be selected as the bull there is intense competition and it is good to be selected even though the status confers no privileges. Still, people will recognize that you are a bull and will remark on it. *Gerewol* is an affirmation of primordial Borroro characteristics and the bull is also and in part the result of a harmony brought about by charms and ritual knowledge. A bull must have beauty but must also be protected by magic. Sometimes there are dry bulls, ones without seductive powers.

213

P46

September 15th 1978

Since midnight I have been listening to the wind
and thunder that have brought a threatening sky to
the start of another day of *gerewol*. The Japtoen
danced despite the prospect of rain and I watched
at the height of their performance having been
roused by wind battering my improbable shelter.

It was a surreal assembly of painted and cos-
tumed dancers swaying in front of a fire that sent
clouds of embers and sparks across the desert floor.
The sound of dancer's leg rattles and chorused
voices were alternately swallowed and amplified by
the gathering winds. It was a contest between men
and the elements, something I have witnessed often
since coming to the Sahel. It would not have taken
much for Nature to hurl us all to the furthest horizon, which prompts me to think if but one of the
legion puzzled by Kurtz's dying words in the *Heart
of Darkness* had been in this Africa for the last
twenty-four hours they would at once know the
meaning of: "The horror, the horror."

All morning I waited for the light to appear
but it never came. It was strange to be here and
not to see the sun at all. I took it as an omen that
we should leave and so we did.

We were again in Chintabaradan in a matter
of a few hours. By evening we were in Tahoua,
not far from Niamey. Our departure was abrupt. I
am sure I would have prolonged this journey had
circumstances been better and if, even more

importantly, there was some way to attach ourselves to a band who, like ourselves, were also tran-
sients on a longer journey. We left today and by
now the Borroro will be gone themselves. I would
like to have left in their company but that has not
been possible given our physical condition. Poor
Patrick looks more and more stricken. I am afraid it
will take many weeks for him to recover his health
sufficiently to pursue his search for his own identity
and the world of his adopted Borroro.

September 16th 1978

The *campement* in Tahoua is a near ruin that in
better days provided the French Foreign Legion
with an opportunity for rest and recreation. There
is even a crumbling cement tennis court surrounded by fallen Moorish arches. All that remains
of the colonial life is a bar whose patrons may
never have noticed a change in rulers. Men came
last night in a steady stream for their beer and
whiskey only to disappear into the night. The
restaurant menu boasted stools as one of its
entrées, an attempt to render stews in English.
What we ate was scarcely edible and the evening
ended early. There was little possibility of rest
much less recreation given the determination of
insects and rodents living on wayfarers such as
ourselves. I saw no other guests.

At dawn following a sleepless night, I was in
the courtyard amid the debris of last night's drunk-
enness. The hotel workforce was asleep, covered by
blankets and getting what rest they could. It was
noticeably cool when I awakened my companions
and someone to take action in the kitchen. Soon
we were eating bread, drinking inevitable Nescafé
and wanting Tahoua behind us. I am covered with
the unmistakable lumps bestowed by bed bugs. The
itching is astonishingly intense.

Before leaving for Niamey, we stopped at the
Catholic Sisters where our stored goods were
retrieved, including my malfunctioning camera and
exhausted batteries. The Landrover is full but somehow lighter than when we journeyed to the Borroro.

I feel strangely incomplete and filled by a
vague sadness on leaving even though I am not
sure what it is I would do were I to stay. This
sojourn is over and I don't know what it is that
has ended.

F1

F2

ika hands

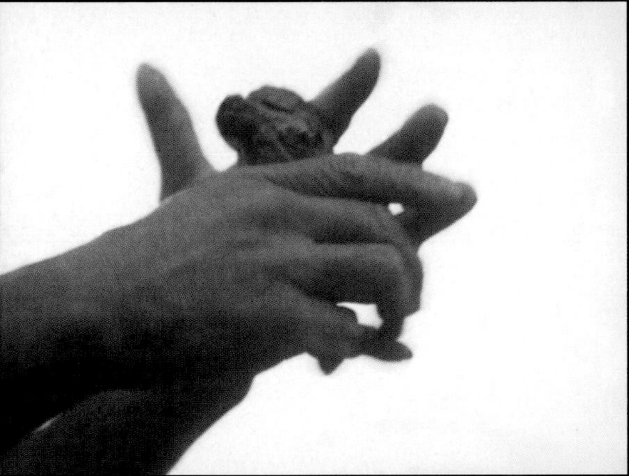

F3

The entries that follow are taken from journals kept with all too slender resolve during 1980 and 1981. They describe my experiences filming a Mayan Indian remnant called Ika who live in the Sierra Nevadas of northeastern Colombia. This work resulted in a film I gave the title *Ika Hands* because of the myriad uses the Ika make of this defining human attribute.

Bogotá, Colombia, November 15th 1980

I know of no major film about what was once a large number of remarkable Amerindian societies both in North and South America including the Hopi, Navaho, or any other of the hundreds of vital and complex cultures that survived well into the age of motion pictures, in fact into the time when Indians became fixtures in one of cinema's most successful genres.

A substantial nonfiction film might have been made had Robert Flaherty been able to do his American Indian project. I remember his widow saying how close they had come only to see the venture die for want of funding. Many years ago I saw a film called *The Silent Enemy* about a Northern Plains group that hunted caribou. It had a few memorable moments but suffered from dramatic pretensions. The Edward Curtis film about Indians of the Northwest Coast is fatally marred by artifice.

Further thinking about the lack of such a film resumed a few years ago when Gerardo Reichel Dolmatoff, the Austro-Colombian anthropologist, got my attention with his book about the Kogi, a Mayan-related people living high in the incomparable Sierra Nevadas of northern Colombia. I was enthralled by his account of young men being trained to be shamans. I wondered, if I could witness that process, whether I might gain entry into an authentic shamanic world and fulfill a filmmaking dream I had for a long time entertained.

On a preliminary visit to Colombia I had met someone in the Institute of Indian Affairs named Yezid Campos. He agreed to serve as a translator and facilitator should I return to undertake a film. He and others made it clear that the Kogi are unapproachable but that if I went to live with another group, the Ika, I would find something very much along the Kogi lines. Yezid is devoted to the Ika and eager to improve his skills and understanding of filmmaking. He can't get those skills in Colombia, and so my coming presented an opportunity which he, with some reluctance, has decided to take. He is wary of *norteamericano* involvement in his country's indigenous affairs, but he found a way to set those misgivings aside.

Yezid met me at the Bogotá airport and we immediately began a conversation about what lay ahead. Genoveve, his fiancée, speaks almost faultless English and is a great help, considering my Spanish has never been conversational. They both were genial and intent on going ahead with the idea of a film about the Arhuaco, as the Ika are sometimes called. We will leave for Valledupar soon. From there it is a day's Jeep ride to San Sebastian, the principal Arhuaco settlement in the Sierras.

November 16th 1980

I am writing in Bogotá's Tequendama Hotel, which is indistinguishable from countless other intercontinental establishments in hundreds of other destination cities for the armies of tourists and businessmen of the world. It is said there are four million people living in Bogotá and that this number grows by thousands every day. The city may now be best known for its thievery. A colonial period can be seen elsewhere but not here in the capital, as far as I know. Rain is frequent and abundant but does not bring any feeling of renewal. Noise and other pollutants burden the air through which people move swiftly and cautiously. A sense of internal siege is everywhere. So far I have met no one who has not been in some way

P1

218

criminally molested and even the wealthy with their ubiquitous bodyguards have no guarantee of safety. I see very little smiling by anyone.

November 17th 1980

Valledupar is an uninteresting frontier city in the lowlands of César Province. This is a region of growing economic importance due mainly to the enormity of the drug industry. Valledupar is a day's drive from Bogotá on a road that is said to be infuriating. It was an hour getting here by a Boeing 727.

We thought we would be immediately on our way to San Sebastian but the driver and his Jeep are otherwise engaged. Instead, we are hoping to leave tomorrow and in the meantime are staying in the apartment of an economist friend of Yezid. The afternoon passed with the usual desultory shopping for small articles that might improve our relations with the Ika: machetes, beads for ritual use, some cloth, and also basic food supplies for our own consumption.

November 18th 1980

I am waiting for the Jeep that is due at any moment. Yezid has gone ahead in another vehicle, carrying baggage, equipment, and supplies. We will rendezvous at some midpoint before proceeding to San Sebastian, the major village in the Ika territory. Last night was a long one on a lumpy bed in a small and airless room. How can anyone do economic theory in these equatorial temperatures? At least I am learning a little about local political tensions between the *costeños*, or coastals, and the *cachacos*, or people of the interior.

November 19th 1980

Just before dark last night we reached San Sebastian, a strange little hamlet with houses arranged in neat rows and surrounded by a low stonewall. The village doesn't look entirely indigenous but I'm told it has been here a long time, serving as a meeting place for populations with conflicting aims and interests. At present such interests belong to groups like the *colonos* who have come to farm, the Catholic missionaries who are here to convert, and the Ika who are trying to maintain a culture under siege. Almost nobody is in the village today except the Comisario, who is

more or less the mayor, his two wives, and a few children. Others are at their more permanent abodes elsewhere in the Sierras. Summer is beginning, and so there is work at the coffee fincas and a need to be in the surrounding countryside looking after cattle, sheep, and goats.

The morning has begun clear and cool with the Sierras looking huge and imposing. Such mountains have a way of making everything else puny and of rebuking human pettiness. The ride yesterday was tolerable even with a driver suffering from severe machismo and making it more perilous than necessary. The last two hours covered considerable vertical distance through innumerable ravines and valleys. The terrain is similar to the highlands in Ethiopia, but there is a great difference in the sophistication of the road building.

Situated on a small plateau about 1500 feet wide, San Sebastian is surrounded by mountains except to the west, where the open terrain slopes downward as far as the eye can see. The approach to the town is through a broad green pasture rising gently west to east. The town itself lies at the western end of the plateau and dominates the terrain that stretches out below. Except for the mission and a few houses belonging to some *mestizo* colonists, there is little evidence of construction. A fine river nearby has many outlying Ika habitations situated near its course. A few centuries ago San Sebastian, by an Arhuaco name, must have been fabulous.

I know little about San Sebastian historically or prehistorically but I have heard a few stories, including one about a German who owned nearby land and commuted from Valledupar in a single-engine aircraft. One might well wonder about this person's politics, considering the large number of SS and Luftwaffe fugitives from justice who fled to Colombia and other South American destinations at the end of World War II.

Today I walked with an Ika who was old enough to have seen the German landowner's aircraft, and what he said made excellent aeronautical sense. There is really only one way to fly in and out of here, and he described how it had been done. I paced off the part of the pasture he said was used and found 1500 feet of more or less flat terrain. The ground is hard and the grass clipped short by fat and lazy cows wandering in all directions. The approach has to start with a letdown over the village and then a turn to the east for an uphill landing. No go-around is possible on such an approach but would be with wind favoring a downhill landing to the west. I am tempted to come back to San Sebastian this way.

But it is not yet certain I will come back and twenty-four hours in Ikaland is not enough to convince me either way. Almost twenty years have passed since setting out for New Guinea and personal circumstances these days make going anywhere a more problematic matter. The New Guinea experience was positive and my expectations at the time were modest. I was willing to commit a large amount of time, more than six months away from my young family, and there were no conflicting demands on me when I returned. I could just sit down and make a film.

I am in Colombia now because I have been imagining making a film about becoming a shaman, a profession that has caught my interest and that I have talked about with friends who know much more about it than I. What I do know is how hard it would be to realize such a film. Shamanism is mostly a state of mind with few outward manifestations to be captured on film. I am not even sure there are any true shamans in these mountains any more. Sometimes I think what I want is to find a shaman to instruct me. The closest equivalent to a shaman in my acquaintance is Octavio Paz. Why don't I get on with the film about him I have been saying I was going to make?

We walked for an hour to the house of a man named Mama Norberto. A *mama* is the highest religious authority among the Ika. They are priest equivalents and repositories of sacred knowledge. You must be born with your umbilicus around your neck to be eligible for mamahood. Countenance, especially with regard to eyes, is also important. Maybe a perilous entry into life is what's needed to guide one through the hazards that await us all.

P2

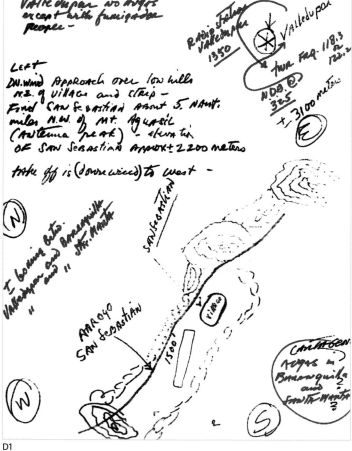

D1

P3

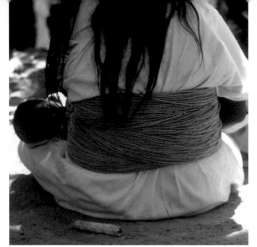

P4

Mama Norberto is an engaging man of about forty who speaks basic Spanish with clarity and humor. His house is on a rocky outcropping at the edge of an abyss walled in by eroded hills rising up to mountains on all sides. After a genial conversation we gave Mama Norberto and his family a number of gifts. The Ika women impressed me with their shortness of stature and immensity of girth. I wondered if most of them were pregnant because obesity is not common, at least for men.

November 20th 1980

I managed to fall into a substantial torrent rushing past some of the outlying houses of San Sebastian. It might not have happened had I not been trying to cross it carrying a number of things I wanted to keep dry. Twenty years ago in the Baliem Valley I had no difficulty overcoming such obstacles.

I am writing while sitting in the main *concurrua* of the district. A *concurrua* is a men's house with multiple sacred meanings and functions. A women's *concurrua* exists, too, but it is little more than a place of social gathering. The architecture of the *concurrua* represents the world itself. The structure is shaped like a mountain, as one might expect, is almost perfectly round and has a pointed roof. According to Ika cosmology, the *concurrua* is believed to have its inverted double repeated directly beneath it, providing a twin, subterranean, and palpable though illusory world.

We are here to continue our conversations of yesterday with a more senior and influential priest. His name is Mama Marco and it is on him that I have pinned my hopes for making a film about the Ika. Mama Marco is a strict traditionalist who is dedicated to the well-being of the Ika and their culture. He has not learned Spanish, which impedes the conversational pace but gives the participants

time to think carefully about what they should or should not say.

Mama Marco lives in a small village named Mamingeka, a difficult day's walk from San Sebastian. Today he has said we may visit him in Mamingeka and has agreed to prepare us spiritually for that journey. This preparation is also intended to make things propitious for what is being called my *trabajo* or work, which is using cameras and tape recorders to explore worlds like the Ika's.

Mama Marco has a wonderfully serious, almost sad face that is deeply lined after a life of at least sixty years. He moves deliberately and smoothly from one task to another and nothing is hurried in his voice or gestures. Our visit with him today follows time spent together yesterday. Yezid is concerned about the welfare of these people but feels that by our exercise of right behavior he can lay some of those worries to rest. He is overanxious in my mind and too ready to proclaim colonialist mea culpas in front of anyone who will listen. But the fact is no one appears to be listening.

Yezid is in his thirties but seems not yet to have much confidence either in himself or in finding fraternity with the Ika. He is deferential when forthrightness might serve him better. He is walking on eggs I think are mostly imaginary. I wonder if he can ever meet the Ika on equal terms with such deep misgivings about his own cultural baggage. After working six years with the Ika, he does not speak their language with any fluency and, as far as I can tell, has no deep understanding of them. His interest is more ideological than anthropological, and his inability to speak either Ika or English could be a problem for us all.

Another Colombian, Eduardo Villareal, was also with us today. He has left medical school to help Yezid and to be in the glorious Sierras among the indigenes. Eduardo speaks English but no Ika. He moves even more slowly than Yezid but is clearly enchanted by the Ika and enjoying his freedom from the indignities of urban life. His purpose is singularly and admirably personal. He spends his time cooking and enjoying the rusticity with which he copes admirably, making fires, hauling water, fetching wood, and otherwise taking enormous pains to be self-reliant. His and Yezid's labors preoccupy them and that is possibly the foremost reason for them to be here.

Yezid and his companions have the use of several houses in San Sebastian. Two are for dwelling, one is for cooking and two others serve as a schoolhouse and a modest clinic. There are almost no books in the schoolhouse and no medicines in the clinic. Both Yezid and Eduardo appear to enjoy their privations and speak of their sacrifices as a way to win the affection of the Ika. This premise came under discussion this afternoon. The exchange was neither long nor particularly deep, but we were able to present our views about a number of things relating to our differing approaches to living with and learning from the Ika. In the end, I felt Yezid agreed he and his companions might not be convincing the Ika to accept them for egalitarian reasons, and that repudiating parts of their own cultural inheritance was not going to unite everyone in a common cause. He and Eduardo may also have realized that the way they live was satisfying their own needs but had little to do with what was expected of them by the Ika. All these observations came up not because I wanted to critique their methods but because I wanted to suggest that their lifestyle might not be helpful to filmmaking. Making films is very physical and nothing should be left to chance. Cameras are heavy and need constant attention. Nothing is as important as rest and nourishment. You cannot play house and make films at the same time.

It is my third night in San Sebastian due to the late arrival of the mules we need to take us to Mamingeka. I write lying in a sleeping bag liberally sprayed with insecticide in an effort to resist an invasion of fleas that have kept me awake for the last two nights. Both of my arms are swollen from their attentions and I'm told bedbugs are next. This experience is uncomfortable so far and one for which I admit having wavering enthusiasm. Compared to Yezid and Eduardo, I have little of the kind of dedication by which they seem possessed, but we shall see who prevails.

November 22nd 1980

I am writing about two remarkably punishing days that began yesterday when it dawned cloudless for the journey to visit Mama Marco in Mamingeka. We had four mules for three persons and a considerable amount of camera equipment. Otherwise, we were remarkably unencumbered. I took a few bits

of clothing, a toothbrush, soap, a towel from the Bogotá Tequendama, my Swiss army knife, a small flashlight, cigarettes, and a lighter.

We set off with fresh mules over relatively level terrain that lasted only an hour before the footpath turned abruptly upward, twisting into the rising hills. Footing grew problematic as the ascent steepened. Usually it is an eight-hour walk but it took nine owing to a wrong turn. Even the Ika can lose their way. From time to time we had to abandon our mounts so the beasts would continue. When the trail began to descend, the walk was easier and the mules did not object when we climbed back on them for the last few miles. But downhill has always been as difficult for me as uphill. It is cultural I suspect. Even compared with the Dani, the Ika have the strongest legs I have ever seen. They could have danced all the way, up and down, to Mamingeka. They do not tire.

We reached Mamingeka late in the afternoon exceedingly tired but the sight of this diminutive habitation perched on the lip of spectacular hills restored my spirits. The village looks in an easterly direction over an immense valley to a mountain range that encircles this world of Mama Marco like the walls of a gigantic fortress.

P5

223

Because at first I could see no other villages, I felt as though we had discovered our own small universe and were the only ones in it. The cone-shaped peaks of the distant mountains were wreathed in the filmiest of scattered cirrus, milky but transparent. This universe was totally and overwhelmingly silent until the inevitable dogs caught our scent. Happily, they are not as belliger-ent as Balinese dogs but are quite cowardly and content to slink into the shadows. The pigs show the greatest interest in people and they gave an appraising look as we arrived. Pigs are the scarabs of the Sierras with a particular fondness for human excrement. Dealing with pigs is an unusually prob-lematic enterprise. When defecating, one abandons the main trails for reasons of privacy but the sub-sidiary paths are those used by pigs, sheep, dogs, and goats. These trails are mere scratches in the sides of almost vertical hillsides on which few if any trees grow. This means one is both exposed and subject to sliding, ignominiously, downward and half-dressed into the village. Maintaining a squatting position takes great concentration of mind. Even with no pigs in attendance, defecating hereabouts is a hazardous business.

I cannot help marveling at the exquisite geom-etry of these people's lives. They persevere on a challenging hypotenuse, literally clinging to a mountainside.

In this culture there are no places to sit, and I have brought nothing with me for that purpose. Women use the ground whenever they are not standing. The men are more inclined to use a rock with which to elevate themselves, if only slightly. Put there for sitting purposes, a few flat stones encircle the *concurrua,* but I am hesitant to use them and anyway they are not as comfortable as one would hope.

So much is happening all at once that there is little opportunity for reflection, especially since I have abandoned the daily use of my journal and rely now on flawed memory.

Mamingeka is Mama Marco's village in that he is its one clear and undisputed figure of authority. There is also no question regarding his Arhuaco identity. His homespun clothing consists of a three-quarter length sleeved jacket and trousers made from spun lamb's wool. All men wear a hat that is knitted from wool by the women. While men wear sandals, women are barefoot. Just as all men wear the same clothes, all the women dress alike in large, near-white cotton smocks. Sometimes weaving results in a stripe or two of darker wool in male garments. The Ika costume is arresting even at its most minimal and has an ampleness that allows for great freedom of movement and for wrapping oneself against the evening chill. Its effect is one of considerable formality, and seeing everyone dressed alike suggests a willingness to abide by tradition. At the same time, the costume is marvelously casual and adaptive to the requirements of Ika life.

Another article of dress is the ubiquitous *mochila,* or woven bag. These bags are of either wool or flax and made only by women in several different sizes. No man is without at least one *mochila,* since they are required for items in constant use. One bag might have coca leaves for chewing or for giving in greeting. Another will contain a lime gourd and such other things as tobacco paste, a cup, string and cotton for offerings, matches, perhaps a flashlight, and even a transistor radio in rare instances. There are other bags for other things depending on need. Men frequently carry a machete sheathed and hanging down their back. They can carry all of what I have described and another thirty or more pounds of sugar, bananas, or some other burden straight up a mountainside with no apparent effort.

The extraordinarily plain women's dresses are held in at the waist by several loops of cording. They also wear fancy beads in large quantity but no hat. Often the women will have a large string bag hanging down their back from their neck or head. Men carry their *mochilas* slung over their shoulders and across their chests so they can reach into them with ease. String bags are slung backwards from their foreheads when they are carrying heavy loads.

The children dress in little smocks meant only to keep them covered. The clothing seems an afterthought, a gesture of modesty perhaps. The fabric is machine-made like the cloth used for their

P7

F4

225

P8

P9

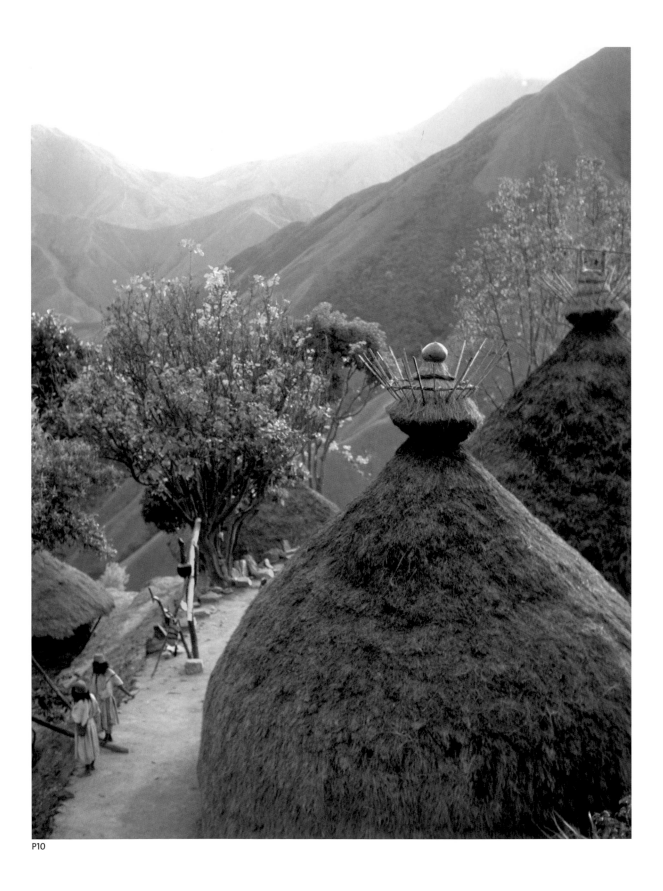

P10

mothers' dresses and it too has no color. Apparently only men's clothes are hand-loomed, which takes a long time, a large amount of wool, and is done only by men. On average, I am told, a man has between three and five sets of tunics and trousers.

I find the way the Ika dress arresting in its contrast to that of most of the world. Maybe only in China do clothes have such uniformity. Something else might be at play with the Ika, such as pleasure, even pride, in looking the way they do. I see no signs of embarrassment about how they dress. They do not yearn for castoff pants and T-shirts the way the Hamar or Nuer in Ethiopia did. I wonder how long Ika traditional dress can last without lapsing into the folkloric. Now there is only a hint of quaintness about their costume, but they may not be able to withstand the persuasiveness of modern merchandizing much longer. What I have learned tells me the Ika are still stubbornly resisting assimilation and practicing a variety of strategies to do so. They also feel beleaguered, especially by the *colonos* who would gladly take their land. I have a sense of doom as I write these words and fear that Yezid's well-intentioned rescue efforts may not be enough to keep this culture intact.

When we got to Mamingeka my uppermost thought was rest but that was not to come until after a bowl of rice and onions given to us in the *concurrua*, situated on a little hill above the village. These remarkable structures are quite large, serving as temple and men's house, and accommodate a variety of activities at all hours of the day and night. They are continually astir with men simultaneously sleeping, talking, singing, drumming, flute playing, joking, farting, killing scorpions, searching for fleas, telling long stories, or humming into an immense gourd whose opening last night was a few feet from my ear.

I had found a place on the hard dirt floor in preference to an empty hammock, an invention that has never allowed me to sleep. I was close to the front entrance in the interest of fresh air but not so close as to be exposed to the night cold. Unfortunately, the floor sloped steeply toward the doorway and so my head had to be aimed inward in the direction of the fire and Mama Marco's groaning gourd. Eventually, I was able to find enough that was soothing in the singing to fall deeply asleep.

November 24th 1980

I awoke with the sun rising above the mountains in the east and beginning to pour through the entry of the *concurrua*. If I could be in the same spot on December 22nd (or would it be the 23rd?), the sun would, if calculations made when it was constructed were right, come directly through this opening and exactly bisect the temple. It should happen again on the same dates in June. Perhaps I can be here for that event and see how the Ika express their fascination with astronomical events.

I got to my feet, descended the slippery hill sloping down from the *concurrua* and took a path leading to a sizeable stream a few hundred yards from the village. Here I managed a sketchy wash and awakened somewhat more completely. By the time I was back in the *concurrua*, all its residents were up and going about their early morning tasks. Soon more food appeared in the form of stew made of yucca, potatoes, and plantains. The dish was warming, full of starch and utterly agreeable.

I wondered what would be required of me physically as the day unfolded. Maybe I was not the only person feeling the effects of the long march, though I failed to see evidence of exhaustion in any of the Ika who regularly spend their time scampering straight up these formidable hills. As it happened, most of the day was spent in the vicinity of the *concurrua* listening to stories and watching Mama Marco do his work.

His work consists of periodic preparation of offerings to the gods and is called *moronzama* or *aburu* in the Ika language. These terms refer to all of Mama Marco's ministrations on behalf of his community including pilgrimage and other ritual acts. His, the *mama*'s, work never ends, it would appear. As sage/shaman/diviner/confessor/historian, a *mama* is obliged to maintain harmony among all men, not just in the Sierras but wherever they may dwell including but not limited to America, England, France, and China. He is able to do this by virtue of his deep knowledge and ritual expertise. His is a considerable, thankless, and clearly futile task.

I have not yet seen any rituals, only the preparation of the little offerings that accompany them. I'm not at all sure, as a matter of fact, that Mama Marco will tolerate such curiosity on my part regarding his sacred duties. I must wait and see.

P11

Despite these and other misgivings, I managed to get some images of the men around the *concurrua* as they went about their chores. I doubt there is much inactivity, given the demands of a farmer's life. They must herd, cultivate, and gather, leaving little time to sit around the temple.

Dusk in this vertical landscape begins in the late afternoon, following ten hours of the brightest daylight. The sun works clockwise around the *concurrua* where I have spent much of the day watching Mama Marco. We sat on the stones outside the *concurrua* protected from the sun by overhanging eaves of thatching. Here and there a few trees provided additional shade. The Ika are mostly indifferent to the sun and anyway have hats, long hair, and ample clothing for protection.

The night following our arrival, we had longed for something to eat but no one had prepared anything and nothing seemed forthcoming. Unlike me, the Ika do not eat, go to bed, or wake in the morning according to some more or less fixed schedule. Work, play, eating, and socializing happen more randomly or when there is an urgency. Sleep for me finally came, despite the Ika practice of not resting if a story is being told or someone wants to play a flute or drum. Maybe the casualness of Ika habits in eating and sleeping

mitigates stress in their lives. It seems eminently reasonable to eat when you are hungry and sleep when you are tired (as La Rochefoucauld once wrote, adding that being human also included making love at will).

Once again I awoke before dawn, alert and alone in my wakefulness. Finding a spot on the hill behind the *concurrua*, I watched as the day dawned and thought of other such hours in other geographic extremities. I am reminded that filmmakers are creatures of light and we do well to keep our eyes open as much as possible. Writers, by contrast, strike me as being more denizens of darkness.

I watched the scene for an hour longer than it took for the sun to rise above the eastern range and found myself wondering where the sun had been while I was sleeping. Underworlds are obvious answers to such questions and the Ika have invented a complex set of such propositions in answer to them. My theories were limited in these respects and I mostly luxuriated in the shifting of color from deep indigo to daisy yellow. As soon as the sun had warmed the village into motion, I left my perch behind the *concurrua* where I had been sitting near some puzzling, unoccupied structures that I later learned were shelters put up for the newly betrothed. These small dwellings were about 150 feet apart, one for the bride and the other for the groom. I'm told that as part of a ritual that ultimately unites them the newly wedded spend two or three weeks out of each other's sight in their respective huts.

Food mysteriously appeared this morning, arriving in a gourd filled with corn, beans, and yucca. I ate well and drank a little coffee before joining some men who had gathered outside. Mama Marco acted a little as though he should entertain me. Our agreement, made in San Sebastian, was that I come to Mamingeka and learn what I could by observing the life that went on around me. I would be the student and leave the role of teacher to him. Of course, I scarcely know my teacher and my teacher does not know me or with what aptitude I will absorb his teachings. But all teachers and surely all shamans of whatever proficiency are themselves students of theatre. They need its devices to practice their craft. Mama Marco, for all his reticence, is no exception and today underlined the point.

P12

F5

P13

F6

The morning went by watching Mama Marco do magical turns. I do not mean sleight of hand but more song and dance in which he indicated his repertory of ritual gestures. Though interesting to watch and even to film, I sensed that the performance was intended for the camera and would last more or less as long as the camera was going. I never felt that what I was watching was watered down or adulterated. On the contrary, I had the impression Mama Marco's self-esteem was such as to indulge in nothing of the sort. Like all Ika, he has implicit faith in his traditions and is not about to engage in playacting. Whether they have the will and endurance to guide their *hermanitos* (everyone who is not Ika) through the turmoil they see engulfing the world is another matter.

I have no illusions that I will be admitted to the sacred life of the Ika and, even if I were, there might be no way to film what I was shown. It will be much easier for me and for Mama Marco if we stay on the plane of the ordinary where everything is in the open and I can make images of what I see. Yesterday I shot two magazines and today twice that number. The footage may only survive in an archive but at least I have begun the process of making a film and done so by centering my attention on the principal player in this remarkable community.

On the next-to-the-last day in Mamingeka, we were told relatives of Mama Marco would press cane to make sugar that is sold down valley. The pressing would be done not far from the village and I decided to spend the time watching rather than filming on the theory that this happened with some frequency. The process was interesting but that is all. The press is crude but efficient and the activity, lasting all afternoon, ended when the extracted juice had been boiled to a paste and poured into moulds. The resulting bricks, called *panelas*, are small or large depending on which forms are used. Later someone will put the bricks on a mule and take them to market.

F7

F8

P14

233

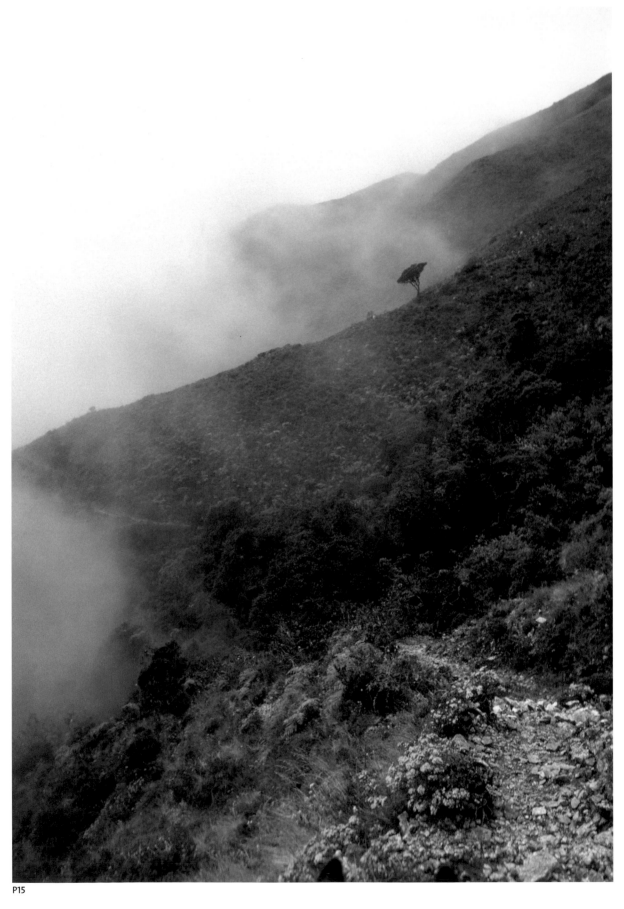

P15

Back in the village, we discovered another gourd with yucca, plantains, and potatoes had been left for us in the *concurrua*. To my delight, a few bits of recently slaughtered sheep had been added.

That this was our final night pleased Yezid more than me. I had become hardened in ways that made it more appealing to stay longer. Yezid, I'm afraid, was feeling the strain of thinking he had brought to Mamingeka human pollutants from the outside world. I happen not to agree but understand his misgivings. I had no sense my being here presented any problem at all, most certainly not for Mama Marco. Yezid feels conflicted and clearly welcomed the idea of departing. An additional reason to leave was his unequal battle against what the Ika call *pitu*, a venomous bedbug to which Yezid has been losing ground steadily.

Once more the moon's near fullness in the eastern sky has lit the night almost to the point of extinguishing the heaven's ordinarily brilliant starriness. Casting deep shadows wherever it shines, the moon's brightness mocks my infidelity as a nocturnal diarist.

I was not expecting a rousing night in the *concurrua* but was wakened by men who came in late for a concert they decided to give that lasted until dawn. I went back to sleep only when the flute and drum fell silent and all that remained were the soothing tones of a mouth harp.

November 25th 1980

The stay in Mamingeka has been shortened owing to the lack of mules to take us back to San Sebastian. Mama Norberto was also feeling unwell and torn between being in close proximity to his mentor Mama Marco and returning to the greater comforts of San Sebastian.

The departure for San Sebastian was preceded by a virtual torrent of food. This bounty is not what happened on our arrival and I am at a loss to explain why there were now fried eggs and bananas. Were we being sped on our way or pitied for the journey that lay ahead?

Before setting out, I did some farewell picture taking involving almost everyone in the village. The excitement was considerable, especially among the young. Had I more film, it would all have been used. For once I was in short supply. It was a sign though that Mamingeka had touched me in some

P16

way. But Nikons are a nuisance both for me and for my subjects. They are big, noisy, and disruptive especially in this tranquil Ika world. I think Ika dignity is offended by their clattering. I must find a better solution.

Our way back to San Sebastian took us 300 feet straight up the mountain to Mama Marco's son's village. He had asked us to stop there and when we arrived yet more food and coffee was provided. I did not learn the name of this community but it had a *concurrua* once presided over by a widely revered *mama*. The village shared with Mamingeka an imposing situation on a high, rounded hill rising behind the dwellings. This hill was said to have particularly sacred properties that imbued the village and its *mama* with much sanctity. After an hour of friendly talk, we set forth wondering if the lightning in the sky the night before would mean a wet trail or perhaps a day of rain. If this were to happen, our trip would be far more difficult and even dangerous. But the clouds bore no rain and only enveloped us in a fine mist. At times, this made forward visibility difficult but the mules were unabashed, never looking further ahead than a few feet. The diffused light brightened the landscape and intensified the color of grasses and wildflowers that grew in great profusion.

November 26th 1980

I lost little time finding water for a wash that was long overdue. The sun was strong and my spirits improved. San Sebastian was nearly empty, and the Comisario said he himself would leave the town as soon as we did. Tomorrow we will go down the mountain, taking with us a young Indian who has decided to explore the world beyond his cherished Ika homeland. He has persuaded his parents that it is a good idea. The boy, who is about eighteen and whose Spanish name is Gonzalo, has been helping in the little school Yezid started here in San Sebastian. Gonzalo can blame his loss of innocence on his aptitude for education.

P17

the impulse to preserve

Mama Norberto thinks Gonzalo should not go without spiritual preparation and so we all took part in making offerings of cotton and string. The ceremony was held inside the *concurrua* and lasted almost two hours. Mama Norberto officiated despite his persisting ill health and showed an authority that rather surprised me. Apparently his ritual attentions were directed to my own as well as Gonzalo's well-being.

November 27th 1980

Mama Norberto's magic succeeded up until a few miles from the Valledupar airport when a tire suddenly went flat. It was quickly fixed and we were able to leave on schedule. While in Bogotá I will try to see Reichel Dolmatoff, who has been so helpful since I first came to Colombia, and also Reichel's son-in-law who has suggested we work together in the Amazon. Maybe some day that could come to pass. But why do I even consider another desolate geography to probe another disappearing remnant of humanity?

I have little affection for Bogotá. Perhaps I have not seen it in a way that does the city justice. More likely the problem is that I cannot speak enough Spanish. The city teems with violence and the constabulary looks insufficient, uninterested, and complicit. No window is unbarred, the doors are triple-locked, and guards keep watch over everything. Purse snatching, mugging, and assassination are daily occurrences. As to its outward appearance, Bogotá has little that is for me visually appealing. Everything is gray and horizontal. The streets are strewn with refuse. Nothing looks old enough to fall into ruin. Historic Colombia is not here but at lower elevations. As to personal appearance, the average Colombian, male or female, is uniformly plain. The cuisine is no different.

November 30th 1980

I reached the airport early this morning but it was late afternoon before we neared Jamaica. Advertised as nonstop, my flight has already put down in Medellín and Barranquilla. The aircraft emptied at Medellín, which must be the reason for having gone there, and Barranquilla may have been required for refueling. It would have been difficult to depart Medellín's high, narrow airport with enough fuel to reach JFK.

P18

These two weeks have been positive, especially the days spent in Mamingeka. I am content with the idea of coming back for *veranito*, the little summer, that arrives in June. The weather then will make it possible to get around quite easily. As these thoughts come to me others do as well. They concern the question about what coming back can accomplish. I have woken from my dream of being transported into veritable shamanic realms. Mama Marco is impressive but will never achieve the magical flight we are told to expect of such people, and which Castaneda has said he many times experienced in his dealings with Don Juan. These thoughts of mine might be fantasy but they have been compelling enough to get me this far. I am willing now to settle for less. I wonder what kind of film remains when such fantasy is subtracted.

I am now sure that I want to make a film about the Ika, emphasizing the priest/shaman figure of Mama Marco, I have no thread or theme to tell the larger Ika story. Nor have I hit upon a metaphor to express the meaning of their exemplary thoughts and habits. So far there is only their appealing idea of being responsible to the whole earth and needing to instruct and correct their little brothers, who cause Mother Nature so much grief.

I note the Virginian shore sliding southward under the left wing. There will be no more open water now.

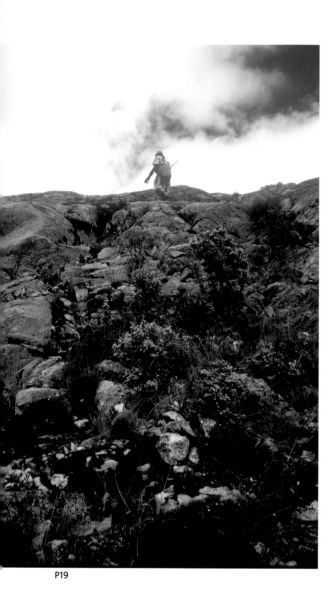

P19

May 28th 1981

In the months since leaving Colombia, I thought often about Gerardo Reichel Dolmatoff's description of how the Kogi trained their shamans, and their journeying into magic and spirituality had become fixed in my mind as a subject for a film. I was also enjoying the writing of Mircea Eliade and may have conjoined the two authors in ways neither intended by them nor advisable in terms of what they were saying. It was Eliade's inclusion of magical flight in his definition of true shamanship that captured my fullest attention.

My thoughts about returning to Colombia came to include flying in my own aircraft with Robert Fulton, warmest of friends and another pilot absorbed by the idea of magical flight.

En route to Bogotá, we landed first in Cartagena, where we met the usual customs and immigration people for whom our papers were apparently in order. Bringing my Cessna into this problematic country was arranged by family acquaintances of the fiancée of Yezid Campos, the Colombian social worker who had helped me on my first visit to the Ika, a group that lives close by and is similar, in essential ways, to the Kogi. He had agreed to use his contacts to bring Fulton and me into their world.

Once through airport formalities, I managed to find a place to store our many and heavy boxes and we flew this afternoon to Bogotá nearly empty. It is better to fly small airplanes light in Colombia, especially in the mountains. The flight was routine until the final phase when we were asked by the controllers to thread our way through some passes to the airport. I was glad the weather was not worse. Most of the flying until now has been pleasant, even the four hours over water from Jamaica to Cartagena when progress was indiscernible and only the hands of our watches seemed to move.

May 29th 1981

The standing rule in Colombia is that no foreign aircraft can stay longer than ten days. Ten days is enough time to do any amount of trafficking in drugs but too short for me to do serious filmmaking. Every moment in Bogotá has been spent trying to arrange a permit enabling us to stay longer than is usually allowed. The problem has been less the unwillingness of people to make this arrangement than the absence of a telephone system by which to negotiate it. The telephone in Bogotá is an instrument of subtle torture. It has a dial tone and numbers ring, however the response is almost invariably a busy signal or a voice saying *no contesta* or *ocupada*. So one dials and redials until a human voice is reached and connection is established. After many hours, we were able to set in motion a plan to circumvent the regulations. The next problem was that it would take time to procure the letter we needed to indicate our exempt status to officials wherever we happened to land. Thursday was a holiday and Friday was the day we wanted to start for the mountains.

We left Bogotá on Thursday, when everything was closed, on the assurance that Yezid would fetch the permissions letter and bring it to Valledupar by Friday. I wanted to use the good weather for getting to the coast and, besides, our things were in the office of a travel agent who would be away on the weekend. The flight to Cartagena was through dramatic cloud buildups of immense size but no aeronautical concern. We arrived in time for dinner and to get some rest.

While Fulton loaded the aircraft, I went to the tower to file a flight plan for Valledupar. On reading our destination, the tower chief, who badly wants a ten-gallon Texan sombrero, asked how we could be thinking of going to Valledupar since it is a restricted airport. "But Valledupar is not in the

F9

restricted area as you can see by looking at your chart." "No, it is not in the restricted zone, but all airports except those with customs and immigration facilities are restricted to Americans. You must have special permission from Bogotá to land anywhere else. I will radio Barranquilla to ask them to ask Bogotá for permission."

After three hours at the airport, word came that the only person able to give permission was not available. He was in a meeting. We heard this as the lightning of late-afternoon thunderstorms appeared in all quadrants of a darkening sky. We were trapped by increasingly menacing circumstances. What could be done to free two unlikely Americans from the regulatory mess made by failed U.S. drug policies? Only, I supposed, the way all problems are fixed anywhere, by privilege and influence.

DATE 19 81	AIRCRAFT TYPE	AIRCRAFT IDENT	ROUTE OF FLIGHT FROM	TO	NR INST. APP.	REMARKS AND ENDORSEMENTS	NR LDG	AIRCRAFT CATEGORY SINGLE-ENGINE LAND		MULTI-ENGINE LAND	
5/28	C 185	4814E	Bogota Col.	Cartegena Col.		ADD 1 Qt 50W TEX AD at TACH: 300.6 to 104	1	2	9		
5/30	"	"	Cartegena Col.	Valledupar Col.		ADD 1 Qt 50W TEX AD At TACH: 303.4 to 114	1	1	4		
5/31	"	"	Valledupar Local			Overflew San Sebastian VIA Atanacil - Rain & Storm	1	1	1		
6/4	"	"	Valledupar Col.	La Mina Col.		STOL work - One Strip - Main Gear Flat -	4	1	5		
6/4	"	"	Valle du Par Col.			San Sebastian & Sierras Aerial Photo to 15000	1	1	5		
6/5	"	"	V. du par Col.	Codazzi Col.		STOL WORK @ AG Strip Mr. Itangara-	4	1	-		
"	"	"	V. dupar Col.	San Juantian Col.		Fulton Made 1st Lndg.	1		5		
"	"	"	San Seb. Col.	Codazzi Col.		Aerial photo @ 12,500 STOL @ Codazzi Strip	4	1	-		
6/10	"	"	V. du par Col.	San Seb. Col.		@ 16 + Feet over Abv of Sierra peaks & Lakes	1	1	5		
"	"	"	San Seb Col.	Codazzi #3 Col.			1		6		
"	"	"	Codazzi #3 Col. Local			6 STOL Lndgs. + T.O.S	6		7		
"	"	"	Codazzi #3 Col.	V. dupar Col.			1		3		
7/6	"	"	V. dupar Col.	Becerril Col.		8 STOL Lndgs. + T.O.'S	8	1	5		

I certify that the entries in this log are true,

PILOT'S SIGNATURE

TOTALS THIS PAGE	15	5
AMT. FORWARDED	447 6	9 8
TOTALS TO DATE	463 1	9 8

D2

May 31st 1981

It is the eleventh day since departing Hanscom Airport in Bedford, Massachusetts. At 3 p.m. this afternoon I was circling the village of San Sebastian in the Sierra Nevadas of northern Colombia looking through holes in a widely broken layer of clouds for the Jeep that was meant to have brought Fulton there by road. I was able to do this because of efforts on the part of Yezid's well-connected fiancée to free us from our detainment in Cartagena. She managed to get part of the job done in that we were able to proceed from Cartagena to Valledupar on a temporary permit good for flights to and from Cartagena, Valledupar, and San Sebastian until the 10th of June. This was the date I had intended to be in Cartagena to meet Adele Pressman, who will come to the mountains.

Bogotá chose to use June 10th as the limiting date for our flights in the restricted zone that included the Sierra Nevadas; so civil aviation must be asked to extend our permit up to the time we will have finished the work we have come to do.

I have been far too unmindful of the enormity of our request to jump into an airplane and fly off to an abandoned airstrip in these Sierras, mountains that are under intensive marijuana cultivation managed by a mafia overseeing the operation from planting to exporting. No one except the indigenous Indian people, a few *colonos* or *mestizo* farmers and the mafia itself has access to this entire region. It is extremely dangerous to move along any except a few major roadways. Having an aircraft makes it possible to get in and out of the Sierras quickly, if you are granted immunity from the soldiers and police whose job it is to stop traffic of every kind. Even though it is their job, they rarely seem to be doing it. Anyway, whatever they do has no effect on the amount of drugs being transported out of the Sierras, down onto the flatter La Guajira countryside and to the airstrips used to fly the drugs into the United States.

Nevertheless, yesterday we left Cartagena with our hard-won permission, much to the surprise of everyone at the airport. No American in their memory had ever obtained such permission and it is easy to see why. Those using the airspace have no need of it. They have their own airstrips and fuel dumps. Why tell the authorities who you are by asking for permission to break the law?

It was an hour and fifteen minutes to Valledupar flying quite low and knowing nothing about the weather en route. Information about such things is difficult to get in Colombia and a power outage in Valledupar meant there was no way to even ask about weather locally. The large buildups of clouds obscured much of the Sierras but a few breaks revealed a series of peaks and valleys of modest proportions. The light was soft as we made our way to the airport while off toward the mountains a veil of mist hanging over them created an air of huge mystery. It was over there somewhere that we would find the Ika.

Yezid Campos was at the Valledupar airport awaiting our arrival. Soon we were in town getting supplies needed for my second visit to Mamingeka. The *supermercado* was short on some things but provided nearly all we would need, especially if we are able to persuade the Ika to share their food supply. I have told Yezid repeatedly that I could not make a film and cook at the same time.

I worry about the problem of eating and also of access to San Sebastian by aircraft. I could not tell if it would be possible to land as I flew over the abandoned strip today nor was there any sign of Fulton on the ground. Being able to use the strip will depend on how much rain has fallen or will continue to fall. I'm told that *veranito* is on its way but by the look of the sky this evening, I would say little summer was having trouble making an appearance.

June 2nd 1981

Fulton came back to Valledupar by road with information that the San Sebastian strip was too wet for use. I'm surprised he was willing to submit to so much travel by car. He has the nervous system of a Siamese cat particularly when it comes to automobiles. He says, with some accuracy, most drivers do not know how to drive. They are always turning to avoid something not there or braking when it isn't necessary. So his body is asked to respond to false signals, or signals that relate to false information and that is a strain that tires him no end. The strip being too wet means we proceed by road and wait for drying winds to make it serviceable.

We left at 9 a.m. and three hours later were in San Sebastian, having had a far easier time than the

P20

day before when it took Fulton five hours and several episodes of extricating wheels stuck in the rain-damaged road. We were met by a few staff members of Yezid's Institute who were returning from a meeting in a *concurrua* about an accidental fire in someone's house. They are very nice people who work with Yezid, when he is not in Bogotá, on such matters as the health and education of the indigenous population. They are young, inexperienced and, I'm afraid, inexpert. They spend much of their time in domesticity, housekeeping, and cooking and so are not likely to malpractice. I have not yet seen any actual teaching or health care but the staff has an egalitarian outlook and wants badly for the Ika to like and admire them. Their worst fears are that they might offend their Indian brothers and sisters.

It was explained to me that there were problems owing to competing factions among the Ika themselves. There are the advanced, politically speaking, who take on roles such as a Comisario, and there are other Ika leaders who are more traditionally minded called *mamas*. As I learned from my visit last fall, a *mama* is guardian of an esoteric domain to which the Ika are profoundly and unquestioningly committed. A *mama's* knowledge is deep and covers an immense complexity of both practical and cosmological systems. I want to think, without any assurance of it being true, that a *mama* is also an approximate shaman. It is this thought which drew me in the first place to these particular Indians.

My major concern at the moment is the weather. The abundant rain has been spoiling gardens and otherwise endangering lives through flooding. We cannot go, as I had hoped, to spend a week in Mamingeka because the trail from San Sebastian leads along perilous cliffs and ridges now too wet for the mules to find decent footing. If a mule cannot walk these trails, I have no doubt we would fare even more badly. So Fulton and I

have been going out in the morning when it isn't raining to level the abandoned airstrip. At the moment, the road across the meadow that in November was smooth and dry is now deeply rutted by the missionaries' Jeeps going back and forth between their compound and the town. Even when the rocks and ruts are removed, the strip has its own peculiar problems. It was never a proper airfield in the sense that one could land in opposite directions according to the requirements of the winds. This is a one-way strip because the approaches are such as to not permit a go-around, owing to rapidly rising terrain to the east.

Fulton and I are reminded of a place called Chintabaradan in Niger where in 1978 we were marooned for what felt like an eternity waiting to be told where to go for the Borroro *gerewol* I had wanted to film.

I find little that interests me in San Sebastian though I am sure upon close examination I could be charmed in unsuspected ways. An air of transition caused perhaps by the circumstances of its situation at the end of a road pervades the settlement. Its population of Indians is courted by Catholic missionaries and government social workers locked in a struggle with *mestizo* farmers doing their best, slowly but surely, to dispossess the Indians of their land. It is a rich and dynamic arena of social change but I have always found it hard to grasp such matters in a visual way. Words are better at describing what is happening here where traditional life gives way to the winds of change and modernity. When I look at San Sebastian, I see cultures colliding but the evidence is not visually engaging: just the usual assortment of plastic pails, nylon clothes, radios, and sunglasses. I am trying to pay no attention and to go to Mamingeka where there are no schools or missions to distract either the Ika or me. But we must wait for what I was told was the superior magic of a Kogi *mama* to undo the prayers and spells that brought on these rains in answer to a serious dry spell. It is a condition that so far no amount of Ika sorcery has been able to countervail.

I have accepted the offer of a ride to Valledupar made by a friendly Catholic brother, Fray Felipe, who had heard I wanted to go. This spontaneous gesture of friendliness is the first I have known since we arrived and it is probably one of the few times anyone in the government cadre has spoken to anyone from the Roman Catholic Mission. These two entities are at sword points most of the time. But we may be considered neutral.

The party included the kind Brother, his assistant, and an architect who is supervising the Mission's plans for expansion. They occupied the front seat. A very large woman whom I was told was helping at the Mission took up most of the bench seat on one side in back. Fulton and I with modest baggage settled into the remaining space on the other side.

Fray Felipe turned out to be an excellent chauffeur with considerable experience going back and forth to Valledupar. He was also a hugely amiable person whose good humor was frequently tested by the road's condition which had not improved much in the past few days. At one point, just before Pueblobello, we encountered an overturned Jeep that had been traveling in the opposite direction. It was in a place too narrow to accommodate more than one vehicle at a time. So we were required to extricate the vehicle, a feat accomplished largely by the enthusiasm and expertise of Fray Felipe. He threw himself into the task with immense humor and good will. It was not a simple matter because the Jeep had managed to fetch up perilously close to the edge of an abyss at least 2000 feet deep. Its driver was a soldier and the cargo that had been off-loaded was an eclectic collection including bags of rice, hundreds of eggs, boxes of salt, candy, assorted fruits, dilapidated luggage, and half a dozen disconsolate passengers. After two hours of heaving and lifting, the Jeep was restored right-side up to the road and we resumed our downward way to Valledupar.

June 4th 1981

I began toiling to perfect my short and rough-field landing technique. Fulton is such a master in these matters that I despair of ever gaining his proficiency. My bonus after an hour of trial landings was a flat main tire at La Matua, a scar on the floor of this valley used by aircraft flying fumigation runs. Whatever they are spraying smells deadly. We didn't have the right tools and it took hours to assemble what was needed from what was offered by interested passersby.

P21

Once again aloft, we headed for San Sebastian to airdrop the shovels and picks I had bought at the market this morning. Yezid had asked that we donate some gardening equipment to the Ika. These tools will also be useful in our efforts to improve the landing strip that still looked very small and rough. I think it will take more time to improve the field and for the sun to dry the landing area.

I want to think this airplane can be less of a burden even if it gets us to San Sebastian in minutes as against entire days in a Jeep. I realize that the plane has been a distraction, really a secondary occupation, ever since deciding to take it such a great distance. The film project gets lost in the exertions required to make flying possible. I search for justification without much success. One improbable thought I have entertained lately is to put together, filmically speaking, the reality of metallic aircraft flight and the fantasy of magical shamanic flight. I even imagine filming a shaman piloting the aircraft.

As I grapple with such ideas, my mind reverts to a more practical matter (not a hopeful sign for getting on with filmmaking) and that is the actual look of this airplane. Ever since Fulton and I brought it to Massachusetts from Minnesota, its appearance has troubled me. Ultra white with large decorative elements in bright red, the aircraft also has lettering announcing that it is fitted with Robertson's short-field takeoff and landing equipment. The plane definitely lacks the subtlety of appearance required by a shaman/pilot. It should be more transparent, closer in tones to the sky. So I have decided it must be peeled of its garish paint, which means finding someone who can do such work and quickly.

June 5th 1981

When I left San Sebastian earlier in the week with Fray Felipe, I did so reluctantly, not wanting to take a step down from the Sierras but also because it would mean being in the noxious frontier outpost of Valledupar. Still, this stay at sea level has given me an opportunity to further practice takeoffs and landings. We do this at the Corazzi strip that used to be the main airport but is now a much shortened version of its former municipal self. It is not far from the mechanic's shop where we had the punctured tire fixed. Nowadays, it is bisected by the main road making in effect two airfields, both of which we use in our practice flying.

I asked a mechanic if he would strip and polish the aircraft. He looked a bit stricken for reasons I don't entirely understand but said he would and for a reasonable price. I wonder if he thought we wanted to change the appearance of the aircraft in order to confound the drug police. Any small plane, especially one in Valledupar, is suspect from the moment of landing. It is going to be hard to convince anyone that we are using the plane to make a film about the Ika. The Ika? An airplane? To land in the mountains in a field of stones not used by an aircraft since a former Luftwaffe pilot utilized it following the Second World War? It will cost $600 to get the paint off and shine the aluminum skin to a dazzling silver.

Fulton and I set out for San Sebastian in the late morning. It was cloudless and hot but the landing was without incident owing largely to Fulton's considerable skills and our carrying so little weight. The wind was brisk from the west and we landed downhill, the way all takeoffs will have to be made. On landing, throngs of children in their white tunics rushed to greet us, smiling broadly. No adults were around because today they are at a meeting to talk about which laws have precedence. There are Ika laws that are really conventions and *colono* laws that are frequently statutes with more weight than custom. These two groups are at constant odds owing to the fact that the Ika resist the *colonos* at every turn and especially their aggressive grabbing of land. It is not a happy place this well-named San Sebastian.

Having demonstrated that the strip will suit our purposes, we went back to Valledupar in the middle of the afternoon. I had hoped we could also look at the sacred lakes we knew to be in the vicinity of Mt. Bolivar but the cumulus was building and we had no oxygen. To get a good view, we would have to be well above 15,000 feet, too high not to risk hypoxia. So we flew to the Corazzi airstrip and gathered our belongings for another night in Valledupar. Tomorrow we will get fuel from the *fumigación* people who spray incredible amounts of toxins on the local crops. Fortunately, we had to walk only two blocks to the one restaurant we have found reliable, the Palacio de Asado, truly a palace of steak.

June 8th 1981

In the last two days the weather may have finally turned from winter to little summer. The sun is brighter and the skies are clearer. We have made several landings at San Sebastian carrying in baggage and supplies. We have even been able to penetrate northward to glimpse the heretofore-obscured peaks and upper ranges of the Sierra Nevadas. They are undeniably beautiful but I wonder whether we will ever experience them from the ground. The lakes lying at the southern end of the range are said to be sacred and look pure and deep. The Ika say each lake contains a serpent and that the waters are the homes of their ancestral mothers. The peaks, on the other hand, for inescapable symbolic reasons, are thought to be the homes of their ancestral male parents.

The whole range is compact and uniquely so in comparison with the Alps or the Himalayas. It comprises no more than about two-and-a-half million acres of which the Ika occupy less than a fifth. The Kogi, who are neighbors to the Ika, share much with them in cosmological thinking. In fact, the Kogi have an even more elaborate view of how the world was formed and is maintained than their fellow believers, the Ika.

By now our airmanship is convincing but then I never thought otherwise, at least about Fulton's. We also are convinced of the utility of our small aircraft having seen its load-carrying capability and its obvious convenience as a way to come and go in the mountains.

We returned from our excursions to San Sebastian where we met with Yezid. I talked with him and two of his more politically minded colleagues about what I hoped to accomplish. They appeared to enjoy the formality of the discussion and the opportunity to share their thoughts about the undertaking. One of them said that he saw my project as a confrontation between two mules: I did not know the Ika and the Ika did not know me. What he saw must have been the spectacle of two stupid animals banging their heads.

After two hours, the sky conditions prompted our departure, which was easy on takeoff but soon showed us what it might be like when the ridges are obscured by deteriorating weather. We found a way through a pass at Aguacil and coasted down to the broad valley that points toward Bogotá. Once in the lowlands we decided to do more short-field practice and went to a strip I had noticed when flying into Corazzi. We went to it and did landings and takeoffs until a truck came with many people looking like picnickers. When I shut down I was told the strip was private and that I should leave. I said we would but then noticed an enormous tractor with a huge trailer parked in the middle of the strip. I think it was there to convince us of their seriousness. Finally it pulled aside enough for us to get off the ground and return to Valledupar.

There is a general tension here owing to the drug business that dominates all else in this region. Northern Colombia is the epicenter of major marijuana commerce and the La Guajira peninsula where most of the drugs are transshipped is not far away. So practicing landings in a stripped-down American registry Cessna on what amount to dirt roads in distances of five or six-hundred feet understandably brings up questions about where we might be going and what we are doing. The people who told us to leave had alerted the military police who met us on landing at Valledupar. We were at once subjected to a thorough search of both the plane and ourselves. I'm sure they were puzzled to find nothing. I am also sure they were mystified that they were not being paid either by us or by our sponsors in the Colombian drug world. We were eventually released when a lieutenant realized a mistake had been made but the privates and sergeants were reluctant to give up. Somewhere, they were sure there was evidence of our true intentions.

This experience was not pleasant mostly, I think, because I saw there could be no recourse from a police that is a law in itself and is manned by largely uneducated recruits. The element of unpredictability is what is so unsettling. I am impressed by the absence here of lawfulness as I know it even in the more hostile and violent American urban environments. The other day I was getting a flashlight at a small bodega in a busy Valledupar street when an immense brick hit the sign hanging above my head just as I was going in. I only glimpsed the face of the young man who had flung it, not at me but at a policeman who was still fumbling for his pistol. It was pure and lawless rage.

June 9th 1981

We are relocated in Cartagena, an agreeable place to be if only for the old city and its public spaces. There is a restaurant here to which we invariably return. It is called La Fregata and I have not been disappointed yet.

The rains have been impressive in size and duration so I have no doubt that the San Sebastian strip is unusable. Besides, Adele is coming tomorrow on Avianca's only weekly nonstop from New York. She may be with Mary Beth, Fulton's new wife. I think Fulton hopes she will come even more than I hope she will not. I see no way for her to join us in the Sierras. Fulton has told me his premonitory senses tell him she is coming and that she will join us. He also said that his premonitory judgment has never failed. I am not feeling good about needing to discredit his sensibilities but maybe she will not even be on the plane.

We are staying at the Bolívar, a small hotel in El Centro. Unlike the high-rise tourist hotels near the beach, it is not without some decadent appeal. The small streets in the city's center are a little like Ibiza and are filled with tourists who have been told they must see the old city. It is well worth the effort now that some of its colonial remains are in the process of restoration. The rich of Bogotá are getting their hands on ruins and making vacation houses of them just as has already happened throughout the Mediterranean world.

What I find missing is any vitality or animation. I watched for an hour sitting under an enormous equestrian statue of Simón Bolívar as people walked about in the city's major square. Their movement was joyless and I detected no music of any kind in what they were doing, which is a vast contrast with, for example, Haiti, an entirely different Caribbean culture. A general gloom is in the air and I do not know how to account for it. People are stiff and uncomfortable beneath their shapeless and dreary clothes. The mingling of Black, Indian, and Spanish blood has not resulted in much to remark upon with regard to physical beauty or grace.

June 10th 1981

The once-a-week nonstop from New York to Cartagena has been delayed five hours for what we are told are necessary repairs to the Cartagena airport. It is now to arrive at 8:30 p.m., which is well past sunset when I had thought no flights could land. I think the repairs must refer to runway work that was ongoing when we landed more than ten days ago. Pilots of the world, I am told, are unwilling to land at Cartagena for all kinds of reasons including inadequate lighting. But it seems Boston is on the same list of airports considered black holes. I have never landed at Boston's Logan but Cartagena doesn't seem that bad.

Adele was on the ground at 9:30 p.m. and we were eating at La Fregata an hour later. We were the only people in the garden of this lovely villa that sits on the boundary between the old and new cities. There is no Mary Beth and so Fulton's premonitions have finally failed him.

June 13th 1981

We are still in Cartagena when we had supposed we might already be in Mamingeka, the village where we intend to spend the days ahead. We are now two weeks behind a schedule made in a mood of apparent optimism. We also are victims of bureaucratic inefficiencies regarding our special permission to fly the Cessna in airspace used largely by drug cartels. The letter to extend our authorization never came despite assurances it would. We went to the airport and were told we could not move. We went back to the hotel and learned the permission would be at the Cartagena tower by early morning. We went back to the airport and were told it had not arrived and the copy that had been sent to Barranquilla was not enough. It was neither stamped nor signed and thus could easily be a forgery. An hour before the airport closed for runway repairs and Bogotá closed for a

weekend of no work, a telex arrived with the explanation that the permission had been lost and then found in the Civil Aviation files at El Dorado airport in Bogotá. The tower chief was quite unbelieving but could find no further reason to keep us on the ground. To leave I had first to file a flight plan, obtain stamped approval from the tower, pay parking and landing fees, obtain a stamped signature from Civil Aviation in Cartagena, bring the flight plan back to the tower, do a run-up and preflight. At last we took off and the flight from Cartagena to Valledupar proceeded in foul weather with rain at all altitudes. Still, we kept going, reaching Valledupar early in the afternoon. Fulton flew on to the San Sebastian strip to see if we could go there in the morning but he had to turn back due to heavy rain and thunderstorms. In fact, little summer has not arrived.

June 14th 1981

Another day is lost owing to our Jeep chauffeur being late and so we spend another day and night in the tedious environs of Valledupar. I completed arrangements with one Don Jaime Rodriguez who said he would strip and polish the aircraft. Despite some disquieting signs of incompetence, I am entrusting to him one aircraft and $300 in down payment. My hope is that it will not only look differently than it has since last winter in Minneapolis but that it will assume a new meaning in my life. We all take the time to wash clothes and ourselves in anticipation of it being harder to do these things when we go to live with the Ika.

P22

P23

June 15th 1981

Five of us left this morning by Jeep for the mountains we could see quite easily through an early mist. We plan to return to San Sebastian from Mamingeka on the 25th, two days after a festival during which it is said there will be many drunken *colonos*. So we could not have taken the aircraft even if it were available without fearing some harm might come to it.

Once in San Sebastian our thoughts turn to the next leg of this journey, which will be an arduous combination of mule ride and shanks' mare. We do this wishing it would take less time to get started, all of us agreeing that San Sebastian is not a pleasant stopover. There is tiresome intrigue among the Institute personnel and any Ika unfortunate enough to live nearby. The Institute is engaged in raising the Ika's indigenous consciousness, something I feel the Ika have no difficulty doing quite well on their own. But such thinking would deprive these urbanites from Bogotá of their sense of sacrifice on behalf of their tribal brothers. I don't see much fraternity on the part of the Ika but that is what the Institute wants ardently to foster. So also do the brethren of the Catholic Mission but they are said to be even less successful playing this game.

I heard tonight there was a murder of an Ika man by another Ika while they were drinking in Pueblobello. How this will be resolved depends on whose law prevails, the Ika's or that of the *mestizo* farmers. I sense that it will be academic since the only effective law is that of superior force which belongs to whoever has the guns, and this is not the Ika.

We retire early to damp beds and the inevitability of fleas.

June 17th 1981

The 16th was a day of further waiting for more mules, for guides who have not shown up, and for the rain to stop. The 17th dawned unpromisingly overcast but we felt the familiar desire to be on our way. Some mules and donkeys have been collected in the Comisario's compound and a few Ika guides have come to lead us to Mamingeka. One of them is a young person of about seventeen or eighteen whom I had gotten to know a little in my first brief visit last November. His name is Efrian and he has

one of the sunniest dispositions I have ever encountered. He is bright and intent on learning English. He also has a great curiosity about why I am in his country. His real employment is as a priest-in-training with Mama Marco. One of the things I have noticed about Mama Marco's role is how consuming it is of energy and time. The work never ends. Our other guide is slightly older but appears to have his own gentle disposition.

We wanted to leave before dawn but rain delayed us yet again. It was mid-morning when we were on our hesitant way. The problems relate mostly to the condition of the trail which, in turn, depends on the amount of recently fallen rain. Footing is difficult under the best circumstances and when it is not dry the animals struggle to stay upright and are not always successful. When they lose their balance, they can fall a great distance if it happens at the edge of an abyss, and there are many between San Sebastian and Mamingeka.

The shortage of mules and the condition of the trail have meant we will have to leave behind most of the camera equipment and wait for it to be brought separately. There are five non-Indians in the initial party, Adele, Fulton, Yezid, Genoveve, and myself. Only Fulton seems to be happier afoot, though he was given one of the few mountable animals. It took four hours to reach the stopping place where one rests for the final climb to Mamingeka. Everyone was tired. Rosa, our cook, was vomiting and faint, Fulton was exhausted by his walk and all of us wished we were more than just halfway. Of course, none of the Ika showed any sign of fatigue. For them, what we were doing was routine. They delighted in the verticality of the journeying, whether ascending or descending.

Apart from its difficulty for the traveler, the countryside was memorably beautiful. It was hard to keep my eyes on the trail where they were needed almost all the time and I regretted not lingering to better take in the wider scene. Happily, the weather remained fair with clouds shrouding us only late in the day as we made the last long descent through a welcome mist to Mamingeka.

I decided to walk the last few miles less from any consideration for my excellent mount than in the hope of recovering some obedience in the muscles of my lower body. I also wished to test my stamina at an altitude higher than the sea level to which I am accustomed. The last hundreds of feet convinced me I am not a mountain man and I arrived in Mamingeka more in gratitude than triumph. I am happy to be here once again and the prospect of a lengthy stay fills me with pleasure and relief.

June 18th 1981

Today was our first full day and it was taken up with domestic chores such as arranging where to sleep, how to eat, and wash. These are really the only essential requirements and they can, of course, be met in a number of ways. The people of Mamingeka did not know when we would arrive and so nothing had been gotten ready for us. There was no house in which to sleep and put our things and so we were in the men's and the women's *concurruas*. The men's was just as I remembered from my November visit, not particularly suitable for rest. My fatigue was such that no amount of drumming, talking, singing, spitting, or flute playing made the slightest difference. We ate nothing for want of an arrangement for cooking and from pity for poor Rosa who had fared so badly on the trek.

June 19th 1981

Today dawned in a thick fog or low clouds, depending on how one views these matters, and ended in torrential rain. The little summer continues having difficulty making its appearance. I only hope it is not too little to be noticed. I was also hoping the cameras and other equipment would soon arrive. I feel bereft without them at hand and my mind occasionally turns to the trail we have been over and to questions of whether the beasts carrying this burden will keep their footing. But no one came as would be expected on such a day and I went to bed both wet and worried. Adele and I are in a little storeroom that has been emptied for us in an effort to provide some privacy. It is private except that it is also where Rosa prepares what looks already like dwindling supplies. Fulton and I had collected all kinds of things in Valledupar but when we left San Sebastian for those days in Cartagena, Rosa may have been using what we had purchased to feed her friends and relatives.

P24

Fulton is dismayed by these arrangements. He is not accustomed to eating without a menu and our plates of noodles with a slice of Spam are really not enough for his large and discriminating appetite. For myself, I am delighted not to be spending time worrying about cooking and cleaning. Whatever we have or do not have is fine with me.

In almost no time, the principle of reciprocity has begun to take effect and the wife of Mama Marco, the spiritual head of this community, presented us with several eggs and boiled yucca root. I am counting on this expression of sociability to make our meals more interesting and our relations more normal, but I am not at all sure there is much surplus in the frail and limited economy of the poor but industrious Ika.

Still, there is plenty of sharing going on all the time. The Ika male's invariable greeting is to give and receive from the obligatory *mochila* of coca leaves that every man above a certain age has hanging from his neck. In this gesture, much of how they feel about living together is repeatedly expressed.

June 20th 1981

Today the ceiling was higher than it has been, high enough for Mama Norberto, a disciple of Mama Marco, to come to Mamingeka from wherever he stopped yesterday in the rain. He had with him what I have been fretting about these past few days. Everything was wet but the magic of plastic and Mama Norberto's American poncho have saved the cameras, film, and other important articles from permanent harm.

By mid-morning the sky had cleared and Mama Marco began the preparation for what he had been planning from the time we arrived, a short journey eastward and down the valley to some sacred stones. I filmed him making and assembling the little packets of string and cotton that are used as offerings and which are part prayer and part payment to the Gods.

All of us were obliged to make offerings having just arrived from our different worlds. Doing this would grant us a measure of spiritual cleanliness and some degree of protection during our stay. It was a lengthy but not a solemn task, more like a church social than a liturgical exercise.

P25

P26

Everyone was smiling and happy to be engaged in something carrying the promise of benefit. In fact, the glow of faith was evident everywhere.

We were told that, if we thought hard about food, such thinking would help manifest its abundance and variety. The trick was to project such thoughts into the tiny balls of cotton held behind one's back in a gesture meant to resemble a person carrying a great load of fruit or vegetables. When sufficiently infused by right-minded thought, these balls are arranged in left- and right-hand mounds along with bits of string tied in knots. These are wrapped in dry leaves, tied once again and given to Mama Marco. He then starts to chant his prayers holding the balls firmly in his hands. They are finally collected in a heap that is transferred to a bag already full of offerings given to him by other members of his flock. There were several such bags. I could see that Mama Marco, as the priest for a large circle of parishioners, was a busy man. Given his unhesitating sincerity, I did not see how he would have enough time to discharge such a heavy burden of obligations.

Our plan was to go tomorrow on a pilgrimage to the gods but as luck, or the gods, would have it, I pulled a muscle in my back lifting something. I asked for a postponement of twenty-four hours to see if the spasms would abate. It was agreed to do this but with the solstice coming on the 22nd, we could not postpone the journey further. The gods had to be fed before the solstice arrived.

The past two nights have been utterly cloudless revealing an astonishing collection of stars which, with an almost full moon, have been bright enough for reading. I would like to do that and to write also, but there is no furniture in this society of deep

thinkers for either of these activities. When people want to sit, they use their haunches or the men go to the little stone thrones arranged on top of a small hill where they spend their time talking and where Mama Marco can often be found doing his work.

The process is slow but we are learning to adjust to our much simplified lives. We eat and sleep in a hut filled with smoke, insects, furtive dogs, visiting Ika, and occasional chickens. It was constructed by a method known as wattle and daub, an armature of interwoven saplings plastered with mud. The house is round like almost all traditional Ika dwellings and not more than fifteen feet in diameter. Inside it is dry, thanks to a foot-thick thatch of stout grass that is the residence of a multitude of insects. They appear content to stay in their straw abode whereas the fleas, ticks, flies, and mosquitoes are ravenously interested in their human companions. Every day our arms, legs, and necks are aflame with their poison and even the strongest repellent, so effective against the mosquitoes of Maine, seems only to stimulate their craving for yet more blood.

I was able to do some filming today despite my back, which has in fact improved. Mama Marco was here because we have put off the pilgrimage until tomorrow. Fulton is helpful as always but chafes a little when asked to do things my way rather than his own. I have always admired the optical quality of his image-making but have sometimes thought content suffered at the expense of form. His images are pure and the light is frequently arresting but while the effect is satisfying to the retina, the mind, at least my mind, hunts for meaning. The result is, musically speaking, a bit like listening to scales and not melodies. But he has taught me much about what light can shape. I am trying to show him what light can say. This life we are leading is clearly a challenge for Fulton. He is helped through it by some comforts he brought with him, including a small flute, a Walkman, his favorite cigarettes, and a few pints of grain alcohol. He told me the alcohol was recommended by a mentor, William Burroughs, whose own travels have taken him into a number of obscure planetary corners.

P27

P28

June 21st 1981

Pilgrimage day began with beautiful weather and we made our way downhill to the east for the first hour. There was only one mule because the others had not been found by the time we left. This meant we were heavily burdened, my having decided to bring the Aaton and Bolex cameras, a tape recorder, and other necessities of filmmaking. Fortunately, I had the help of a strong young Ika who carried the Aaton. I was particularly happy he was there for the return uphill. It fascinated me to see how little encumbered he was by the considerable weight on his back. Growing up in this mountainous landscape has developed his body in ways mine never was or ever will be.

At the end of ninety minutes walking, we arrived at the first of the sacred spaces, near a cascading stream about sixty feet wide and responsible for an enormous din. It was difficult to hear Mama Marco singing above the roaring water and most of the quiet, recitative chanting was lost in the tumult. We moved on through a succession of groves, rock formations, caves, and other holy sites until mid-afternoon when it was time to start back to Mamingeka. The evening sun plummets into these valleys with almost no warning, making it even more difficult to do steep climbing along the narrow trails.

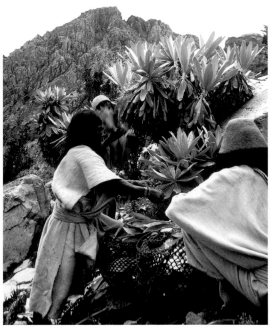

In the morning descent we were able to gather a few edible fruits such as mangoes and limes that grow only at a lower altitude. A thousand feet make a big difference and owing to the wide range of ecological zones in the Ika habitat, diet can be very different depending on where one lives. Elevation also determines what crops to farm and what animals to domesticate. The range of elevation in which these choices are made is from about four to twelve thousand feet.

Mama Marco has been in fine form throughout the day and has paid little attention to the cohort of gringos following him wherever he went. He is a serene and cultivated man whose mind is filled with knowledge gained during a long apprenticeship in the priesthood. He seems never to sleep but is always busy leading the already burdensome life of an adult Ika and the even more taxing life of a *mama* responsible for the well-being of a large and dependent community. I notice when using the camera that, although he is not at all self-conscious, there is a faint suggestion of concern in the midst of his cordiality that whoever will see what he is doing will acknowledge his performance. In this regard, I think I have found an almost perfect subject in that Mama Marco can sustain a high level of involvement out of both self-interest and a feeling of general responsibility while, at the same time, he will not use the camera as a means of promoting his already considerable self-regard.

I suppose his performance constitutes borderline acting but I cannot think this in any way subverts the process by which the camera finds significant expression. I have no idea what it would be like to say to Mama Marco: "Be yourself." I have a feeling it would result in mere perplexity. The few times I have asked someone to do something for the camera, the results are usually hilarious renderings of what should be ordinary bits of behavior. On the other hand, I am sometimes most convinced by roles in films played by nonactors who have obviously been directed. How can things get more real than in *Bicycle Thief*?

A few times on this pilgrimage to these sacred places I felt I was witnessing something approaching rapture. I could not possibly have instructed Mama Marco in the fine points of that condition. I can only thank him after the fact for achieving it.

June 22nd-24th 1981

The days pass with alarming rapidity. They are a
blur of major and minor events, sacred and profane
and I am using my limited film stock faster than
anticipated. If the present pace is maintained, my
supply will be gone by the middle of July, well in
advance of when I had thought we would be going
home. It is not that I have been spendthrift. Nor do
I feel the 25,000 feet I brought is especially parsi-
monious. That amount provides for a total of
twelve hours of screen time, which is generous, if
the main concerns are visual and not documentary.
There have been only a few times when I wanted
sound recorded at the same time as image, a strategy that always wastes film, and Fulton for the
most part is making time-lapse sequences that are
notoriously economical of film. Often he begins
before the sun rises or sometimes at the end of the
day when the light bends around the encircling
hills as it hurtles into the ravines. He does all this
with a hand-operated Bolex, making it a very
tedious task. I am awed by his patience but can
easily understand his fascination with the process.
The results are condensed lightshows with frequently spectacular optical effects. It almost doesn't
matter that there is little if any content.

As might be expected on the solstice, we
became involved with celestial issues, particularly
those relating to the sun. The Ika and, even more,
the Kogi are known for their astronomical accomplishments. They are more than mere lovers of the
heavenly bodies. They are keen observers of many
of them. Among those to which they pay particular
attention is the sun and they have made a system-
atic study of its behavior. I was told the sun's journey across the sky would be watched with
particular attention on the solstice but I did not
sense this to have been the case. I was also told
there was a fear among some of the sun's devoted
observers that it might not rise at all but return to
its origins and plunge the world into perpetual
darkness. To ascertain that the sun was observing
its habitual practices, one needed to see at a critical juncture whether it had reached a little notch
between two peaks off on the eastern horizon. This
is what is meant to happen on the solstice and,
apparently, it did.

P30

Mama Marco has the responsibility of providing the sun with adequate worship. This is what he
has been doing in the days leading up to the 22nd
by making offerings of cotton balls and bits of
string wrapped in leaves, offerings that were
charged through correct thinking with an abundance of nourishing food and other wealth. In
Mamingeka there is a sense of relief connected
with the fact that the sun is where it should be and
has not retreated to a nether world for having been
slighted by those who should have worshipped
with greater fervor and generosity.

Today Adele, Genoveve, and Yezid climbed on
mules and set out for San Sebastian. It was important for me that Adele was here in Mamingeka to
comfort and encourage us all. Yezid will come back
in a few days and stay with Fulton and me until
sometime later in July. Adele returns to Cambridge
and Genoveve to Bogotá. I hope Fulton will survive
what I think is an ordeal for him. He has a cold
that will not subside and his situation in the *concurrua* where he has chosen to sleep does not allow
for much peace or quiet. There is also some doubt
in his mind as to what his role is or should be. I
see no problem because he is here to help however
he can. He is good at everything, trusted implicitly,
and his mind is as important as his hands. For
Fulton things are made difficult only by reason of
our reduced living arrangements. For me there are
fewer problems because I am content with what I
am seeing and with giving thought to putting it in
a film. The place is undeniably one of beauty, even
mystery, and we are among people of exceptional
complexity and character. Except for the occasional
stab of fear that I will not avoid the pitfall of the
picturesque, I find the situation both difficult and
engaging from the filmmaking point of view.

June 25th & 26th 1981

I have decided to take some moments to reflect a little on what has been happening since we arrived on the 17th at this village/cosmos called Mamingeka. I do this seated on a rude bench using another bench for a desk. It is not a familiar posture for writing or anything else for that matter, but that is possibly how it should be while living with this outlying remnant of ancient Mayan culture situated in the midst of sacred mountains and valleys.

I am outside the temple or men's *concurrua,* which is on a raised place as one would expect of the Mayan imagination. People come here for the same quiet introspection I am pursuing myself. My writing excites the young who have gathered around me. Maybe they think I am trying to solve the vast cosmological problems that absorb their own elders' thoughts.

P31

This morning, typically, I was awake by first light. It has been a clear day except for some inconsequential puffs of cumulus off to the east. My waking was in synchrony with the arrival of Rosa, our missionized Ika cook who comes every morning bringing fire from a neighbor's hearth. She uses it to kindle the remains of a previous fire that goes dead at my elbow during the night. Fires are encouraged into life here in the Sierras by gusts of wind created by powerful lungs. The fire starts amid the first of many clouds of dust and ash produced on an average day. In every house, every movement raises dust from the bone-dry floor and until night, when movement stops, it permeates everything: food, beds, clothes, one's innermost being.

It takes many minutes to boil water and then to stir in the coffee to make the first of several cups of this delicious beverage. Apart from coffee, we are in short supply of nearly everything. Either we miscalculated badly or there is still some leakage of our stores. But this is more than half expected since we are required to put into circulation things we have brought. It is one half of the reciprocity whereby gifts are made to us of avocados, eggs, milk, and sometimes lamb or goat. I welcome this arrangement in that a supply of fresh vegetables is worth more than any number of cans of Spam. I also welcome the effect this mutual dependency has on the relations we enjoy with our Ika others. Food is the great unifier even if it means sleeping near the smoking forelegs or neck and head of a freshly slaughtered goat. We are to eat the ribs for lunch and then stew the rest for dinner tonight. This should correct the slow physical decline brought about by our mostly vegetarian diet. We are weakening and a goat may restore our waning strength.

It is important there is enough energy to meet the exigencies of filmmaking in this environment. Yesterday was particularly active in this regard and last night I began thinking about what I was doing here as a filmmaker. Much of what I have so far done has been to cover a number of activities such as pressing sugarcane, shearing sheep, and making lime and tobacco paste. These are hardly more than little stories of mostly routine bits of village life and as yet I have developed no ideas about their having any larger significance. All I can say at this

P32

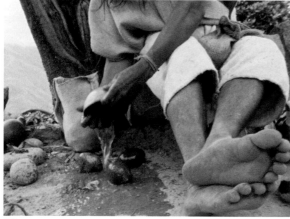

F10

point is that I am diverted but not inspired looking through the viewfinder. Now may be the time to explore the spiritual side of things which, after all, was my high-minded intention at the start. It was a shaman's inner life I wanted, not a pictorial chronicle of mundane activities.

The closest I have come to anything of this kind is to watch the patient divining done by Mama Marco. This involves a small calabash of water and a hollowed-out bead that is dropped into the water so as to make bubbles as it falls to the bottom. The bubbles are read as replies to questions posed before the bead was dropped. There have also been many occasions when Mama Marco has done his cotton ball work but this and the divining have not yet given me access to the thoughts behind the behavior, and I have not conceived of any imagery that would even begin to convey what those beliefs might be.

Another mode to explore could be surrealism in order to provide an alternative imagery for registering the sober realism of daily life. What imagery though? Maybe the short pixilated sequences Fulton is doing can serve or, maybe, something huge and almost unrecognizable, but belonging to Nature, like the enormous condors that go sailing by. There are also elements such as clouds, smoke, or fire itself that might take on some additional meaning. But I keep returning to the enigmatic divining cup into which the little bead is dropped in hopes of answers to questions that cannot be found in other ways.

Most of the necessities of Ika life are provided in solutions such as the way rope is made from maguey leaves, gardens are cultivated on hillsides, and cloth is woven from the wool of sheep. These are all measures taken to survive according to a set of long-established practices but they cannot deal with such problems as sickness, whom to marry, or what to name a child. For these matters the divining cup is needed and so is the sacred knowledge of a *mama*. I think I must find a way of learning about these aspects of their lives too. Maybe the journey I have promised myself to the sacred lakes high in the Sierras above Mamingeka will provide imagery of the kind needed. Meanwhile, I stare at the little gourd cup balanced on its three leveling stones and think about questions I would put to it were I a *mama* or simply myself.

P33

The Ika laugh frequently and appear to get much pleasure from play on words. I cannot understand their language but it is expressive and melodious. I have been told the language is not, technically, tonal, which is to say there is no phonetic significance to its various notes, but it is nonetheless musical and a delight to hear. At this moment in their history, some Ika are learning Spanish by listening to the occasional radio or from interaction with the encroaching *colonos*. The Ika play with Spanish words, too, but not with the same delight.

June 28th 1981

It is Sunday afternoon and I am sitting outside Mama Marco's house with chickens pecking interminably at the dry earth under my feet. They are said to belong to the inner ring of life here in this village that is both so structured and so organic at the same time. Besides chickens there are people, dogs, and a few cats. All these creatures are fenced in by wood, stones, or thicket so that the life beyond the ring cannot penetrate. Most of them leave their droppings inside the village limits. Outside the ring are the mules, goats, cows, pigs, and sheep. Such animals and adult humans defecate beyond the village limits under the watchful surveillance of pigs, which appear to survive mainly on human excrement.

P34

F11

F12

Yesterday we went with Mama Marco to a particularly sacred site, one that is importantly related to the domain of food. There was mention of eagles and mosquitoes but beyond the fact that the place in question was a long way off, not much more was said. It lay to the northeast and the way led along a path that went straight down from the sugarcane mill. We were afoot because the terrain was too difficult for mules. Fortunately, I had Ika helpers who carried whatever I did not need to have in my hands. The trail at first was steep and I had difficulty staying balanced carrying thirty pounds of camera down an almost vertical, gravel-strewn path. It was so steep that my ears felt the pressure differential as we descended and the ecology changed radically before my eyes. It was suddenly tropical and there was fruit, unseen near Mamingeka, growing temptingly within my grasp.

After two hours of walking, the path turned upward into a canyon closed by a hill at its further end and carrying a stream that rushed toward us with considerable force over huge boulders and with a deafening roar. Suddenly, around a turn in the riverbed, there was a great foaming pool of blue water fed from some hidden source. The canyon had narrowed to a virtual crack between steep, moss-lined rock walls. The Ika slowed their pace to determine the best route up the narrowing canyon and indicated that we were close to our goal. By this time, I was exhausted and sore-footed from walking on the torrent's rocky bed.

It looked as though I might have to scale the dank walls above the river in order to join the Ika who were quite comfortable with this maneuver. But within moments I could hear the waterfall that was our destination; it lay only a few hundred feet ahead. In the pool beneath this glorious cascade Mama Marco, with his white skirts tucked up under his belt, was standing up to his thighs in water. It fell to his left from the lip of a ridge sixty feet above our heads, sending up clouds of cooling droplets that reflected a sun also falling through the trees on the far side of the gorge. The moment was the closest I have seen Mama Marco come to ecstatic possession.

He had traveled this long and difficult way in order to give offerings to the Mother of Food who is thought to dwell in this magical space. I had struggled to keep behind him with my camera poised for filming and I longed to be making images when the time came. Yet when we arrived, I was assailed by a feeling that I should not intervene in any way and the previous urge to inflict my own mark on the occasion suddenly disappeared. It was enough to simply witness this vital expression of Nature and man's worship of it. I was at a curious loss to put a cinematic face on the event.

Eventually I did attempt some image making but not, I suspect, with notable success. I continued to regard the scene as one that ought to remain undocumented, that to film it was in some way to defile it, to situate it in an irrelevant time and space. I will be interested to see the results when the film is processed. I doubt the footage can possibly convey the intensity of the experience I lived.

After making his offerings and capturing what appeared to be a fledgling owl from its nest somewhere under and behind the falls, and after filling a sack with the food produced by the many birds we disturbed by coming here, Mama Marco started home. This food is in fact what the birds defecate but it is used in offerings to the gods.

Mere exhilaration was what carried me yesterday back up the three hours of mountainside to Mamingeka.

F13

F14

Today I awoke at dawn hoping to find the *concurrua* sufficiently well lighted to film the slow awakening of the men who slept there last night. Fulton was up and had started another time-lapse sequence of the rising sun. He is, even at this moment approaching evening, above and behind the village making another sequence of the failing, late-afternoon light. I was only moderately successful inside the *concurrua* as there was too little light and not much human activity. Even Yezid slept on in his garish imported hammock that I must remember to ask him to move to a dark corner.

Later in the morning Mama Marco said I should come with him to some sacred stones that lay above the village to the west. I tried to decline his invitation, having been on the pilgrimage yesterday to the glorious waterfall of the Mother of Food. He seemed a trifle hurt and told me it was "*muy cerquita,*" so we set out with me being, this time, my own bearer of the camera. I did this despite a promise to myself that I would, in the interest of preserving strength for the act of film-making, always have someone willing to share this burden. Endurance contests have less interest for me now than in the past.

The trail led upward and we passed groups of rocks with names like Father of Dreams and Father of Vomiting until we came to a place with the name *Gwi Achina*, or Bad Father, an interesting rock formation. Mama Marco climbed onto it as I began to film. There was no room for me but I came as close as I could. The whole scene lacked the grandeur of yesterday but the view behind Mama Marco was open to the east and his performance was totally accessible.

I will join him any time he asks for my company on his worshipful rounds. I have learned that it is essential to follow him almost anywhere he goes. He is the center of my interest in this Ika world.

F15

June 29th 1981

The day began cloudless with the sun rising rapidly into the sky. Ironically, as the weather improves, there has been a general deterioration in the community's health. In the house between where I am sleeping and the *concurrua* there is a family with several children all of whom have dreadful coughs. Their house seems almost to shake as their lungs gasp for air. The mother brings me a bowl of milk every morning.

When I arose, three stricken mothers of coughing children had gathered outside the *concurrua* to make packets of offerings they will hand to Mama Marco. Usually this sort of thing waits until much later in the day when women have finished their daily chores and so I sense urgency in what they are doing at this early hour. It has been decided that *moro*, a Spanish word from the time of conquest, lurks nearby, ready to bring death. Something has to be done to persuade the *moro* to depart.

The relatives of Mama Marco continued their worship near the *concurrua*. Soon they were discussing the immediacy of death and the need to work harder and faster. Gathered there were the son of Mama Marco who is himself a *mama*, Mama Marco's wife, and one or two other women with small and unwell children. They left in the early afternoon when I had been busy at my own work for more than eight hours and Fulton was still above the village completing still another time-lapse sequence.

He has not come down since early morning so I have sent something for him to eat. By nightfall he will have to stop for lack of light. In the storeroom where I live, a woman came in while I was eating. She was with her daughter of about five years and they both were making *mochilas*, something all women do. I was astonished by the child's faultless ability to manage this complicated task. I don't think I have ever seen such perfect imitation of an adult by a child. I must see if I can put it on film.

I am told that nine levels are structurally represented in the building of a proper *concurrua*. The first is a horizontal stringer about three feet from the ground. Most thoughtful people belong to the ninth or highest level. The whole edifice is held up by the four fathers of earthquakes.

P35

June 30th 1981

I sense today an odd bending of time as I find myself midway through the year. Everything has slowed a little as happens on trips like this where all is at first novelty and excitement and then a pause ushers in the next phase. The Ika could not be more hospitable and courteous. While they are almost perfectly agreeable to my joining them in their daily lives, I have never felt harassed or bedeviled by their curiosity about me. Privacy seems to be a virtue in both our worldviews. They go directly and vigorously about their own lives with absolute composure. Their intimate lives, of course, elude me entirely, that and real understanding of their cosmological thinking.

Chronic upper respiratory ailments plague everyone at the moment. Even Fulton is afflicted. Day and night there is a constant lung-wracking that claims attention the way coughing fits do in churches during Sunday services.

I have taken an opportunity to talk a little with Mama Marco about plans for the next days and for the period following the 16th of July when I hope to have come back. My biggest desire is to accompany him to the sacred lakes, wherever they might be. He has agreed in principle and says three or four days might be required to complete the journey there and back. I also want to take Mama Marco in the Cessna to Santa Marta on the coast. I have vague notions of taking him, as sorcerer, into the clouds and, once there, to test his affinity to the realm of flight. I suppose I should be prepared to stay aloft and obscured by clouds long enough to see what happens, but then this may all be only daydreaming.

Going to Santa Marta is what Mama Marco does from time to time in keeping with the requirements of his work. There, in Santa Marta, is the Caribbean and at its shore are the shells, rocks, and fishy things so valuable to a mountain shaman. Ordinarily, Mama Marco would walk to Santa Marta over the Sierra Nevadas, which might take a month. I am offering him a daylong excursion, there and back. My plan is to go at the very end of my stay, late in July. My thoughts of coming again in December are not yet firm. It depends on what I have managed to do, which I will not know until I see the rushes on my return to Cambridge. For now

I worry most that I will have exhausted not just the raw stock but my limited store of ideas about how to get on with this perplexing business.

July 2nd 1981

Yesterday I visited some gardens belonging to Mama Marco a short walk beyond the sugar mill. There he and his family cultivate several crops that are staples of the Ika diet. The garden is on a hillside so steep it was almost impossible for me to stand upright. Cultivating it is curiously easy owing to its extreme pitch that puts the soil almost in your face as you lean in toward the hill. No Ika working there seemed to have the slightest difficulty even when carrying a hundred or more pounds of plantains on his back. Shooting these scenes was demanding and watching me trying to stay balanced with the Aaton somewhere near eye level caused a good deal of merriment for those watching.

While walking home, Mama Marco saw or heard a snake in a banana tree and quickly killed it. I gather snakes are not protected under Ika convention, especially this kind that belonged to the cobra family and is thought to be quite dangerous. I could not stop thinking about all the banana trees I had put my hand into to get a grip on something while walking about in these hillside gardens.

As if he had not exerted himself sufficiently while cultivating his garden, Mama Marco put himself to the task of gathering firewood on his way back to the village. By the time we had reached the entry gate, he was carrying an enormous load of dead limbs that will be used for the fire that burns continuously in everyone's house.

Today I woke early after a night of spectacular lightning throughout a star-filled sky. Continuous and leaping from cloud to cloud, the lightning was most prodigious to the east and the lowlands off in the direction of Venezuela. Fulton and I both wanted to film it and we spent a few hours trying. Even prodigious lightning is an elusive subject, however, so I am not sure we had any success. In the morning, we filmed the rising sun that came up in a sky as clear as I have ever seen.

In a brief and beautiful little ceremony in the early forenoon, Mama Marco baptized some plantain, corn, yucca, onion, and two kinds of sugarcane, the plants most common to Ika gardens. Now

P36

it is dark and we repeat our habitual, evening meal. This near-ritual starts with Rosa and her daughter finding something to cook. Tonight it was rice, yucca, and a chicken I had insisted we buy in the village. She begins her work while it is still light so that it can be done with a minimum of groping. We are now only three, Fulton, Yezid, and myself, who are eating Rosa's food, and I am presently the only one living in our all-purpose storeroom. The smoke is thick, especially around mealtime. There is no outlet for it in the roof and our doorway is often blocked by large Ika women who come to chat with Rosa or to have a coffee.

My place is against one of the two uncluttered walls a few inches from the stones that steady the cooking pots. Someone is always blowing on the fire to keep it going, which creates yet more smoke and clouds of drifting ash. Keeping as close as possible to the mud floor is the only way to avoid the nearly unbreathable air. This assault upon the lungs has not, of course, diminished my delight in cigarettes. In fact, if anything, I am smoking more and with greater pleasure than at any time in my life, including childhood days behind the family cow barn lighting up corn silk I was told would burn but never did.

Tonight we were early for our meal after a relaxed late afternoon during which a swarm of parrots flew formations overhead for almost an hour. I was amazed and kept wondering if I could film it but also thinking that by the time I got my camera, the parrots would be miles away.

The menu is beans, rice, and chicken. We eat sitting on the ground because there are no chairs. It is an effort because unfamiliar muscles are required in this most familiar of all activities. There is no light to find a spoon, no place to put a cup of water without it spilling, nothing to remove red-hot pots from the fire. There are also the hunger-maddened dogs that brazen their way into our midst in search of scraps, famished chickens with their broods of hungry chicks pecking at crumbs falling from our plates, and the food-aware Ika who sense there will be residual beans and rice available when we are finished.

The meal advances hesitantly accompanied by halting conversation. I have long ago exhausted my limited store of conversational Spanish and Fulton creates mayhem with his complicated inter-rogatories directed at Yezid who is essentially flummoxed to the point of despair. Fulton will then trivialize language and ideas mercilessly in a play on words and puns that go completely over Yezid's head. I think Fulton is trying to distance this experience through a process of abstraction. He is not ready to treat it as reality worthy of his undivided attention.

By late evening the meal is over and the debris of utensils, dishes, and pots is pushed against the wall beside the door. Here, too, is where food stores are kept, including a tethered chicken waiting to be plucked and eaten. The condemned chicken is not more than two feet from my bed that now boasts the luxuriousness of not one but two thin foam pads following Adele's departure. I thought this chicken too sad a sight and so have found a place outside my dwelling for it and other ill-fated poultry.

Fulton and I wander outside and up to the *concurrua* in an effort to clear our lungs and minds. Tonight, one of Mama Marco's sons was busy heating coca leaves. I tried to film this but I have no confidence the little lamp I brought was sufficient illumination. To get the mystery of these dim interiors is a lighting problem of some magnitude and I have no equipment to get it right.

The coca leaves are heated slowly in a huge, blackened ceramic pot that sits on the glowing embers of the *concurrua* fire and are stirred carefully until they turn to a consistency close to tar. This is Fulton's entertainment tonight as is something or other every night. He keeps shifting his place in the *concurrua* in an effort to find some modicum of peace and quiet. These attempts have not been especially successful and he looks more haggard every day.

I return to my storeroom under a sky filled with stars and lightning bugs. Is it not an indication of mating when they illuminate themselves to become targets of desire? Lightning flashes complete the symmetry off toward the notched hills far to the east. I duck through my doorway hitting my head for the hundredth time.

July 4th 1981

It has been a rainy Fourth, not what it's supposed to be on my favorite holiday. The atmosphere is dismal, and there has been something of a slowing of the pace of things. I feel it has quite a lot to do with the prevalence of illness.

Our replacement cook/helper came yesterday. She is an Ika who married an Ika who no longer lives a traditional life. She is quiet and pleasant. Rosa was not much help as she dragged herself around in her absurd blouses and skirts, usually wearing two or three at the same time.

Yesterday, Mama Marco's brother Manuelo came from San Sebastian where he is some sort of leader. It was a surprise to see him because Yezid had expected to leave today for talks with him in San Sebastian. He can do it here I suppose. I have not been told what the nature of these negotiations with people like Manuelo are, but I suspect from what I do know that the intention is to foster a more self-aware and demanding Indian solidarity.

It is fine for Yezid to stay with us even if he is not able to speak either Ika or English with any fluency and so is somewhat isolated from both parties to our enterprise. He is also notably listless for which I have no ready explanation. I am afraid, too, that he is not sure what I am doing. At the start, there was some hope that he could learn filmmaking by watching but without a common language it is hard to make much progress. He can see me film what interests me but I wonder if it is what interests him. He also may be getting sick in the same way so many others are here in Mamingeka.

July 6th 1981

Around mid-morning I heard there would be some interesting work done in the *concurrua* by our resident *mamas*. Before getting this news I was trying to do some interesting work of my own down in the lower courtyard to which I retreated in the belief that my attention had been too concentrated in the upper courtyard where the *mamas* divine and devotees worship. Everything was getting too esoteric, too obsessive and I felt the need for something basic. I knew this could be found down in the lower part of the village where people lead a major part of their daily lives.

While filming in and around one of the houses, a gust of energy swept past me hurling a tray full of slops to the pigs. It was one of the more becoming ladies, the one who smiles with such intensity. She turned around and almost ran back up the hill to the little corral where she had been roping goats. The goats then led me on a chase back to the village and to Mama Marco's wife who blessed them and then to some boys who slit their throats.

At the *concurrua*, in Mama Marco's use of shells and stones that were chipped, broken, and much meditated upon, I saw more and better magic than I have until now seen. I then took a walk to the sugar mill, beyond that to a deadfall trap sprung by some game birds, and eventually to some boys who fetched and plucked them before going to work in their father's garden. Finally I came back to the village to witness elaborate censing of everyone in clouds of expensive smoke and vigorous chanting by Mama Marco.

After dinner we did more of our own work in the dark interior of the *concurrua*. It is late evening and Fulton has collapsed, as will I in moments. Yezid left at dawn for San Sebastian to pursue his political agenda. Only four more days are left before we ourselves go to San Sebastian and only 1000 feet of film remain unexposed. In two days there will be a forty-eight hour baptism and a small child's life is hanging by a thread. I pray that I will be gone before it dies. I cannot remember being so short on supplies even in New Guinea when, at one point, I was eating only songbirds. At least there were plenty of them. Yezid is to send back some of the film and rice we have stored in San Sebastian. If he does not, there is less reason to hold out and be further exhausted by these boundlessly energetic people.

P37

265

P38

F16

July 7th 1981

The most recent twenty-four hours have gone at an even slower pace than the previous twenty-four but there have been clear indications that some ritual or other is in the wind. Yesterday two goats were killed and quantities of yucca processed in a way that I am told makes it intoxicating. Today when I returned from what has become my own ritual bath at the bend in the trail to the north, an enormous cow appears to have been rather messily hacked to death. I think these are portents of more than the Ika's chronic anxiety about food. The hints I get from some scraps of Spanish spoken by the few Ika who command any of this language are that two of one of Mama Marco's son's children are to be baptized. This information is in conflict with Yezid's view that baptisms are done only in December.

Being one-third fewer in number, our own food problems are somewhat improved. Now there are eggs, milk, and an occasional avocado. We also have benefited from the recent carnage wreaked upon the herds. All this plus some rice and noodles should keep our strength up sufficiently to reach San Sebastian by the evening of July 11th. On the morning of the twelfth our Jeep hire should be waiting to take us to Valledupar. That day or early the next, I expect to repossess the aircraft and have flown it to where Fulton and I are invited to spend a few days of rest and recreation at the finca of Genoveve's parents.

I have reached a point where I welcome a brief respite from Mamingeka, although I am glad to say I am also at a place where my heart is quite won over and my head wholly open to the idea of a much deeper involvement with this village and its inhabitants. Both adults and children come nearer every day. I detect no fear and much amusement in what we are doing. The Ika are certainly not without humor, which endears them to me but not, I'm afraid, to Fulton who has seemed ready to leave almost from the time we arrived. He said the other day that he has expressed all he has to say about the Ika in what he has done with the Bolex. Despite his disquiet, he has been wonderfully considerate and an immense help. He more than anyone else needs relief from this wearying place and some building up for the long walk to the sacred lakes. Every day I am able to go farther and carry more weight less breathlessly, but the lakes are very high and far away.

July 8th 1981

While true that I can go up steeper inclines carrying ever more as the days go by, it is my spirit that is now flagging. I trust this is not apparent to those around me. It has something to do, I am sure, with the interminable coughing, retching, spitting, whining, and tantrums I hear from all directions. These are no longer background sounds; they are dominating the aural landscape. I listen to distressed humanity from all quarters, day and night. It is in my face, sitting, standing, or lying down. Mucous and vomit pour forth. Gobbets of expectorate fly in all directions. Tears come in floods. Everyone is fatigued by constant heaving and coughing. I wheel and dodge, duck and run. I recoil a hundred times a day. The village closes in just as it becomes more friendly and familiar. I retreat in the face of misery arriving from all directions. Pigs charge at me in mid-defecation. Snarling dogs plague me for scraps of food. Hens, cats, and roaches scavenge me into corners where hunger, thirst, and fear congregate with black flies, lice, fleas, ants, spiders, and other ravening insects.

The work suffers as I suffer. I don't feel centered, forgiving, or even interested; so the eye wanders and so does the camera. Why shoot at all? Why not shoot everything and go home? I can find nothing mysterious about illness and disease. A boy gasps for breath even as I write. He is in the house next door and his fit will last an eternity. I would love to have clean feet and I long for the eleventh when I will leave all this sickness behind. Why isn't that sick child dead? It should be and will be. The film could use it. Mama Marco is just

P39

barely holding things together. What more can he do? He works continuously for health and equilibrium. There isn't any time for humanity at large, only for that child who will have to die, that child or some other child. The Ika say they are my Big Brothers. In fact they say they are humanity's Big Brothers but they themselves are struggling to breathe, gasping for their next breath.

I filmed a sick child being bathed who flung himself to the ground in despair from choking on bacteria that will not go away. When will Mama Marco realize that wads of cotton and string are not enough? He himself is coughing badly but he has bought some aspirin today from a trader who came through with a mule load of urban nostrums.

July 10th 1981
I awoke to a steady rain that has been falling for about three hours. I'm reminded of New England where this is so common. Mama Marco predicted rain but for yesterday not today. He left early this morning with quantities of offerings under a sheet of plastic I had bought in Valledupar to keep our equipment dry on the backs of mules. He said he was going far away but I did not press the issue of accompanying him even though I wanted to go at least once more on one of his local pilgrimages. He returned at nightfall.

I spent much of the day on the upper terrace sensing that something was astir. It had to do with the rumor I have heard that Mama Marco's son, Cornello, wanted two of his children, a boy and a girl by different mothers, to be baptized. I have already described part of the prelude to this, the animals butchered and yucca fermented. But Mama Norberto has left as has Mama Marco and Manuelo. So it was Mortimero, another son of

Mama Marco, who got things going. Mortimero is something of a *mama* himself, dreamy and bemused most of the time. The ceremony was interesting but hardly intense and took place outside the *concurrua* from early morning to midday.

The two mothers, almost exactly spherical in shape, seemed a bit dull-witted but maybe it is from the shock of realizing the extent of their servitude under Ika rules of conduct. Both look pregnant and both possess two children of approximately one and two years. Their continual fecundity may be a way to offset a high rate of infant mortality.

After the ceremony, there was a brief celebratory moment during which relatives of the baptized children ate corn that had boiled all morning. They sang a few songs that reminded me of what I heard last night when they performed a little dance. The event was social in that only those connected to the baptismal family had gathered. I was not impressed by it as spectacle, but was charmed by the silent gliding of the women with bare feet doing a sort of *Paso Doble* to flute, drum, and rattle.

Today I find myself with less than one roll of film remaining, which means there is no more than seven or eight minutes of screen time left before I must get more. I cannot remember being in such short supply though I have always calculated the amount to bring as less than what might be needed under the most demanding circumstances. I do this, I think, in the belief that being chronically short makes what film there is more valuable.

I have brought fifty ten-minute rolls for the Aaton and Fulton has the same number of three-minute rolls for the Bolex. Fulton may need more because he tends to shoot as long as there is anything left. What is clear at this moment is that filming is over for the day.

In the midst of my writing these words, Mama Marco came by for coffee and conversation. After I had given him a few small presents, he started his customary declaiming upon several matters that mostly eluded me. I never really know what he is saying on these occasions but I detect a good deal of repetition both in tone and phraseology. These speeches sound a bit like sermons that are dusted off and given again and again. What most impresses me, though, is his vitality and capacity for work.

I am ready to leave tomorrow after sunrise. Everything is packed and the mules have been persuaded down from their pastures in the uplands. It will have been twenty-five nights on a hard mud floor when I leave this remarkable place. I feel much stronger though maybe ten or more pounds lighter. I also am confident I will not get lost in this strange wilderness of hills and valleys and that the people among whom I am living have now taken me into their confidence. I may have sensed the coherence and continuity of their lives too late to do much good filmmaking, and I am running low on both real time and screen time but I will come back in another season, if I feel certain enough there is something to be gained by doing so. I wonder though. December is a long way off.

July 18th 1981

Back in San Sebastian I am conscious of my abandonment of this already much forsaken journal. It has been more than a week since I put down any thoughts at all in a time of substantial change in my emotional status. One whole continent of love and care has sunk beneath the horizon with my sister Isabella's death. I learned of it on the night of July 12th from Adele when I called after flying to Cartagena from the Corazzi airstrip near Valledupar. Fulton and I had just come down off the mountain. I was told she had died while reading. She always read, Belle did, to sleep and to death. She read everything and very fast. I remember our father not believing her when she told him she had finished a book; he would quiz her and she would answer correctly and he would go away scratching his head.

Because Genoveve's family had a road accident that nearly took a life, our visit to their place was no longer possible. Yezid came with us so he could book a flight to Bogotá. There he became extremely ill with the respiratory complaint that has brought everyone to their knees. He was sick enough that we had to wait several days for him to return to Cartagena and bring him with us to San Sebastian.

Cartagena was purgatorial for many reasons, including terrible heat. I felt a strong desire to depart for the United States but before going home I was determined to take Mama Marco to the seashore in Santa Marta and then to let him take me to the sacred lakes. We reached San Sebastian on the seventeenth to discover that Mama Marco had kept his word and was waiting for us to fly him to Santa Marta.

I did some filming of him in the aircraft and on the beach in Santa Marta where he collected auspicious shells and pebbles. In all, it was a busy day of buses and taxis as well as noisy rides in the Cessna, rides that never approached magic flight as I had naively hoped. The day ended with my showing him his village from the air. He seemed exhausted for the first time since I'd met him but he sang while looking a bit distressed by the sheer magnitude of the day's experience.

We flew back to San Sebastian thinking we would be setting out immediately for the lakes. But Yezid is still not well and those who were to go upward have decided to wait a day to rest, cook some food, and prepare their sacred offerings. My patience is dwindling but I have made peace with the loss of another day.

F17

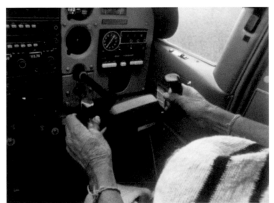

F18

Today the weather was fine and I was able to persuade Fulton to be with me in the air by early morning. This followed an incident too improbable to imagine. I had gone to my customary grove of trees above the cemetery west of the village to empty my bowels but before I was able to pull up my pants, several pigs had made a lunge for the space between my legs. I was alarmed by the ferocity of their attack and hurled immense stones at their heads in what could only look like a determined defense of a mound of feces. Suddenly, I was overwhelmed by the absurdity of what was taking place in this battle to protect my excrement and I retreated in confusion.

Following this insane standoff, Fulton and I climbed into the Cessna and began a day that reached exceptional heights of beauty. It was also one that came dangerously close to calamity.

We began by doing aerials of the higher elevations of the Sierra Nevadas, up beyond where the *mamas* go in search of sacred lakes. The day was utterly clear and the aircraft sufficiently light to climb to where we would have no difficulty having excellent views of these extraordinary formations. We were quickly at 18,500 feet and in a space more intense in its silent perfection than anything I have ever before seen. Foolishly, we lingered at this height paying little attention to the fact that, in the parlance of aviation, our time of useful consciousness at this altitude was steadily diminishing. Still, we went on filming yet more of this vast snowscape.

The gauge indicated sufficient fuel for the descent to Valledupar. I had installed a fuel-flow meter just before leaving for Colombia thinking it

might help as we planned some of the lengthier flights, particularly those over water. On this flight we needed only to drift down the mountainside with what appeared to be ten gallons remaining, more than enough for the short lateral distance remaining to the runway threshold. As we leveled off at 1500 feet, the engine stopped. Six gallons remained or so the fuel-flow meter indicated. But six gallons, we realized later, though a real amount, was also the number of gallons of what is called unusable fuel. We were hypoxic enough to have forgotten this most basic aeronautical fact. Too far from the airport to glide with a dead engine, we lined up to land on a dirt road that appeared under us and which, we discovered later, was where most of Valledupar's brothels were located. As we assumed an attitude appropriate for landing, enough fuel made its way to the carburetor for the engine to restart and take us to the end of the runway.

We fueled and returned to San Sebastian where tomorrow we will set forth by foot for the lakes that had been close to fatally mesmerizing yesterday from the air. Yezid is still sick and will not come.

July 24th 1981

We came down from the mountain yesterday after five days going to and coming back from the sacred lakes. We were at 10,000 feet yesterday at dawn on our way down – cold, hungry, and unspeakably tired. Following sunrise, I began the last leg of that ordeal with the same muscle pulled once again in my back. Each step was an intricate problem in the geometry of locomotion over rocks, marsh, and loose turf while towing a hungry mule by a lead it had chewed to bits two nights ago. Once unleashed, it had disappeared down the mountain and was therefore unavailable until found last night. Fulton had probably surpassed his limit of endurance. He had a serious cough and insufficient clothing. We existed on cheese, peanut butter, and saltines. The fires smoked but, for lack of dry wood and oxygen, there was never a flame.

We reached San Sebastian at a little past midday and saw immediately that the wind was strong out of the west. There was no question but that it was there to encourage us to depart, even with a heavy load. This we did without the slightest hesita-

F19

P41

tion and also without Yezid who had recovered but whose presence both Fulton and I felt would mean dangerous additional weight. We collected our meager belongings and lifted off for the last time.

The story of this walk to the lakes is best told in the images made as it unfolded. What will never be seen is the hardship it entailed in lost sleep, lack of nourishment, and exhausting work. Mama Marco appeared almost to float above the stony paths and marshy glens while at the same time worshiping in dance and song as he went. He seemed never to stop for anything but, when he did, he was never really at rest. Certainly his hands were not. When he wasn't scraping his lime gourd with a wand of wood, he was putting offerings into rocky crevices, blowing his conch shell, or hurling incantations at the semi-gale that blew each day. It is his hands that I have fastened on and that will certainly play a visual role when the time comes to make this film.

P42

P43

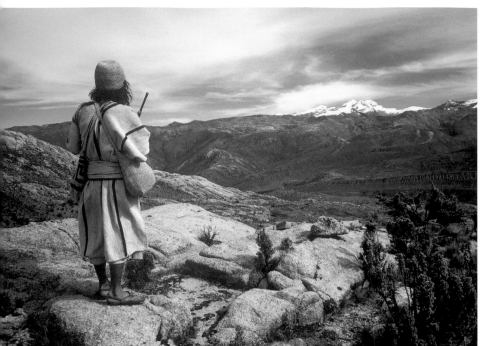

P45

I am profoundly sorry not to have had the heart to stay in San Sebastian and learn more about this extraordinary man. What was it that persuaded me to leave? The wind, the coprophiliac pigs?

I sit in Cartagena's Aero Civil office waiting for signatures that will permit a flight to Barranquilla for fuel of which there is none here. So, it means yet another local flight before departing Colombia definitively. I am told, too, that I must return to Cartagena and pay another landing fee before leaving the country.

On the ramp the Esso employee whom I tipped outrageously weeks ago says he can give me fuel but everyone else says there is none. He still says he can and there is an interminable palaver. But first I must get the receipt for the landing fees with a stamp and signature because without that I cannot get a letter written to Esso saying I have paid my fees and hence entitled to fuel. All the documents have to be retyped because there will be no flight to Barranquilla after all and there will only be yesterday's landing fee. One hour more and I have the receipt and a letter to Esso. The fuel goes into the aircraft and the bags come out of the fireman's shack where they were stored while we were in Barranquilla where we never went.

At immigration and customs I am told my aircraft is unauthorized and I must pay duty on it. I say I could not possibly be flying an unauthorized aircraft this long in this country. "But there is no *aduana* stamp on your documents and so you must pay the duty on the aircraft." "Let's go see the chief of customs."

The chief is someone I insulted two weeks ago for making me walk all over the airport in order to send a suitcase by airfreight. He doesn't recognize me. There must be many people insulting him. He says to go to the main customs office to get stamps on my flight plans. This I do with the tower person who wanted me to bring him a ten-gallon hat from Texas. They talk the situation over and agree what I am being asked to do is odd but then say I should pay them something and they concoct a figure. I even it out in their favor because I no longer have any pesos and they type a spurious receipt and apply a magic stamp.

Now, five hours later, all is ready. I miss the Ika after these brain-numbing experiences with civilized Colombians. We arrive in Willemstadt, Curaçao, at 4 p.m. There are no submachine guns, no plainclothesmen, no narcs, no thugs. The people at immigration are friendly, believing, trustful, and helpful. Our legs can scarcely support our diminished bodies to a taxi that actually works and does not career into oncoming traffic.

P46

F1

F2

F3

P1

P2

Cambridge, Massachusetts, April 1985

I am about to begin viewing the footage of *Forest of Bliss*, the working title I'm using for the film that I have just shot in India. I will use a flatbed-editing table so that I can stop now and then to make notes. The journal I so carefully kept during the shooting is lost somewhere in the waters of the Gulf of Maine. I foolishly left it in a bag that I placed on the pontoon of a plane and it got swept away on takeoff. The reason for setting down my thoughts as I watch these images is so that I can try to recapture the experience I had while making them.

Often, when I look at film I've shot, I'm able to recall much about the day, even the instant I was looking through the camera's viewfinder. Such recollections are sometimes quite detailed. I might remember, for example, what I was wearing or had had for breakfast, what persons were with me and what we said to each other. I think there is little question that innocent fragments of sensory actuality can evoke a whole array of memories. In the account that follows, I will try to make use of this striking property of film to recover what I was feeling and thinking as I worked.

Another purpose of this note taking is to discover how to use these scenes to make a film. But for now, even though it will mean passing over whole sequences of images, I will include only comments about those that provoke important memories and responses.

We arrived in Delhi on the 5th of December, 1984, and stayed only a few days. Adele Pressman and I, our infant son Caleb, and our indispensable friend the anthropologist Ákos Östör, took an afternoon train on I think the ninth scheduled to arrive in Benares the next morning. Contrary to what I expected from recent Indian Railway history, the train was two hours ahead of schedule. The people who were to meet us were of course not there and so we struggled into two ramshackle taxis with almost half a ton of film equipment and another hundred pounds of baby paraphernalia on top of the ordinary adult baggage one tends to drag around the world. We got to our Benares address while it was still dark, about 5:30 a.m. and climbed to the second floor of a house above the American Institute of Indian Studies in which Ákos had found a place for us to live.

Our quarters were modest and quite ugly in a failed attempt at modernity. The space felt hard and cold, especially the cement floors onto which Caleb would continually fall as he learned to walk. But we made rapid adjustments and our domestic arrangements were never an issue. The location gave me easy access to the parts of Benares in which I knew I wanted to work. This feature out-weighed all other considerations and we simply abided our distinctly un-princely circumstances.

I realized that I had to dive unhesitatingly into this city if I was going to come out of it with a film. I had thought at length about what Benares meant to me. Much of what I felt was colored by my first encounter with Manikarnika Ghat, the Great Cremation Ground, which I had stumbled upon while wandering alone and lost on my first visit to Benares in 1975. That decade-old con-frontation with death and the industry surrounding it would play a large part in how I approached my task. Because my knowledge of India was limited to what I had read in college and to a large num-ber of novels, written by Indians, to which I had recently taken a strange fancy, this project was never destined to be academic.

In 1961, when I was planning work in New Guinea, I can remember how bound I felt by anthropological scruples. I had not yet formulated a working distinction between fact and truth, doc-ument and insight, observation and vision. This accounts for the tension I now see between the

F4

> *In saying* Forest of Bliss *is a personal film, I mean that subjectivity played an important role in how I shot it. I had been in Benares several times and made a visual plan to pursue certain themes and motifs: steps, wood, marigolds, and bamboo poles. I also had a helpful sense of the shape and weight of the object I wanted to realize.*
>
> RG [from a letter]

F5

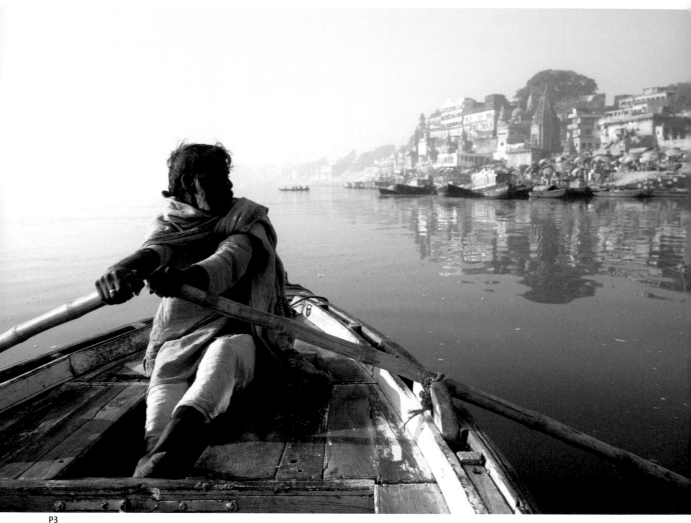

P3

requirements of science and of art in my film *Dead Birds*. In Benares, I expected to be free of those kinds of concerns and yet, quite apart from the almost purely acrobatic matter of inserting oneself bodily into the crowded alleyways, there was the conceptual predicament of how to make sense of the chaos I saw in Benares as a whole.

It was usually around five in the morning when I tried to write. I remember those occasions well. Everyone was asleep, though Adele and Caleb would have spent much of the night struggling with chronic coughs and ravenous mosquitoes. There was seldom electricity due to nightly power outages. Illumination was a kerosene lamp, if there was kerosene, otherwise a candle. I tried in these fits of crepuscular journal writing to examine the thoughts I was having as I made the images I am about to screen, uncut rushes sorted into two categories, wild and synch sound. Wild means footage that is not accompanied by simultaneously recorded sound. It is footage resulting from my solitary use of a camera, almost always without a tripod. Synch-sound footage was shot with someone else recording sound at the same time, almost invariably Ned Johnston, a former student and my general assistant. These notes will be concerned almost entirely with filming I did with sound being recorded at the same time.

The footage I am looking at was shot on the 11th of December 1984, soon after getting to Benares. I think it might even be the next day. I cannot be sure because I have also lost the little diary in which I noted my whereabouts on a daily basis. These first shots are of a man rowing me in his boat down the river. There are closeup details of the oars as they rotate in the makeshift oarlocks. Other shots show the blades of the oars going into the water. Sometimes one sees in the background, rather obscurely and a little out of focus, the city of Benares on the west bank. The east bank is largely deserted. I had selected my oarsman out of any number of others in Benares because he was a denizen of Asi Ghat, close to our living quarters. (The *ghats* are stepped embankments along the river and have different names.) From the time I first began thinking of making a film in Benares, a boatman was an essential figure in the larger landscape. Boats and boatmen put me in mind of my own mythology, of the Styx, of crossing a river and getting to the farther shore.

P4

The scene I am watching is of Manikarnika Ghat. It is actually about 300 feet south where a carpenter is filling holes in the bottom of an old boat with new pieces of wood. I am trying to convey an idea of what goes on behind and beyond the boat. I want the boat, in some way, to stand for redemption. After all, it is being reborn, remade, reconstituted. Beyond this boat is one of the most powerful locales in the vast and sacred geography of India. This is where Vishnu used his discus to dig an enormous hole that was then filled with the sweat of Krishna's asceticism. Now it is a place of utmost sanctity for millions of practicing Hindus, but especially for those who come here on pilgrimage or, simply, to die.

Dying in Benares is something devoutly sought. Many people not only stay here to do that, but come here for that reason. It is believed that dying in Benares is a release from the necessity of rebirth, a way to escape the endless wheel of life. In the background is the cremation ground with images of the devout seeking salvation. In the foreground, the old boat is being rehabilitated for another cycle of life on the holy Ganges. Anybody who knows Benares would know where we are.

I'm showing details of the boat; it's full of holes and the carpenter is shaping new pieces of planking to repair the underside. I remember this day very well. I had felt extremely lucky to find this particular work in such close proximity to Manikarnika Ghat and to be able to use it to distance the immediate immensities of the burning ground. As might be expected, taking pictures at the burning grounds is fraught with problems, official and unofficial. Everyone has an opinion and frequently it is vehement. The longer I stayed in Benares the more I learned about the workings of the police and the management of the burning ground. In fact, far greater access was tolerated, often for a sufficient bribe, than I had assumed would be possible.

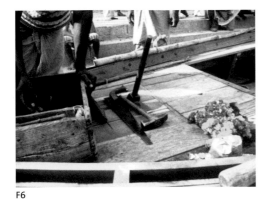

F6

Some shots in this sequence have modest interest in that they show process. I was happy to work on something redemptive in a place filled with an abundance of pain and sorrow. I must remember that such thoughts are imposed by me and do not at all reflect the views of Hindus. For them, Benares is a place of and an opportunity for exultation.

I left this location after shooting perhaps three or four minutes of film. I remember wanting to calculate how long it would take for the carpenter to finish the job so I could go back periodically to keep up with what was happening. This way I could use it as a device for indicating the passage of time and of suggesting that things do have a way of improving, even in Benares.

Now the image is of some steps leading down to a landing on the water and they're covered with the silt of the previous rainy season's flooding. I remember making a few shots of men cleaning the dried mud off this *ghat.* Each year an enormous labor is devoted to retrieving the steps from the silting that occurs when the river rises during the monsoon. Shooting the steps was a way to impart a sense of season. This is the time of the year when the steps are exposed; seeing the mud taken off can suggest they were recently under water. The stairways themselves are also an important visual motif. I had decided long before coming that steps would be important indicators of transition: between life and death as much as between the river and the city. One goes down the stairways to reach the river and up to reach the city. They also lead, of course, to the crema-tion ground. This is the first effort I've made to

work with steps but I am sure there will be many more such images in this footage. Anyway, these steps are being cleaned off and I think this mate-rial has some promise.

The scene changes to what we indelicately called the shitting *ghat,* which is what it was. Architecturally it is a beautiful stretch of the embankments, not far north of Asi Ghat and near a large, umber-colored palace where there is so little happening that people, but really only males as far I can tell, use it as an outhouse. The place is quite appalling up close. It is easy to understand why it became deserted. There is always a vast collection of human ordure which, though irregularly swept up, never fails to assault the nostrils.

As I watch this roll of film, I see that I am working on the theme of steps all the time. For example, a few birds are hopping about on some. A dead dog is lying in shallow water at the bot-tom of others. I also see boys with reels of string who are flying kites from other steps. At Harishchandra Ghat, boats are unloading sand that has been dug up on the far shore, sailed across the river and unloaded. This is an almost Mesopotamian scene of big barges filled with sand and then emptied by people carrying it in baskets down a gangplank and up an embankment of yet more steps. There it is thrown onto a huge pile that is constantly added to and subtracted from as it gets used throughout the city.

My images are simple portrayals of this oddly absorbing scene. In the editing, I may try to use the material to indicate the idea of the farther shore. For me, sand has a distinct association with time, termination, and death, as in expressions like "the sands of time" and "the sands are running out." In the scenes I'm watching there is an added surrealism of what look like colonies of human beings picking up one bank of a river and deposit-ing it on the other. It is ant-like, relentless and unvarying.

At this moment I am looking at scenes of boys on the *ghat* near Harishchandra playing with their kites. Kites are exceedingly lively devices. They animate the environment with their darting and fluttering. They have a happy spirit. At the same time they are frail and vulnerable and at the ends of easily broken strings.

F7

F8

F9

F10

F11

I see that I am showing the bamboo poles that prop up the boat under repair. Bamboo was another motif I had wanted to pursue since first noticing that the litters carrying the corpses were made from it. I tried to develop this idea in several ways. I found a carpentry shop where litters were made and spent considerable time there. Later on, I was alert to the use of bamboo in many contexts. I wanted to use those images the same way I would use marigolds, wood, and sand.

A roll labeled #4 starts with images of the *ghats* as I float by in a boat, usually one taken in the morning from Asi Ghat to go downriver. The first scene is an oar in use. I can remember first trying to keep the oar out of the frame but here the oar is very much in the frame as we float past the umber-colored palace near the shitting *ghat*. As the roll continues, the camera drifts past the sterns of the large sand-carrying boats that beach nearby at Harishchandra Ghat. I can see the effort I was making to go obliquely at the material, especially the death material. It shows up in shots like these where I'm looking at the river and what's on the river but the background is where I want the eye to migrate.

I am searching the river for meaningful imagery, mostly birds and marigolds both of which I intend to develop as themes when I edit. Marigold plants have little orange and red flowers that are used to adorn not only all the deity figures but also the corpses. They are the offerings made by ordinary people worshipping in the temples or wanting to make a religious gesture as they go about the city.

Suddenly there is an image of a dog trying to get a bleached human corpse into its mouth. The animal's gotten hold of a foot or part of a leg and is trying to drag the whole thing onto the shore. The image is gruesome but I'm not sure anybody will even know that it's human and not just an anonymous lump of meat. There's no synchronized sound for this. I will be able to use this moment to bring particular sounds into association with a particular image and that way develop the meaning of a key scene.

It is still early in the morning and we're passing the Dhobi Ghat. The Dhobi belong to the caste that washes clothes from early in the morning into the hottest part of the day. It seems such a futile undertaking, putting dirty clothes into this river in

F12

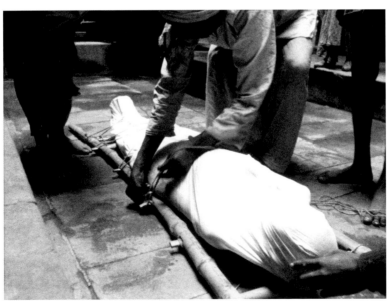

F13

F14

F15

order to make them clean. But, in fact, they become clean and their wearers are thought to be among the subcontinent's best dressed. The sound is nice in these shots of the laundrymen.

I'm on the eastern shore in the early morning and a dog is busily gnawing meat off unidentifiable ribs. I think they are animal and not human. There are more scenes of carrying sand onto the sand barges. After this sequence, there emerges a marvelous scene of dogs fighting early in the morning on the same, farther shore. I am certain this will be an image somewhere near the beginning of the film maybe setting up the whole idea of dogs as guardians of the gates to the other world.

A boy is flying a kite at Manikarnika Ghat and it's tossed by the thermal updrafts from the funeral fires. It was always tantalizing to shoot the kites. They are extremely small objects in a vast sky and by the time I had framed the shot and found the focus they were usually gone.

Filming was frequently a nightmare. Sometimes I would have to shoot with drastic framing to keep onlookers out of images. Often I would abandon a shot because of the press of bystanders. I finally resorted to carrying my Aaton

in a plastic garbage bag and, when I wanted a shot, remove it and have it back inside almost before anyone saw what I was doing.

There is not only the literal garbage in the streets but the cacophony that is Benares. Many of the shots I'm looking at now have the water in a temple tank in the background as a neutral element. Only it's not very neutral because it's the most lurid green I've ever seen. I suppose the green is the result of a calamitous invasion of algae following some profound chemical breakdown. It's almost fluorescent.

The working title of the film, from the time I first began thinking of one, has been *Forest of Bliss*. Filming something on the gathering of wood to be used at the cremation grounds seemed to resonate nicely with this title. Obviously the title is meant to convey more than the simple meaning of the words. I have in mind all the wonderful ambiguities of a "forest" and of "bliss." A forest is enchanting and also forbidding; bliss is joy and a danger. The cremation ground is sometimes called "Forest of Bliss" in the sacred texts. I think my pleasure in this title comes from the suggestion of both a place and a state of mind. Forests can be intimidating and so the idea of a forest of bliss is, for me, a strangely entrancing notion.

I seem to have made many shots of wood being dumped on the ground, dragged out of trucks and piled onto people's heads. The background noise level is very high but I think it is faithful to what was going on at the time: radios, car horns, train whistles, and much else. It was hard to isolate particular sounds such as what was happening with the wood because of the high, overall noise level. But the sounds are almost as necessary as the pictures. They certainly are evocative.

On the 20th of December I was apparently at the flower market to continue establishing a marigold theme. Part of the life history of a marigold is that it passes through this market. I remember many difficulties on this day because of the crowds. Besides, everyone seemed more concerned with what I was doing than what they were there for. Nothing is particularly compelling about any of these scenes. I believe, however, I can make a little sequence out of the gestures of buying and selling the garlands. It is all essential to worshiping a deity or decorating a corpse.

F16

F17

I see that I began shooting roll #10 on the 20th of December, 1984. I've walked on toward Harishchandra Ghat and am once again at the place where sand is unloaded. I shot more scenes of that and others of boys with kites. Then I try to float with my camera up the steps to define this space along the river's edge. None of it is working very well. I remember being in low spirits at the time. Caleb was sick, Adele was exhausted, and the film seemed quite impossible to make. The chaos was enormous and I hadn't yet hit on any scheme that might reduce the complexity of everything.

Now there's a shot of a boy running along the steps. I remember asking him to do that just to have something happen. He runs back toward the camera and then down to the edge of the river. I think this is the only time I proposed that someone do something. I'm near the water tower close to Asi Ghat. I can hear the pump in the tower going like crazy. A man is cooking his meal at the very edge of the river. His whole life is spread out before him and he seems about to fall into the water. The sound of the pumps nearby is very strange.

My camera is now hanging out of a scooter taxi coming very close to rickshaws, trucks, and pedestrians going the other way. The sequence is not successful. The recorded sound is less impressive than the reality and the roads were too bumpy to keep the camera steady. It's strange that these scenes don't convey at all well the insanity of Benares traffic, the anarchic madness, delirium really, of those streets. Unfortunately the sound is not up to conveying this absolutely mind-shattering experience. The pictures don't succeed either. On the contrary, they have an almost choreographed look to them, like big production numbers in a Broadway musical.

Camera roll #14 starts with an exterior scene at the Mukti Bhavan, a hospice for the dying. Brought here by their poor relatives, old people are looked after for about ten days by which time they are expected to have died. This hospice, like most others, was founded by a rich Indian wanting to gain favor with the Almighty. It is a place marked indelibly by the poverty of its clientele.

The next scenes are of little girls playing hopscotch in a courtyard just outside a temple near our house. I'd seen them through the window and wanted to work with them, partly because I have

P6

been told that hopscotch is a cosmic game, like getting into heaven by playing Parcheesi or chess for that matter. Hopscotch must be another version of a diagrammatic path to the realms above and beyond. Most importantly, I thought it was a charming game, especially the way these girls played it. Abstruse symbolism is not what matters in film.

The next sequence was shot back at the Mukti Bhavan. At first I thought I shouldn't do anything there. It seemed too grim to be waiting at the bedside of some old person about to die. But as time went by and I watched, this place became more and more moving. Whoever came there to die did so with a joyful expectancy. I wondered though, whether, even while they were hoping to die in Benares, they were not also entertaining the possibility of a postponement.

The relatives of the Mukti Bhavan inmates talk with gladness and serenity about the event that is expected anytime and how relieved they are that the person they love will be given the opportunity to depart the world forever, a gift granted only those who manage to end their days in Benares.

I'm back again in the Mukti Bhavan hoping to see the floor being washed. I thought that doing something with that floor could make a telling image, particularly if someone were to die and I was there to film what happened.

F18

F19

F20

This first washing of the floor was not as good as the one I filmed later, as I remember. I also see a slight leaking of light in the lower left corner of the frame. I didn't see that in the first quick overview when I was separating this footage, but for some reason there is a leak or a reflection on the left side of the frame and I don't know why. It's not serious, but it's there. The trouble with this particular washing of the floor was that they had already started by the time I was ready and instead of a dry floor that gets wet, it's a damp floor, which gets wetter.

In the foyer of the building, four people, the stalwarts of the attending staff, are sitting opposite each other, chanting Hare Krishna and doing a pretty animated job of it, primarily, I suspect, for the reason that they are being filmed. Now there is a scene of attendants getting ready a tray with cups of Ganges water, incense, camphor, and other small objects they take upstairs during their periodic tours of the hospice rooms.

The attendants are knowledgeable enough in ritual practice to lead these brief services or *pujas* even though they are not priests. They're going up the stairs now and into the rooms to give the Ganges water and other comforts to the dying. I have made two sequences in which water is given to these desperately old people. Both are quite convincing even though the sound of the gong is so loud the words of the mantras can't be heard. I hope it will be possible to do something in the mix by running the words on a separate track. I followed the procession down the stairs and back out through the courtyard, but not that successfully.

I'm back in a gully, one of the many narrow lanes in Benares that serve as byways for people and animals as well as drainage ditches, garbage dumps, and sewers. It's such a long distance down this gully you can't see what's happening at the other end. Many people are gathered around some musicians who are dancing at the head of a cortege, really more a parade than a cortege, with a corpse all finely done up with brocades and silk. I move a bit closer and can see the litter being carried on the men's shoulders. A large box is also being carried. I don't know what it contains; maybe offerings. Behind the box are the mourners and behind them is another litter. Of course, a

F21

F22

F23

F24

woman comes and stands directly in front of me, just as I'm trying to frame a shot.

The next scene is of an old blind man coming down a wide stairway, knocking at each step with his stick as he comes, talking to somebody that passes by. The steps are otherwise empty and he's just feeling his way along with his stick. The stick defines the steps.

Next there is a shot of a cow eating marigolds, something I was always watching for. This image communicated the whole idea of life recycling. The garbage and trash gets reborn in the digestive systems of the dogs, cats, cows, water buffaloes, and everything else that creeps, crawls, and flies.

In the next camera roll I follow a Bengali family as they take a dead relative upriver to Manikarnika Ghat in a boat. They have some musicians with them in the boat who sing devotional songs as they row along. My filming here is an example of unnecessary reticence, hanging back more than was required to allow people their privacy. Clearly I hadn't yet decided how close I was going to get to some of the things I wanted to film.

The family reaches Manikarnika where boats are pulling up to the shore. There are shots of birds coming to little bamboo perches anchored in the river. Next are shots of marigold garlands floating along with the current; we're quietly drifting through a whole seascape of garbage and trash. It's impressive just as a view of the Ganges. The whole scene looks fantastic and even a little exotic or beautiful instead of what it really is. Kodachrome has a way of redefining everything in its own, mostly saccharine terms, what Sontag called "aestheticizing."

I'm back on the *ghats* themselves, back up on the steps, about midway between Manikarnika and Asi Ghat where a few men have taken their nightingales out for an airing. There's an old Benares custom of training these birds to wrestle with each other at a certain time of the year. This event was to begin soon and today the cognoscenti were admiring each other's nightingales.

I went back several times to the Mukti Bhavan hoping to find people washing the floor. Finally, I think I had to say, "Please don't wash the floor until I get here." Every morning, whether or not someone had died, the floor would be washed. I had missed this five-minute event on several dif-

F25

ferent days but this time they managed to wait for me. The first part of this camera roll has shots of a man splashing water on the floor and then washing it with a broom. In the background, the attendants are chanting their almost continuous round of devotional songs. The chanting is quite loud and almost overwhelms the sound of water being splashed on the floor and the brooms spreading it around. Next I'm filming a sequence of ritual activities that took no more than ten or fifteen minutes of real time. Everything was unfolding very quickly and with great novelty for me.

A corpse is brought down the stairs in the Mukti Bhavan. The body had to be one of the three resident ladies, but I wasn't sure which. Everything, such as the kinds of things gotten to prepare her for her final journey, indicates that for this funeral there is very little money. The corpse has been wrapped in a simple white cotton shroud with only one small scrap of silk draped over it. I've seen other bodies literally festooned with yards of this gaudy stuff. This corpse has only one string of marigolds and a few lonely sticks of incense.

Camera roll #22 was shot on New Year's Day, 1985, in Sarnath, where the Buddha is said to have given his first sermon. The sequence begins with a shot of an interior courtyard where women are making garlands of marigolds. They are stringing blossoms into long strands. A puppy is in the midst of this activity. The animal is very small and playful and begins to chew at the blossoms. Again, this puppy and all its mates in the city and down on the *ghats* will be important figures in the film. The dogs of Benares are quite formidable.

As I watch this scene, I see it is an especially peaceful passage. But as I'm transported by these images back to the time I was making them I am reminded of how numerous the obstacles were to getting on with filmmaking. I hear again the hundreds of children that crowded the entranceway to what seems in this shot to have been a peaceful courtyard. I see the women who were so wary of me they kept pulling their saris over their heads to cover their eyes. There were airplanes overhead and scooters and motorcycles roaring by on nearby roads. On that day almost all the problems confronting the filmmaker in India were present.

I am looking now at shots of flower sellers outside one of the major shrines in Benares. A man is selling garlands exactly like the ones made in Sarnath. More scenes show people walking up and down the stairs near the Dom Raja's house. He is king of the Great Cremation Ground of Manikarnika Ghat.

At a certain point I must have gone home from the gullies and come back the next morning to Mithai Lal's house. Mithai Lal is the healer at the Durga Temple and this shot was made in his house early in the morning. He's doing a *puja* or small ceremony to venerate the Mother Goddess. This early morning shooting is done with about two candles' worth of light. A single weak and intermittent electric bulb burning way off to the left is giving almost no illumination. I'm using a wide-open, super-speed Zeiss lens and the quality of the image is not beautiful. But it's usable. It's hard to keep these very short, super-speed lenses in focus when nothing can be seen in the finder owing to darkness.

Roll #25 begins at the same place on the same day. Mithai Lal, the healer, is still doing his morning *puja*. It's very noisy both inside and outside the house. He has his little drum going and does his whole routine. Finally, he picks up an enormous bronze bell and begins to ring it and, of course, the sound drowns out his voice and the voice of another person who's there. I think it's his wife. What he's doing is a homespun *ariti*, the great culmination of a temple *puja* in which sounds climax in a frenzy of bells, voices, drums, and chattering monkeys. Mithai Lal blows the conch shell with a good deal of authority. It's a fine view of him praying to his goddess, blowing his shell, belching, and coughing. He ends the ceremony by banging his head on the floor in what I assume is a gesture of utmost devotion.

I'm watching roll #30. There is a man bringing a child's corpse down the steps of the *ghat* in his arms. It is wrapped in a dirty white shroud. He's

F26

P7

F27

F28

about to place the body in a boat from which he will drop it in the river. I just happened to see this scene developing very swiftly out of the corner of my eye. I don't know how clear what is happening will be to an audience because I never got close. In the foreground there is a goat eating marigolds; the whole thing is quite somber. It's a cold, wet, and gloomy day. A stone is being carried on someone's shoulder down to the shore and no doubt will be tied to the little corpse. A man who sells milk gets off the boat that will be used to ferry the corpse. There are shots of tying the body onto the stone that will take it to the bottom of the river. Then the boat is launched, as usual, quite awkwardly. They push off from the shore and start for the middle of the river.

A roll begins at the shrine of Ragul Pandit, a self-appointed priest, early in the morning. He has started his *puja* and is reciting the thousand names of Vishnu. Ragul is dressed warmly as he enunciates the mystic names of Vishnu while at the same time pouring water over a lingam from a pitcher shaped like a tiny trumpet. There's barely enough light in the shrine to film. It's early in the morning and the shrine is cave-like behind its shuttered windows. Dark objects that hang on the wall are painted in a murky hue.

The scene shifts to the exterior of the shrine where a woman is doing devotional exercises in the courtyard. Another shot or two is of sweeping the steps at Dashashwamedh. I kept trying to film sweeping for reasons not entirely clear even to me, except that it is such a common gesture in India. The act speaks clearly to the necessity of keeping rubbish from burying the city.

I see that it is the day of the relaunching of the boat whose repair I have been filming for some time. The men are gathering the ingredients necessary for blessing the boat. The main figures in this little drama are the boatman-owner, the carpenter, and his assistant. It's really they who are doing the ritual and who, curiously, appear to know what they are doing. As I indicated earlier, I wanted this sequence about the boat to suggest something more than a repair. It was also to be the rebirth of an important element of life in Benares. I wanted this repairing and relaunching to help redeem things such as death, corruption, and chaos. Here

was a boat that must have had a busy history and has been brought ashore to be remade. Finally, the time has come when it is ready to be a boat again. I like the idea of the boat launching to be happening next to the cremation ground where the dead are about to take another kind of voyage. Boat and people are actually at a place where each will make a crossing. The boats will be going to the farther shore, which is what these bodies are also doing, it's believed.

I didn't know the carpenter was going to do a *puja* before launching the boat. For days the men had been saying they would launch it the next day and of course they were never quite ready to do that. But when I arrived on this day they were ready and I even think they had been waiting for me since I had been asking them so many times about it. Since starting the filming of this boat I tried to play the foreground off against the background. Today the boat is being given a new life and the dead bodies are headed for eternity. Someone looking at these shots of the boat might not actually see what's happening in the background where hundreds of people are bringing their dead to be burned. The scene is extraordinarily busy but it's also quite far away. At the moment when the boat is actually launched, a joyful procession comes down the *ghats* bearing a richly decorated corpse. At this point it is pretty clear what is happening at the cremation ground.

I'm not sure it's possible to take in this remarkable simultaneity because what's happening in the foreground is interesting in itself. What's going on in the background is, in turn, absorbing enough that someone might assume all or part of it is contrived. The reality is that it was real and here it is on film. The images have a terrific density. They are almost too rich.

Roll #40 was shot on a morning when Ragul Pandit took his morning bath in the river. The scene starts with a slight focus problem because I was not able to see well through the finder in the dim morning light. There are also moments when the sound recorder is not functioning correctly. I finally got decent focus and the actual bathing part is quite beautiful. In fact, when Ragul goes into the water the scene is very special. The sun is coming up at this point, so I'm getting a good exposure

F29

F30

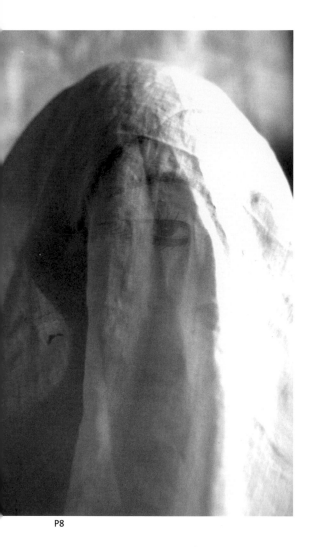

P8

F31

with a little bit more of a morning character to the light. The gong sound is so loud that it distorts.

Roll #41 is a continuation of the morning *ariti* done at Ragul Pandit's little shrine at Dashashwamedh. Ragul was one of the people I had chosen to take a major part in the film. I never knew how much time I would get with him or how many different things we would do together but I always felt comfortable with him and did whatever I could. He had a lot of confidence in himself and a rare intensity. I liked the way he projected himself into situations. Nothing about him was retiring or the least apologetic. He knew what he wanted and he liked being who he was, a self-made priest.

Roll #45 begins in the gullies near the huge woodpile you pass to get to the river. People are splitting and piling up wood, a lady is collecting cow dung to make fuel patties, and a man is sweeping up around where he weighs out the wood. A radio is blasting in the background incessantly. In these Manikarnika scenes there's always a radio producing either music or a cricket match. The next sequence is of the weighing out of a load of wood. What I saw in this image was the suggestion of equivalence in a human being to a measure of wood, to a certain volume and weight of wood. After the wood is weighed, it is piled on a helper's head and brought down to be stacked at one of the empty positions on the cremation ground. Then a body is put on the pyre, a little more wood is put on the body and sacred fire is used to touch it off.

I am looking at images of the making of clay idols. The idols are Saraswati figures. Saraswati is the goddess of learning and we were in Benares at the time of the festival honoring her. The figures are purchased by students who parade them through the streets and down to the river where they take them in boats and dump them into the Ganges. What I have done is simple documentation of how these idols are made by the Bengali craftsmen. It's a popular art that has been horribly vulgarized by lurid colors and vapid poses. The iconography is straight out of the Bombay film industry and has little connection any longer with the folk traditions of rural India.

Roll #47 is the first of my more direct efforts to come to grips cinematically with Manikarnika proper. I began, I so well remember, in the little shrine below the Dom Raja's portico. I went there first because I didn't want to start in the midst of the burning ground itself. I wanted to prolong my tactic of indirection. What caught my attention at the shrine were little birds pecking at some marigolds piled up on the lingam. It's not a beautiful shrine but then I didn't find many in my travels through India that were. But this particular shrine is in the middle of people carrying wood for the cremation fires and doing other errands. I'm still hoping wood will be suggestive of the atmosphere and meaning of Manikarnika. Wood is such a central part of what happens here that it should be evident no matter how indirect my camera.

The next roll has material that feels quite abstract. Clouds of smoke obscure facades of buildings and things are happening in a backlight that makes them harder to comprehend. Great loads of wood are dumped on the ground creating explosions of dust. At the end of this roll there are scenes in the gully behind Manikarnika of the workers asleep in their wood shop. A huge goat that's always at Manikarnika is rubbing its horns on the wood. I believe this goat belongs to the Dom Raja. There are some water buffalo and cows going through the gullies.

These rushes skip to the 19th of January at Mithai Lal's house. I went there to go with him early in the morning to where he bathes. That sequence begins here. I'm trying to pull an exposure out of nowhere. It's so early in the morning the sun hasn't come up. Mithai Lai manages to just

F32

F33

barely move, making his way in a gingerly fashion down the steps and through the gullies, groaning every foot of the way. Finally, the light is better. Every once in a while there is a dog in the frame, which greatly pleases me. The far side of the Ganges can also sometimes be seen.

Mithai Lal lives just above Manikarnika Ghat so when he leaves his house he goes along what I called Manikarnika gully. It's a familiar landscape by now, with its stacks of wood, beggars, shops, and tea stalls. Many people are going this way to their various morning activities. The light at the point where Mithai Lal starts down the stone steps of the *ghat* itself is much nicer. Over the far, eastern shore the sun is a ball of redness. Mithai Lal begins his bath in a mood of high hilarity and he maintains his good humor until we are back in his house.

The next shots at Manikarnika are of a steaming pile of charcoal and of water buffaloes munching straw. A boat filled with wood is docked at Manikarnika and lies in the background ready to be unloaded. A corpse, in fact two corpses, are carried into the gully and just dropped at my feet. I had no idea this was going to happen. I guess the litter bearers decided to buy something they needed in one of the nearby shops. Anyway, there was great commotion since these gullies are only a few feet wide and two corpses have been put down right in the middle.

The final scene on this roll is again in the gully at Manikarnika. Some men are buying a pot to use in a death ritual. On some camera roll to come, I trust, this kind of a pot will be seen being broken. The action was something I tried to film more than once.

Camera roll #52, also shot on the 19th of January, has more of Mithai Lal bathing in the river and then on his way home up the steps of the *ghat*. Mithai Lal is in a genial mood this morning. I suspect that he is most mornings, but this one especially. As he goes up the steps he is laughing and clowning with passersby. He takes a great interest in whomever he sees and in what he's doing. Mithai Lal may be infirm but he has his wits about him. He performs small worships as he goes back up to his house. The progress is slow and not self-conscious. The images of Mithai Lal are quite

telling in the way they reveal Hindu faith. It's a soft and gentle series of gestures arising from one man's daily devotions.

I see that I'm again trying here and at other times to make steps and stairways a visual motif. I'm showing human and animal feet on steps, steps being swept, slept on and prayed on. People lie dead on steps, bang their heads and go into trance on them. Steps are part of a threshold, of a transition to another space or another time. I'm really asking that they be a figure that embraces the notion of going to another realm, that of the farther shore.

In the gullies a woman sells marigold garlands. A body goes by on the left and, inevitably, people look at the camera. The next shot is of a blind man walking in the gullies. I don't know how he manages without sight to get through these crowded lanes but he seems to know exactly where he is. In some uncanny way he avoids the worst hazards. He bumped into one motorcycle and he stepped in one cow dropping but two mistakes are pretty minimal over a distance of several hundred feet even for someone with the sharpest eyes.

On the burning *ghats* there's a woman at one of the fire pits salvaging the bigger bits of unburned wood. One shot is of a dog sniffing in the cooling embers of an old fire, looking for something to eat I'm afraid. The roll runs out on a very low-caste woman gathering scraps of charcoal. She swears at me. Then, oddly, she is amused by my persistence.

The Durga Temple is the subject of camera roll #56. I'm doing more with Mithai Lal. On this roll the *ariti* starts and Mithai Lal collapses to the ground. It's not a very dramatic collapse but nonetheless he ended up prone and stayed that way as long as the *ariti* lasted. The temple courtyard is extremely dark and full of shadows. It amazes me to think that I have tried to get away with shooting a film as difficult as this one after months of not using a camera. It is like someone thinking they can give a piano recital without practicing.

I'm at the fire pit behind which Mithai Lal sits in the Durga Temple. He's up to his old tricks of pouring clarified butter into the fire and shouting

F34

F35

F36

F37

outrageous advice at his clients who sit docilely around the pit.

At the end of roll #61, I made a few shots of the hundreds of bamboo litter poles propped up outside the Dom Raja's house. They're a form of tribute paid by those who have taken their corpses to be burned on his cremation ground. I recall that I went frequently to the Dom Raja's house hoping to find something that conveyed the somber mood of his place.

Down on the *ghat*, at the bottom of the stairs leading to the river, a body is being immersed. Cows are on the same steps eating straw. A man is circumambulating a corpse preparatory to lighting the fire. There's a long sequence of a man burning a small bunch of things and then throwing them into the river. I really never knew what he was doing. I think he may have brought part of a body, using it to stand for the whole. The dogs are looking to see if there's something they can eat. I have a feeling that the part the man wanted to burn was all he could manage to take with him to Benares.

On the Asi Ghat in the morning the women do their *puja* around a small tree and the lingam under it. This material is slightly soft. I don't know why. Maybe the angle of the sun is diffusing the light. There are shots of feet going around a lonely tree. Candles are lit at the base of the tree. A combination of these shots could be nice: the circumambulation of the tree with feet and heads going around.

I am starting to look at roll #66. It is a scene of a body being taken down an alleyway. There is no sound, probably because it was one of the frequent occasions on which I was alone. All the time I was in Benares I was certain that cinema vérité was not an appropriate way to work. I feel this wherever I'm working but in Benares I felt it even more strongly. There are much richer and more suggestive possibilities doing sound and image separately.

The next scene is at Manikarnika of a man throwing a pot over his shoulder. This happened very suddenly. Things kept coming into my peripheral vision and I was frequently so surprised that I was not always able to make the shot. There are more scenes of the river, traveling through marigolds, rotting marigolds floating on the surface. Birds are tearing meat off a carcass in the

water. Bodies are being put on the fire and bodies are already on the fires burning.

Roll #68 was exposed on the 27th of January. The first shot is of a woman doing her morning *puja* in the gullies. She tosses flowers at carved deities. It's early in the morning. There are scenes of cows in the gullies and a man actually feeding marigolds to a heifer. Two beggars come into the gully. A man pushes a leper in a cart. It's an extraordinary scene. Three kids come and stand in front of me. Another body comes down the gully.

There is a scene of a man breaking a skull. Another throws a skull into the river and up on Manikarnika Ghat is a corpse that arrived by boat. Several shots show this corpse waiting for the chief mourner to get shaved. This roll also has a sequence of making rice balls in the image of a man. There are shots of the body ready to be carried over to the place where it will be bathed in the Ganges. A great disappointment for me was running out of film exactly as they were carrying it down to the river.

I pick up the same event again on roll #69, at the bottom of the steps. The female members of the family put Ganges water, ladled up with their cupped hands from the river, into the mouth of the corpse. About ten or fifteen people file by, each with handfuls of water.

Camera roll #70 begins with a journey on a boat loaded with wood. This is the day I got on one of the wood barges at Raj Ghat and went down the river with it to Manikarnika. The details, the different angles, the glimpses of the river and what's going on at the river's edge will be useful in editing. Later in this roll there's a series of dead animals being brought down the steps at Dashashwamedh; a donkey, a cat, and a dog are simply and casually dragged down the steps to be pitched into the Ganges.

The next scenes are of the two people whom I had asked at the very end of the trip to sing about Benares. It was a late and halfhearted attempt to find a musical dimension for the film. I sometimes wondered if the sound was too unsparing without it. We eventually found a man whose voice and melodies I liked but I had difficulty arranging a time for him to sing. I asked another singer, but he could never remember the words. I had to give him crib sheets that kept getting into the shot. The first images are impossible visually but maybe not as musical passages. The singers were, in the end, quite enthusiastic and did their best. It has a slightly comic opera look to it, so I doubt if the scenes will ever be used. The shots that show the skyline as the men are singing seem to work in a strange way. It's a little hard for me to evaluate just how banal the whole thing might be.

The first images on #76 are closeups of Mithai Lal. They're nice. In one sequence he's getting up from his trance/catnap during the *ariti* in the temple. It's fine except that the images are dark because the fire in the pit has burned down to nothing. A long, quite interesting passage goes on for about a minute of Mithai Lal beginning his healing after his brief nap and, although it's dark and you don't see him very well, the voices are clear. The sequence may not get into the film, but I think it's a good piece of substantive filmmaking showing precisely what's happening. The bells in the temple are destroying the intelligibility of the track, but that was true all the nights we were there. Near the end of the roll Mithai Lal gets up and dances a little jig.

The beginning of roll #77 has more of the Durga Temple but then the images change to the next morning at Asi Ghat. I suspect I was running out this magazine in a gesture of abandonment. One shot shows the two old Dandi monks who went to bathe at Asi Ghat every morning. It's a little better than past efforts because the scene is not too cluttered. There is one good sequence of these old ascetics, the blind one coming into the water, feeling his way, and then both of them later drying themselves in the sun.

The roll ends with a quintessential Benares image: two men squatting in the distance. The Ganges is nearby and the sun will be up in a matter of moments.

N.B. The reels with the wild footage — the ones shot when I was alone and no sound being recorded — contain the visual heart of this filmmaking effort. I will not attempt to describe these scenes because there are too many and they are too varied in content. I will just keep looking at them in an attempt to learn them as if they were a new vocabulary.

P9

304

P10

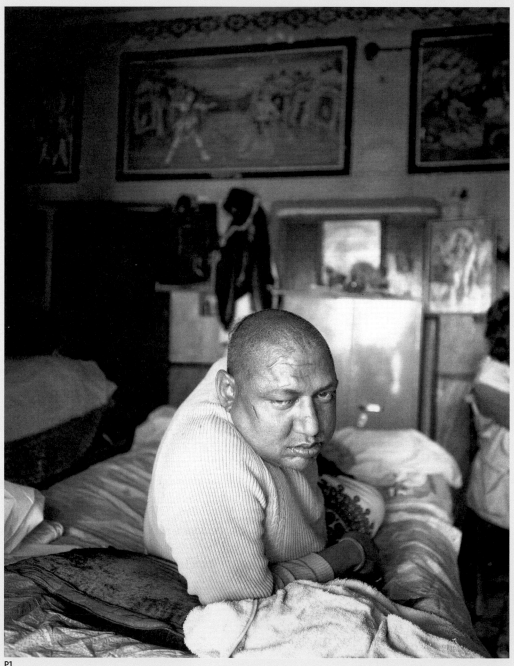

P1

city of light

Looking at photographs can awaken a sense of privilege in that they appear to promise, apart from other enjoyments, that you are in the presence of something arguably authentic. After all, what you see, trapped in particles of silver, might, if it is a negative or a glass plate, be the very light that illuminated the moment in question.

No doubt almost everyone born by the last half of the twentieth century knows how to take a photograph and even the rudiments of its photochemistry, but only a few have begun to inquire into the nature of the photographic transaction. Stanley Cavell is one. About it he says, "A photograph emphasizes the existence of its subject, recording it, hence it may be called a transcription." Cavell is concerned with such matters as the nature of reality and of experience, and so he is genuinely, promisingly distressed with what it might mean to seem to be looking at reality (in a photograph or a film) and not actually doing that.

About a year ago, Benares was for three months the subject of ambitious transcription in film, photography, and sound recording. I had gone back there to make *Forest of Bliss*, a film over which I had pondered at length following an initial, unsettling visit ten years earlier. My film, as well as the photographs made mostly by Jane Tuckerman and Christopher James, are testimony to what Susan Sontag calls "time's relentless melt." I take her words to mean that every transcription in photography (and film) is a reminder of the continuousness of life, as long as life continues and, if it doesn't, of its mortal nature.

In James' photograph, the Dom Raja, one Kailash Choudhury, looks balefully at us as we look back at him supposing, maybe, this is the way he looked on January 24, 1985 (the day his "likeness" was captured), but giving little heed to the fact it is not the way he would ever look again.

Of course, time melts not only people but also everything under the sun. Styles and customs appear and disappear, buildings rise and fall, landscapes are obliterated in the blink of an eye, the click of a shutter. The next Dom Raja to rule the cremation grounds of Benares may, in the coming years, compete with electric crematoria furnished by a municipality concerned with the pollutedness of the sacred Ganges.

Cavell again: "One may also think about photography as transfiguration." I have tried on occasion to do this and find it is as suggestive as thinking of it as transcription. I sometimes wonder, though, if images like those by James and Tuckerman don't make the point on their own. It seems to me that what these photographers may have done without even knowing it is to grasp certain fragments of experience that they see as speaking for something larger than the fragments themselves, perhaps during a Cartier-Bresson moment. I think Tuckerman's dogs do this and so do James' bamboo litters. The dogs and the litters have been transfigured by photography exactly because, as images, they can claim no reality. But they can and do represent more and other than what they appear to be.

F1

stone, birds, air, and water

We did not really know each other, Basil Wright and I, though we did meet once many years ago when we were both too shy to say much. He must have sensed my worship of him as a filmmaker, more particularly my gratitude for his having shown me how moving the moving pictures could be.

We began a timid correspondence a few years ago that might have flourished if his eyes had not betrayed him with cataracts. For him, this darkening of the world might have seemed like the last scene in his great *Song of Ceylon* where the patient and serene Buddha is enveloped in blackness by the "dark and monstrous forests through which no man might pass without peril." Surely there has never been a more passionate (or sonorous) voicing in all of cinema than when these words of the seventeenth-century sea captain and preanthropologist, Robert Knox, were spoken by Lionel Wendt 250 years later.

Wright's was a long life I see from the *London Times* obituary sent me by a friend and fellow admirer of this quiet poet of film. He was almost halfway into his eighty-first year when he died, a long enough time one would suppose, considering his accomplishments, to be appropriately loved and admired, even to have been invited into the company of cinema's masters.

I cannot judge how his own countrymen came at last to regard this man, whether he ever, indeed, was acknowledged by England's film establishment as one of very few men or women who possessed a transforming cinematic vision; someone at the same level, let us say, of Jean Vigo. I tend to doubt it because that establishment, like our own, is almost wholly preoccupied with the story film, its stars, its budgets, and its gossip.

Wright is largely unknown in my country but then so is Vigo and anyway that is all beside the point. The point is that Wright is embedded in our common cinematic sensibility. In 1934, and earlier and later, but especially then, he showed us how to see differently and better. He was only twenty-seven years old, yet he was revealing a world that no one had ever looked at in quite the same way. For example, the dancers in the last section — I am tempted to use the word movement — of *Song of Ceylon*, which is called the Apparel of a God ("for the light that shines for a fathom round his body"), achieve an ecstatic abstraction by virtue of the way they have been filmed.

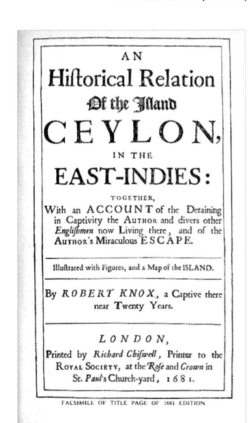

AN
Hiſtorical Relation
Of the Iſland
CEYLON,
IN THE
EAST-INDIES:
TOGETHER,
With an ACCOUNT of the Detaining in Captivity the AUTHOR and divers other *Engliſhmen* now Living there, and of the AUTHOR's Miraculous ESCAPE.

Illuſtrated with Figures, and a Map of the ISLAND.

By *ROBERT KNOX*, a Captive there near Twenty Years.

LONDON,
Printed by *Richard Chiſwell*, Printer to the ROYAL SOCIETY, at the *Roſe* and *Crown* in St. *Paul*'s Church-yard, 1 6 8 1.

FACSIMILE OF TITLE PAGE OF 1681 EDITION

D1

F2

Wright also made relationships through editing that were astonishingly courageous and quite amazing in the way new perceptions emerged from the observed actualities. It did not matter that these were frequently commonplaces. Their humanity drew strength from the fact that that is what they were.

I am reminded in this connection of the almost literally transporting spirituality he evoked in the Buddha segment, near the beginning of *Song of Ceylon*, where stone, birds, air, and water are joined to create an abiding atmosphere of holiness. Such an outcome would not seem likely, if one were to look at the shots singly and silently. Occasionally they are not even particularly well photographed. They sometimes stutter and shake and, by now, they have lost their original glory of tone, brilliance, and definition. We are heirs to such corrupt versions of once pristine work. But when looked at assembled by this masterful cutter, under the spell of Wendt's voice, "Chakra lakshana," hearing the tintinnabulation of those relentless bells guiding the senses into novel excitations, the effect is transfiguring. We are in his grip and we are changed forever.

If I could choose my cinematic inheritance, I would ask for equal parts of Andrei Tarkovsky and Basil Wright. If there is a more wondrous opening to a narrative film than that of Tarkovsky's Andrei Rublev, *I haven't seen it, and if there are more lyric nonfiction passages than occur in* Song of Ceylon, *I have not seen them either. After seeing their work, I am more certain of my own humanity, surely the real test of a higher anthropology.*

RG [from an interview]

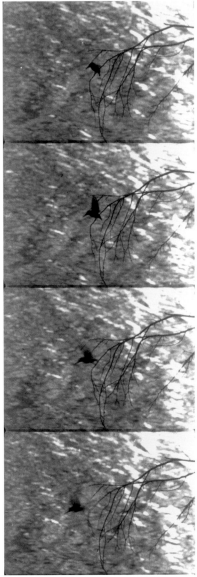

F3

P1

going back

I first went there (the Grand Valley of the Baliem) to describe in words and images people who lived in a place that reminded me of what Eden might be like had such painful pastimes as ritual war not been invented. Going back would mean seeing how much further from Eden they had strayed.

RG [from an interview]

This text is taken from a longer essay written following a visit in 1989 to the Dani of West Papua (formerly Netherlands New Guinea) with whom I lived, enthralled, for half a year in 1961. To that text, I have added lines from notebooks and diaries kept in 1989 and in 1996. On both visits, I was accompanied by my closest of friends and frequent collaborators, Robert Fulton, Richard Rogers, and Susan Meiselas, and by my wife Adele Pressman and our two young sons, Noah and Caleb. Richard Rogers died of complications arising from an unavailing battle with melanoma in 2001 and Robert Fulton flying his aircraft through unforgiving turbulence a year later.

Peter Matthiessen, with me in 1961, told me to think hard before undertaking such missions only to be disenthralled. He said I would most likely find more heartache than anything else.

In some ways he was right, but heartache had already set in and more was to follow. I had learned, before setting out, of major transformations in the world he and I had known: holy stones into Holy Communion and bows and arrows into AK-47's.

These would of course be sentimental journeys, but I had taken many of them before and since, in idle reverie and recurrent dreams.

Not long ago the Grand Valley of the Baliem River, high in the central mountains of Indonesia's West Papua, belonged more to legend than reality. For hundreds of years it had escaped the notice of all but a handful of the most adventurous, a circumstance which, until relatively recent days, allowed a population of warrior farmers called the Dani to flourish in a Stone Age of dazzling and inarguable authenticity. In 1961, my companions and I spent more than half a year in that astonishing landscape, describing in images and words a vivid but fragile world. We had come at the invitation of the Dutch who were then governing this final remnant of their East Indian empire, and who had grown concerned with the way events were propelling the Dani and other delicate societies into a dubious embrace with modernity. Even then it was clear that the Dani, far from slumbering like flies in some eternal amber, had already started on a course of rapid and perilous change. I wanted to see for myself how almost three decades had transformed these people's lives. While I was sure I had many reasons for my return, I knew that more than anything else I wanted to see the Dani individuals who, when I came the first time in 1961, had come to mean the most to me — Weyak, Wali, Kurelu, and Pua.

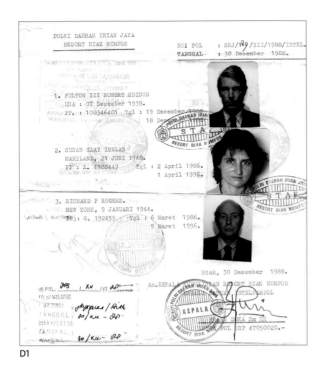

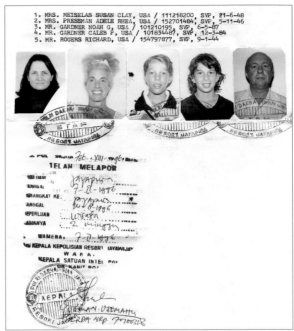

D1

D2

My reunion with Pua, after our long absence from each other's company, began as I, making my way along the Aikhé to the village where Pua now lives, met a man who somehow recognized me and I he. It was Siba, Pua's older brother. He knew why I had come and instantly called out, in the inimitable Dani manner, PUA-A-A-A-OOOOOO, the last vowel propelled into space by a musical escalation of pitch and volume. Immediately I heard the answering call indicating that Pua had heard and would be on his way. In a matter of moments, a figure of unmistakably familiar gait came through a grove of bushy trees. This man of middle age displayed all the distinctive attributes of Pua the boy I had known many years before. We exchanged countless and, for me, strangely unreal greetings. Who, I asked myself, is this imposter I'm told is the child who lived, just yesterday, the life of a stone-age swineherd?

With a growing collection of people I had known in 1961, we walked toward Pua's model village where he brings to life bygone days. I did not realize at first that we were in the Dani equivalent of such phenomena as our own Williamsburgs. The village looked quite familiar until it was clear that no one lived in it. No animals, fires, or crying children were present, only a full-scale diorama waiting for people to animate it like some back-lot movie set. Pua used a strange word to describe this village. He called it his "lodgment." I finally understood this was what he thought a place where tourists spent the night was called. He explained that he had arranged everything so tourists could come to it and experience authentic Dani life. Even benches for onlookers, covered by projecting eaves to shade the noonday sun, were placed inconspicuously between the principal Dani-style houses.

The tourists could come individually or in groups and stay at his lodgment for as long or short a time as they wished. None of these facilities had entirely

P2

P3

satisfactory sanitary arrangements, and Pua talked to me about this problem. He realized how important it was to how people viewed the prospect of staying at his lodgment. In any case, no one was in residence that day. Tourists were in fact quite rare and, because Pua was by no means the only guide to reenactments of the Stone Age, the few that came to the valley were spread rather thinly. At a certain point, Pua must have decided that as a creature of two worlds, the Stone Age into which he was born and the Sony Age into which he was moving, there lay a promising opportunity for self-improvement. Like many others, he would concoct a Dani World and offer his services as an expert guide.

Pua told me that what convinced him to offer the tourists a taste of the Stone Age was that many of the people who were visiting the Grand Valley had come looking specifically for him, for the little swineherd they had seen in my film *Dead Birds*. These travelers also came with copies of his photograph or the photographs of Weyak, Wali, and Kurelu they had xeroxed from books or articles published many years earlier in *Life*, *Stern*, *Paris Match* and elsewhere. Such travelers, who were mostly European, were exceptionally conscientious to have prepared themselves in this way. By no means is it an average tripper who books the basic hostelries of Wamena, the airport town in the Baliem Valley. This valley is advanced tourism on any scale of difficulty and those who finally get there are likely to have begun with more than a casual interest. Pua and I parted that day with his asking me to promise I would come so he could kill a pig for me.

Soon after finding Pua, I began looking for Weyak. I had been told he was still alive and living near a minor tributary to the Baliem in a village I had often passed on my way to and from the salt wells in 1961. When I last saw Weyak, there were no vehicles and, therefore, no road. Now many trucks, vans, and motorbikes are in constant motion up and down a road that runs like an incision left by a planetary undertaker. While in 1961 the trip by boat and foot from Wamena to Kurelu took several hours, now it took only minutes by minibus. In no time, I found Weyak close to where the little tributary was spanned by a noisy metal bridge. His house lay in a hollow that collected the dust and noise of traffic on the nearby road. Though his eyes were failing, Weyak had no difficulty recognizing his long unseen friend, though I am certain he was as shocked by my appearance as I was by his. Almost thirty years, much of any lifetime, transforms us all. Like Pua, but with less enthusiasm, Weyak spoke of how he would entertain tourists, and he showed me a house he was building where he said they would stay.

I was reminded of photographs seen years ago of those remarkable and, at one time, prevalent delusions in the emergent world called "cargo cults." I recall clearly one in which there were two or three natives who had made a mock airplane out of scraps of wood and put it in a little clearing betokening an airport. The architects of this fantasy lived next to their creation for weeks, waiting for a real aircraft to land and disgorge its cargo of splendor and wealth. Weyak was building a similar sort of lure, one that would attract tourists and make him rich.

Weyak once built houses that had great beauty and utility. He would never have lived in the house he showed me.

Soon darkness began to settle over the valley, and I left Weyak telling him I was staying at the Indonesian guesthouse near a settlement called Jibika, and that he should come and visit whenever he could. He asked me to return and to stay in his new tourist house, and I promised I would. He said he would kill a pig for me and steam a net full of sweet potatoes.

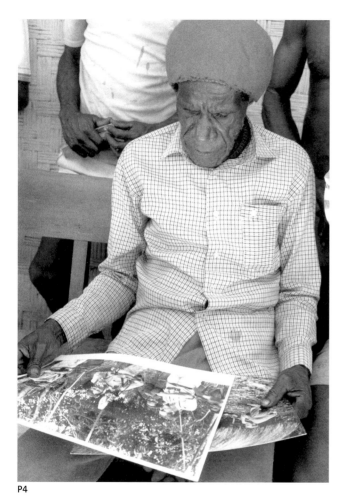

P4

The next day I went to find Wali at Wuperainma, the village in which he has been living since I left in 1961. We met in an embrace fueled equally by conspiratorial memories and forlorn dreams. While covering me with ardent kisses, he drew me gently but powerfully into the darkness of the same *honai*, or Dani's men's house, I entered with such misgiving so many years before. Almost at once, Wali started the ritual weeping done when greeting loved ones after a long absence. It is a great, sobbing dirge in which quantities of real tears are shed for the time not spent together, and also as a measure of the happiness regained.

We, Wali and I, were once again unable to put into words many of the thoughts and feelings that crowded our minds. Yet, despite the fact I had lost nearly all the Dani language I had ever learned (never more than what could be exchanged with an average two-year-old), I knew what he was trying to tell me because he looked at me in the same old confidential way as he listed the things he needed. He kept mentioning a radio and some pants that would fit. I longed to know what it meant to him not to have wars or victory dances and how the ghosts were behaving now that no one was avenging anyone's death anymore. How could he or any of my other stone-age friends live without the things that made their lives so magical? I never got answers because the questions were too complicated to put in words and, anyway, the talk always came back to what Wali wanted from me. I left with him insisting that I tell him when he should plan to kill a pig.

When I reached the guesthouse where I was staying, I was told Kurelu was waiting for me. He had heard I was in the Grand Valley and he had come wearing short pants, a ragged T-shirt, and a cloth fedora that had required cutting off most of his magnificent head of hair. He greeted me in his customarily grave, distant, and oddly quizzical manner as though he was not quite sure he should be

318

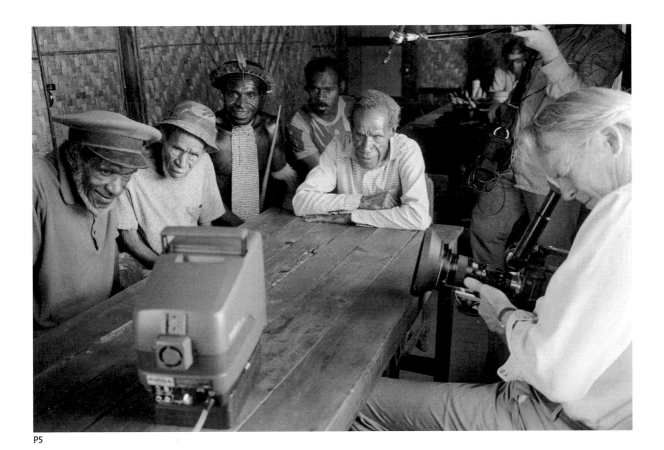

P5

allowing this meeting to take place. Even Kurelu, whose name also serves for an entire region, including several Dani villages, and so now is a destination painted on travel brochures, minivans, and signposts, had his own needs to be heard. I would never know precisely what these were because Kurelu was too dignified to ask except obliquely, and I had no heart for asking.

Something I wanted to do, if I ever returned to the Baliem Valley, was to show *Dead Birds*, the film I had made on my first visit. As far as I knew, the Dani had never seen it, though I was told the Protestant Mission had somehow obtained a videocassette that was shown from time to time to their guests. The people I wanted most to see it were Pua, Kurelu, Wali, and Weyak. Kurelu was not in the film the way the others were, but the whole undertaking, in important ways, was as much about him as anyone else. From the beginning, I had thought of him as epitomizing everything enduring about the Dani. He would be not only my best and most telling critic but also my judge, one of the few who were entitled to say I had passed or failed as a teller of this particular tale.

I am not sure what I myself think now about this vexing object called *Dead Birds*. I confess, though, to feeling that by showing them the film I was doing something good for Pua, Weyak, Wali, and Kurelu. Part of me felt they had become too willing collaborators in the changes that had taken place in their lives since 1961. How could they tolerate so much compromise with what had been such a compelling life? I may even have thought the film, in some mystical manner, was more real than they themselves and that it might even keep their world

319

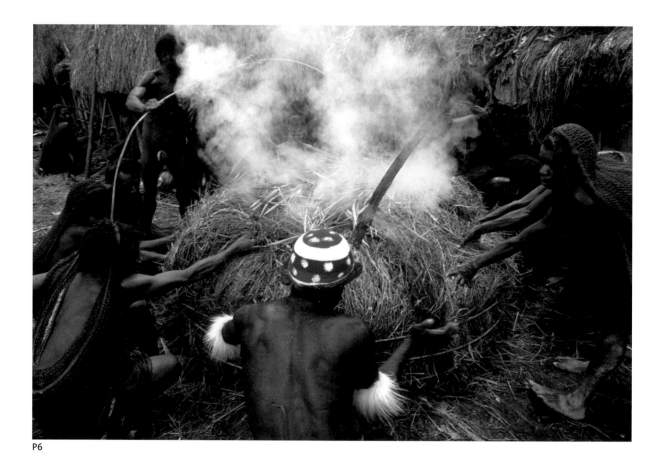

P6

from crumbling away entirely. Anyway, bizarrely, the film had become for me a repository for the Dani soul, the amber in which they were in fact imbedded.

Pua, Weyak, Wali, and Kurelu came to the guesthouse, miraculously, at the appointed hour. I had decided that, as the film was running, I would film its unlikely audience in the hope of finding some meaning in their responses. I remember being careful that all of them were seated in a way that gave them the best possible view of the puny video monitor I had brought. I also wanted to be sure they knew when the film had started so they wouldn't miss the opening sequence that establishes its central metaphor. In attending to such subtle matters, I had forgotten that the voice they heard telling them their own myth at the beginning of this film was mine, and so not one of them could understand a word of what was said.

I soon realized it hardly mattered what they heard and saw that day. Their pleasure was not in the shape but in the content of what they watched. The film could have begun in the middle, or gone backwards and not forwards, or have been composed of any of the thousands of scenes that had been left out when I edited it so scrupulously more than twenty-five years earlier. No doubt they were greatly entertained by what they saw, but there was also little to indicate they were particularly moved by any of it. I wonder though, if anyone can look at themselves in some much earlier manifestation and not be touched at all. Weyak's eyes watered more I fear from fatigue than anguish and both Pua and Wali were filled with mirth and astonishment but, when it was over and getting dark, they wanted to be taken home in a minivan. Kurelu said very little, but since his village was nearby he hung back and stayed for dinner.

I left the Grand Valley not long after showing *Dead Birds*. I made another visit to Pua, Wali, and Weyak, and they came a few times to see me, but we never talked about the film or what had happened to the world it resurrected. The only pig I saw killed was at Pua's lodgment where we went to film some German tourists he had discovered in Wamena and had persuaded to watch him prepare an authentic stone-age feast. I hoped that Wali's and Weyak's pigs would wait for me until I went back again to the Grand Valley. Kurelu, who never promised me a pig, died on January 26th, 1990.

D3

P7

Just as I made final plans in 1996 to return a second time to the Grand Valley, I received a message telling me that Weyak had died. Weyak, the hero of my film *Dead Birds*, was now himself a dead bird, and the news brought on immense longing for another chance to see and be with him, another chance at life itself perhaps. This news of Weyak's death hit with greater force than I had thought possible. For weeks I had been anticipating, almost rehearsing, our reunion. Instead, this simple but deep and warm person had gone away. Of all the figures in that faraway landscape, Weyak was the one adult to whom I was closely attached. It was Weyak and Pua, who also had died, whom I cared about the most.

I realized for the first time how profoundly fraternal my feelings toward Weyak had always been. Weyak knew no English and I too little Dani to exchange more than the simplest thoughts. Still, we were the staunchest comrades imaginable under these or any other circumstances. We were fast friends providing whatever we could to make our different but continually intersecting lives enjoyable. I am sad that I will not be able to tell Weyak how important he was to what I was doing and to the person I was becoming. Since I planned this trip in part to take my wife, Adele, and my sons, Caleb and Noah, to see the Grand Valley, it was fitting that we screen *Dead Birds* in preparation for our visit. Weyak was entirely alive for eighty-five minutes in what was, in so many ways, his film.

We reached West Papua by way of Djakarta and Biak. We later flew into the much improved airfield in Wamena, and, after an overnight stay in a hotel, drove up the valley to Wuperainma, where Wali still lives and where I knew him thirty-five years ago. Before long I was listening to Wali as he once again recounted the story of my arrival in his midst many years ago. It was long in the telling and much embellished by whatever process of mythologizing has gone on all these years. As I listened to the translation of what Wali was saying, I felt I was in the presence of actual myth making, hearing something I knew well being given a new meaning through conflation, exaggeration, and distortion. I recorded Wali's performance, which means it can be put with other accounts of the same story, perhaps one of the main reasons for having come this great distance.

Wali appeared to have an entirely new set of wives and several children about whom I of course knew nothing. But he was unmistakably himself: commanding, cajoling, and entreating in his customarily tense and nervous manner. We spent hours going through the ritual of greeting after a long absence.

We left Wuperainma as darkness gathered with great suddenness as it always does in this valley. Plans were made to return for a longer visit in a few days at which time we said we would spend the night in one of Wali's little make-believe family houses set up for the tourist trade that has never materialized. Wali's bungalows are functional but they have produced few if any of the intended results. I think, in fact, that these have been built for two or three years and we will be the first to use them. I find something ironic in all this. We who discovered Wali and introduced him and his community to another reality are the first to be welcomed into one that is pure fiction.

The next day we were without our interpreter and spent our time in the mostly disheartening pursuits of third-world tourism. The main market of Wamena was busy with trade from early in the morning until late in the afternoon. Many Dani walked many miles bringing to it their pathetic commodities in hopes of a sale. The women brought sweet potatoes and specialty foods such as garlic, tangerines, and bananas. There was never much on display in front of them as they squatted in the refuse and mud, talking all day with their friends from other villages. The women seemed never to look up, coming to life only briefly when a straight hair, as Indonesians are called, stopped to make a transaction that was always swift and never affable. The women stayed until they had nothing more to sell, or until it was getting dark and they had to start on their often lengthy journeys home.

Dani men brought heavier things like hewn lumber, which is in great demand in this construction-crazed place. As best they could, they resisted the contemptuous offers of the Indonesians who openly exploited their dominion over these ragged survivors of a once gloriously coherent society. The Dani men seemed more naked than ever in their partly Western, partly traditional dress.

The market, unlike many others I have seen from one end of the world to the other, both repelled and dismayed me. Listless and grim-faced, the event had none of the frequently joyful energy that fuels the human byplay typical of traditional markets, and was instead more a place of squalor infused with great sadness. I wondered if it was a sadness I provided, or if there could ever again be any happiness in the valley as long as the Dani were slaves in what were once their own gardens. I was barely able to make images, even with the little Sony video camera I had brought instead of my customary Aaton. I was equipped as a simple tourist and so, naturally, found myself treated as one whenever I put the camera to my eye. Whoever was in my view asked, really demanded, payment for what I was doing. Anyone using a camera had to pay something to whoever was subjected to its torment. At first, I could not accept these new rules, having years ago borne away a treasure of imagery without giving a thought to com-

V1

V2

P8

pensation. Gradually, however, I saw there was no way to escape the new order or the inequality of the old transactions, and I, too, began handing out the required amounts, which were usually tiny, varying only fractions of a cent according to the wishes of the individual concerned.

A few Dani men were veteran posers who covered themselves in soot-blackened grease and put on traditional dress to beg for their pictures to be taken. Sometimes they demanded outrageous sums. Others were less practiced in this way and simply whined for anything, never sure what it would be.

I found a back street behind the central market where I could see Dani living out their destiny as a conquered people. Their rulers, the Indonesians, came there to buy, on the cheap, things like wood planks and long poles. One of the Dani's most developed skills was basic carpentry. In 1961, I thought the things they did with wood to be among their most elegant achievements. In those days, I saw evidence of a remarkable sensibility in the fences they made from slabs of wood fashioned by stone adzes, and in the thresholds of the main gateways to their villages made from found tree roots and put in place in a Japanese manner.

In the back streets of Wamena in 1996, the Dani's traditional skills were used to produce building materials for a rapidly growing immigrant community. The Indonesian buyers arrived by motorcycle, helmeted and aggressive, to get what they wanted for as little as possible. The Dani had trouble dealing with their imperiousness, and I admired the few holding out for a reasonable price. On another corner there were young Dani with bicycle rickshaws they filled with three, four, or even five extravagantly dressed Indonesian women and children in town to do the household shopping.

Many of the Dani men, who would have been warriors and farmers a generation ago, rent rickshaws from an Indonesian to make enough rupiahs to buy food, tobacco, and other essentials. They were good at pedaling, given their enormous leg strength from centuries of climbing these fertile valley walls. No warmth or amiability was to be seen in the interaction between served and server, owing to the vast physical and cultural distance between them. It cannot be so different from the red and white encounter in America of the 1800s. The Indonesians were contemptuous of what they regarded as backward and heathen Dani. The Dani were intimidated by powerful invaders and had no way to assert their traditional claims and interests.

Coupled, I think, with their social inequality, was a pervading shame on the part of the Dani male. In 1996, they were transparently alone and vulnerable in their nakedness, a nakedness that was not at all diminished by the few scraps of torn and inappropriate Western clothing to which they had fallen unheeding heirs. Traditionally, a Dani male, beginning at about five or six, would be literally naked except for a hollow gourd covering his penis and tied by string to his waist. It was protective only of excessive modesty. Without it they felt undressed. In the old days, losing this device, called a *horim*, was mortifying in the extreme and no time was lost in restoring it to its proper place. Even in the heat of battle, losing one's *horim* was almost as great a calamity as being struck by an arrow. In adopting Western clothing through edict and other pressures, the Dani male has lost his *horim* and cannot feel other than humiliated as a result. He is deprived of not just an aspect of dress but an emblem of his own manhood.

On first encountering a Dani wearing his *horim* which, depending on personal taste, was straight or curved, long or short, narrow or wide, my reaction in 1961 was partly disbelief. Here was an otherwise convincingly human being with an outlandish decoration perched on his penis, sticking up sometimes higher than his shoulder and often embellished with a bit of rat fur at the tip end. It was worn not to protect vital anatomy but to assert dignity and maintain masculine pride. With it a Dani male was content and whole, without it he was threatened and incomplete.

The Dani were seen by Indonesians to be fit objects of fun and derision, and it was their penis gourds that created the most laughter and scorn. The Dani seemed to be trying to decide what discomforted them most, scarcely concealed contempt for looking like savages or the embarrassment of a life without their *horim*.

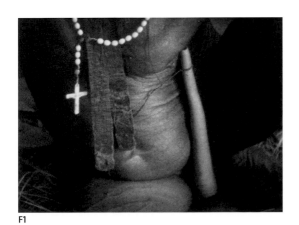

F1

F2

V3

V4

On the way back to see Wali again, and to spend the night in one of his tourist huts, as I had promised, I wondered what I hoped to accomplish by again visiting the Grand Valley of the Baliem. I think I was looking for a way to put an end to my long involvement with a world I entered in such high excitement long ago. Wali, on the other hand, had a more precise agenda. He had already said he would like me to take him to America, or at least to Djakarta. These destinations had meaning in Wali's view of the world as places of power offering him a chance to regain some of the influence and wealth that have eluded him for most of the years since I left in 1961. Wali supposes that by going to America, he will return laden with treasures that he is persuaded hang everywhere like grapes on a vine.

Wali's nature also had a more mundane and practical dimension. He had a specific list of needs that included a radio, a chain saw, clothes, a pig, and cigarettes. These were his immediate requirements, especially cigarettes to which he had by his own admission become addicted. He could no longer make his own the way he did before factory-made alternatives entered the valley. Only old men and women could be seen smoking the hand-rolled cigarettes using tobacco that in 1961 grew in every village and were wrapped in leaves from a common shrub. With no other stimulant and no ceremonial warfare, the Dani had become a population of filter-tip chain smokers.

On the path to Wali's village, we passed unpromising fishponds introduced by the Indonesians to provide an outlet for Dani enterprise and a dietary supplement for the increasing numbers of immigrants. We arrived in Wuperainma in the early afternoon where a noticeably motley contingent of older men and young boys were welcoming us with an unconvincing version of *etai*, or victory dancing. What it most certainly lacked in vigor and sonorous depth, it made up for in sheer friendliness. Once inside the village where I had spent such long and memorable hours, it was clear that Wali had arranged for a small feast, cooked in a steam pit, which would be the main event in a diminutive ceremony of welcome.

Significantly, Wali apologized for having no pig. He mentioned something about there being none nearby and that such an oversight would never happen again. The women and girls set about quickly readying the stones and gathering the ingredients. We would try to eat before dark.

326

V5

V6

While we waited the two or so hours for the vegetables to cook, Caleb and Noah played with a small army of Dani children. They had a frisbee and some whiffle balls, which seemed not to daunt or confound the Dani in the least. I remembered how passionately the children played their own games when I was here long ago. By the time the steam pit was ready to open, my boys were extremely tired and both had found fast friends.

We ate as much as we could of the many different kinds of sweet potato prepared by Wali's women. Wali also orchestrated more *etai* singing and dancing but it was of a sadly desultory kind, a debased rendering of what I had always looked on as triumphal music making, outdone only in my experience by the otherworldly chanting of the Borroro of Niger.

When darkness had enveloped us, we began thinking of the night ahead. The guest quarters were next to Wali's compound and in some ways mimicked quite well the structures in which he and his family lived. On looking closer, I realized no Dani would use them as they lacked such essentials as a place for the fires that, above all else, made Dani dwellings habitable. Fires were and still are the only defense against mosquitoes and the frequently cold and dismal days. Fires were also the focus of social life, where women gathered to cook and gossip, children played, and everyone ate. Dani fires should never die out. If they did, the Dani would too.

We arranged sleeping bags and a few possessions like flashlights, insect repellent, and a bottle or two of trustworthy water in anticipation of some rest, if not sleep. We all knew this first night in a Dani village would not be without its inconveniences and were prepared for almost anything except what Wali, to my astonishment, had arranged: a serenade by what must have been the entire village population which, on a signal I never saw, filed into our confined quarters. This gesture was Wali's grandest yet, a tribute that expressed his concern that we hold him in high regard while also indicating his waning but still sufficient influence over people who once regarded him as their undisputed leader. The singing, which was of a kind I had not heard before, went on for an hour or more. During a rare pause between songs, if that is what they were, I was able to tell Wali by unmistakable body language the fact of our collective fatigue.

I was ashamed of my lack of endurance but realized my days as a participant observer had probably ended some time ago. These days I listen and watch less to be informed by what I hear and see than to search for personal meaning. Wali left, graciously, telling me to be sure to latch the rickety door with the bent nail provided. He said we should keep it shut against any animals that might want to explore our space for anything edible. I assume he had rats uppermost in mind.

Despite the unyielding floor and concerns for poisonous centipedes that are known to roam uninhabited living spaces, we all found sleep before rising at daybreak.

Many different kinds of sweet potato were ready for us in the family house, and Wali made tea that he laced with fresh orange juice. It eased the hoarseness he developed during yesterday's vocal reception exercises. By eight we were on our way to the Third Annual Baliem Cultural Festival, a major reason I had come at this particular time. I had heard that the event included mock wars staged by ex-warriors from local villages, and I was curious to see what had been preserved of this spectacle that drew me to the Valley in the first place. In 1959 I read with

P9

immense excitement the Christian and Missionary Alliance communiqués to their flock about thousands of plumed warriors, contrary to Christian precepts, firing arrows and hurling spears at each other in daylong efforts to kill and maim each other. Thirty-five years later I wanted to see a reenactment of what was once authentic ritual warfare. I wanted also to have a chance to film or, more precisely, videotape what I saw.

When we reached the festival, a few miles northwest of Wamena, on this first day of a weeklong schedule, the heat was intense and I marveled again at Dani stamina. They have stupendous energy, which they are more than willing to devote to what might easily be seen as play. Some young men had come a great distance, perhaps ten miles on foot, to compete in a bicycle race balancing precariously on battered and unstable bikes or to run a ten-kilometer footrace across uneven garden lands.

These and other such events are the invention of an imaginative mayor of Wamena who has decided to put his town on the international tourist map by whatever means possible. There are not many places the intrepid traveler can go to see any of what this mayor has concocted. Just the mock warfare between groups of recently emerged stone-age warriors makes compelling travel literature. Yet this festival had attracted fewer than a dozen who qualified as actual tourists. Other than us, there was only a handful of middle-class Indonesians from the shops in Wamena or Jayapura, formerly Hollandia.

The day's entertainments included the bicycle race, which no one could see as it wound its way through neighboring gardens and villages, a pig race in which the mostly female owners encouraged their pets to scamper across a finish line, a wedding ceremony whose authentic antecedent I had never seen but wish I had from the look of the reconstruction, and the mock wars and raids that had an eerily real look to them, as if those participating had not only not forgotten but had been quietly practicing all this time.

As I watched, I did not think I was witnessing any particularly historic battle, or even examples of renowned strategy by some well-known war leader of the past, but I did think I was watching competent demonstrations by men who had been engaged in real ritual warfare not so long ago. Could it still be taking place in the remoter parts of these highlands? I think almost certainly it is. We were told in fact that the reason the mayor had not come to his festival was that he was trying to put a stop to a feud in the southern valley threatening to engulf a number of villages in old-style hostilities.

The Dani were the object of everyone's curiosity. They were objects of scorn as well, of course, for their savage looks and supposedly barbarous ways. They were the ones with gourds covering their penises and long hair matted with pig grease and soot. They were at once pathetic, frightening, and hilarious and, as such, much sought after for photo opportunities. The Dani understood perfectly their marketability; that is, they could sell themselves as the curiosities they knew others took them to be. Many did so with considerable skill, striking convincing poses as aggressive, even dangerous, savages.

Once, when Caleb was only two or three, we took him to a much advertised event called, I think, King Richard's Faire somewhere on the way to Cape Cod. It was based on the idea of re-creating the world of knaves, knights, and maidens along with all the relevant animal life of the medieval world. We went hoping for some combination of instruction and amusement but found little of either. I worry that even the most enthusiastic jouster cannot bring real conviction to his feats of daring after weeks of falling off his horse, and I wonder, too, when the Dani will succumb to the same ennui.

CINE KODAK
BLACK AND WHITE

(Safety Film)

KODAK (A/asia) PTY. LTD.
MELBOURNE - AUSTRALIA

D1

fixing time

I do not know at what point in time I began my life as a filmmaker. Might it have been the day I could at last reach the shelf where my father kept his 16mm movie projector? It was a Bell and Howell, the kind that had a heavy, round metal base and was made so as to bend in the middle in order to slide, miraculously, in and out of a velvet-lined box that smelled mysteriously of celluloid and electricity. At some point I became the projectionist at our passionate family screenings of Laurel and Hardy, Our Gang, and Charlie Chaplin. I knew that Chaplin was funniest, but Our Gang touched me deeply with its almost true accounts of children trying to outwit a problematic world.

My father also had a 16mm camera that he used to document the antics of his offspring. I have inherited what has survived of this troubling chronicle. Nowadays I can hardly bear to watch it. He seems never to have captured in those little yellow boxes of black and white film anything except joy, and yet I remember the business of growing up to have had its painful moments. Perhaps my memory is no less faulty than my father's camera, but I think the greater certainty is that his camera, like all cameras, could be no more telling than the hand that held it.

Some desire to stop time and even revisit certain of its passages must have played a part in my father lifting his camera to capture our somersaults and pony rides. He may have been thinking only of a way to preserve happiness. But for me, fixing time in particles of silver held all the promise required by my youthful inclinations toward art.

As I got older, I would sometimes open the long wooden box that held the tightly wound and silvered screen, slide the projector from its snug housing, thread up a reel getting pungent with neglect, and allow myself a furtive look at the enchantments of a long forgotten summer.

At a certain point, I came into possession of my own camera and have, ever since, wondered how it should be used. Forty years ago there were no schools in which to learn filmmaking like the ones there are now in London, Paris, Rome, or even in Cambridge, Massachusetts, where I myself sometimes teach. We all learned by doing and watching those we had reason to think or to hope knew more than we did. We also learned by going to films whenever the opportunity arose.

As I absorbed more and more examples of every available kind of film, I gradually and unexpectedly grew to prefer nonfiction. My first inclinations had been toward narrative, especially as practiced by such innovators as De Sica and Rossellini, who could create so much life from such thin but touching stories. I was also dazzled and sometimes perplexed by what was known then as experimental cinema. Here Maya Deren was my chief delight. Of Maya's films, I am still fondest of *Private Life of a Cat* that she helped her husband Alexander Hammid make, and also the pictorially arresting *Study in Choreography for Camera*. I think these two were and still are more engaging of the heart and more visually commanding than her denser, surrealistic work. I have always thought it significant that her final, unfinished attempt to document the practice of *vodoun* in Haiti was, in the end, her sincerest acknowledgment of the power of actuality.

Of all the films that entered my consciousness in those days, Basil Wright's *Song of Ceylon* appealed in some essential way both to my sensibilities and to any budding ambitions I might have had as a filmmaker. I do not think I was particularly aware of its importance to me at the time. The subtle genius of the film is easily obscured by the obvious charms of Flaherty's *Nanook of the North* or the technical mastery of Riefenstahl's *Triumph of the Will*. I have no idea how many times I have seen Wright's film over the years but each time I do, it reveals new evidence of an astonishing capacity to make images that convey feeling and mood at the same time they are representing, indeed preserving, the world of actuality. When I noticed this happening with other films, like Franju's *Le Sang des Bêtes*, Vittorio De Seta's *Bandits of Orgosolo*, and in some of Dziga Vertov's less-mannered efforts, I began thinking that it was perhaps possible to give utterance to inner feelings about the world by the adroit seizing of it with a camera. For a young man with appropriately intense feelings but no demonstrated talent for expressing them, this discovery was an alluring prospect.

P1

Soon there was no doubt but that I should set about finding an answer to the question of where and how to point my camera at the world. Perhaps this was when my life in filmmaking began but my Protestant background instructed me not only to work hard but toward some purpose, preferably the kind that is improving both to one's soul and to one's surroundings. Idealism was very much in the air. World War II was over and the Cold War had not begun. We were told there would be no wars if people were fed, housed, and educated. Among those saying this was the great Scottish reformer/producer John Grierson, armed with the curious notion that nonfiction film was the best teacher in a world just waiting to be taught. This idea gave an air of evangelism to what came to be called "the documentary." For me, the possibility of doing something that might lift up humanity and also belong to the realm of art was certainly exciting and drew strength from Larkin's dictum that an impulse to preserve is at the bottom of art. On looking back, however, I realize that except for some of the early films by Humphrey Jennings, Lindsay Anderson, and especially Wright, I am not particularly attracted by much of what came from the Grierson movement. Too much of it is a trifle bleak and earnest. The goal to instruct was certainly admirable, but the work often seemed to lapse into preaching. Besides, more Larkin-like impulses began to agitate my mind.

Longings to capture human reality in ways that might reveal its essence or significance fully asserted themselves by the time I began making *Dead Birds*. That was in 1961, a time when I had already absorbed what I most enjoyed in my brief, formal study of anthropology, and also when I had abandoned any thought of a life in social science. My commitment to filmmaking grew out of one of anthropology's intellectual sources, Moral Philosophy, rather than any of its mainstream doctrines.

I was bewildered by such dismal notions as functionalism and structuralism, theories that had in some miraculous way overlooked people entirely. The most appealing concept then current was the connection between culture and personality. In this I found a sensible way to organize my thoughts about the human condition. Its basic premise of there being two fundamental engines of experience whose interaction shapes our lives is related to an underlying theme I detect in many of my films: the tension between individual will and cultural constraint.

While thinking about the cinematic inspiration upon which I drew such a long time ago, I sometimes wonder whether Grierson may not have had more of an influence than I had supposed. In his voluminous and skillful writing, I do not remember him ever making the observation that film could serve as means of moral inspection or even contemplation, but his sometimes high-mindedness about our ethical obligations to improve the human lot coincided with some of my own preoccupations both then and later. The important difference that I see between his views and my own is that I would prefer any moral to be drawn rather than pointed, and I am more concerned with contemplating than improving our ethical natures.

West Papua, where I made *Dead Birds*, was a place largely unknown to even travelers and anthropologists, the two callings specializing in distant and obscure geographies. I went with companions who would arrest time in their own way, in words, sound recordings, and countless photographs. I hoped that what I did with a motion picture camera would engage the eye as it satisfied my urges to preserve. Even in 1961, it was the formal qualities of images (was I still in thrall to Vertov?) that interested me as much as the information they contained. I have always thought the technology employed to make a film, compared to the thinking that instructs its use, is a matter of relatively little consequence. Beautiful films can be made with minimal means, and an abundance of means frequently results in just the opposite. In West Papua, many years ago, I was adequately but modestly equipped. At least nothing technical was going to submerge the ideas informing the image-making.

High on a list of things I wanted to do was to make a film about particular individuals through whose lives and situations the film's themes and narrative threads could be developed. Among other things, this decision meant the camera would not be used for passive observation but as an active agent in disclosing the identities and recounting the experiences of some individuals but not others. I wanted to see all I possibly could of the context within which these individuals existed, but I wanted to do so by deliberately limiting my gaze to an exploration of the space they occupied. I was interested in entering the lives of a few real and identifiable people. I was not at all interested in making a film about an abstraction like society or about items on an ethnographic laundry list.

Once, a long time ago, a professor of anthropology who had just seen *Dead Birds* told me: "You sure have some beautiful data." I think he thought I was in the enviable position of being able to put the film through some kind of methodological processor. What he didn't know was that filmmaking is itself transforming, and what he was calling data had already lost their existential virginity.

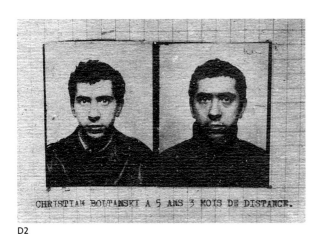

CHRISTIAN BOLTANSKI A 5 ANS 3 MOIS DE DISTANCE.

D2

Two things that determine much of what happens in our lives are circumstance and chance. They play equally important roles in the telling of nonfiction stories. The chance nature of reality draws our attention to one thing instead of another, setting in motion the combination of eye and hand movements that point a camera in this direction and not in that. Something compels us through another kind of urgency to follow as we preserve what we see.

When I started the filming for *Forest of Bliss* I knew that my freedom to move about the city of Benares would be limited by a variety of circumstances — rules, conventions, and even my own hesitation. Owing to my foreignness, there would be places where I would not be immediately welcome. One of the places important to me was the Great Burning Ground, the cremation area called Manikarnika Ghat. My inadvertent stumbling into that extraordinary place ten years earlier had filled me with a panic that I kept coming back to Benares hoping to relieve. On the shore of the Ganges very close to Manikarnika, a man was repairing a battered old boat and I saw in this wreck a chance to pictorially enter the space from which I felt excluded. Every day I visited the carpenter who was repairing the boat, filming its gradual restoration and at the same time getting physically and emotionally more ready to enter the larger space that included, a few hundred feet away, Manikarnika Ghat. Finally, when the boat was finished, I moved onto the Great Burning Ground. This way I managed to insert myself in sacred space and to preserve the commonplace story of a carpenter rebuilding a boat.

Chance often plays a decisive role in what finds its way into nonfiction films and sometimes seems almost to overwhelm all other considerations. Occasionally these coincidences result in such a powerful rendering of reality that transposing them to the screen runs the risk of such moments being seen as artifice. This is where actuality outperforms imagination, out-fables the fabulous. While shooting *Forest of Bliss*, I went to nearly absurd lengths to get an image of a kite falling from a great height onto the far shore of the Ganges. Kites were being flown by hundreds of children every day, but in spite of the innumerable opportunities they provided, I was never happy with what I saw in the viewfinder. I was driven by the idea that, if I could make this image, I might be able to convey a heightened sense of finality, of loss. My thinking was that when its string broke, a kite was departing forever.

334

Late one afternoon coming home down the river, I saw a boat leaving the city shore with what I could see was the shrouded body of a child. I knew from experience this bundle was being taken to be dropped into the river. As I filmed the scene, I could see a number of kites sailing above the river on their way to the opposite shore. In what might have been my third or fourth shot, one in which the child's body was slipped overboard into the river, I saw in the distance a bright red kite simultaneously entering the water. I do not think this coincidence of burials means to anyone else what it means to me, but I am sure that chance, which had brought these two events together, resulted in an image of intensified and extended meaning. But the story does not end here. I learned shortly after shooting these scenes that the child who was put into the Ganges had fallen to its death flying a kite from the parapet of a building close to the river's edge. Chance was beginning to weave an improbable web of circumstance. Were there ever to have been a voiced commentary in *Forest of Bliss*, and if I had said how this child died, and if my words had been spoken at the very moment when the screen pictured the bundle being put into the river, and if at that very moment a kite was falling into the water a short distance away, audiences might understandably object to an apparent contrivance.

The lesson here may be that it is easy enough to leave out something that strains credulity, but much harder to grasp what is happening before one's eyes and to do so in such a way as to be pointing the camera in the right direction at the right time. These kite-falling stories are precisely the kind for which life is the unique source and that, if watched carefully enough, give people like me the opportunity of fixing and preserving them, possibly in the service of art, on film.

I have no formula for determining what is and what is not filmic, to use a slippery term, by which I mean subject matter that has convincing affinity to the medium. I am quite sure no rules govern these matters. Everything depends on knowledge, insight, inspiration, and talent. These scarcely measurable and mostly unteachable attributes tell me that film is an art form and we should welcome, not despair of the fact.

RG [from an interview]

P1

And that will be England gone,
The meadows, the meadows, the lanes,
The guildhalls, the carved ~~pews~~ choirs.

D1

meadows and carved choirs

In his prose collection *Required Writing,* Philip Larkin says: "The impulse to preserve lies at the bottom of all art." I found this while hero-worshipping poets whom I envied for the way they could explain things my camera could not. The sentence was so immediately cogent and heartlifting that I had no hesitation carrying on as a nonfiction filmmaker, inquiring into the marginal worlds of warrior gardeners, nomadic herdsmen, farmer narcissists, and even artists. I have also taken from his poetry Larkin's clear instruction that what people should be doing is finding more and better ways of making things endure, one of which is to preserve our feelings and thoughts. For Larkin (and for myself at times) this task has looked pretty daunting, considering the outrages arrayed against humanity. But clearly the work is not impossible, since the fixing of experience in poetry (almost the way photographic crystals are fixed in hypo) means that some things do have a chance of surviving. No doubt an inherent conservatism exists in these acts and in the impulse behind them. Larkin, despite an occasionally Tory cast of mind, was passionate about Jazz, but I am told he was deeply offended by Charlie Parker's musical unconventionality. He also hated the idea of travel and stayed most of his life in the provincial city of Hull where he was the university librarian. In a recent review of his collected poems it is said, "[Larkin] cherished, probably more than anything else, an England he perceived in [his poem] 'Going, Going' to be rapidly vanishing":

> And that will be England gone,
> The shadows, the meadows, the lanes,
> The guildhalls, the carved choirs.

Larkin was not just sentimental about a changing landscape. His response was much larger in meaning and sprang from his experience of life that he pictured in terms of meadows and carved choirs, and that set in motion an effort at preservation that he elected to perform by inventing a few hundred miraculous poems. Like any artist, he found a way to describe these experiences in language that not only defined and preserved his feelings but also made them available as new experiences to others. If this was not so, why would we be moved by his verse, and why would anyone think what they read might be art?

As I ponder the question of what relevance Larkin's thoughts about art might have to my own work, I realize his notions persuade me that when I make an image of some urgent aspect of my own experience, I am not only responding to the impulse to preserve, I am making an object that can itself be seen and felt. As a filmmaker, I find enormous excitement in realizing that experience has not been replicated but that it has been recast or transfigured using the medium of light. Even if one wanted to preserve reality, and some social scientists do, such efforts are doomed to fail. The impulse Larkin identifies can only aspire to art.

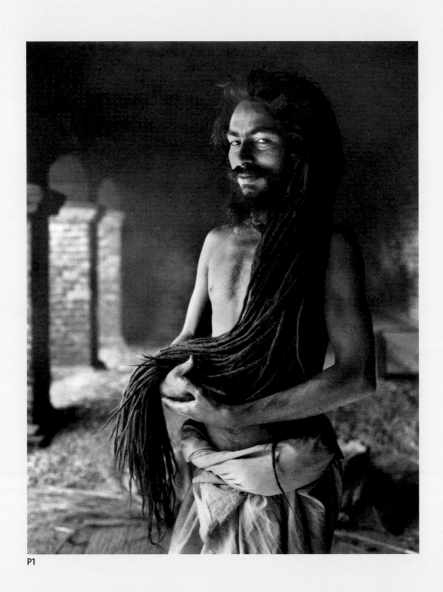

P1

holy men

Kevin Bubriski has been making photographs in a serious way for over twenty years and his exhibition, "Sadhu: Hindu Holy Men," at the Williams College Museum of Art, includes twenty-three examples of his work drawn from the latter half of this period. All of it was accomplished in Asia, specifically India and Nepal, and is confined for thematic purposes to images of Sadhus, the frequently fierce and always vivid exemplars of ascetic piety who thrive throughout the subcontinent and beyond.

It is, I think, the way in which virtually all the figures in these images look at Kevin and so also at me and all others who see these photographs that is so striking and that fills the act of meeting their gaze with so much tension. For example, there is the man, ambiguously male, cradling his armful of matted dreadlocks who looks from the corners of his eyes and seems to say, "Is this what you want?" and the man warming his hands at a small fire whose look is of such ill-concealed anger that he may or may not be about to strike you with the trident stuck in the ground next to him. In another photograph three figures are crouched in the foreground of a scene from what must be a Kumbh Mela (a great religious fair) with its stage set of walking, motorcycling, beggar-cart-riding
figures stretching back into obscuring mists whose collective look is enigma itself. Are they asking for something in their seeming piteousness or do I detect a faintly derisive smile suggesting, perhaps, a hope that Kevin will not linger as they try to warm themselves under a sunless sky?

What gives these photographs such an abundance of tension between observer and observed comes from the manner in which Bubriski approaches his subjects. Here I mean that this photographer like most photographers and other depicters of experience (anthropologists, travelers, journalists, filmmakers) will, if they are any good, more or less intuitively and more or less self-consciously adopt a style or working method. With Bubriski, the method meant providing his subjects with a good measure of autonomy in how they presented themselves. He may have wanted these (holy) men to act out their Sadhuhood, to say something about who they were and how they should be regarded.

Now this is not a particularly common way to elucidate the meaning of behavior, or at least it wasn't until about twenty years ago when I stopped following the methods and purposes of the social sciences. Nor is it particularly common among photographers or filmmakers, except of course for those practicing outright contrivance like food and fashion photographers and directors of other still and moving fictions. What is interesting for truth seeking is that Bubriski has hit upon his own kind of semifiction, upon a way of fashioning, to use a word close to its Latin derivation. The man with the abundant and dreadful tresses is given light and space to adopt (I think) a pose that was almost certainly not given but taken. It is his act of self-revelation that is then caught by Bubriski at an exacting moment in the playing out of the man's disclosure. The photographer knew at what instant the languid hands, the light-defined face and torso and, above all, the faint smile beneath a conspiratorial glance camera-ward perfectly concatenated in time to provide a fictive truth.

Many of the photographs in this remarkable exhibit bear a similar stamp of origin—most obviously that of the gentleman who demonstrates the tensile strength of his phallic member by hanging from it what looks to be a very heavy stone. This is a practiced bit of vaudevillian sainthood on a par with the mongoose and cobra act outside tourist hotels on the Indian subcontinent. Still, Bubriski has done something photographic despite the threadbare quality of the expression itself. Something more is in the eyes of the Sadhu in question than would be there had the lens not opened when it did. Opening a lens and pointing a camera are the essential means of photographic and cinematographic invention. This is true whether special Bubriskian fictivity is at work or the imagery is the result of life seized accidentally.

More might be said about how Bubriski is, I think, showing us the way to a deeper and more penetrating photography of people and place. Let me only say here that he belongs to an honorable tradition of such work and will, I am certain, be guiding us through new and important precincts of the human experience for years to come.

For most people there may not be much that is either interesting or erotic about a naked holy man walking in the snow, but I do think that exposure to the elements in such an unprotected way can be a telling and disturbing image. I also think some understanding about human limits can be gained from seeing it or, at least, this is how I felt when I had the impulse to film it.

RG [from an interview]

P2

P3

P1

isle of dogs (a treatment for a film)

On New Year's Eve 1888, an aging but still physically powerful fisherman named Joseph Auguste Néel paid a visit to his seagoing colleague Francois Coupard in the cabin where he lived on L'Isle aux Chiens, a small island in the harbor of St. Pierre, France's lonely outpost in the North Atlantic. At a certain moment and for reasons that were never entirely understood, Néel disemboweled his friend with a fishing knife. Both men were single and in their early sixties. Though acquainted, they were not thought to have been particularly close.

Following the murder, Néel attempted to row his fishing dory from St. Pierre to the neighboring coast of Newfoundland but was driven back by high seas and strong winds.

Soon after, he gave himself up, was taken into custody and eventually put in a small prison located near the center of St. Pierre. It was built for lawbreakers of the usual kind, drunkards and petty thieves. Néel was the first murderer in the Island's history and so something of a celebrity at least to the local inhabitants. There was a small balcony outside his locked room from which Néel frequently engaged in conversations with his fellow townspeople as they strolled about the town. The gist of his thoughts in these exchanges had to do with his not understanding why he was being held prisoner having already confessed to the crime. He argued that he was well known to everyone and that, furthermore, his detention meant he was neglecting his fishing.

Everyone knew that in a life of more than sixty years he had never harmed anyone and there was no reason to suspect that what had happened to Coupard was anything but a tragic mistake, accidental and irremediable. He reminded people that he had many lobster traps set out around the islands and that they may well be holding a growing population of prisoners of their own. All of this was quite true but no one was able to fathom the significance of what Néel was saying or, for that matter, what the public prosecutor, Marcel Aragon, had in mind when he ordered him incarcerated.

St. Pierre was then, and still is, inhabited by no more than a few thousand souls. The two main islands, St. Pierre et Miquelon, and the much smaller Isle aux Chiens amount to less than one hundred square miles of forest and grudging farmland resting on vast ledges of rock. This scarcely known outlier of French civilization has never been much other than a place to lead a hard life in an economy devoted almost entirely to fishing, though there is some evidence that it participated in illegal shipments of alcohol during the short lived American Prohibition. But bootlegging was not to enrich these islands and there was no other circumstance with the possible exception of the Néel affair that would ever bring these isolated people to the attention of a wider community.

It is in the hope that the story of Néel's curious homicide has a certain rueful instructiveness in the continuing moral struggle to comprehend our violent natures that its principal features are set forth here.

For weeks Néel was held in his somewhat improvisatory confinement while the persons responsible for civil harmony on St. Pierre pursued the proper legal course prescribed by French law. Aragon, inexperienced as he was in capital crime, consulted his superiors in the Ministry of Justice in Paris via the transatlantic cable that had just been laid. Messages came and went with urgent frequency. In the end, the directive from the Ministry was clear: Néel must be indicted and tried for murder under the existing code of justice. There would have to be a proper trial with prosecutors, defenders, jurors, and a judge.

It seems possible that the way in which Néel's case evolved was due in part at least to the perceived clarity and urgency with which procedural questions posed by the public prosecutor in St. Pierre were answered by the efficient and relatively instantaneous cable transmissions sent from Paris. Things began to gather an unaccustomed momentum and had about them an air of almost cosmopolitan importance.

Once the trial began, it was clear that it, too, would proceed with a certain inevitability as to outcome. After all, the accused had admitted his deed and, though there were no witnesses, no one had reason to believe otherwise than that he was telling the truth. The attorney defending Néel could only hope that his client would be shown mercy for what clearly had been a singularly vicious but, more than likely, unpremeditated act. In fact, the entire population of the islands had arrived at a similar point of view and looked upon the trial as more a demonstration of its gradual inclusion in the modern world than a reflection of any wish to torment Néel unnecessarily. There was even some feeling that he had already suffered enough and that there was not anything that they, sitting in judgment as fellow islanders, could think of to make the crime any clearer in its meaning.

Néel was, in short order, found guilty of murder and, according to the relevant Napoleonic statutes, sentenced to death for his crime. Not immediately appreciated by the island's entire population, which by the end of the trial was in nearly absolute thrall to the drama of the proceedings, was that capital punishment in the late nineteenth century in France had to be accomplished by means of the guillotine.

Another volley of messages were sent to Paris in search of responses to such questions as where to find a guillotine, how to operate one once obtained, etc. Answers came back assuring the islanders that they would have access to a traveling guillotine presently in Martinique in the West Indies and that it would be shipped to St. Pierre at the earliest opportunity. Meanwhile Néel, though confined, was in continuous communication with his jailers and various acquaintances with whom he could sometimes talk through the window or from the balcony of his makeshift prison. He knew what direction his case was taking almost as soon as the cables were sent or received in the little telegraph office nearby. The news that a guillotine was on its way from the Caribbean dismayed him but mostly because his mind could not grasp its ultimate significance. He explained it by supposing

P2

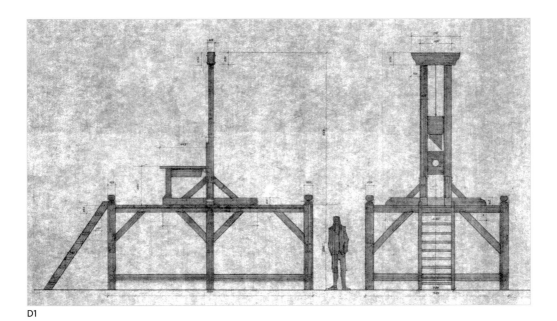

D1

that the state, *La France*, was still exhibiting its formal or ceremonial face and that talk of a guillotine was simply part of the weeks of oddness that he had recently experienced in the courtroom.

One particularly foggy morning nearly three months after the trial, the inhabitants of St. Pierre awoke to see a large wooden crate hoisted from the deck of a small freighter that had docked the night before. News of this cargo had spread quickly and dozens of onlookers gathered to watch the proceedings. The crate was an enormous object, twice the height of a man and nearly as broad as it was tall. An open cart drawn by two docile mares stood waiting on the pier to transport it further. When the crate had been unslung from the ship's derrick, a group of burly fisherman shoved and pulled it onto a cart that had been backed into position. Two gendarmes armed with rifles stood close giving the occasion a curious solemnity.

Once secured to the cart, the driver urged the mares in the direction of the police barracks where the crate would eventually be opened. They walked on either side of the wagon as if to ensure its safe passage on the road along which silent knots of people watched as it passed. When the unlikely procession had reached its destination, the crate was unloaded and left on the parade ground in front of the barracks. It was mid-morning and dense fog was still hanging low across the island. A chill was in the air and most people went inside to stay dry while they wondered what would happen next.

The crate was opened when the weather improved and it was soon discovered that the contents had been disassembled for shipment. It was hardly the working guillotine they had expected and so the commandant of the police summoned the island's best carpenters to put it back together. There were no instructions for doing this and messages to Paris elicited little more than encouragement. Fortunately, as far as infernal devices went, this one had a chilling simplicity depending, as it did, almost entirely on gravity.

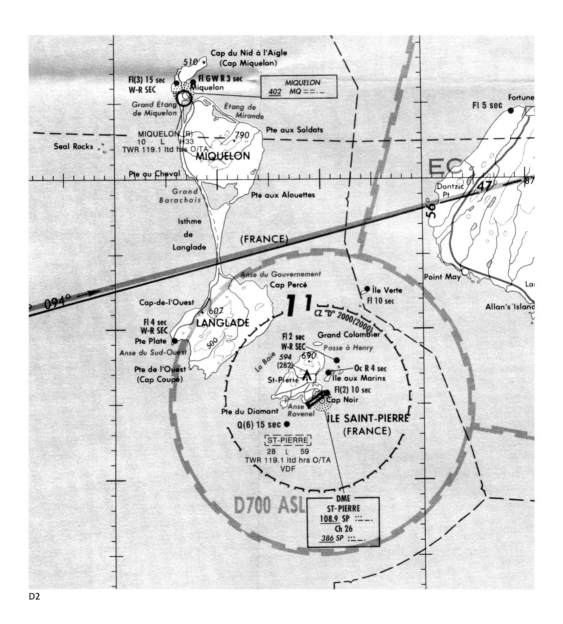

D2

The reassembly went forth rapidly. Néel could not see what the workmen were doing but he could hear snatches of their conversation as well as most of the noises the workmen made as they carried out their work. Once the blade was installed and could be made to fall whenever the catch holding it aloft and in place was released, those in positions of responsibility wanted to be sure it had the necessary precision, heft, and sharpness to separate a man's head from his body. They could think of no other way to find out than to test the device with such unsuspecting stand-ins as sick sheep, immense codfish, and the occasional pig donated by the town butcher. Finally, after a series of experimental beheadings and a few minor adjustments, everyone was satisfied they had a mechanically reliable way to carry out Néel's sentence. At this point another chapter of this story began.

Several months had passed since Néel had committed his crime and it was midsummer when the only unfinished business was the appointment of an executioner. Telegraphs from Paris on this point were adamant in their requirement that the person who would drop the blade come from the condemned's community. It was quickly seen that such a person would be difficult to find. Not only did no one step forward, no one could be made the least interested. In fact, everyone whom the public prosecutor thought to ask shrank from his grasp explaining that he was too busy or offered some other excuse. Weeks passed and there was still no candidate. At that juncture it seemed as if not finding an executioner might constitute a kind of technical flaw in an otherwise seamless legal process and, perhaps, even invalidate the whole proceeding.

Such thoughts may have given comfort to those who had never had much heart for the zeal with which the trial had been prosecuted, but Néel took quite a different view. He could not any better understand why someone would refuse the thousand francs, a more than handsome wage, offered for his execution than he could comprehend how things had gotten to where they were. His had been a case in which justice, though swift, may not have been especially well served and this he vaguely sensed. As required by the laws of France, whose influence on the trial was apparent through the miracle of electric communication, Néel was represented by counsel. His defense on the other hand could not be said to have been especially spirited. He had begun, in effect, with no case at all since he freely and frequently admitted the crime he committed on that recent and lonely New Year's Eve. His lawyer did attempt to persuade the court to act with lenience considering the absence of any motive and no previous history of violence. But it may have been the very cold-bloodedness of his deed that persuaded the judge that Néel had committed an unpardonable act.

For Néel, who could not explain his feelings on the fatal night even to himself, the court's view in this regard was quite mysterious. He still felt warmth and concern for his neighbors and he still expected to continue living as a fisherman.

> If I were asked what I do in genre terms, I might say I am a story-finding filmmaker. I go into the real world and see something I want to tell people, something I think is important. There is a story about Omali Inda in Rivers of Sand, about Weyak and Pua in Dead Birds and about a city in Forest of Bliss.
>
> RG [from an interview]

347

The nightmare of New Year's Eve was receding and he hoped the commotion that surrounded him would end. Instead, it seemed to gather ever more momentum even as the dilemma resulting from failing to find an executioner persisted.

Despite everything, the date for Néel's execution was set for the 24th of August at 5 a.m. Only weeks remained in which to complete all arrangements and it was thought propitious when an executioner was at last found. It was one Felix Hulot, an unemployed teacher who had lost his job owing to a longstanding problem with alcohol. Hulot owed substantial sums at the few bistros and bars that served him drink and though he first refused the court's offer on the strength of his acquaintance with the accused, he decided to accept in the hope of settling his outstanding debts.

It was the time of year when St. Pierre's short summer began giving way to autumn. The days were noticeably shorter and darkness lingered into the time when fishing people rise. Fog frequently settled on the town and turned the familiar landscape into a puzzle of obscured waterways and hidden streets. One heard but often could not see what went on. In the days before Néel's execution, there was a greater silence than usual until it was broken one afternoon by the hammering of nails into the boards on which the guillotine would stand. An open place in front of the police barracks where the constabulary exercised and formed up its units for parades was chosen so as to afford something of an amphitheater in which those who chose to attend might have an unobstructed view of the stage upon which the guillotine would stand. It was about a half mile from the place where Néel was held and so it was decided that he would not be asked to walk on the morning of the fifteenth, a mere week off. He would be taken in a coach, an enormous black affair with immense springs and huge wheels that was sometimes used as a hearse, if the deceased's family felt grand or had no cart of their own.

Hulot was spending much of his time drinking and enjoying his sudden celebrity. He spoke confidently about his desire to acquit himself honorably and professionally when his moment came but those who would listen at all simply nodded in mute accord.

At two o'clock in the morning of the 24th of August, the curate of St. Pierre's parish church came to hear Néel's confession. Néel lay awake on his bed with his eyes shut after being given a large meal and one of the police commandant's better cigars. His mood was thoughtful but not at all agitated, as if he still was not convinced what had been decreed would ever be carried out. It was the middle of a very dark night, one on which the sky was wholly obscured by fog and the only sound to be heard was from the horn in the lighthouse at the entrance to the harbor.

The two men spent the next hour recalling the tragic circumstances of New Year's Eve. For the first time Néel appeared to recognize the horror of his act, the simple truth that he had pitilessly if not deliberately caused his friend to die painfully. It was more difficult for him to comprehend the subsequent furor of imprisonment, trial, and sentencing. Néel had always been a quiet and solitary person. He asked nothing from his community of neighbors and friends than that

P3

he be allowed to fish and live alone in his small house on L'Isle aux Chiens. He regretted the commotion caused by his feckless act and wished sincerely for that to end.

At 4 a.m., two gendarmes came to his room and escorted him to the carriage that had drawn up to the entrance of his so-called prison. He climbed in with the priest and, escorted by a dozen armed men, the carriage started for the parade ground, not yet discernible in the early light. There were now many people walking along the same road from their houses in the town to join the large group of onlookers already gathered in the barracks' square. On the stage, where the guillotine had been placed, stood the commandant and Hulot. Below it on the parade ground were some dignitaries including the mayor, the public prosecutor, various court personalities, and the telegraph operator. In another group stood Hulot's wife and a few of her family and friends.

When the carriage stopped at the foot of the stage, Néel got out with the priest and was quickly led up the few steps to where Hulot and the commandant stood waiting. Hulot had followed Néel's arrival intently from the time he first could see the carriage emerging from the mist as it creaked toward him along the muddy road. He kept turning to the commandant for a sign of encouragement or comfort as he shifted from foot to foot in an effort to quell his growing fright. It was when Néel stepped from the carriage and started toward the stage that their eyes first met and Hulot's heart began to weaken as he realized that, after all, he was not be able to do what he had agreed to do.

Hulot turned to the commandant and whispered: "I cannot do this work." At first the commandant said nothing but smiled wanly and looked extremely puzzled. He asked Hulot what he meant and was told again, "I cannot do this work." The commandant then motioned to the public prosecutor who came onto the stage and was told what Hulot had said. Néel, standing only a few feet away, overheard enough of the conversation to understand the predicament in which all suddenly found themselves — the authorities, the public, and he himself. It was then that Néel decided he must persuade Hulot to do what he had agreed to and he began to gently explain that, by saying he would not, Hulot was causing an embarrassment for everyone. The trial was over and the judge had pronounced the sentence of death. The guillotine had been sent, put in good working order, and the public was waiting for justice to be served. At a few moments after 5 a.m., with the cries of seagulls filling the morning air, the great shining blade clattered down and the awful work was done.

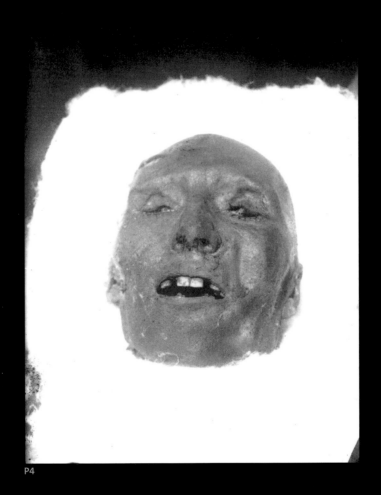

P4

Just. *adv.*

1. Exactly; nicely; accurately.

The god Pan guided my hand *juſt* to the heart of the beaſt. *Sidney.*

just representing

The idea of linking the techniques of cinema to the purposes of anthropology in the hope of getting new and different takes or angles on what it means to be human goes back to the invention of the medium itself, almost exactly 100 years ago. The first thoroughly innocent experiments in capturing actuality seem to have been inspired by the same intuitive grasp of what constituted the medium's essential nature as now, when the marriage between film and anthropology is still being proposed. The earliest, quite unself-conscious achievements of film were no more than naive observations of quite ordinary behavior, such as Lumière's primitive documents of workers leaving a factory or of a baby being fed.

Margaret Mead, half a century later, chose to adopt the same principle and felt no need to go more than a few halting technical steps further in her cinematic effort to learn anthropologically by recording the way babies were bathed in five different societies. Before and after Mead there have been innumerable small and large-scale attempts to exploit the documentary or recording capabilities of cinema as the search has continued for greater understanding of people's behavior.

There must have been some common hope underlying all these efforts, such as that the astonishing thirst of film for detail and precision would anchor the vagaries of theoretical speculation and interpretation. But this union between cinema and the so-called science of man has not often lived up to its promise. Depth and intensity have been absent from most of the work done by generations of practitioners of not just ethnographic but all other varieties of nonfiction filmmaking. That work has irrefutable importance as documentary evidence that will remain an important gazette of diverse but transitory cultural experience. But a dismayingly large part of this same work has an earnest and threadbare quality stemming from the effort to avoid even the suspicion of hidden fictive intentions. Most representations of the world of actuality try but inevitably fail to achieve the impersonal, nonfictional objectivity so dear to social science. Such concerns may have begun to lose their urgency, however, because maintaining the boundary that for so long has separated nonfiction from fiction filmmaking looks like not only a mistaken principle but also a limiting strategy.

In his *Preface to Shakespeare*, Samuel Johnson offers many thoughts about why what Shakespeare wrote was so true to life, so convincing, so unarguable in its portrayal of human experience. Near the beginning of that remarkable essay is a sentence that seized my attention and changed my thinking about the methods and even the purposes of actuality filmmaking. Johnson wrote, "Nothing can please many and please long except just representations of general nature." I vividly remember the excitement I felt as these words made clear the possibilities available to,

P1

353

among others, filmmakers with documentary inclinations. He did say, did he not, that just representations would please many and please long? He also said, for the benefit of those still dubious about such matters: "The irregular combinations of fanciful invention may delight a while, by that novelty of which the common satiety of life sends us all in quest; but the pleasures of sudden wonder are soon exhausted, and the mind can only repose on the stability of truth." Repose? Stability?

No other writer may have seen into as many corners of the human heart as Shakespeare, but it was not until I had read what Johnson thought that I saw Shakespeare's fiction was not just a way to represent but a way to represent justly. To know what Johnson intended in his use of the word "just," I consulted his own dictionary where he wrote, "JUST, adv. 1. exactly, nicely, accurately 'the god Pan guided my hand *just* to the heart of the beast.' Sidney etc." One must only, I thought, find a way to observe (and represent) exactly, nicely, and accurately. It makes no difference whether the world observed is actual or imagined since (according to Johnson) the method is suitable in both instances.

For a long time I have been struck by the way certain passages in fiction films have had an uncanny claim upon my credence and have no difficulty at all convincing me of their truthfulness despite my own once formidable skepticism. If fictional prose used justly can depict unarguable facts of life, why, I began to wonder, might the same not also be true for imagery used in the same manner? What about those scenes in films that haunt you with their poignancy as they conjure compelling fragments of life? For example, consider the intimacies between the two principals in *Woman in the Dunes,* Teshigahara's documentary fantasy about an entomologist who inadvertently becomes the prisoner of a woman living at the bottom of an enormous sand pit. The situation, which would never be found in the annals of ethnography, is one that, despite the immense improbabilities contained in the very premise of this curious account, is utterly convincing as a depiction of not just one couple's predicament but of general human nature.

Or what of that fantasy of impossible revenge and retribution in Vigo's *Zéro de Conduite* where miserable schoolboys all but demolish the world of their adult oppressors? No attempt is made in this film to create a world that mimics any recognizable reality. On the contrary, Vigo provides the boys with entirely unlikely means to realize their aims of righting what is wrong by empowering them through slow motion, pixilation, and other optical distortions. He is, in fact, constantly intervening with the generally perceived look of things. The children are asked to participate in a fiction that with, and perhaps because of, its absurdities justly (exactly, nicely, accurately) represents the common inner desires of all schoolboys.

How, one might ask, can it be said that by distorting reality we get closer to some kind of truth about reality? Has not conventional wisdom required the documentary gesture to be as faithful as possible in its rendering of actuality? Was not cinema vérité, which could see and hear the truth twenty-four times a second, the straightest road to the promised land of ethnographic or any other realist filmmaking? So indeed one has at least hoped and even believed up to the present day. But for some time now there has been a growing interest in what might be called the blurred genre phenomenon as it applies to cinema. This condition results from seeing the supposed differences in the scope and goals of filmmaking as being altogether arbitrary and that much of what comprises the act of filmmaking is shared across genre boundaries.

What this may mean is that, if the true nature of film resides in its capacity for storytelling, the true calling of all filmmakers ought to be the employment of its fictive capabilities. In terms of particular strategies, what this approach also argues is that the practice of actuality filmmaking is not, and cannot be, free of distortion any more than the practice of narrative filmmaking can escape the inherent tendencies of cinema to imitate physical reality. By distortion I mean the effect achieved in film through the use of the variety of ways there are to alter reality as perceived by the naked eye. Every cinematic glance is informed by the innumerable choices made that direct that glance from near, from afar, from high up or low down, in color or in monochrome, and so on through a considerable technical repertoire.

In some essential way we filmmakers are all, regardless of our genre tendencies, engaged in the same task, telling stories with moving images, images that assume their shape and effect through obedience to our choices and commands. One person's report on the way a woman carries a child on her hip is not going to be the same as someone else's report on that same event. Inevitably there will be as many stories using the same language but employing different terms as there are tellers of stories. Whether any of the many ways of telling a simple tale has passed Johnson's test of just representation will depend on how it has been told.

The Encyclopedia Cinematographica *has its usefulness, and the fragments of time that are stored in its separate rolls of film are important notations in the larger human story. Yet even these fragments are utter fictions, faithful and uncooked as they may appear to be. For all their supposed innocence, they are prodigious transformations of actuality—altered in dimensionality, rhythm, color, texture and context, to name only the most obvious. So the idea that combining a variety of fictional elements through editing undermines film's (uncut) objective integrity is to fail to grasp the very nature of reality.*

RG [from a letter]

V1

V2

V3

P1

P2

Spain, June 1997

I have come to Spain to make a film about the painter Sean Scully. My first day with him was the tenth of June starting the morning after I had flown to Málaga from Barcelona. I came with Bob Fulton whom I had asked to join me for part of this enterprise. He would work with a Steadicam and in time-lapse, both specialties at which he excels.

Sean was at the Bishop's Palace, which is more or less in the medieval center of the city. The building is a relatively ordinary but large structure magnificently refurbished with marble floors and polar-white galleries. Sean was there to supervise the installation of a large exhibition of his work including big paintings, pastels, and photographs that had just come from Bilbao where it had been at the new satellite Guggenheim Museum.

Francisco Jauraute, said to be one of Spain's leading contemporary-minded curators, was directing a small but expert crew of helpers maneuvering gigantic Scullys with a minimum of equipment into position to be hung. I began immediately to film the proceedings. More accurately I began video-ing inasmuch as I was using a new, highly portable digital video camera.

While I have always shot film, I thought that using video might allow me to experiment with a variety of effects not readily available using film but that are familiar to anyone who has watched

V4

contemporary television, especially MTV, which occasionally goes some distance toward developing a new visual grammar. The effect that especially interested me was one that renders a blurred, almost smeared, look to things. The results produce a world still convincing as to its reality and surprisingly novel in its formal rearrangement.

Francisco Jauraute and his diligent assistants worked steadily, stopping only for the traditional midday meal and a long rest between 2 and 4 p.m. The work resumed in the late afternoon and didn't stop until late evening when it was time for Spanish dining. Sean was less involved as the exhibit came closer to being hung and began to devote much of his attention to a newly hatched sparrow that had fallen into the courtyard from its nest at the top of a giant palm tree. With no mother to provide for it, Sean did everything but mouth-to-beak resuscitation and eventually the bird gave a few faint shudders of life. When the exhibit opened, the sparrow was flying. I used it as a little metaphor in the small video piece I put together about the Málaga exhibition.

June 12th 1997
Today I started doing what I had only imagined months earlier, a sequence of Sean's parents, Holly and Tony, dancing the Paso Doble in the galleries hung with their child's pictures. These two are convincingly in their seventies and not in the best of health. Father and son, according to Sean, have not been on good terms for a long time. The meeting here in Málaga was to be a way to find some reconciliation.

P3

V5

V6

Tony is dressed like any respectable Englishman on holiday and speaks English with scarcely a trace of Irish accent. As for their dancing, Sean tells me they are ranked second in their class or category. I am not sure what this means but will know more when I see them perform.

The galleries are on the first floor and make a continuous space of one long section and two slightly shorter ones at right angle. The space is very beautiful. Tony and Holly were not happy with my suggestion that they dance uninterruptedly from one end of the galleries to the other. They didn't think this would be, choreographically speaking, consistent with the spirit of the dance. I did not find out why or, for that matter, what the true spirit of the dance was but settled on their trying with their own choreography to do what they were comfortable doing moving from gallery to gallery. I could always later unite any separate segments into one sequence.

I was struck by their inflexibility not then knowing they were as much enthusiasts as dancers. Still, I very much wanted them in the film and it was clear they had put considerable store by the opportunity to be a part of their son's installation.

June 13th 1997

Holly and Tony came dressed for their roles, she in basic gypsy and he as toreador. They were soon taking practice turns to an accompaniment provided by a tape of popular Spanish dance tunes played on a small boom box. After a short rehearsal, we started filming. The idea was to do it with one camera on the small Steadicam Fulton would operate. I chose a point on the tape where we could start each long take and we began in the first gallery. I asked Sean to stand in a corner so that the camera could discover him as it moved through the space. I also asked him to move during the shot to different corners of the gallery so that

he could be discovered in more places than one in the same scene. I hoped that way to create a little mystery about where he stood in terms of the paintings that stayed in fixed positions. It took almost an hour to do all four galleries and at the end both dancers were visibly tired, almost exhausted I'm afraid. It will be interesting to see if it works in the editing.

June 16th 1997

I flew back to Barcelona on Friday evening, June 13th, so I could film Sean in his studio. Fulton and I went there today and we worked with two cameras. One was set up for time-lapse; the other Fulton used for a few Steadicam scenes but mostly I used it during the hours Sean was working. I tried to use it in a way that probed the act of a painter painting.

Sean decided to begin with the biggest untouched canvas available in the studio and did a lot of work the first day, every moment of which was recorded by the time-lapse camera set up in back. With an uninterrupted record in time-lapse of the work done each day, I would have a document lasting about two minutes at the end of a week or ten days. I thought this might provide an interesting visual dimension, although I didn't know what use it would be in the editing. We will see.

June 17th 1997

The paint put on the big canvas yesterday was still not dry enough to start painting over and so Sean worked on a smaller canvas. He began immediately making marks, with a crayon I think, to divide the plane of the canvas into a grid to paint bands of color. Much of the day was spent on this small painting and it underwent several transformations before being put aside to resume work on the larger and more important canvas.

I wanted to find ways to use video to get something different than what is found in most painter films. One idea was to attach a miniature digital camera to Sean's arm while he was painting, or even while he was just sitting and looking at what he had painted. I experimented with this notion before leaving Cambridge by taping such cameras to a student who did karate, and the results were promising.

V7

V8

V9

V10

V11

V12

Sean has a black belt in karate and one of the scenes I planned to do was his kata, his routine. For this I would use a Steadicam but I would also attach the little cameras to his hands. When we replayed some of the imagery made this way, Sean thought it interesting, and I, too, thought it revealed something not commonly seen. What I particularly liked was the blurring effect from using a slow shutter speed. It was dreamlike and rather unreal.

I liked this, and I also liked how much Sean cared about film. He not only cared but he knew about film and would talk about actors he liked and movies he wanted to see again. Though we didn't always agree on these matters, it was clear his enthusiasm was real and his acquaintance with the medium serious. He would quote lines of familiar dialogue, and he would talk about serious independent film work. One night we went to see the latest Greenaway film called, I think, *Pillow Book*, and at a point not too far into the film, we stood up in simultaneous dismay and left.

N.B. These brief notes are from recollections of the contents of a journal I kept with uncommon fidelity on a laptop snatched from me in a brilliant con at a Barcelona bus stop.

V13

Artists get up in the morning, pick up their tools, and go about the business of making sense out of what they see around them. The sense making is what they do and the sense is their results: their paintings, movies, books, or poems. In Passenger, I wanted to see how Sean Scully made sense.

RG [from an interview]

V14

P1